D1156532

William Ward Watkin
and the
Rice Institute

William Ward Watkin
and the
Rice Institute

Patrick J. Nicholson

Gulf Publishing Company
Houston, Texas

William Ward Watkin and the Rice Institute

Gulf Publishing Company
Book Division
P.O. Box 2608 □ Houston, Texas 77252-2608

10   9   8   7   6   5   4   3   2   1

Library of Congress Cataloging-in-Publication Data

Nicholson, Patrick James, 1921–
    William Ward Watkin and the Rice Institute/
    Patrick J. Nicholson.
        p.   cm.
    Includes bibliographical references and index.
    ISBN 0-88415-012-7
    1. Watkin, William Ward, 1886–1952.
  2. Architects—Texas—Houston—Biography.
  3. Rice University—Buildings.   4. Houston
  (Tex.)—Buildings, structures, etc.   I. Title.
  NA737.W39N5   1991
  727′.3′092—dc20   91-27421
                                                            CIP

To the memory of William Ward Watkin, FAIA.

The Rice Institute that he helped Edgar Odell Lovett and Captain James A. Baker transform from a charter into reality now moves into a new century as a major university of high accomplishment, worldwide recognition, resplendent architecture, and unique potential.

CONTENTS

Acknowledgments ix

Chapter One 1

Chapter Two 29

Chapter Three 51

Chapter Four 75

Chapter Five 116

Chapter Six 170

Chapter Seven 196

Chapter Eight 251

Epilogue 322

The Projects of William Ward Watkin 330

Bibliography 340

Index 343

ACKNOWLEDGMENTS

Acknowledgments are found within the text, but more are due:

More than three decades ago, Annie Ray Watkin (Mrs. Henry W.) Hoagland began to collect and preserve materials relating to her father's remarkable career, both at the Rice Institute and as a practicing architect in the far different Houston of more than a half-century ago.

One of the results of her dedicated and successful efforts is this book. It is based in major degree on materials in the William Ward Watkin Collection at Rice's Fondren Library, as well as on material in Mrs. Hoagland's own records and files. Rare and especially meaningful photographs are included. The research and writing for this project was supplemented by many interviews and conferences with Ray Hoagland.

Since beginning her work in earnest on the Watkin collection in 1962, Mrs. Hoagland has greatly enriched the holdings of Rice University, her alma mater (BA '36 and MA '44), in Fondren Library's Rare Book Section and Woodson Research Center. She has compiled and provided invaluable data and detail on the earliest years of the Rice Institute that could have been lost to succeeding generations.

Nancy Boothe of the Woodson Research Center has been helpful many times during the three years since the inception of this project. Her knowledge of the Watkin Collection and of the archival materials within the Fondren Library in general is exceptional.

Steven J. Fox, AIA, a critic and historian of wide knowledge and rare discernment, provided important assistance through his *Monograph 29: Architecture at Rice* and his willingness to check the manuscript for accuracy in architectural matters.

Clayton Umbach, with his efficient and knowledgeable crew at Gulf Publishing Company, has once again proved the ability of that remarkable organization, headed so long by my neighbor and friend Fredrica Gross Dudley, to produce books relating to Houston's lengthening history and the people who have helped shape it.

Elizabeth Raven McQuinn, who edited William Ward Watkin and the Rice Institute, is also due special mention and thanks.

I write this on May 19, 1991, one hundred years to the day since Secretary of State George W. Smith signed and certified the charter of the William Marsh Rice Institute for the Advancement of Literature, Science & Art.

Patrick J. Nicholson, Ph.D.
Houston, Texas

CHAPTER ONE

A stunning masterpiece of architecture (". . . brilliant,
astounding, enduring . . .") on a flat prairie . . .
World-renowned giants of learning at a three-day
academic festival in burgeoning 1912 Houston . . .
Emerging roles for Captain James A. Baker, Edgar
Odell Lovett, and Ralph Adams Cram . . . William Ward
Watkin, a young architect from Philadelphia and Boston,
comes to Houston and decides to stay . . . Of William
Marsh Rice: his earliest days in Massachusetts;
entrepreneur and leading citizen of Houston,
1838–1900; the chartering of the Rice Institute and a
surprise lawsuit . . . Forgery, embezzlement, and
murder in New York City . . . Captain Baker saves the
day, a magnificent endowment, and the Institute

I.

There it stood in the hazy, still-summerlike morning of October 12, 1912: a stunning masterpiece of roseate-pink brick, pale gray granite, richly toned marbles, and colorful tiles standing in contrast to elegant white marble columns and bronze-green metal balconies.

Built in the "round-arched" style of a gifted architect entering the prime years of a brilliant career, this was the Administration Building of a new and innovative university. The structure, nucleus of a resplendent master plan, rose abruptly on 300 acres of flat prairie farmland three miles south of downtown Houston, a brash yet booming Texas city of slightly fewer than 80,000 people. Although Houston was a relatively young city, it had already developed a unique culture, combining the gentility and traditions of the Old South with the ambition and energy of the West.

The Administration Building was arguably the finest academic building designed and constructed to such exacting standards. This three-story model of excellence was 300 feet long by 50 feet deep, with a basement running the entire length. A vaulted sally port, surmounted by a four-story tower, was flanked by arching cloisters facing a

1

courtyard. As one of many unique, elegant, and effective touches, marble capitals depicting the storied pioneers of letters, science, and art had been carved in place by an Austrian sculptor. The building, now Lovett Hall, was and remains the heart of the Rice Institute.

To the strains of a now-forgotten march ("My Dreams of the U.S.A.") performed by the Houston Municipal Band, an academic parade of eminent scholars and administrators wound its way toward the courtyard. The procession was led by President Edgar Odell Lovett and the six other Rice Institute trustees, additional distinguished guests, speakers in the dedicatory ceremony now unfolding, and the original faculty of nine. About half of the first 77 students followed behind. They had matriculated just three weeks earlier.

As Dr. Lovett and his fellow trustees, together with other principals, took their places on a platform directly in front of the sally port, the remaining persons in the procession joined the audience already seated facing the platform.

Texas (indeed the entire South) had not seen anything like the triumphal parade of academic giants that launched the final event in this exhausting three-day celebration opening the new university. The distinguished guest list was clearly a tribute to President Lovett's year-long journey throughout western Europe, Russia, and even Japan to extend personal invitations to the academic festival. The 250th anniversary of Harvard College in 1886 and the few comparable events in the history of U.S. higher education had, of course, attracted a far larger group of distinguished guests. Regardless, this was a major academic event, distant though it might be from more hallowed halls of established tradition. It was clearly unparalleled for an institution barely under way.

Those in the march that Saturday morning of October 12, 1912, included the six speakers of the preceding two days, each of them a scholar of wide and deserved repute. They included Rafael Altamira y Crevea of the ancient Spanish University of Oviedo, a leading authority on the history of jurisprudence and consultant to many of the nations of Latin America; Emil Borel of the University of Paris, a world-class mathematical analyst; Senator Benedetto Croce of Naples, a renowned Italian critic and editor who spoke on the philosophy of aesthetics; Hugo de Vries of the University of Amsterdam, celebrated botanist and expert on the developing theories of heredity pioneered by Charles Darwin; Sir Harry Jones of the University of Glasgow, discussing recent trends in metaphysics and social reform; and Sir William Ramsay, who had been awarded the Nobel prize in chemistry for highly significant studies at the University of London. Sir William's address, the most widely publicized, was on the new field of transmutation of chemical elements. It stimulated research by future Nobel laureates in this field of growing significance.

Six other distinguished scholars from universities as widely separated as Leipzig, Christiania (Norway), and Tokyo had prepared formal papers for the occasion. These were published, along with all the proceedings and details, in a formidable three-volume publication commemorating the dedication (*Book of the Opening, Volumes One, Two, and Three*).

As the academic procession wound its way to the platform that historic morning, one of the unusual sights was the diversity of academic regalia displayed, ranging from the striking, cardinal-red robes of a fellow of the Royal Society of London to a variety of multicolored hoods, resplendent in the Texas sunlight. A velvet beret of deepest orange contrasted with the usual academic headpieces of blackest mortarboard. As the colorful procession advanced, a welcome breeze brought the temperature near seventy degrees, far cooler than the high eighties of the preceding two days. However, those in the procession found a new difficulty. The fine, pinkish gravel selected for campus walks had not yet arrived, and they strode along at some discomfort and risk over coarse, rough gravel laid down as a base [1].

Despite this minor detail, the Administration Building was in its full glory for the historic dedicatory ceremonies—". . . brilliant, astounding, enduring: rising out of the barren brown prairie . . ." as Sir Julian Sorley Huxley, a young luminary of the original Rice Institute faculty would later describe this lasting jewel of the new university.

II.

The history of the Rice Institute did not begin on that Columbus Day of 1912, which saw the end of three days of academic festival and celebration culminating in a relaxed excursion to Galveston. There had already been three decades of happenings preceding this dedication, and they resembled a convoluted Dickensian plot. The plot turned in the beginning upon a complex merchant and investor, William Marsh Rice. Part recluse, part community leader, Rice was also a far-sighted philanthropist and benefactor. The plot turned as well upon forgery, embezzlement, and murder; upon lawsuits and bitter, lengthy controversy that preceded the actual inception of his Institute.

Much as in the novels of Charles Dickens, however, there were those who worked effectively to remove the many, sometimes bizarre, threats to founder Rice's magnificent legacy—a unique educational institution for his adopted city of Houston. Four principals brought his plans to reality, pointing the way to ongoing achievement.

The first of these men was Captain James A. Baker, a brilliantly able, suspicious, indefatigable, and public-spirited Houston attorney [2]. The second was a uniquely well-educated and prepared astronomer–mathematician–administrator: Edgar Odell Lovett. He knew where to seek and how to achieve true excellence. The third man was not only a distinguished architect, but a writer and thinker described by Franklin Delano Roosevelt as ''a towering figure [in] our cultural life.'' This was Ralph Adams Cram, the prime source of an inspired overall concept (plus specific plans for a first complement of pivotal buildings and infrastructure) for William Marsh Rice's Institute. The concept and the projects completed through 1915 still influence not only the greatly expanded physical plant of what has become the Rice University, but the institution's thrust and very being.

This book is the story of the fourth man, William Ward Watkin. An architect on the staff of Cram, Goodhue & Ferguson, Watkin arrived in Houston on August 17, 1910, as the personal representative of Ralph Adams Cram. Only twenty-four at the time, he assumed, almost overnight, a crucial role in turning his firm's plans for the Rice Institute (on which he had been working for almost a year) from paper to reality. Fully intending to return to his native Boston upon completing his assignment at Rice, he instead remained in Houston for the remainder of his life. There were many reasons for this: a principal reason, however, was that young Watkin quickly became an invaluable link and a human synergist between Captain Baker and his fellow trustees, President Lovett, and Ralph Adams Cram.

Sometime before 1912, William Ward Watkin came to the decision to remain in Houston, a decision that affected many persons, the Rice Institute, other Houston institutions, and a number of the city's leading families. Born, raised, and educated in the northeastern United States, this was a major decision for him as Houston was not only a city of fewer than 80,000, but was half a continent away from his native Massachusetts. It was also a city with distinctly different ways of life, traditions, and, most certainly, climate.

What he must have seen while still in his mid-twenties was opportunity in a town that had the earmarks of a metropolis-to-be, populated by whole-souled, farsighted people. Further, he saw in Rice an institution of rare potential, meticulously planned from physical plant and landscaping through curricula, faculty, and ultimate goals. In an important meeting with President Lovett, Watkin proposed the formation of a Department of Architecture, with allied courses in art. From the beginning, this would fulfill the charter's intent to establish and maintain an institution dedicated to the advancement of art, as well as of literature, science, philosophy, and letters. The proposal was accepted with enthusiasm, and Watkin was named department chairman.

Within a year or so after the actual opening of Rice Institute for classes on September 23, 1912, the young architect was assigned significant administrative duties outside his teaching responsibilities. This was an indication of the growing confidence that Edgar Odell Lovett had in him. Watkin would also establish meaningful, lasting relationships with his fellow faculty members, which would prove to be increasingly important. Virtually all of the original teaching staff, as was Watkin, were young bachelors, although many soon married and had children. Living in a neighborhood near Rice, sometimes in adjacent homes, they formed close, permanent friendships. Such similar ties facilitated the development of an effective core faculty in the earliest days of the institution.

As early as 1915, Watkin began a tradition of involvement in community life in areas where he could provide important professional advice or assistance. He proposed the establishment of a civic center to the mayor, and spoke and wrote increasingly on matters of special import to his expanding adopted city. He soon became a vital connector within the Institute itself, and between the infant university and burgeoning Houston.

III.

To understand the development of Rice University, one must first look at the background of its founder, William Marsh Rice. How did Rice, a young man of fifteen with only three years of formal education, accumulate capital of $2,000 while still in his teens? How did he have the foresight to emigrate to the still-primitive settlement of Houston at twenty-two, amassing what became the nucleus of a tremendous fortune and founding an internationally renowned university? Probably through a combination of unique forces and factors. Central among these were the singularly fortunate qualities of Rice's own character, and the choice of reliable, highly competent advisers and abettors. The men he chose, along with their successors, carried out his objectives while bringing them to new levels of accomplishment.

David Rice (1790–1867), the father of William Marsh Rice, provided some admirable genes, attributes, and predilections for his son. David came to Springfield, Massachusetts, in the valley of the Connecticut River, when he was just twenty-two. A skilled mechanic and metalsmith, Rice learned that there was work and opportunity in the expanding Springfield Armory, seventy miles due west of Boston on the Connecticut River. He and his young wife, Patty Hall Rice, moved to Springfield late in 1812.

From a modest beginning in the forging shop, David Rice rose steadily at various armory jobs to one of the most exacting: boring gun barrels. This led to the very responsible position of Inspector of the Middle Watershops. Meanwhile, he and Patty were blessed with five sons and five daughters, and became the first admitted to the local Methodist Society when it was organized in 1815. Their second son, born in March 1816, was named for a Methodist preacher, the Reverend William Marsh [3].

David Rice received only minimal formal schooling. Nevertheless, he served as tax assessor and collector, and as representative to the General Court of Massachusetts. He was a staunch supporter of the Methodist Church and of broadly available education. A photograph late in life shows him as a handsome man with an open, rather angular face, close-set eyes, prominent cheekbones, and a full head of hair. There is clearly the impression of a serious and reserved yet reasonable man, concerned with the welfare of his community, his family, and of others.

William Marsh Rice's maternal grandfather Josiah Hall (1753–1855) was another striking, forceful personality who must have left his mark upon his grandson. Again, a photograph provides clues to appearance and distinctive traits. This likeness, from the 1830s, is of a sturdy, still fine-looking man, staring directly into the camera with eyes described as "of piercing blue." The hands are clenched in front of him, with the resoluteness of a seasoned veteran of the War of Independence who has lived a full life but continues to look forward. Josiah not only volunteered at twenty-two (soon after Lexington's immortal militiamen were killed by British redcoats on April 19, 1775), but signed on for two more enlistments after being wounded. Alive and in reasonable health at the age of one hundred and two, he had received a veteran's benefit of bounty land the year before under a new act of Congress.

These then, were some of the influences playing upon William Marsh Rice as he entered the Classical High School in Springfield as a 12-year-old. Many must have remained with him through the years to come, even though young William persuaded his father to allow him to leave school three years later to take a job as clerk in the local family grocery store. While still nineteen, he borrowed the money to purchase and stock his own grocery store in a better location much closer to the Armory, repaid the note before the due date, and made $2,000 "free and clear." By 1837, still technically a minor, he was loaning out money to carefully selected borrowers, but only against the security of valuable real estate or personal property.

Only a few months later, as the spreading effects of the Panic of 1837 began increasingly to be felt, William Marsh Rice was looking well beyond Springfield for new fields of opportunity. As he searched for a more favorable setting in which to invest not only his capital but his more intangible assets of experience and judgment, young Rice learned of the new "city" of Houston in the faraway, infant Republic of Texas. The *Springfield Republican* carried (usually disparaging) notes about the "Texians" and their chances of joining the United

States. Earlier accounts of Texas included the stirring victory over Santa Anna at San Jacinto and Houston's designation as the temporary capital of the new nation.

The *New York Herald*, often read in Springfield, was one of the Eastern newspapers in which James K. Allen and his brother Augustus C. placed their glowing advertisements about Houston: ". . . located at a point on the river [Buffalo Bayou] which must ever command the trade of the largest and richest portion of Texas . . . warrant(s) the employment of at least ONE MILLION DOLLARS of capital, and when the rich lands of this country shall be settled . . . [will] make it beyond all doubt the great interior commercial empire of Texas."

Rice, an eminently practical man even at twenty-two (the critical age at which both his father and grandfather had taken decisive steps that shaped their lives), took the Allen advertisement with a grain of salt. He must have been impressed, however, by 1838 data vouched for in a 1942 publication by the Bureau of Research of the University of Texas: ordinary cloth from the United States, selling in Springfield at retail for $6 fetched $20 in Houston; $6 boots went at $18; and lumber, some of it imported from as distant a point as Maine, brought an astronomical $150 per thousand feet. Butter was 75 cents a pound, eggs $1 a dozen, and the lowly sweet potato, $4 a bushel. It was enough to make a merchant–importer eagerly anticipate huge profits.

It has never been confirmed whether or not young Rice invested his capital in a stock of goods and placed it on a small steamship bound for Galveston, only to have ship and cargo go down in the Gulf of Mexico. In any event, he was obviously not greatly taken with Galveston upon arriving there early in the fall of 1838, and he moved on to Houston sometime in October.

IV.

When William Marsh Rice became a Houstonian in 1838, the little town had been legally incorporated and organized, at least to some extent. A distinguished guest, the noted naturalist and artist John J. Audubon (who had just completed his four-volume *The Birds of America*), reported that there were 800 houses plus as many tents in Houston in the summer of 1837. Within a year, almost as many additional homes, mainly of logs, had been added, along with two hotels and a "shopping area" of more than a dozen stores. The rare bears and more frequently seen panthers had left the town site, retreating to the more desolate areas upstream.

A "direct wagon road" had been opened to San Antonio "traversing country now so well populated that travelers were able to reach a house each night." Moreover, the Philosophical Society of Texas had been organized, and there were advertisements in the tiny local newspaper, the *Texas Telegraph and Register*, for a ". . . GENTLEMAN capable of taking charge of a SCHOOL." There was talk of building a sawmill to replace the one at Harrisburg burned by invading Mexicans, as a growing flood of settlers poured into Texas from the major entry point at Natchitoches on the Louisiana border.

Curiously enough, William Marsh Rice did not immediately turn to merchandising, the apparently promising field in which he was primarily experienced [4]. Instead, the young entrepreneur was first involved in private banking (commercial banks had been specifically forbidden by the constitutional convention of 1835), real estate, and leasing a small hotel and other properties.

On February 12, 1839, Rice received a "headright" grant (under which the recipient agrees to make certain improvements within a specified period of time) on 320 acres in the Harrisburg area. This may well have encouraged Rice to turn his maturing judgment and keen foresight increasingly to the interlocking areas of land, lumber, cotton, and transportation, and to major real estate investments in Louisiana as well as Texas, several of which were to have a tremendous impact upon the early and continuing development of the Rice Institute.

The growing number of wealthy plantation owners up and down the Brazos and the dozen or so cotton buyers in Houston did not escape Rice's canny eye either. He was soon dispatching a small fleet of delivery wagons to the Richmond area southwest of Houston in a booming trade with the plantations, and doing everything with cotton except the risky business of growing it. In the process, he became an incorporator of the Buffalo Bayou, Brazos, and Colorado (River) Railway, the solution to late summer and autumn rains that often made it impossible to get cotton to Houston.

Further demonstrating his exceptional foresight and ability to discover money-making opportunities, Rice bought thousands of acres of prime Louisiana forest land starting in the 1850s and continuing until shortly before his death. He had a standing order with agents for stands of "first-class longleaf pine," and some of his huge acquisitions, at an average of about $2.50 per acre, turned out to have sizable oil and gas deposits beneath them.

By 1850, Rice was able to considerably widen his ongoing contacts with, and generosity toward, members of his family back in Massachusetts. There were many gifts, including major assistance to his aging parents in the purchase of a new home, and help for his married sisters and their children. When the Massachusetts economy remained anemic in contrast to burgeoning Houston, he brought his older brother, David, Jr., and the youngest of the Rice boys, Frederick Allyn, to help with his expanding undertakings [5].

Frederick married Charlotte Baldwin, the widowed niece of both Mayor Harvey Baldwin and Mrs. Augustus C. Allen, in 1854, an example of the tendency, at the time, toward intermarriages between prominent Houston families. His brother William had done the same four years earlier. On June 29, 1850, William took as his bride Margaret Bremond, the 18-year-old daughter of Paul Bremond, a sophisticated and elegant man who was president of the Houston & Texas Central Railroad [6].

V.

Still a few months shy of thirty-five, William Marsh Rice launched a distinctly different phase of his life. There were no children, but his marriage was apparently a stable and happy one. Margaret Bremond Rice lived quietly with her ever more prosperous husband, active in the various church and women's organizations and "benefits" of the time.

In 1863, Margaret Bremond Rice fell desperately ill, possibly of the dreaded yellow fever that remained the scourge of hot, mosquito-ridden summers. She died on August 13, 1863, only thirty-one. Characteristically, Rice showed little outward emotion, but there must have been the natural reaction of depression and the tendency to withdraw as he struggled with the grief of his loss. In the fall of 1863, he left Frederick in charge and moved some of his operations to the Mexican cotton and shipping center of Matamoros, where the Rio Grande flows on into the Gulf of Mexico. There, and in Monterrey, capital of Nuevo Leon, he was in a chaotic yet profitable market where gold was the medium of exchange and cotton could bring a dollar a pound.

These travels, of which little is known, took Rice much farther afield, to Havana. He did not return to Houston until August 1865, months after the final surrender at Appomattox. A note in William Marsh Rice's own handwriting states succinctly: "The war broke up my business." Before credit collapsed in the Gulf Coast area and, for that matter, throughout the Confederacy, the William M. Rice Company was sold in Houston at public auction. Its founder then expanded the substantial banking connections he had already established in New York City.

Early in 1866, Rice bought his parents a new home at Three Rivers, just north of Springfield, and told them of his plans to spend more and more time in the East, specifically in New York City and in New Jersey's nearby suburban Middlesex County. It was both a true and a significant disclosure. Rice would retain his close ties with Houston for the remainder of his life, while expanding the activities leading to the chartering and eventual opening of the Rice Institute. But he was destined never to live again in the elegant house where Margaret Bremond Rice died. In spite of continuing and new businesses and major investments in Houston, from that time on, Rice would only infrequently visit the city.

On June 26, 1867, William Marsh Rice took as his second wife (Julia) Elizabeth Baldwin Brown. There remain conflicting reports regarding Elizabeth (Libbie) Baldwin Rice, variously described as a tall, handsome woman ". . . of wondrous eyes . . . always happiest when doing for others . . . ," and as an unhappy, ambitious social climber. There are no doubts, however, regarding the exact wording and potential impact of her final will, signed on June 1, 1896, and probated soon after her death on July 24, less than two months later.

Elizabeth Baldwin Rice has remained a woman of some mystery. Few, if any, knew her well. Her innermost feelings or ambitions were apparently never disclosed to Rice, although the meager record of their relationship shows no evidence of his ever having treated her with anything but marked kindness. One would suspect that the impecunious years with her first husband, the "unremarkable" John H. Brown, followed by a return to Houston as an impoverished widow employed as a housekeeper, left her with almost a compulsion to gain the high social position held by her older sister Charlotte (Mrs. Frederick Rice), or her aunt, Mrs. A.C. Allen.

In a new marriage and lifestyle, William Marsh and Libbie Rice lived in New York City hotel suites and apartments half of the year before removing to Houston to stay with the Frederick Rices or with Margaret Bremond's sister Harriet and her husband Samuel Timpson. They travelled to the metropolis and returned from there in a luxurious new drawing room and "Pullman Palace" accommodations on the Houston & Central Texas. Rice had helped to negotiate an agreement with the major railroads running north and east, which allowed Houston–New York City passengers to travel with only a single transfer, which was made in St. Louis.

By 1895, she and William Marsh Rice were listed for the first time in the New York City Social Register; had taken a lease on a handsome, newly furnished, and considerably larger apartment on Madison Avenue; and seemed to have attained some standing in the complex society of the Eastern metropolis. In Houston, a comfortable apartment in the new annex to the Capitol Hotel was being prepared for them. This apartment was the scene of what Elizabeth Baldwin Rice must have regarded as her arrival, at long last, at the summit of Houston society. She gave a reception in her new home for Jefferson Davis' daughter Winnie during the thirtieth reunion of the United Confederate Veterans Association. Society reporters for the Houston and Galveston newspapers went on for days about the "stunning elegance" of the affair, complete with a small orchestra and hundreds of guests, the ladies uncomfortable but determinedly fashionable in heavy satin gowns in hot, humid mid-May.

Returning to New York for the summer as was their custom, Elizabeth and William Marsh Rice stayed on for much of the winter of 1895–1896 because of Rice's involvement in a series of complex business negotiations at the time. She suffered through a siege of pneumonia and, when the weather remained unusually cold and disagreeable, they went to Houston at the end of April, a time that ordinarily found them en route to New York City.

In mid-May, Elizabeth Baldwin Rice had a severe stroke in the apartment at the Capitol Hotel annex. This left her paralyzed on the right side, with speech impairment and some evidence of mental disorder. On June 1, 1896, she signed a new will about which her husband knew absolutely nothing. Drawn by Orren T. Holt, an attorney who had moved into the Capitol Hotel annex with his wife (who quickly established a close friendship with the ailing Elizabeth), it was based on the contention that Mrs. Rice and William Marsh Rice were both legally residents of the state of Texas. She was, Holt maintained, therefore entitled to one-half of all community property acquired by her husband since their marriage.

Among Elizabeth Baldwin Rice's many bequests were ten percent of her estate to Orren Holt for his service as executor, about $400,000 to various members of the Baldwin family, and $250,000 to establish the Elizabeth Baldwin Home for ''indigent gentlewomen.'' There was no mention of the William Marsh Rice Institute. The will was witnessed by Orren Holt's mother-in-law and sister-in-law. This detailed document, had it been accepted as valid, would have greatly diminished both the endowment of the Rice Institute, and the funds available to move it from concept to reality.

VI.

Nearing sixty, William Marsh Rice began to consider some major, ongoing project or institution that he could endow with his growing fortune. He noted Cooper Union, the institute founded by Peter Cooper for the education and training of ''the workingmen of New York City,'' and visited the uptown campus a number of times. He went to Philadelphia with John Bartine, his Plainfield, New Jersey, lawyer, to obtain detailed information on Girard College, founded by Stephen Girard to educate ''white orphan boys.'' And when his nephew and namesake William Marsh Rice II (Frederick's son) entered Princeton in 1875 to study engineering, he visited the nearby New Jersey institution several times.

Impressed greatly by the concepts of both Cooper Union and Girard College, and by the opportunity that Princeton was providing his nephew (in a changing United States where higher education would obviously be increasingly important), Rice had Bartine draw up a will for him in 1882. This will provided for the building and endowment of the William Marsh Rice Orphans' Institute, to be established at his Green Brook estate after his death.

Fortunately, Rice had gradually increased the time he spent in Houston, starting in 1879. An investment of consummate importance to the future Rice Institute was made: rounding out his purchases of Louisiana timberland, 50,000 acres of prime longleaf pine in Beauregard Parish was obtained from the federal government at $1.25 per acre, which would be left to the Rice Institute in his will.

Rice was drawn ever more closely into the circle of influential Houstonians who were to become the original trustees of the Rice Institute. One of these community leaders was Cesar Lombardi, who had emigrated from Switzerland to New Orleans with his family at fifteen. Educated by the Jesuits in the Louisiana capital, he had become a key official of W.D. Cleveland & Company (wholesale grocers and cotton factors), and president of the Houston School Board. In the latter post, he was ever more conscious of the need for a public high school in the growing "little city." The project was regarded as expensive foolishness in many quarters, and was turned down almost unanimously when Lombardi requested financing in the late 1880s. Soon thereafter, he decided to tackle his longtime friend and frequent visitor, William Marsh Rice, on the proposition.

One of a series of letters preserved in the Fondren Library at Rice recounts how Lombardi locked the door of his private office against interruptions, and discussed the need for the high school with Rice for more than an hour. He told him that Houston, ". . . where he had made his fortune . . . should become the beneficiary of his surplus wealth . . . [in a] monument to his memory that would not crumble with time." Rice promised to give Lombardi an answer soon, and when this was not forthcoming, the latter called on the financier. He was told to put his plan on paper and send it to Rice in New York. Some months later, Lombardi visited Rice in New York. They had what seemed to be an encouraging discussion about the high school, but an entire year went by without any decision or further news regarding the proposition.

Another highly significant letter from Cesar Lombardi tells the happy sequel to his protracted and unsuccessful campaign for a public high school in Houston:

"Then one evening Capt. James A. Baker, who was Mr. Rice's attorney, came to see me and told me that Mr. Rice had just arrived from New York and wished to see me next day . . . [when] I called upon him, he told me that what I had told him the year before about devoting a part of his fortune to educational purposes had made an impression upon him . . . he had come to the conclusion [however] not to erect and equip a High School because the City . . . was under obligation to do that . . . was able to do it, and should be made to do it. Instead, he had planned to endow an institution of learning separate and distinct from the public school system . . . planned largely upon the Cooper's Institute in New York and to be known as the Wm. M. Rice Institute of Literature, Science, and Art . . . while he would begin right now to make provision for financing the Institution, he did not wish to put his plans into effect during his life time, but only after his death."

The founder also asked Cesar Lombardi to join him and Captain Baker and his younger brother, Frederick Allyn Rice, as charter trustees of his Institute. The invitation was apparently accepted on the spot.

Captain Baker had obviously been hard at work for some time when the Lombardi–Rice meeting was held sometime in late April 1891. The application for a state charter for the Rice Institute was signed by the original seven trustees on May 13, 1891, and formally received and registered by the Texas secretary of state in Austin six days later on May 19. Baker, one of two lawyers among the seven, was already a central figure in the new enterprise, as he would be for the next half-century and more. He counseled William Marsh Rice on the selection of the five other trustees, as did businessman Emanuel Raphael [7].

Much as his friend Lombardi had done, Emanuel Raphael had called on William Marsh Rice, requesting major support for public libraries tied into the public school system. Rice gave him the same answer he had given Lombardi: let the city support any such undertaking. However, the two men began a lengthy discussion of the new plan for the Rice Institute. Raphael was so interested, and Rice evidently so gratified at his positive reaction, that the younger man left with two crucial assignments: to help Captain Baker and the founder put the plan for the Institute down on paper, and to recruit the remaining trustees to serve with the Rice brothers, Baker, and Lombardi as incorporators and members of the first governing board.

Raphael was asked to accept the appointment before he left the meeting, and agreed to do so. He had the agreement of the two other charter trustees, James Everett McAshan and Alfred Stephen Richardson [8], within days, and apparently made valuable contributions to the wording of the institutional charter, as he would many times during the twenty-two years he served on the governing board until his death on April 16, 1913.

All seven charter trustees were members of the evolving Houston aristocracy, although from widely differing backgrounds. Captain James Addison Baker, Jr., was born January 10, 1857, in Huntsville, Texas. His father had come to the pleasant, prosperous county seat of Walker County as had so many others there, from Huntsville, Alabama. And, like James S. Abercrombie, wealthy oilman, industrialist, and philanthropist; Judge J.A. Elkins, lawyer, banker, and master politician; and Robert Scott Lovett, eminent lawyer and U.S. secretary of defense, Baker came the seventy-five miles directly south to Houston to make his name and fortune.

The relationship between Captain James A. Baker and Rice continued to be of the utmost importance to the genesis of the William Marsh Rice Institute. During all the years of its first half-century, from 1891 until Captain Baker's death in Houston on August 2, 1941, Baker and the Rice Institute were ever more closely associated.

VII.

William Marsh Rice was demonstrably a man who looked before he leaped. As early as 1875, he had been convinced that he wanted to devote the bulk of his mushrooming fortune to an institution capable of helping the deserving, needy young. As this basic conclusion emerged in growing detail, it became both broader and more specific. From an orphanage in New Jersey, the mutation progressed in the charter and objectives of the Rice Institute to the establishment and maintenance of a public library and an "institution and Polytechnic school" in Houston, Texas.

The institution was to be ". . . for the Advancement of Literature, Science, Art, Philosophy, and Letters" (later shortened to the far less cumbersome "Letters, Science, and Art" on the rings worn by graduates). There was nothing specific concerning the Polytechnic school, but the charter provided broadly for "procuring and maintaining scientific collections; collections of chemical and philosophical [?] apparatus, mechanical and artistic models, drawings, pictures and statues; and for cultivating other means of instruction for the white inhabitants of the City of Houston, and State of Texas . . ."

The unfolding plan, however, included other, quite specific and significant elements that the founder himself insisted upon: In order to proceed from concept to reality, Rice signed a "deed of indenture" on May 13, 1891. This involved a $200,000 note from Rice to the trustees, at six percent interest payable annually. Of far more consequence, Captain Baker drew up, with help from Emanuel Raphael, four deeds of gift from Rice and his wife, Elizabeth Baldwin, that would become the lifeblood of the neonate Rice Institute. The gifts comprised seven acres along Louisiana Street just south of downtown Houston, a 10,000-acre tract in Jones County near the county seat of Anson (named for the last president of the Republic of Texas), the historic site of the Capitol Hotel (soon to be the Rice Hotel) at Main and Texas, and a donation of the utmost importance: the 50,000 acres of choice pine forests Rice had bought in Louisiana's Beauregard Parish for $62,500.

Rice himself added two other pointed provisions to the deed of indenture and related documents in the plan that was now taking definite form. As Rice had told Cesar Maurice Lombardi, while he would begin right now to make provision for financing the Institution, he did not wish to put his plans into effect during his lifetime but only after his death. This was an obvious reflection of his innate modesty and of the distaste for publicity that had continued to grow as Rice moved through middle age and into his final years.

And while he had full confidence in the six men chosen to serve with him as charter trustees, Rice had the following stipulation inserted in both the $200,000 deed of indenture and the four deeds of gift: if a difference of opinion should arise between the party of the first part (the founder himself) and said Trustees as to the investment or expenditure of such funds, then the decision of the party of the first part shall control. The canny Yankee in Rice had remained intact, even in his seventy-fifth year.

Controversy did not arise. The founder continued to work long hours on Institute matters with Captain Baker, with his brother Frederick, and with Lombardi and Raphael, the latter having developed into both a trusted adviser and close friend. Rice also conferred regularly with two other trustees, James Everett McAshan and A.S. Richardson, who had, as did their peers, specialized knowledge and experience of specific value, plus membership in Houston's elite banking, business, and professional circles.

VIII.

Captain James A. Baker, elected chairman of the Rice Institute governing board, a position he would hold until his death in 1941, remained the central figure among the trustees. He proved his worth many times, especially in connection with a crucial lawsuit involving the will of Mrs. William Marsh Rice. This document, the talk of Houston for months, was a dagger pointed straight at the heart of the Institute when it was filed for probate in March 1897 following Elizabeth Baldwin Rice's death at the age of sixty-eight in 1896.

Just entering his eighth decade, a time when he might have looked forward to relative peace of mind and the opportunity to look back in retrospect upon what had already been an eventful life of achievement, the widower William Marsh Rice was faced with another shock: Orren Holt, the second Mrs. Rice's attorney, as executor filed her will for probate in Houston's Harris County courthouse. Captain Baker was about to enter center stage again, this time as champion and defender of the entire concept and future of the Rice Institute. His crucial roles as chairman of the governing board and lead attorney for both founder and Institute suited him ideally for this position.

Elizabeth Baldwin Rice's will was admitted to probate almost eight months after her death. Her husband had several legal avenues through which to attack the will, among them charges of collusion, mental instability, and lawful place of residence. He chose the latter, and Captain Baker filed suit in United States Circuit Court in Galveston, claiming that his client was a resident of the state of New York at the time of his marriage to Elizabeth Baldwin, had been since, and remained so. If upheld, the claim would negate the second Mrs. Rice's attempt to seize ownership of one-half of community property under Texas law.

It was soon apparent that one certain aspect of the case would be its duration in the courts. The legal questions involved were complex, and the sums involved increasingly large. Further, the entire situation would become even more confused by a slowly forming specter of forgery, embezzlement, and murder.

William Marsh Rice returned to New York City and his still active life, seeing to his myriad investments and the ongoing financing of a number of his enterprises in Houston, elsewhere in Texas, and in Louisiana. He was able to spend a great deal of time in the East because of the faith he had in Captain Baker, the other trustees of his Institute, and a vital addition to his staff, Emanuel Raphael's brother-in-law, attorney Arthur B. Cohn. Almost from the time he hired Cohn in the summer of 1893 (when the new employee was barely twenty-two), Rice knew that he had discovered, through Raphael's strong recommendation, a jewel of honesty, integrity, and dedication to task. Cohn exhibited these admirable qualities with others, while steadily gaining in judgment and in the respect of his elders.

IX.

Even as Rice paid ever-increasing attention to his health [9], the elements of an entangled plot that proceeded from fraud and forgery to murder were falling into place around him. He had employed in Houston the 21-year-old son of an impoverished farmer working a few acres "out in the country." This was Charles Freeman (Charlie) Jones, who had worked at a variety of small jobs in the area after completing grade school. Rice needed a jack-of-all-trades who could act as manservant, sometime cook, handyman, and messenger between the 500 Madison Avenue apartment and the downtown banking centers that were the locus of financing for his many business ventures. Jones was an agreeable young man who got on well with people, and was seemingly honest and trustworthy. He was hired for a trial period at $25 a month, plus board and keep, and went on to New York with his new boss in May 1897 as Houston's thermometers climbed rapidly in the first heat wave of late spring.

A new character, attorney Albert T. Patrick, appeared on the scene, as Orren Holt continued to seek evidence in support of his claim that the Rices had been legal residents of Texas, and that Elizabeth Rice's will was therefore valid. Patrick dressed well, spoke in a manner that seemed to quell any suspicion, and made an excellent appearance overall. Orren Holt knew of Patrick, although his information concerning him must not have been too complete. He retained the younger practitioner to uncover absolutely anyone who had known William Marsh and Elizabeth Baldwin Rice in New York City or at the Green Brook estate, and hopefully obtain from them testimony shoring up the contention that the Rices had been legal residents of Texas.

While seeking depositions, Albert Patrick soon discovered Charlie Jones. It was easy to arouse in this pliable, unsophisticated man fear over the prospect of his 83-year-old employer dying suddenly, or discharging him to wander the alien streets of New York City unemployed and without means.

The solution, Patrick suggested, was to watch carefully for opportunities to provide for himself (and for lawyer Patrick). Charlie Jones' meager salary had been twice doubled, and was now at $100 a month. However, he had reportedly become something of a womanizer and had increasing need for additional income. He joined the evolving conspiracy at once.

After one or two amateurish attempts at having Rice sign a fraudulent will, Jones turned to even more criminal projects: he slipped mercury tablets into the old gentleman's food and medication in an attempt to murder him. From Galveston, Jones' brother also mailed him six ounces of chloroform, which Jones did not immediately use as the overall plot was proceeding under the direction of Albert Patrick, who tended toward far more sophisticated approaches.

Patrick, meanwhile, practiced Rice's signature endlessly. Since Charlie Jones now typed much of his employer's business correspondence, the attorney signed a few letters going back to Houston. His forgery had reached a point where it escaped even the eye of the meticulous Arthur B. Cohn.

What would culminate in murder was now moving rapidly toward the final turn of events. The details have been recorded in most complete, scholarly, and interesting fashion in Andrew Forest Muir's papers and research notes, admirably edited by Sylvia Stallings Morris. To briefly summarize:

Albert Patrick prepared a fraudulent will assigning major portions of William Marsh Rice's already tremendous estate to him. The forged document carried the same date (June 30, 1900) on which two notaries public had witnessed Rice actually signing other documents, all of which were legitimate. However, there were major problems remaining for the master plotter. First, William Marsh Rice was still very much alive, and an inheritance cannot be had before the testator dies. Moreover, Orren Holt had to be dealt with. It had become increasingly important to settle Holt's attempt to validate Elizabeth Baldwin Rice's will and thereby obtain one-half of her husband's property for the widow's estate, including a huge legal fee.

A reasonable compromise, Patrick felt, would get Holt out of what had become a considerably larger picture. When Patrick cautiously inquired about Captain Baker's position on a compromise, however, he was given a blunt and discouraging reply. Baker told him that there was overwhelming evidence clearly establishing that his client, William Marsh Rice, had not been a legal resident of Texas at the time of his second marriage. And the trial, after many delays, had been firmly set for November 1900.

Nature intervened on September 8, 1900, with a monster hurricane demolishing Galveston and causing enormous damage in Houston. Many of Rice's best properties were torn asunder, in particular the Merchants & Planters (Cottonseed) Company Mill. It was devastated by winds in the 150-mile-per-hour range, and then burned after huge smokestacks collapsed. When the telegrams began arriving from Houston, Charlie Jones reported the progressively worse losses to Albert Patrick. He also kept his co-conspirator closely informed concerning Rice's plans to draw upon a then tremendous cash balance of $250,000 for emergency repairs. The money was in the New York bank of S.M. Swenson & Sons. Much of it would be depleted almost immediately in a series of $25,000 drafts as repairs began and continued.

Patrick knew that he had to act, and quickly. It was already Saturday, September 22, when the overall situation was revealed, and Jones told him that the first $25,000 draft from Houston had arrived for presentation to Swenson & Sons on Monday. Patrick gave Charlie some oxalic acid, a poison calculated to encourage cardiac arrest in the elderly, with instructions on how to administer it to the ailing Rice, in distress because of the catastrophic losses in Texas. When Charlie gave it to him, though, Rice promptly spat it out, complaining of the bitter taste.

Patrick then ordered Jones to administer the chloroform, mailed from Galveston, through a makeshift cone made from a towel. This was done by Charlie about 6:00 p.m. on Sunday, September 23, his employer having gone to bed at an unusually early hour, and this attempt was successful: William Marsh Rice succumbed to the chloroform. As soon as Rice's physician pronounced him dead, Jones relayed the news to Albert Patrick, who came over at once from his rooming house.

There is often a slip-up that allows even the most carefully planned "natural death" to be uncovered as the murder it really was. Patrick, arriving soon after at 500 Madison Avenue, called in an undertaker. In his usual officious, self-assured manner, he instructed the mortician to cremate the body while he made arrangements for a brief funeral ceremony the next day. Jones had, in the meantime, placed a brochure on cremation near the top of a pile of current papers on Rice's desk, to appear as if his employer had been considering such a procedure.

The undertaker had unexpected news: Because of the intense heat required, he needed at least a full day to prepare the cremation furnace. There were other fortunate developments for the Rice Institute the very next day. One of Albert Patrick's confederates appeared soon after S.M. Swenson & Sons opened with a $25,000 check made out to "Abert" Patrick and apparently signed by William Marsh Rice. The check was not accepted for payment because of the Abert/Albert error, and aroused the suspicions of Eric Swenson, a senior partner in the bank. Swenson had the good judgment to consult James W. Gerard, a young attorney under retainer to the firm. Gerard urged his client to send what would become a historic telegram immediately to Captain James A. Baker in Houston: "Mr. Rice died last night under very suspicious circumstances. His body will be cremated tomorrow morning at nine o'clock."

Baker consulted at once with his fellow trustee and executor Frederick Allyn Rice, the founder's brother and closest living relative. Their telegram was back in New York City within an hour or so. It ordered an immediate halt in any plan for cremation and announced their departure on the afternoon train for New York. Meanwhile, the invaluable James Gerard worked on through Monday and most of the following night. He went to the district attorney, to William Marsh Rice's physician, and finally (after midnight) interviewed Albert Patrick in the presence of a senior detective from the district attorney's staff. An autopsy was ordered; Rice's vital organs were removed for minute examination and chemical tests.

Soon after Captain Baker arrived in New York City, he discovered the existence of the so-called "Patrick" will of June 30, 1900. This limited total bequests from William Marsh Rice to his Institute to $250,000. Baker sensed at once that he was confronted with a monumental instance of fraud, forgery, and murder. He stayed on in New York, working constantly with the district attorney and his capable staff, and with James Gerard.

Within two weeks, Albert Patrick and Charles Jones had been charged with forgery, and were safely behind bars in the Tombs, the city's dreary prison. Then Jones was read the damning evidence from the coroner: His employer's organs showed the presence of mercury in potentially fatal quantities. Charlie lost whatever composure he had, and broke down completely. He accused Patrick not only of being the man behind the complicated plot to seize control of Rice's fortune, but of having chloroformed the founder.

Time spun on, with enormous publicity from the more sensational of New York City's newspapers, and very full coverage from the conservative *Times* as well. Albert Patrick was released on bail supplied by a wealthy relative, but was arrested at once on a new charge of capital murder. After two attempts at suicide, Charlie Jones finally admitted that he had administered the chloroform, but there was soon testimony that William Marsh Rice could have been dead when the cone was placed on his nose.

Albert Patrick was found guilty of murder in the first degree on March 26, 1902; the sentence was death by electrocution at Sing Sing. Jones was given probation, returned to Houston with a brother, and shot himself to death more than a half-century later, in nearby Baytown. After long litigation and the resetting twice of execution dates, Patrick's sentence was reduced to life imprisonment as one of a series of commutations by the governor of New York during Christmas week of 1906. A full pardon was granted in 1912, and William Marsh Rice's murderer left to make a new life in Oklahoma, where he died in 1940 at seventy-four.

Captain Baker had saved the Rice Institute twice, once even before the jury issued its verdict on Albert Patrick, by halting the cremation of William Marsh Rice. Orren Thaddeus Holt, just elected mayor of Houston, was still pursuing Elizabeth Baldwin Rice's community property suit almost six years after her death in 1896. Mayor Holt saw, however, little hope of establishing Texas as the legal residence of the Rices at the time of their marriage. Baker and his co-executors and trustees could now see far more clearly the probable dimensions of William Marsh Rice's estate, even in 1902. There was also an obvious and growing need to keep faith with the founder, and with those he was to help so much down all the years to come, by getting on with his Institute.

Captain Baker settled with Orren Holt and the estate of Elizabeth Baldwin Rice for $200,000 (less than five percent of the endowment that was eventually turned over to the executor/trustees of the William Marsh Rice Institute), on February 6, 1902. It was an especially trying time for Captain and Mrs. Baker and their family. Their oldest son Graham was desperately ill of pneumonia, and died a week later.

Notes

1. Few of those present knew that Rice Institute had narrowly averted an embarrassing problem in planning the academic proceedings. Until one week before, a cantankerous but financially agile farmer, Charles Weber (who had been paid the then exorbitant price of $50,000 for 7.152 acres immediately adjoining the Administration Building), still had an unsightly fence perched on Institute land next to that splendid structure. The fence was removed just in time, in part because of the diplomatic abilities of President Lovett. He called upon Farmer Weber, drank supposedly beneficial well water with him, and convinced Weber that an ancient survey he had depended upon was in error.

   The farmer was reportedly mollified both by Dr. Lovett's courteous manner, and by the $50,000 paid for his land. He had already purchased ten lots along Sunset Boulevard, in what would become the attractive Southampton addition, for a fraction of the $50,000. His comfortable new residence would soon be under construction on the best of the lots, and he anticipated handsome profits on the remaining nine.

   Emergency plans, now unnecessary, had already been worked out to route the October 12 procession from its starting point at the first residential hall so as to avoid Weber's ugly fence. Ground crews still had to fill in large puddles south and northeast of the Administration Building. These had remained from heavy rains in late summer, delaying final completion of an underground tunnel system. Large potted shrubs were brought in to hide a construction shed and a temporary railroad spur to the west.

2. James A. Baker, Sr., practiced law in Huntsville, Texas, with State Senator Leonard Anderson Abercrombie. His son, Captain James A. Baker (the title was from the Houston Light Guard, a highly skilled, highly social, military drill team composed of the city's more prominent young men, which performed in holiday parades and at formal balls, dedications, and other special events), was educated in the excellent public schools of Huntsville. Huntsville had prized good primary, secondary, and higher education from its earliest days.

   Because of the military tradition in his family and throughout Walker County, young Baker was sent to Texas Military Academy at Austin, a high school popular with Huntsville boys during and after the Reconstruction era. The Bakers had in the meantime moved to Houston, where, in 1872, James

A., Sr., joined the prominent law firm of Gray & Botts, founded in 1866 by Peter Gray and W.B. Botts. Peter and his father, William Fairfax Gray, were old-line Houstonians who had helped to found Christ Church in the 1840s. Members of the Botts family, a name now associated with the legal profession in the city for almost a century and a half, were equally well known.

Captain Baker was employed by the firm as early as 1878, after his years of "reading law" were rewarded by admission to the bar at twenty-one. The firm had by then become Baker & Botts, and would so remain until 1887. Less than a decade after he joined the rapidly expanding firm, the name was changed again, to Baker, Botts & Baker. This was in recognition of the major clients Captain Baker brought in for what was increasingly identified as Houston's leading association of attorneys. Foremost among these clients was William Marsh Rice, who had expanded still further into undertakings that included banking, real estate, milling flour, dredging, lumber yards, railroads, and compressing and storing cotton.

3. David Rice gave the land for Springfield's Methodist Chapel, named for the celebrated Francis Asbury (who died in March 1816, the same month in which William Marsh Rice was born), first bishop of his denomination to be consecrated in the United States. When his town's "Classical High School" opened in 1828 with a curriculum featuring geometry, algebra, and the mathematics of surveying, he backed the new institution with both influence and cash. Later, he would help establish and serve as a trustee of the Wesleyan Academy, a Methodist preparatory at Wilbraham.

4. It was 1844 before William Marsh reentered merchandising, this time as a partner with Ebenezer Nichols, who had risen to the rank of major in campaigns against both Mexicans and Indians on the Texas frontier. The firm of Rice and Nichols, "merchants and forwarding agents," provided the early foundation of Rice's soon-to-be-expanding fortune. Rice & Nichols began by bringing in staple groceries and farming supplies from New Orleans via Galveston. Soon they added everything from harnesses and office supplies to the elegant New York silks, satins, whalebone, and modish hats that Houston's increasingly sophisticated society demanded.

5. William Marsh Rice's brother, David, sometimes described as the handsomest man in town, was really interested in a military career. He became a colonel in the Texas Rangers, thereby outranking William Marsh Rice by nine military grades; the latter had enlisted as a private in Sam Houston's short-lived campaign against the Mexican invaders of San Antonio, and returned to civilian life in the same exalted rank. Frederick Allyn, however, would become his brother's right-hand man in everything from the pivotal William M. Rice & Company through a cotton compress, vastly extended real estate operations, the Merchants & Planters Oil Company, timberlands, railroads, and even an explosives factory.

6. The wedding between William Marsh Rice and Margaret Bremond was held in Christ Church (the site for today's Episcopalian cathedral) where Rice had been a vestryman since 1845. It was followed by what Houstonians would remember for a generation as the town's most brilliant social event yet: a beautifully decorated and expertly catered reception at the groom's Capitol Hotel that reflected Paul Bremond's knowledge of French cuisine, decor, and wines.

   After an eight-month honeymoon in New York City and various resorts in the East, the couple returned to make their home in what has been preserved as the "Nichols-Rice" house. Ebenezer Nichols began the residence before he moved to Galveston to more closely supervise key operations of Rice & Nichols, and sold it to his partner before it was finished. Among its many features, still seen in Sam Houston Park, were splendid floors and fireplaces, a rosewood staircase, and a completely separate kitchen adjoining the house in the old style of Mount Vernon.

7. Emanuel Raphael was a 44-year-old native of Birmingham, England, whose father, Samuel, had been the rabbi for Houston's relatively small Jewish population since the early 1860s. Raphael had launched a highly successful career in business as a teenage laborer helping to build telegraph lines on railway rights-of-way. He came to Rice's attention as a clerk for the Houston & Central Texas, and became head cashier of the Houston Savings Bank while still in his late twenties. In 1884, at thirty-six, he was named president of the Houston (Electric) Light & Power Company.

8. James Everett McAshan was born in La Grange, the historic, prosperous county seat of Fayette County (named for the Marquis de Lafayette) on October 20, 1857. He came to Houston as a teenager when his father Samuel Maurice launched a banking career that soon had him serving as chief cashier and ranking operations officer for T.W. House's powerful private bank. House served on many directorates, and was among the most prominent of Houston's bankers and industrialists. His son "Colonel" Edward Mandell House was also a banker, but would soon be far better known as a key adviser to President Woodrow Wilson, and as an expert on international affairs. He was so skilled that he was sometimes known as the "other secretary of state."

   The younger McAshan, named a trustee at thirty-three, was a teller at the T.W. House bank in his twenties, and quickly regarded as one of the more promising of a new generation of Houstonians. An organizer of the South Texas National Bank in 1890, he was its first head cashier and chief operating official. During the ensuing third of a century, James Everett McAshan was a leader in the local and state financial industry, president of the Bankers' Association of Texas, and a foremost figure in Houston's business and social circles. His son Samuel Maurice II and his grandson Harris McAshan would both become presidents of the South Texas Commercial as the family dynasty in banking continued down the years.

A.S. Richardson, as he preferred to be called, completed the extraordinary range of specialized knowledge, experience and business, and professional and social connections represented by Rice Institute's seven charter trustees. An attorney born August 16, 1830, he had long service in the railroad industry in Texas. He was named secretary of the Houston & Central Texas as early as 1870, and served as master in chancery during the financial difficulties of the Houston East & West Texas Railway. William Marsh Rice knew Richardson well because of their joint interest in the H&CT, and the latter's long service as a vestryman at Christ Cathedral. He also dealt with his fellow trustee when Richardson was a member of the Texas Legislature and secretary of the City of Houston.

9. William Marsh Rice exhibited even more ability and success in business as he moved on into his eighties. He had little difficulty in recalling minute details, or in moving logically toward the attainment of major objectives. However, there were growing tendencies to retreat into some of the life patterns of the semi-recluse and into hypochondria. Ironically, the diet he devised for himself was essentially what he would have been given (at enormous cost) at most of today's faddish health resorts. It consisted primarily of a rough-ground cereal of bran and oats, home-baked whole grain breads, little meat, and plenty of the freshest vegetables, eggs, and milk.

CHAPTER TWO

The trustees can finally move ahead . . . $4 million in
hand, and more in prospect . . . The search for a
"superintendent". . . President Woodrow Wilson of
Princeton makes a recommendation . . . Edgar Odell
Lovett, a brilliant young scholar from Bethany College
with doctorates from Virginia and Leipzig . . . Princeton
or the Rice Institute? . . . Dr. Lovett is formally named
president . . . Clarifying some basic concepts:
University or Institute? Financing? . . . Vital problems
of location and architecture . . . A world-girdling trip
from Houston to western Europe to Russia to Japan . . .
The appointment of Ralph Adams Cram, an architect of
"the liveliest imagination and creative thrust"

I.

Almost eleven years had passed since the Rice Institute was
chartered on May 19, 1891, and two more would elapse before the
trustees had the founder's endowment actually in their possession.
The situation changed greatly, however, in a period of less than eight
weeks, beginning early in February 1902. The resolution of the suit
involving Elizabeth Baldwin Rice's will, together with Albert Patrick
being found guilty of murder and the June 30, 1900, ''will'' being
adjudged a forgery, opened a new era. The trustees could now begin
to move ahead in certain crucial areas, in anticipation of receiving a
sizable sum within a reasonable period of time.

The areas on which they focused were long-term financing,
academic planning, finding a specific location for the Institute, and
selecting a president. Each of the seven trustees had formidable
experience in finance, although this varied among them from the
legal approach of Captain Baker to that of the president of a utility
company and from high-level business executives to that of Houston's
foremost bankers. With the tangible, long-awaited receipt of William
Marsh Rice's estate of $4.6 million on April 29, 1904, they began to
protect and augment this handsome corpus.

Academic planning could have understandably been a field that the executor-trustees would bypass pending the arrival and expert advice of a first president. Rice had clearly indicated his intent to establish a free, nonsectarian, post-secondary institution for white students, male or female, to be located in Houston, Texas. There the plan became somewhat murky: Was it to resemble Peter Cooper's Union? Stephen Girard's College? What of the Public Library and Polytechnic School? And how would one interpret ". . . cultivating other means of instruction for the white inhabitants of the City of Houston," in Article Two of the charter?

Only the nephew of William Marsh Rice, William Marsh Rice II, named to replace the deceased Alfred Stephen Richardson in 1899, had even attended a university. Nevertheless, the trustees were highly intelligent and well-read men, further broadened by executive and management experience. Emanuel Raphael, who with Cesar Maurice Lombardi had met with William Marsh Rice as early as 1886 on the need for additional educational facilities in Houston, toured a number of Eastern institutions in 1906, primarily those in Philadelphia and New York City. Captain Baker had asked him to make this trip, and to prepare a formal report for the governing board on his findings.

Emanuel Raphael's report to the trustees was in considerable detail, extending from endowment and other financial aspects through curricula, physical plant, and makeup of the student body. Significantly, Raphael did not visit a single university. He did include college campuses in various settings, with differing missions. Among them were Girard College, Cooper Union, Brooklyn's Pratt Institute, and the Drexel Institute in Philadelphia.

The selection of an appropriate location for the Rice Institute was also on the agenda for the governing board at this time, with the seven acres the founder had donated on Louisiana Street an early favorite. Another key item appearing on the agenda for the first time late in 1906 was the search for a chief executive (who was in the beginning termed a "superintendent") for the new institution. Emanuel Raphael was asked by Chairman Baker to compose a letter to the presidents of many of the best-known U.S. colleges and universities, seeking recommendations. A few prominent national figures (including President Teddy Roosevelt, who had become something of an honorary

Texan during a stay at San Antonio's Fort Sam Houston with his Rough Riders) were also sent the letter.

The William Marsh Rice Institute could have taken a quite different direction through this search. After a month or so, the dean of the Teachers College at Missouri State University, Albert R. Hill, was the leading candidate, based on recommendations of the presidents of both Cornell and the relatively new Leland Stanford University. Arthur Lefevre, a distinguished mathematician then serving as Texas' state superintendent of schools, also stood high among the nominees. After Professor Hill had so impressed the governing board that he was almost offered the post, Thomas Woodrow Wilson, the president of Princeton who was to later become president of the United States, also sent in a nomination.

Wilson's nominee was Edgar Odell Lovett, a highly recommended 36-year-old who had graduated with highest honors from well-regarded Bethany College and the universities of Virginia and Leipzig. He had progressed with meteoric speed from instructor to full professor of mathematics at Princeton in the three years from 1897 to 1900.

II.

Edgar Odell Lovett was born in Shreve, Ohio, some twenty-five miles southwest of Akron, on April 14, 1871. His ancestors included Scotch pioneers seeking a new life on the western frontier, and a "German evangelical preacher." Lovett's parents were staunch members of the Disciples of Christ (the Christian Church). The Disciples had their beginning on the frontier during the last decades of the eighteenth century, in an era of great revival movements within the Protestant churches. They yearned for a return to the "ancient order," free of sectarian creed and devoted to Christian fellowship, in a church stressing the fundamental importance of the congregation.

When their son had completed high school with superlative grades at age fourteen, the Lovetts sent him to Bethany College [1], the small but splendid institution at Bethany, West Virginia. Lovett not only became the valedictorian of the Class of 1890; he exceeded the highest average yet recorded at Bethany, that of the storied James Beauchamp (Champ) Clark, a graduate two decades earlier. Clark, speaker of the U.S. House of Representatives for eight years, narrowly lost the Democratic nomination for president in 1912. He was defeated by Woodrow Wilson on the forty-sixth ballot.

After graduating from Bethany at nineteen, young Lovett taught mathematics for two years (1890–1892) at Western Kentucky College in Mayfield. This was followed by a stellar career at the University of Virginia, Thomas Jefferson's renowned institution at Charlottesville.

At Mayfield, he met Mary Ellen Hale, a freshman student at WKC whose father was a leading citizen there. Major Henry M. Hale, a veteran of the Civil War, had been in the midst of bitter controversy as Kentucky tried to remain neutral in the developing conflict of that war.

Like Lovett's parents, Major Henry Hale was a stalwart member of the Disciples of Christ, and a supporter of Bethany College. He was a direct descendant of Kentucky followers of Barton Stone, who helped Thomas and Alexander Campbell found the denomination in 1832. Hale took an immediate liking to Lovett, who had similarly deep ties to the Disciples, and who had begun to call on his daughter, Mary Ellen. The young couple realized that it would be a long courtship, as Lovett wanted to complete his ambitious goals for advanced degrees and academic promotion, and the popular Mary Ellen had other suitors. But in 1897, after he had been awarded the Ph.D. from Leipzig University and gained a coveted post at Princeton, Lovett married Mary Ellen Hale.

The five intervening years (from 1892 to 1897) had been extremely busy ones for young Lovett. Attracted primarily to mathematics, and extremely adept in the field, he had turned more and more to the vital areas of highly sophisticated measurement in which mathematics and astronomy intersect. These were spheres of research and newly revealed knowledge of particular interest to scientists in the last decade of the nineteenth century. His papers in leading journals began to draw widening attention.

An unusual opportunity became available at the University of Virginia: an opening for a graduate assistantship in astronomy at the Leader McCormick Observatory, at the time one of the best of such campus-related facilities in the nation. It was an ideal appointment for Lovett. His studies and research had closely followed the work of Marius Sophus Lie, Norway's great mathematician. Lie, his brilliance in complex calculations amplified by the development of powerful new telescopes, had opened new areas of geometry with his pioneering work in celestial mechanics and measurement.

Lovett soon developed and had approved a unique academic program. As a crucial part of the Ph.D. in astronomy, Lovett was allowed to go to Leipzig to study with the illustrious Lie. Lie had moved on from the University of Christiania to the University of Leipzig. This institution, established in 1409 in northern Germany, was widely known as a source for Ph.D.s singularly well-equipped for a career in either high-level research or in university administration. It was becoming more and more apparent that the young scholar from Shreve, Ohio, and Bethany College would be admirably suited for either field of endeavor.

III.

Lovett was clearly a true Renaissance scholar. At Charlottesville, he had immersed himself not only in the increasingly intricate studies of mathematics and astronomy, but in classical Greek as well. In the little spare time left to him, he had played violin in the campus orchestra, and somehow worked in quick visits to see Mary Ellen Hale in Mayfield. The University of Virginia enthusiastically accepted him not only as a candidate for the doctorate in astronomy, but also for the master of arts degree in Greek.

At the June commencement ceremonies of the University of Virginia in 1897, Lovett was awarded the M.A., Ph.D., and B.A. as well. After further research and study both at Leipzig and the Norwegian University of Christiania, the University of Leipzig granted him the doctorate in 1896. The following year, he was appointed lecturer in mathematics at both the University of Virginia and the University of Chicago. Then came an invitation that would shape his future and—starting a decade later—the history of the Rice Institute.

Princeton University, with a traditional and increasing interest in expanding mathematical knowledge, offered Lovett a post as instructor in mathematics. Other more immediately lucrative appointments were available to him, some at the level of full professor. Faculty membership at Princeton, however, carried prestige plus the opportunity to serve under the chairmanship of the renowned mathematician and astronomer, Charles A. Young.

Moreover, although the 26-year-old new Ph.D. was not aware of it, fateful elements were falling into place: William Marsh Rice II had graduated from Princeton in 1879 and one of his classmates was Woodrow Wilson, who had earned the Ph.D. in political economy at Johns Hopkins and joined the Princeton faculty in 1890. Wilson, named president of his alma mater in 1902, would become a friend of Lovett, and quickly recognize and reward the junior man's abilities.

Princeton also provided the economic stability that made it possible for Lovett to marry Mary Ellen back in Mayfield, soon after classes began in the fall of 1897. And, in a progression that could only be described as meteoric for an institution of such distinction, Lovett won quick promotions. Within a single year, the neophyte instructor was promoted from an assistant professor to the rank of full professor in 1900. Then, when Chairman Young retired in 1906, the coveted chairmanship went to Lovett. The stage was set for the trustees of the embryonic Rice Institute, as they stepped up their search for a president to head their new institution.

Many years later, in the summer of 1944, Dr. Lovett would set down some of the captivating details of how he came to be chosen by the trustees. His selection was in large part because of the board's decidedly positive reaction to the candidate during his visit to Houston in mid-April 1907, especially after a long interview with members of that board on the evening preceding his return to the East.

Asked for an opinion, the Princeton professor gave it, clearly and with supporting logic. This naturally appealed to the mature businessmen and attorneys with whom he was meeting. Of various proposed sites, the seven-acre tract on Louisiana Street inherited from the founder was "far too small," in Lovett's opinion, and also too near Houston's expanding downtown commercial area; the "ranch beyond the city," acquired as an investment by William Marsh Rice in present-day Bellaire, was "too far out." The "old golf links" (site of the original Houston Country Club on Rice property adjacent to Jefferson Davis Hospital and Buffalo Bayou), an isolated plot in what is now Riverside, another just west of the University of Houston, and "wooded acreage down the Ship Channel" had similar and other disadvantages.

By far the best location, Dr. Lovett concluded, after being shown it and each of the above, would be in the area "along the (trolley) tracks on Main Street." Property was available there at a quite reasonable price from George Hermann, another philanthropist. Hermann had expressed much admiration for William Marsh Rice's original gift to the Institute in 1891. Two years later, Hermann had indicated that the founder's generosity influenced his own decision to offer land in this location for a charity hospital, and for a future park. Hermann Park was to provide lasting protection from commercial invasion for both Rice Institute and the elegant subdivision of Shadyside, just north of the Institute's principal entrance on Main Street.

And, having recommended a location upon which the trustees would soon agree, Candidate Lovett gave them another extremely important piece of advice: "Have in hand a comprehensive architectural plan before breaking ground for anything." [2]

IV.

Edgar Odell Lovett was quickly a strong favorite of the trustees, but it would be almost eight months later, during Thanksgiving week of 1907, before they voted unanimously to offer him the presidency. He wrote many years later: "I arrived in Houston one night [April 10, 1907], [and it was] about six months before the trustees took any further notice of me." [3]

It was decided that the invitation to Dr. Lovett to accept the presidency should be extended in person by William Marsh Rice II. The founder's nephew had received an unqualified commendation of the trustees' choice from Woodrow Wilson, whom he would also call upon while back East. Rice went to Princeton nine days before Christmas, four weeks after the unanimous vote of the governing board.

During a cordial meeting with Rice, Lovett seemed to be torn between the Rice Institute and his excellent connections and prospects with Woodrow Wilson. The Princeton president, perhaps already contemplating an entrance into politics, had advised the young professor to seize the opportunity in faraway Texas, as much as he was valued where he was.

Lovett told Rice how greatly he was honored by the invitation to become the founding president. Rice offered him a $7,000 salary with a home provided, plus a five-year contract. In reply, Lovett mentioned the obvious advantages of guiding the new institution even before it had curricula, faculty, staff, a physical plant, or for that matter, specific objectives. However, he told Rice that he would like to consider the matter further. Contracts, he added, were in his judgment out of place in higher education.

William Marsh Rice II suggested that the offer lie on the table for thirty days while the candidate made up his mind. Lovett accepted this, and spoke of how much he had been impressed by all the members of the governing board during his visit to Houston the preceding spring. Rice then left for Houston, where a meeting of the trustees was convened soon after his arrival to hear a detailed report on the Princeton interviews with Lovett and Woodrow Wilson.

Captain Baker reacted almost immediately, in a classic letter that is preserved in the Fondren Library archives. It strongly urged Dr. Lovett to accept. After praising the candidate for his high qualifications and, additionally, for his insight and candor, Chairman Baker cannily emphasized two telling points. He hinted clearly that the original $4 million had grown substantially in less than four years (which it had), and pointed out that the trustees "practically without . . . experience in educational matters . . . will be disposed to give you a very free hand." Then came the strong summation, worthy of a master lawyer who knew how to plead a vital cause: "The opportunity . . . is an unusual one, and however promising may be your prospects at Princeton, you ought to be slow in declining [it]. Such an opportunity comes rarely to one so young."

Within days, Lovett wrote to William Marsh Rice II. He would accept the presidency so graciously offered him. He had been to see Woodrow Wilson, who congratulated him on the decision while expressing regret at the loss that Princeton would suffer in his departure. President Wilson had kept Lovett's professorship and chairmanship in effect through the 1907–1908 academic year, but would arrange for him to be in Houston after the midterm break in February 1908.

The trustees of Rice Institute confirmed the appointment on December 28, 1907 in an immediate telegram and following letter.

President-elect Lovett responded formally on the first working day of the new year, with a splendid letter that was made part of the records of the governing board. He promised to work with the trustees in ". . . combin[ing] in the [Rice Institute's] personality those elements . . . largeness of mind, strength of character, determined purpose, fire of genius, devoted loyalty . . . which make for leadership in institutions as in men . . ."

An illustrious founding presidency that would last thirty-eight years had been launched. In time, some would compare it to the presidencies of William Rainey Harper at Chicago, Daniel C. Gilman of Johns Hopkins, Andrew D. White at Cornell and David Starr Jordan of Leland Stanford.

V.

As agreed with Woodrow Wilson, President Lovett came to Houston in March 1908, a month shy of his thirty-seventh birthday. And he arrived brimming full of sound, well-thought-out ideas. Mary Ellen stayed behind with their first two children, the eight-year-old Adelaide and six-year-old Henry Malcolm, until the end of their school year in Princeton. Another daughter, Ellen Kennedy, had died in infancy. Their second son, Laurence Alexander, would be born in 1913.

Lovett had immediate, significant goals as he arrived in the city that was to be his home for the remainder of his long and productive life. He took up temporary quarters at the Rice Hotel and began to plan. First of all, he wanted to clarify and reinforce the vital concept of the Rice Institute as a university. It might be a university starting its existence with a narrow scope, but it was a university nonetheless—a high-level university directed both to excellent teaching and to meaningful research from the very outset. It was not to be another technical institute.

This crucial matter was soon resolved with the trustees, probably to a considerable extent because of Dr. Lovett's memorable remarks concerning the various interpretations of the word "institute" during his April 1907 visit to Houston. And with this fundamental decision came another determination that also pleased the new president. As he had recommended, the trustees would operate out of income without invading the endowment corpus.

There remained many matters, two of them quite essential, in those earliest months of the Lovett administration. The first was to, as soon as possible, get the process of choosing an architectural firm to produce both a master plan and designs for specific buildings under way. The president wanted to be open for classes in September 1910 if at all possible and, of course, in the Institute's own buildings. The idea of temporary, leased quarters was never entertained. Further, more than 130 acres (or about half of the total acreage required for a campus) had already been purchased, much of it from George Hermann. The location was directly across from the future Hermann Park, in the area isolated from commercial development that President Lovett had recommended in 1907. Other tracts seemed to be available, although updated surveys, ongoing negotiations, and the drawing up of contracts could be time-consuming.

The choice of an architect, President Lovett soon came to realize, would have to be deferred until he could deal with another matter that was quite fundamental and even more timely. He was determined to carry out a project unique in higher education: a journey around much of the world to observe practices, evolving trends, and even experiments in higher education firsthand. During this odyssey, he would amass invaluable data and personal knowledge of curricula, research methods and innovations, and the recruitment of faculty. One of his main objectives was to seek out potential faculty members, as well as distinguished delegates to the academic festival he already had in mind for the formal opening of the Rice Institute.

To get the process of choosing an architect under way in his absence, Dr. Lovett was authorized by the trustees to issue an invitation to a dozen of the nation's preeminent architectural firms to indicate their possible interest in this significant commission. His brief letter, issued July 21, 1908, as he prepared to leave on his lengthy journey, was an eye-opener. It began with two sentences guaranteed to gain the attention of anyone in the profession: "In the course of the next twelve months, we shall seek the services of an architect to design the buildings for the Rice Institute at Houston, Texas. This institution starts with an endowment of seven million dollars, and should rank substantially with the representative universities of the country.''

Half of the firms contacted were in New York City. The remaining six were scattered among Philadelphia, Chicago, Cleveland, and Boston. The list had apparently been compiled to a considerable extent by Lovett himself, and filed with a copy of the July 21 letter of invitation. There are notations as to various honors won by the firms selected, in his precise and distinctive handwriting.

Ninth on the list was Cram, Goodhue & Ferguson of Boston, headed by Ralph Adams Cram. The firm had won a national competition in 1902, thereby gaining a coveted contract to devise a new general plan for the expansion of the U.S. Military Academy at West Point. Four years later, Cram was appointed supervising architect for Princeton University.

VI.

As specific planning began for what would involve an absence of ten months abroad, Lovett hired the fledgling institution's first employee, Fontaine Carrington Weems, a member of a distinguished Houston family. He was hired as Lovett's personal assistant and as secretary to the William Marsh Rice Institute. Dr. Lovett had known Weems as a student at Princeton [4].

Weems accompanied Dr. and Mrs. Lovett on this tremendous journey. He would recall it throughout a life marked by unusual accomplishment and adventure. The itinerary was reminiscent of some of the latter-day, world-girdling travels of U.S. secretaries of state. Landing at Liverpool on the first day of August 1908, they went to England's storied universities at Oxford and Cambridge after visiting some of London's most renowned scientific and educational societies.

The next stop was Dublin. In the Irish capital, President Lovett read the first paper presented by a representative of the Rice Institute. He had especially wanted to do this, since Ireland had just celebrated the centennial of the birth of one of his heroes, the famed mathematician Sir William Rowan Hamilton [5]. A mathematics genius, as a teenager Hamilton had discovered an error in La Pierre-Simon Laplace's theory of celestial mechanics; was appointed professor of

Trinity College, Dublin at twenty-two; and gained increasing stature as a mathematician and physicist of international repute during the next four decades.

Lovett's epic journey continued through all of western Europe and into Scandinavia. In Stockholm, he read a research paper before mathematicians and astronomers from the ancient Swedish University of Uppsala, and other representatives of the learned societies of the Baltic nations. In Oslo, his distinguished mentor, Marius Sophus Lie, arranged for him to be presented to King Haakon of Norway, King Edward VII of England's son-in-law.

These memorable experiences, however, were secondary to his meeting with some of the world's leading scientists, men of letters, and presidents and senior officials of renowned universities and learned societies. The men he visited, and their institutions and organizations, were to provide much of the inimitable and long-remembered impact of the three-day formal opening and dedication of the Rice Institute four years later. It was through Dr. Lovett's presence at so many world-renowned institutions, and his interaction with their leading scholars and administrators, that he was able to reap many lasting benefits for the Institute.

After months in England, Scotland, France, Italy, Belgium, the Netherlands, and Scandinavia, the Lovetts and young Weems went on to Moscow. There, in the last decade of a thousand years of rule by the czars, the president of the world's youngest university met Russian academicians widely acclaimed for their research in mathematics, astronomy, chemistry, physics, biology, and engineering. Ivan Petrovich Pavlov, the master physiologist turned psychologist, had just added new luster to the Russian tradition of pioneering scientific investigations. Pavlov was awarded one of the very first Nobel prizes in 1903, for his discovery of the concept of reflex action and its mechanisms.

Finally, nine months after departing Houston, Lovett set out from Moscow on the final leg of his heroic journey: a 4,500-mile trip across Russia to Vladivostok on the new Trans-Siberian Railroad. From this distant, ice-free seaport in deep southeastern Russia, it was only a brief voyage across the Sea of Japan to his final destination, Tokyo.

In the Japanese capital, Dr. Lovett met with senior members of the Imperial Academy, and with the president of this distinguished affiliate of the Imperial University of Tokyo: the Right Honorable Baron Dairoku Kikuchi. Baron Kikuchi, privy counselor to the Emperor Meiji (Mutsuhito) had taken a leading role in the Westernization of Japan, which came about during the historic 45-year reign (the Meiji era) of his sovereign.

President Lovett sensed that it would be a propitious time to invite a high-ranking Japanese scholar, and member of the Imperial household, to prepare a major paper for the dedicatory ceremonies of the Rice Institute. President Theodore Roosevelt had just served (most successfully) as mediator of the treaty ending the Russo-Japanese War of 1904–1905, in a series of historic meetings at Portsmouth, New Hampshire.

Lovett was correct. Baron Kikuchi was pleased to undertake a scholarly presentation on the introduction of Western learning into Japan. This was a unique, timely, and meaningful contribution to the discourse of October 10–12, 1912, and to the massive, 1100-page, three-volume *Book of the Opening* that appeared later. The paper traced historical, political, and philosophical developments from 1543 to 1912. It ranged from the first arrival of the Portuguese (the original *Seiyōjin*, or men of the western seas) to the opening of a college specializing in Western law and theories of economics in Kyoto, in 1912.

VII.

As the long journey back to Houston began in April 1909, Lovett had time to reflect on his travels across half the world. Ideas covering everything from long-range planning, faculty recruiting, and research procedures to the details of student life crowded his mind and fertile imagination. First on the agenda, he resolved, would be the essential matter he had deferred the previous summer. He wanted to examine as soon as possible replies to the July 21, 1908, letter he had sent inviting expressions of interest from selected architectural firms.

Letters reaching Dr. Lovett in Europe told of major new additions to the original acquisition of 95 acres from George Hermann. Tracts from David Hannah, W.T. Carter, August Warnecke, and J.C. League had brought the total holding for the campus very near the total of 300 acres being sought. The five purchases to date had averaged only $647 per acre. Only three small pieces of land were still under negotiation, although the original Charles Weber tract of seven acres was priced so exorbitantly that it would run the average cost up.

In light of the new land acquisitions, it was increasingly important to move ahead with the choice of an architectural firm. Rather than going directly from New York City to Houston, however, the Lovetts made brief stops in Princeton and in Mary Ellen's old home at Mayfield, Kentucky. They had been entertained in London by Woodrow Wilson, who had invited them for a visit on their way back to Texas. Lovett was anxious to do this, both to have Wilson's views on several matters (including the selection of an architect), and to thank him more appropriately for his recommendation of Lovett to William Marsh Rice II and the other Institute trustees.

Dr. Lovett would always treasure a letter from President Wilson to him, accompanying a request from the trustees of the Rice Institute for Wilson's advice regarding a president for their new university. It said in part: ''I need not tell you that there is no man in the Princeton faculty I have counted on more to remain part of us, both in action and in inspiration, than yourself; but I feel bound, when a thing like this turns up, to present it to the man who seems to be best fitted, and let him say whether he wants to be considered or not. Apparently it might be an opportunity to do a very great service to the South.''

From Princeton, the Lovetts went on to Mayfield to pick up Adelaide and Malcolm, who had stayed with the Hale grandparents. Finally reunited in Houston, the family moved into a furnished home on the corner of Caroline and Polk (1213 Caroline), near downtown. The residence, in a then-fashionable and genteel residential area, had been leased by the Rice Institute from Mrs. A.H. Atkinson pending the construction of a President's Home on campus. This prospective campus facility, designed and redesigned and delayed again and again, was not to be built for four decades, and then for Lovett's successor. Lovett himself seemed to have little desire to live on campus, where he spent long and sometimes exhausting hours as it was.

In the Institute offices in the Scanlan Building, replies from the architectural firms invited to express possible interest in a commission from the Institute awaited Lovett's review. Predictably, no one failed to answer. No firm would ignore the opportunity to snare a multimillion-dollar contract. The architectural companies involved had sent resumes of their most impressive commissions to date, often accompanied by photographs and sketches. Correspondence with the architects had been handled in President Lovett's absence by Arthur B. Cohn, the efficient and ever-reliable "A.B.C.," as he initialed files and papers.

Cohn, it will be recalled, was Emanuel Raphael's young brother-in-law. Hired in 1893 at age twenty-two by William Marsh Rice, he quickly became invaluable in the management of Rice's expanding empire. After Rice's murder, he was simply indispensable. Cohn now wore yet another hat, as general agent for the Rice Institute. He served the Institute four more decades in key positions, often as liaison to the governing board on complex projects involving financial management, or on matters as relatively simple, yet important, as remitting drafts overseas to cover Dr. Lovett's and Mr. Weems' salaries and expenses while in Europe.

Edgar Odell Lovett had abandoned his original plan to have the Rice Institute open for classes in September 1910, but he still hoped to be in operation a year later. In any event, it was vital to move with all due speed in commissioning an architect. He decided to reduce the number of candidates to three or four, and then visit the finalists in their own offices. As this proceeded in the summer of 1909, Dr. Lovett was increasingly drawn to the professional accomplishments, and as well to the creative powers, imagination, and personality, of Ralph Adams Cram.

He was quite aware of the possibility that the choice of the Boston architect might be criticized as undue favoritism toward Princeton, where Cram was in his third year as that institution's supervising architect. Lovett made his decision after weighing this and other pros and cons. After a meeting of the Rice Institute trustees on August 4, 1909, it was announced that the firm of Cram, Goodhue & Ferguson had been selected.

President Lovett explained the decision to pick Ralph Adams Cram more than a decade later, in the Houston *Post-Dispatch:* ". . . if you are to take architecture seriously, why do so with a lower ambition than to make a distinct contribution to the architecture of the country while you are about it? . . . obviously, you must start by seeking the liveliest constructive imagination available among existing creative architects . . . . In the end, it was less of an reasoned choice than an intuitive one, for . . . [I] was more impressed by Ralph Adams Cram's imaginative grasp of the elements of the problem than . . . by any one of the . . . other architects who had kindly set themselves to work informally on the problem; so Mr. Cram was chosen supervising architect of the Rice Institute.''

Cram, or members of his firm, must have been known for combining practicality with intuition, for a high-level panel of distinguished scientists endorsed the naming of Cram, Goodhue & Ferguson. This advisory group consisted of Edwin G. Conklin, head of a new laboratory for the biological sciences at Princeton; J.S. Ames, director of the physics laboratories at Johns Hopkins; Samuel W. Stratton, chairman of the National Bureau of Standards; and T.W. Richards, chairman of Harvard's department of chemistry.

The prestige of the panel's members, and their association with institutions in the forefront of new and significant research projects, was widely noted. This had a distinctly positive effect as President Lovett increased his emphasis on another crucial area: faculty recruiting. At the same time, with Ralph Adams Cram actually aboard, he again turned in detail to curricular matters and to planning the formal dedication and opening of the Rice Institute.

VIII.

Ralph Adams Cram was born December 16, 1863, in Hampton Falls, New Hampshire, a tiny town just south of Portsmouth and barely ten miles north of the Massachusetts border on the Boston & Maine railroad. He was the son of a retired Unitarian minister, described as wise and of ''strong character and philosophical insight.'' When barely seventeen, he was sent to Boston on the first day of 1881 to study architecture. This was the profession chosen by his father when Ralph seemed unable to make up his own mind about a career.

Actually, the perceptive Reverend Mr. Cram had noticed how his son, even in childhood, cut out sketches and pictures of buildings from old copies of *Harper's Weekly*, pasted them on cardboard, and arranged them endlessly in different patterns. As a teenager, he was given a copy of C.J. Richardson's *House Building*, and had soon advanced to John Ruskin's *The Seven Lamps of Architecture* and other seminal works in his father's library. There was also available to Ralph a quite good collection of books on architectural criticism and the history of the profession in the nearby school that he attended at Exeter, New Hampshire.

In the yeasty atmosphere of late nineteenth-century Boston, the young architectural student and apprentice was also drawn to music, art, and criticism. He won attention with a letter to the old *Boston Transcript* lucidly protesting a plan to sell the triangle in front of revered Trinity Church (now Copley Square) to a real-estate promoter. Soon, because of an admirable article he wrote on Dante Gabriel Rossetti and his Pre-Raphaelite brotherhood watercolors at the old Art Museum on Copley Square, Cram was offered and accepted, at twenty-two, the job of art critic for the *Transcript*.

Meanwhile, Cram was in the fifth year of his rigorous training as a "draughtsman" and apprentice architect, and already so adept that he won enough in an architectural design competition to (barely) finance a trip to Europe. Richard Wagner was all the rage in Boston at the time, as his works were performed at Mechanics Hall. By selling his editor on a side excursion to the Bayreuth Festival (near the bygone home of the *Freiherren* Cram), Cram stretched his travel money into a sum that would support a much wider tour of some of Europe's magnificent architecture. The *Boston Transcript* was soon receiving insightful reviews of the Ring cycle, sung by artists trained by Wagner himself. And Ralph Adams Cram was wending his way back, slowly but surely, from what would develop into a valuable secondary career as a talented author and critic, to his true profession: architecture.

Perhaps reacting to the beauty of the majestic buildings (and especially to the inspiring churches and cathedrals) he had seen, studied, and sketched in Germany, France, Italy, and England, Cram gave up his job as a newspaper critic soon after returning to Boston. He then spent more than a year as an illustrator and designer and in a thorough review of the writings of John Ruskin.

In the process, Cram became convinced that Ruskin, the noted critic whose influence upon Victorian England was profound, had discovered a fundamental truth: Architects should seek to emphasize spiritual values as an antidote to the growing overemphasis on technology. In Ruskin's view, the profession could best accomplish this by reviving the Gothic style, which alone was true to nature and to the correct standards of morality.

Cram was soon an ardent advocate of John Ruskin, as he would remain, and in time a leader of the Gothic revival that brought him many commissions. However, he also adopted the tenets of the celebrated and eminently practical French architect, Eugene Viollet-Le-Duc. This practitioner was an early champion of the more modern emphasis on prudent, common-sense methods of construction, as set forth in his classic 1875 work, *Discourses on Architecture (Entretiens sur l'architecture)*.

In 1888, at twenty-five, Cram decided that architecture was, after all, his proper field. He had just completed two more trips to Europe, primarily to Italy and to Sicily. During both, additional exposure to the masterworks of the great architects had a markedly positive effect upon him. And in Rome, an experience that would influence him for the remainder of his long life came along: Intensely moved by a midnight mass in the imposing Anglican cathedral, he was instructed in the Episcopalian faith and received into a High Anglican congregation soon after arriving back in Boston. Eight years of study, travel, and reflection, combined with an architectural apprenticeship and employment as an art and music critic, had finally brought him to safe harbor in his true profession.

Friendships and associations outside the field of architecture, ranging from the soon-to-be renowned Bernard Berenson to opera singers, journalists, artists, poets, and priests, had greatly enriched his abilities, experience, and potential. They would also make it possible for Cram to enjoy collateral careers as writer, critic, and professor. Berenson, another devotee of John Ruskin and of Ruskin's *The Stones of Venice*, must have had a particularly strong influence upon him. Cram would later state that ". . . [my Mecca of] Venice really settled the matter so far as an architectural career was concerned."

After a year back in Boston, working as a freelance draftsman and designer, Cram won $1,300 in a competition for additions to the Massachusetts State House. He then formed a partnership with Charles Francis Wentworth, described by Cram as ". . . [a] perfect balance wheel . . . of strong character and rigid integrity . . . combin[ing] sterling good sense, practical ability, keen judgment . . . and genuine enthusiasm for and appreciation of good architecture."

The firm opened in 1889 in a cubbyhole office of eight by twelve feet. Their very first commission was to remodel a tenement for a wholesale liquor dealer. After a short time, the partners made a wise policy decision: to specialize. The field of specialization chosen, the design of Gothic churches, was one of particular interest and competence for Ralph Adams Cram.

The area selected was already experiencing a slowly expanding revival in the United States, led by architects such as Richard Upjohn. Upjohn's award-winning Trinity Church, completed by 1846 in New York City, had brought him three dozen commissions over the next four decades. James Renwick had furthered the trend by using Gothic adaptations in his stunning St. Patrick's Cathedral on Fifth Avenue. The revival was under way, and as early as 1890 Cram and Wentworth would have four church commissions in the greater Boston area.

Later the same year, a brilliant, very young architect, who also specialized in church design, called on the firm. He had won a competition to plan a $150,000 cathedral in Dallas. This was Bertram Grosvenor Goodhue, who had trained under James Renwick of St. Patrick's Cathedral. He joined the firm. Five years later, in 1895, Goodhue was the new partner of Cram, Wentworth & Goodhue, which became Cram, Goodhue & Ferguson after the untimely death of Charles Wentworth in 1899.

The firm expanded into other areas of practice, including the design of small office buildings and homes, even though Cram continued to concentrate on Gothic churches. Cram was the intellectual and creative source for the company. Goodhue was a gifted artist whose ability in fully detailed drawings was phenomenal and widely recognized. He was also a fun-loving, guitar-playing extrovert who added much to the convivial, warm atmosphere that William Ward Watkin would find at Cram, Goodhue & Ferguson as a new employee. Cram pointed out that Goodhue was ambidextrous, a considerable boon when hours at the drawing table grew long.

It was soon evident that Cram and Goodhue made an excellent team, and were further strengthened by the addition of Frank W. Ferguson. This third partner in Cram, Goodhue & Ferguson could deal ably with contractors, suppliers, the "vacillating income" that can often plague architects, and a wide range of design and construction problems.

The decision to specialize in Gothic churches bore additional fruit, as the flow of mainly Episcopal commissions continued. Meanwhile, Ralph Adams Cram gained growing prominence by publishing many papers on the relationships between his profession, aesthetics, and morality. Several of these early publications were to be expanded into books, including *The Gothic Quest* (1907) and *The Ministry of Art* (1914). The firm gained a most significant commission in the field of church architecture, to design a replacement for St. Thomas' Church on New York City's 53rd Street, as the church had been destroyed by fire in 1904.

Even more important to Cram, Goodhue & Ferguson, however, was the emerging trend for Gothic-revival architecture to invade the campuses of the nation. Cram and Goodhue were a major force in the invasion, from the day in 1902 that Cram opened a telegram and discovered that the firm had won the competition to design the buildings for a full-scale expansion of the United States Military Academy at West Point. The job was so extensive that they decided to open a new office in New York City, just thirty miles down the Hudson River from West Point, and place it under Goodhue's direction. However, Cram had a central role at every stage in the West Point project, working in close liaison with General Hugh Scott. The legendary old Indian fighter had been named superintendent of USMA, a choice appointment with which to end his illustrious career.

To some extent, it was through the West Point project that Ralph Adams Cram was named supervising architect for Princeton University. He and General Scott would march together in Princeton's 1910 commencement, at which time he and the USMA superintendent were awarded honorary doctorates by Woodrow Wilson, presiding over his final graduation ceremony.

And Cram's appointment at Princeton, as we have seen, was a considerable factor in Cram, Goodhue & Ferguson being chosen by President Edgar Odell Lovett of the Rice Institute. Even though, as Dr. Lovett pointed out later, there was the matter of seeking out and discovering in Ralph Adams Cram ". . . the liveliest constructive imagination available among existing creative architects . . ."

Notes

1. Bethany College was established in 1840 by a remarkable man, Alexander Campbell. Alexander, with his father Thomas Campbell, a Presbyterian minister and immigrant from Ireland, had founded the Disciples of Christ in 1832. A prolific writer and editor, the younger Campbell became a notable figure in religious circles through his publications, as well as through his striking ability as a preacher and debater. Among his opponents were Robert Owen of the memorable experiment in living at New Harmony, Indiana, and Bishop John Purcell of Cincinnati, an early leader of the Roman Catholic Church in America. Campbell further demonstrated his versatility by initiating forward-thinking scientific farming methods in the Ohio Valley that made him a rich man, and enabled him to help Bethany College recruit and retain the core of an excellent faculty.

2. There were other opinions, clearly expressed by Lovett, that would have meaningful impact upon Captain Baker and his fellow trustees. Lovett recalled almost forty years later-telling them, ". . . it would be well to build and maintain the institution out of income [from endowment corpus] alone." Then came a final observation of the visitor from Princeton, and a telling one. It removed once and for all any lingering doubt that he would speak his mind plainly, even on a matter involving the founder's will, the charter, and fundamental questions touching upon direction and basic objectives.

   "The very designation 'institute' " President-to-be Lovett recalled telling the trustees, "if it did not mean a female seminary, or one for defectives, or one for the colored race, meant an institute of technology. There was some hint of this [in our discussions] that night, so I told them that I could not be a party for any such undertaking that would not assure as large a place for pure science as for applied science. It was an entering wedge away from technology and towards the university idea. I have always thought that it bore fruit . . ."

3. Perhaps it had been difficult to round up a quorum, both before and after the usual summer recess of the governing board. William Marsh Rice II, while awaiting a pronouncement from his classmate Woodrow Wilson regarding Professor Lovett, had been out of the city more than usual, accompanying Captain Baker. They were involved in very significant negotiations regarding

the Institute's timberlands in Beauregard Parish, Louisiana. Cesar Maurice Lombardi, a close friend and adviser of the founder whose views on the selection of a president were particularly sought, had just returned to Texas after several years as president of a grain brokerage in Portland, Oregon. But he was almost immediately called to Dallas to serve as acting president of the A.H. Belo Company, publishers of the *Dallas News* and *Galveston News*. This was after the sudden death of A.H. Belo himself, Lombardi's brother-in-law.

4. Young Weems was the grandson of Captain Benjamin Francis Weems, who had served under Colonel Benjamin Franklin Terry of Terry's Texas Rangers. This legendary regiment was raised in Houston within days after the cannon on Courthouse Square alerted the city to the fall of Fort Sumter in South Carolina and the beginning of the War Between the States. Fontaine Carrington Weems was born in Houston in 1882, graduated from the excellent public high school at fifteen, and worked for five years before entering Princeton in 1902. He was awarded his degree in 1907, at the last commencement Edgar Odell Lovett would attend as a member of Woodrow Wilson's faculty.

5. Just as Lovett, Sir William Rowan Hamilton was attracted to observatories, and spent much of his career at Dunsink, near Dublin, a center for Irish astronomical research. Hamilton's later work on dynamics was important in the development of the quantum theory, and became well-known to members of Rice's early faculties. He is remembered best of all for his pioneering research into quaternions, hypercomplex values that are the sum of a real number and three imaginary units.

C H A P T E R   T H R E E

"The Meaning of the New Institution". . . *Edgar Odell*
Lovett in a masterly address . . . William Ward Watkin
recalls two difficult yet memorable years . . .
Responsibilities seldom entrusted to an architect in his
mid-twenties . . . Mosquitoes, cockroaches, and grits
. . . A site "level and stupid". . . A splendid academic
festival ends . . . The Watkins of Northamptonshire,
builders and collaborators with great architects . . . The
Hancocks of Staffordshire and Danville, ironmasters and
entrepreneurs . . . Of Will Watkin's parents and the
tragic death of his father . . . An early decision to
become an architect . . . Cret, Cram, and the University
of Pennsylvania . . . A memorable trip to England

I.

William Ward Watkin listened intently to President Lovett as the
final formal program of the three-day dedication of the Rice Institute
drew to a close on the morning of October 12, 1912. Dr. Lovett had
prepared a masterful address on "The Meaning of the New Institution," primarily as a historic record of some ninety pages for the
Book of the Opening. The address had been expertly summarized for
his audience, in four sections entitled "Source," "Site," "Scope,"
and "Spirit" [1].

Watkin found his concentration wandering from time to time in spite
of the happiness of the occasion and the meaningfulness of Dr. Lovett's
address. It had been an unforgettable three days, recalling eventful
weeks and months during which he had successfully fulfilled responsibilities seldom entrusted to an architect in his mid-twenties. He could
not help but remember many of the highlights of the memorable two
years since his arrival in Houston on August 17, 1910.

That first night, Watkin had stayed at the old four-story Rice Hotel,
the mosquito netting carefully in place over his bed because of
Houston's dreaded late-summer outbreaks of yellow fever. As he tried
to read more of a recent history of Texas, he thought he had spotted

several mosquitoes on the netting above him. There was no telltale buzzing; on closer inspection, he discovered a very large cockroach that went scurrying away.

Early the next morning, Edgar Odell Lovett had met him in the lobby after Watkin's breakfast that included grits and bacon drippings. From a nearby livery stable, they had driven out Main Street in a horse and buggy to the proposed site of the Rice Institute, a distance of some three miles. The last mile or so was over a rough dirt road with deep ditches on either side. The actual site still had several gates and cattle guards in place. Water from recent rains stood in many low places and, on the southwest boundary, a little stream called Harris Gully was overflowing its banks. Ralph Adams Cram had called the site "level and stupid." It looked as if it might require a topographic survey, and obviously some flood control work.

Other memories came flooding back as the ceremony in front of the Administration Building sally port drew to a close. Watkin recalled long months struggling with the decision of which one of three suggested master plans for the campus to approve, the seemingly endless telegrams to and from the Cram, Goodhue & Ferguson office at 15 Beacon Street in Boston, and the difficulties encountered with complex materials and procedures. During the past two years he had survived a change in general contractors, months of work with tunnel and roof experts, and much work with gifted bricklayers and stonecutters.

But it had all been rewarding, Watkin realized as he looked again at the magnificent Administration Building and the other structures that fit so well into the master plan. The power plant had been finished first, and now the mechanical engineering building, most of the original two residence halls, the commons, and the faculty tower were in place. And he was already teaching and advising the first class in architecture while accelerating the search for another instructor to help with the second class a year hence. Two generations of architects would enter the profession in the next forty years under the skilled teaching and guidance of Watkin, first chairman of the Department of Architecture.

With the formal dedication over, there was an opportunity for Watkin to visit further with his architectural mentor, Ralph Adams Cram, who had paid tribute both to Watkin, his "personal representative" at Rice

Institute, and to his partner, Bertram Grosvenor Goodhue [2], during the ceremonies. That evening, Watkin and most of the original Rice Institute faculty joined Cram and the other distinguished guests at an informal "shore supper and smoker" on the veranda of the then splendid Hotel Galvez at Galveston.

Departure for Galveston had been by train from the new Houston Country Club, which had a railroad siding on its northern boundary adjoining Wayside Drive. The change of pace must have delighted everyone after the deluge of formal luncheons, receptions, dinners, and lectures of the past three days. There was no chance for rest, however. Instead of a long snooze in the soothing sea breeze, the special train left Galveston at eight the next morning for a 9:30 a.m. religious service at the City Auditorium in Houston, featuring a sermon by the Reverend Doctor Charles Frederick Aked of San Francisco, a noted preacher and pastor.

Houston and the Rice Institute had treated their illustrious guests royally. The founder's Institute had been formally launched with an observance worthy of any great university—especially one so young and so distant from any of the prominent institutions that had sent their high-ranking representatives as participants.

II.

Every architect worthy of the name is essentially a builder as well as a planner. The best within the profession watch their imaginative designs become handsome, useful reality. William Ward Watkin, with the blood and genes of English builders well-represented in both his paternal and maternal ancestry, particularly appreciated the quotation on the classical "Tablet to Art" in the courtyard elevation of the Administration Building at Rice Institute. It reads: "Love, Beauty, Joy And Worship Are Forever Building, Unbuilding And Rebuilding In Each Man's Soul." [3]

As early as the first decades of the 1700s, the Watkin family was in Northamptonshire, the East Midlands county known for good brickmaking clay, imposing Norman and Elizabethan churches, stubborn nonconformists, and Sulgrave Manor, the ancestral home of George Washington. William Ward Watkin's great-grandfather William was born at Maidwell, near the county seat of Northampton, in

1790. He was a member of an old Northamptonshire family, a shire the English often abbreviate as "Northants."

In 1815, William, a builder, married Mary Hobson, who traced her Midlands ancestry back to one George Lambley, born in 1593 in Kingsthorpe. Described as a "man of considerable property," William Watkin and his bride soon removed to nearby Pitsford, where he died in 1830, leaving seven children. The third son was William Ward Watkin, for whom his grandson, William Ward Watkin, was named.

Another son of William and Mary Hobson Watkin was William Ward's eldest brother, John, who became perhaps the best-known builder in Northamptonshire in the second half of the nineteenth century. John Watkin (to quote his 1904 obituary) "will be remembered . . . [for] the excellent building work which gained for him high encomiums . . . [and for the fact that] . . . the architects with whom he worked express[ed] their complete satisfaction with the way their designs were carried into affect, and with the character of [his] work."

Between 1862 and 1864, John Watkin, as the builder, brought to reality the prize-winning design of Northampton's Town Hall (Guildhall) by the famed English architect, Edward William Godwin. This remains a classic of the Gothic revival style.

The second major work of John Watkin in Northampton was the painstakingly thorough restoration of the Church of the Holy Sepulchre under the "superintendence" of the architect Sir George Gilbert Scott. The Church of the Holy Sepulchre is one of the few remaining "round churches" left in Britain. The round churches, with their distinctive rotundas, were built in England at the time of the Crusades in the style of the Church of the Holy Sepulchre in Jerusalem. The Northampton church dates back to 1100 A.D. It was built by Simon de Soulis, whom William the Conqueror had made Earl of Northampton. He built it as an offering of thanks for his safe return from the Crusades in 1099.

Sir George was chosen for this exacting restoration because of his design of the Martyrs' Memorial at Oxford. The memorial is based upon the remarkable Eleanor Crosses at Geddington and Hardingstone in Northamptonshire. The crosses mark, with striking effect, where Edward I decreed that there be temporary resting places for the coffin and burial procession of his queen, Eleanor of Castile. She had died in

Nottinghamshire in 1290, and the body was returned to London for interment in Westminster Abbey using these temporary resting places along the route, one marked by the famous Bamburg Cross.

Scott expressed great satisfaction with the way his design for the restoration was built by John Watkin. Only nine round churches were built in England, and of these, the one in Northampton is the largest and best preserved. Watkin was especially praised for his excellent collaboration with the architect [4].

William Ward Watkin's paternal grandfather, for whom he was named, emigrated from Pitsford, England, to New York City following his marriage to Sarah Wright of Northampton on February 2, 1840. They lived on Windsor Terrace, in Brooklyn, until Sarah died, childless, on December 31, 1854. There are records indicating that this grandsire, sometimes identified within the family as "WWW the first," added the middle name "Ward" after arriving in the United States. This was to honor an uncle-in-law (William Ward) and favorite aunt (Eunice Hobson Ward) who had three daughters, two of them lifelong spinsters, but no sons to carry on their family name.

On March 2, 1860, the widower William Ward Watkin married a 24-year-old young lady from Carrickmacross, Ireland, just east of Dundalk Bay in County Louth. His bride was Catherine McCormick. The marriage was solemnized by her parish priest. The couple would have one daughter with the marvelous name of Hepsibah, and three sons: Frederick William, Albert Henry, and Charles Francis.

Frederick William Watkin was born November 19, 1863, at Windsor Terrace in Brooklyn. He married Mary Matilda Hancock of Danville, Pennsylvania, on November 24, 1884, in her hometown, and their only child, William Ward Watkin, was born on January 21, 1886, in Cambridge, Massachusetts. Frederick William's sister, Hepsibah, married Ernest Charles Churchill five months later on May 2, 1885, and lived in New Orleans almost sixty years until her death there on July 12, 1943.

III.

William Hancock of Danville, Pennsylvania, William Ward Watkin's maternal grandfather, literally "grew up in the iron trade" in England. Born at Lainesfield, Staffordshire in 1812, he was the son of an accountant who trained himself, through long study and experience, as an expert in the mining and processing of Staffordshire's abundant coal and iron-ore deposits. As early as the middle of the eighteenth century, these valuable properties had become increasingly important factors in the developing Midlands economy.

By the time he was 25, William Hancock was in Sunderland, the ancient port well to the northeast of his birthplace where the River Wear empties into the North Sea. There the centuries-old trade in the exportation of coal to Scandinavia had been strongly reinforced by a prosperous new shipbuilding industry and successful developments in the manufacture of iron and steel. In 1844, still only 32 years old, young Hancock and his colleague, John Foley, were en route to Danville, Pennsylvania, at the request of a group of entrepreneurs there that had organized the Montour (County) Iron Works. This new enterprise was in the forefront of the ongoing expansion of the city of Danville, located along the Lackawanna Railroad and Susquehanna River, halfway between Scranton and Harrisburg in northeast Pennsylvania. Early English settlers had left their mark in the region, seen in the names of the nearby counties of Northumberland and Northampton.

The Montour Iron Works was built around an experimental concept: a rolling mill designed to produce pig iron with anthracite (hard) coal, rather than with bituminous (soft) coal, which contains a much higher percentage of volatile materials. The anthracite variety has the advantage of burning with an almost smokeless flame, resulting in more efficient operations, allowing for differing and superior iron products. William Hancock had earned a wide reputation as a metallurgist and iron finisher back in Sunderland, and he was soon hard at work in a laboratory at the Danville plant.

After months of experimentation, Hancock and John Foley succeeded in perfecting the use of anthracite coal in producing high-quality pig iron at the new rolling mill. Of even more significance, they were able to achieve the design and manufacture of the first T-shaped rail to replace the U-shaped rail long in use by the railroad industry. In the words of a contemporary publication, they had made available ". . . a new invention so superior that it supplanted the U-rail and was put into general use all over the world."

William Hancock proved to be skilled in management and financial matters, as well as in metallurgy. He was, to some degree, a forerunner of today's experts in mergers and buyouts. This was at a time when it was increasingly obvious that the United States was entering an era of industrial expansion in much of the northeast. In 1847, almost exactly two centuries after John Winthrop of the Massachusetts Bay Company brought his own ironmaster from England to establish a foundry on the Saugus River just north of Boston, Hancock and John Foley purchased control of the Montour Iron Works and renamed it the Rough & Ready Rolling Mill. Three years later, when Foley had returned home to Sunderland, the Rough & Ready was merged into the Glendower [6] Iron Works, a specialized rail mill, as demand for the new trails continued.

William Hancock's sudden death in 1872 at 59, in the prime of what had been a healthy and extremely active life, was termed "a public calamity" by his peers. He was described as the man ". . . probably responsible for much of the development of the iron industry in Pennsylvania . . . upright and honorable to a marked degree."

Twice a widower, Hancock had had eleven children by his three wives. He first married Isabella Emerson, a Shropshire girl, back home in England when they were both in their twenties. She bore him a son and four daughters before dying in Danville when only 36. He next married Mary Ann Reay, an 18-year-old native of the Birmingham area, in the industrial and commercial heart of Great Britain. The wedding took place in Baltimore, Maryland, the city to which Mary Ann's parents had emigrated in 1844, the same year that William Hancock arrived in Danville.

Few brides would receive a more magnificent wedding present from their groom than did Mary Ann. William's gift to Mary Ann was to become a showpiece in the Hancock home and, finally, a national treasure on permanent exhibit at the Smithsonian. It was one of the new concert grand pianos patented by Jonas Chickering of Boston [6], and one of only three built like this.

However, Mary Ann's marriage to William Ward Watkin's maternal grandfather would be tinged with tragedy. There were three children, all born in Danville: Charles P., in 1860; his younger brother, George M., who lived only eight months after his birth in

1862; and Mary Matilda, the mother of William Ward Watkin, born November 14, 1863. Mary Ann Hancock herself would only live until February 1, 1867. She died when Charles P. was seven years old, and his little sister Mary Matilda only three.

William Hancock's third wife, whom he married in 1868, was Mary Jones. They had three children before his untimely death: Harry T., Jane E. ("Jennie"), and Augusta R.("Gussie"). Mary Jones Hancock thus had an infant, a toddler, and another child barely three to care for after her husband's sudden demise, plus Mary Matilda, only eight. Mary's full brother, Charles P., was twelve, and already demonstrating the ability and early maturity that would make him a community and area leader.

Lucy Reay, Mary Ann Hancock's younger sister, had also married and settled in Danville. Her husband, Dennis Bright, was a second-generation native of Montour County and prominent businessman who had risen from the ranks to a captaincy in the Union Army. Lucy had always been very close to Mary Ann, and was devastated by her sister's death. Her loneliness and sorrow were accentuated by the fact that she and Dennis had no children; further, he had been elected as one of the few Republican members of the Pennsylvania state legislature in 1871, making it necessary for him to be in the state capital of Harrisburg several months a year.

In the face of all this, and because of Mary Matilda's love for her "Aunt Lucy," it was decided that Mary Matilda would make her home with the Brights, beginning in 1872. This she did, although remaining close to the other members of the large Hancock clan in Danville. She was especially fond of her full brother Charles P., who had definitely inherited the energy, attractive personality, and entre-preneurial abilities of their father. Charles, after graduating with honors from Danville's high school, founded what became the largest dry-goods store in the area. He then moved on to investing in and directing a telephone company, a street railway, a knitting mill, and the Danville National Bank, after also organizing the Danville & Sunbury Railway. He and his family lived in a splendid home on Market Street, with a summer residence on the Susquehanna River. Danville would remain Mary Matilda's home for much of her life, and Aunt Lucy and Uncle Dennis became her surrogate parents.

There were startling similarities between Mary Matilda Hancock and the man who became her husband—tall, handsome, adventuresome Frederick William (Fred) Watkin. Both were of long-established Midlands ancestry, born in the northeastern United States. Both were children of a second marriage for a widowed father who had emigrated to his adopted country after a first marriage in England. And both were strongly influenced, not so much by their parents, but by family members with whom they established strong and lasting relationships at a critical stage in their own development.

IV.

Frederick William Watkin had been close from childhood to his only sister, Hepsibah, two years his elder. This bond strengthened after the death of their mother, Catherine McCormick Watkin, on August 5, 1877, while both children were still teenagers.

Their father, William Ward Watkin "the first," owned and operated the Ward Hotel on Windsor Terrace for almost four decades, until his death on November 8, 1883. Actually a large boarding house that provided meals, the long-established property in Brooklyn's Flatbush area was well known to businessmen. Hepsibah Watkin had become a friend of Mary Matilda Hancock, perhaps because Mary Matilda and other members of the Hancock family stayed at the Ward Hotel on trips to New York City. The city was only a few hours away from Danville and northeastern Pennsylvania by train.

As the long friendship between the two women deepened, Hepsibah and, in time, Frederick, were invited to visit Danville. A romance developed between Frederick and Mary Matilda while both were still in their late teens.

Another occasional guest at the Ward Hotel was Ernest Taylor Churchill, a young executive with the Whitney Iron Works in New Orleans and brother of Frank Churchill, a prominent architect in that city. However, his trips to New York City and Brooklyn were not all strictly business. He was engaged to a beautiful girl in Flatbush, a friend of Hepsibah Watkin.

When the Brooklyn beauty jilted young Churchill, he began to court Hepsibah, an attractive young woman of twenty-three. They were married in New Orleans on May 2, 1885, in a union that would last almost forty years and would make New Orleans a new center for members of the Watkin family.

Five months earlier, on November 24, 1884, Frederick William Watkin and Mary Matilda Hancock had celebrated their marriage in Christ Episcopal Church in Danville. Both bride and groom had marked their twenty-first birthdays during the week of the wedding ceremony. The Danville marriage, in a church in which Mary Matilda's father, William Hancock, had been a vestryman, was further confirmation of how the Watkins were moving ever more solidly into the ranks of the Episcopalian Church [7].

The bonds between Mary Matilda and Hepsibah continued to strengthen after their marriages, as their new lives gave them ever more common interests. The young couples, however, would establish their first homes in widely separated cities. The Churchills, quite naturally, remained in New Orleans, where they had taken their vows and where both Ernest and his brother, Frank, were active in their respective careers.

Hepsibah Watkin Churchill ("Aunt Hepsie") remained close to her sister-in-law, Mary Matilda, for the remainder of their lives. Hepsibah was the family genealogist who, through correspondence, maintained the link between the Watkin, Hobson, and Fuller lines in America and England. This was especially true after she made a long visit to her Hobson cousins at their imposing home (Ely House) in the ancient Staffordshire city of Wolverhampton, in 1884.

V.

Frederick could have remained with his bride in Danville; the Hancocks had lived there almost a half-century. However, he was an enterprising, independent man of twenty-one, married at the very same age his father William Ward Watkin took his first bride. In any event, Frederick Watkin chose to make his first home with Mary Matilda in Boston, Massachusetts [8].

William Ward Watkin, the only child of Frederick and Mary Matilda, was born in Cambridge, Massachusetts, on January 21, 1886. Cambridge, an ancient part of greater Boston once called New

Towne, was just across the Charles River from 15 Beacon Street, where young Watkin would begin his architectural career with the firm of Cram, Goodhue & Ferguson twenty-two years later.

Frederick William Watkin's venturesome nature soon turned his interests from Boston to less-developed areas of the United States. The nation had increasingly recovered by the late 1880s from the severe financial panic of 1873. The recovery brought about burgeoning prosperity, based upon expansion of the railroads with unprecedented new construction and greatly increased production to support major upswings in population.

Frederick's brother-in-law Ernest Churchill, as a native of Natchez, was familiar with Mississippi, and particularly with the huge southern area of the state termed the Piney Woods. Here were enormous forests of virgin pine that would become the heart of a vast lumbering industry, centered around such towns as Robinson Springs and Lumberton, near the Louisiana border.

The Mississippi economy, left devastated at the end of the Civil War, showed little or no improvement during the difficult years of Reconstruction, through 1876. Another decade was to elapse before the state began to join in the unfolding prosperity seen elsewhere. It was obvious by the final years of the 1880s, however, that timber from the Piney Woods would be of fundamental importance to the national economy. High-quality pine was available there in enormous quantities, and it was increasingly in demand.

Young Frederick Watkin—much as his father, who had immigrated from England—apparently had a great deal of confidence in his ability to make his way in a new environment. Mississippi's timber would certainly have attracted his attention, and it is probable that Ernest Churchill, with his knowledge of the Piney Woods and its potential, helped his brother-in-law find a foothold there sometime in the later 1880s.

There would have been only the most minimal of accommodations for Mary Matilda and their young son in the tiny lumber towns in Mississippi. It was decided that she and Will would remain temporarily in Danville, with Aunt Lucy and Uncle Dennis Bright. Both Fred and Mary, as they were now known, would meet in New Orleans from time to time visiting with Hepsibah and Ernest Churchill, whose own first child and only son (Neil) was born seven months after William Ward. Fred could, in effect, "commute" from Robinson Springs, Mississippi on weekends and holidays.

Then tragedy struck. On June 24, 1892, Frederick William Watkin, only twenty-eight, died suddenly at Robinson Springs, probably from a ruptured appendix. The death certificate shows the cause of death as "gastritis," a broad medical term that could have included peritonitis. This would have been impossible to treat in such an isolated area, far away from a hospital or physician.

Fred was buried in New Orleans, where a younger brother (the 22-year-old Albert Henry) had also come to live. Mary Matilda went back to Danville with her six-year-old son Will to live in the large, comfortable home of the Brights. Will would remain there until, at seventeen, he left to matriculate at the University of Pennsylvania as an architectural student. Mary Matilda would make this her home until the Brights died.

Hepsibah Watkin Churchill would write of her love for her sister in-law and brother, and of their closeness over the years, a half-century later:

"... now it is Will's mother's birthday [November 14], bringing memories. I've missed her . . . more than you can realize. We were young together, and married [together], she on November 24 [1884], and I on the following May 2. Her firstborn, Willie and [my] Neil, were only seven months apart. She sent me Willie's long baby clothes, and I made her some of Willie's short ones in return. Through their baby years these exchanges went on, and all the years since we understood and loved each other yet were entirely different. We both loved Fred, and that tie bound us long ago."

VI.

It was a pleasant and secure although often lonely life for the widowed Mary Matilda and fatherless son William in Danville. Part of the widow's heart would always remain in New Orleans' old Greenwood Cemetery, where her beloved Frederick was buried, but her Aunt Lucy and Uncle Dennis helped her gradually to accept her grief and a new existence in the comfortable Bright home at 152 West Market Street, overlooking the Susquehanna in a particularly desirable part of Danville.

Dennis Bright proved to be an excellent foster father. He and Will roamed the banks of the Susquehanna, a river named for the Indian tribe discovered by the explorer John Smith in the first decade of the seventeenth century [9]. They dug up arrowheads on the site of one of the Susquehanna tribe's settlements, among buried remnants of one of the small palisaded forts used as a defense against the marauding Iroquois, a far more warlike people [10].

Will Watkin, growing up in a household of adults, tended naturally to emphasize propriety and quiet good manners. There was no rigidity, but a marked inclination toward reserved, dignified reaction rather than to spontaneity in any degree. A certain not-unattractive shyness was accentuated by the youngster's extraordinary height and thin frame. When he entered the academically sound Danville High School in September 1899, he was still four months from his fourteenth birthday, but near his adult stature of six feet, three inches. He weighed barely 120 pounds; although maturity would add another fifteen, William Ward Watkin would remain tall and thin for the remainder of his life.

Will (more often William in his late teens) was an excellent student. In spite of his relative shyness, he was popular at Danville High, and very involved in significant extracurricular activities. He served as editor-in-chief of the historic first issue of the *Orange and Purple,* the campus yearbook that was published to considerable acclaim in December 1902. William appears in the very center of a group picture of his classmates. All are in quite formal attire (in contrast to the extreme informality of yearbook pictures today), and Editor Watkin is the most formal of all. He could, indeed, almost take his place in the House of Lords, with a suit, high collar, and tie that would do justice to London's Savile Row.

In another key campus activity, William was a proficient first-team debater. Against Sunbury High School, Danville's traditional rival in adjoining Northumberland County, he took the affirmative of a topic that would be of paramount interest throughout our nation two generations later: "Resolved: that the United States Government should interfere to protect the Southern Negro in the exercise of the suffrage."

VII.

One of the most meaningful developments in young William Ward Watkin's life came in the summer of 1901, when the tall, dignified teenager found a vacation job in the office of J.H. Brugler, Danville's leading architect. Fascinated by this new (and lasting) field of interest, and apparently doing a good job for his boss, he returned to Brugler's employ the following summer. And for good measure, he enrolled in what he termed a "correspondence course in architecture" in the meantime.

In the fall of 1902, William wrote his great-aunt, Hepsibah Watkin Churchill, a significant letter about these experiences. Excerpts show how rapidly he was maturing while only sixteen, a time when most teenagers have virtually no resolute ideas about their specific interests, much less the choice of a lifetime career: "I have been studying architecture by correspondence . . . and for the past two years have spent my vacations in Architect J.H. Brugler's office (here in Danville). Architecture not only presents fascination and variety, but offers a broad field for . . . individuality and advancement."

Watkin had taken a considerable step forward, and now he took another of far more consequence since he had decided that architecture would be his life. Characteristically, with his final year at Danville High School under way, he began at once to make definite plans toward that end. J.H. Brugler had already made him aware of the Department of Architecture at the University of Pennsylvania in Philadelphia, regarded at the time as the focal point of architectural education in the United States. Now he read in the *Philadelphia Enquirer* that Paul Philippe Cret [11], a French architect only twenty-six years old but already with a developing international reputation, was coming to the University of Pennsylvania in the fall of 1903 to head the Department of Architecture.

In Paul Philippe Cret, Watkin was to discover not only a gifted professor and practitioner of architecture, but a man shaped by the unusual city in which he was born and educated. He was capable of transmitting to his pupils the tradition and flavor of Lyons, the ancient capital of the Gauls along the Rhône in southeast France [12].

Young Cret was familiar with the treasures of Lyon's museums from his childhood, and studied them intensively as a student in the related Institute of Fine Arts. He and his classmates also studied firsthand the magnificent Cathedral of Saint Jean. Other well-preserved examples of the best of Renaissance and Gothic architecture were visible in Lyons' city squares. The Town Hall, seat of municipal government, was a notable showpiece of the best in the Gothic tradition, which Edward William Godwin might have studied before designing Northampton's Guildhall in 1860.

"Time and I," the Spanish proverb proclaims, "[will prevail] against any two." A potentially enormous force in the overall development of an individual and a determinant in his success or failure is timeliness. In 1903, timeliness had become a major factor in Watkin's life and career. His now firmly established interest in architecture had coincided with the arrival of Paul Philippe Cret at the University of Pennsylvania. Meanwhile, other developments, all fortunately timed, were under way as young Watkin graduated at the top of his high-school class and was awarded a scholarship to attend the Department of Architecture of the University of Pennsylvania. He fortunately matriculated there in the fall of 1903 as a member of Professor Cret's first class.

VIII.

At that very moment, three of the four persons mentioned as having critical roles in the early development of Rice Institute were active in matters that would later have impact upon William Ward Watkin.

In 1900, William Marsh Rice had been murdered by Albert T. Patrick, who sat under sentence of death in New York's grim Tombs prison. Rice's nephew and namesake, William Marsh Rice II, however, had begun late in 1903 (as a recently appointed trustee of the Institute) to seek the counsel of his fellow alumnus of Princeton, Woodrow Wilson, regarding likely candidates for chief executive of his uncle's Institute. His high-level contacts with his alma mater, as well as with those of his 1879 classmates, were to have a profound effect upon the selection of Edgar Odell Lovett as president of the Rice Institute three-and-a-half years later.

A brilliant and tenacious campaign by Captain Baker was turning William Marsh Rice's Institute into reality, and Edgar Odell Lovett was in the process of a career that would lead him to the first presidency of the Rice Institute.

Ralph Adams Cram, fourth and last of the persons having had a strong, positive influence upon William Ward Watkin, had clearly emerged as a renowned architect in 1903, though still two months shy of his fortieth birthday. Already a leading exponent of Gothic-revival architecture, which he had helped to bring to new heights in designing impressive new churches and cathedrals, Cram also turned his talents and those of his gifted partner, Bertram Grosvenor Goodhue, to commissions for institutions of higher education, particularly at the U.S. Military Academy (West Point) and at Princeton.

The degree to which links and contacts and their timeliness were shaping William Ward Watkin's life was becoming obvious by 1903. How different they might have been, for example, had he begun his studies at the University of Pennsylvania in 1898 or in 1908, instead of 1903. There was one final tie that would benefit Watkin as much as any other. This was the vital link between Paul Cret and Ralph Cram. It was Professor Cret who sent young Watkin to Cram for advice on the best itinerary for a tour of England's Gothic cathedrals and monasteries—a field of architecture in which the Boston architect was perhaps the foremost authority of his time.

It was natural for Watkin, descended so directly from English forebears who were builders, to be interested in the architectural traditions of that country. His interest in Europe must have been strengthened by Cret, raised and taught amid the Renaissance and Gothic treasures of old Lyons.

IX.

Paul Philippe Cret might have known of Ralph Adams Cram even before assuming his academic post at the University of Pennsylvania. Cram, in addition to his rising fame within a relatively small profession, was a leading advocate of the traditional "Grand Tour" of the architectural highlights of Europe for graduating neophytes, preferably as the basis for a formal thesis to complete the requirements for the bachelor of science degree. He had crisscrossed England, France, and Italy (with side excursions to Greece and Dalmatian Yugoslavia), and knew Paul Cret's city of Lyons well.

Further, in 1902 and 1903, when the University of Pennsylvania was searching for a new dean of its top-rated school of architecture, Cram must have followed the search there with attention. He may well have been consulted by the selection committee. Cret would have known of Cram's significant commissions, and been familiar with his prolific writing for the profession.

It was quite predictable, therefore, that Cret would prove to be a particularly timely link between Watkin and the forces moving him toward the evolving William Marsh Rice Institute. Cret recommended that Watkin, the young man with obvious interests in medievalism and the Gothic revival so popular in Britain at the time, seek Ralph Adams Cram's advice on a thesis subject and fifth-year tour abroad.

Watkin had been an excellent student at the University of Pennsylvania, making very good progress toward his degree while participating fully in extracurricular activities and student fellowship. He was active in debate and in campus dramatics, a member of the Tennis Club, and participated in the horseplay in his department that included "sponge fights, sink parties, and 'operatic ebullitions' in draughting rooms." He was no longer William, or Will, the next step down in formality, but "Billy." Still, the top grades continued, and as early as his sophomore year of 1904–1905, Billy Watkin was working more and more under the direct supervision of Paul Cret.

Then came what could have been a major problem and setback. Before starting his fourth year in the fall of 1906, Watkin contracted a serious case of scarlet fever, with complications. This was two decades before Sir Alexander Fleming's discovery of penicillin. Faced with a long convalescence to full recovery, Watkin dropped out of college and spent the fall and winter on his uncle Dennis Bright's orange grove at Orange Springs, near Ocala, Florida.

When Watkin resumed his formal course of study in September 1907, there was a new dedication for him to textbooks, lectures, assigned projects, and drafting tables. The Architectural Society section in the Class of 1908 yearbook explains: "As seniors, we decided that we had come to college to work, and tried to extricate ourselves from the mess of athletics, musical organizations . . . [and other campus activities] in which we were entangled . . . . Schwab, Putnam and Billy Watkin showed us how it might be done."

However, "Watkin" was also prominently mentioned in the "all-star cast" that made the spring musical (The Brain Trust) ". . . the greatest show artistically and financially that has ever been given." And the yearbook section concludes that ". . . common interest in things artistic, working together on the annual play . . . [as well as] the nightly vigils over a stiff problem . . . have cemented our aggregates closer than any bunch of fellows in the College . . . we're proud and glad to have been Pennsylvania men and architects."

As soon as the 1907–1908 academic year was well under way, Watkin went to Boston for the all-important interview with Ralph Adams Cram that his mentor Paul Cret had helped to arrange. Cram has explained in his own words how he and Mrs. Cram began to limit their biennial trips to Europe almost exclusively to England after their three children began to arrive:

> "As children began to come along, it seemed unwise to take babies in any country other than England, and so, every two years we went there for three or four of the summer months, with only brief and occasional trips to northern France. This meant steeping myself in the medieval architecture of Great Britain, which explains in a measure the stylistic bent of the work we did [during] a ten-year period. In 1904, I made a special study on monastic architecture in preparation for a contemplated volume on the particular subject."

Cram did not add that he was now such a devout Anglican that each of his trips to Great Britain included a retreat spent at a Church of England monastery. It was not unexpected, then, that when Watkin left his interview with Cram, he had chosen the title for his thesis. It was to be "Anglican Monasteries in England."

There were even more significant results of his interview at the offices of Cram, Goodhue & Ferguson. First of all, young Watkin was offered a beginning position with the firm, which was already in negotiation for a contract with Rice Institute. Second, he left on an unforgettable trip to England, where he saw the cathedrals, churches, and monasteries recommended by his new mentor. He combined all this with a memorable visit with his English cousins under the guidance of the family historian and master contact, his beloved Aunt Hepsie.

Watkin would recall his trip to England a third of a century later, in a delightful letter to Hepsibah Churchill. He was, in his own words, "only a Yankee, and nothing much to brag about," meeting some "forty or fifty Watkin cousins . . . some of them in top hats, all of them friendly." The visits were at Ely House in Wolverhampton, where another William Watkin had established a large family in a comfortable old manor at the marvelously named town of Leighton Buzzard.

In London, he stayed at the then fashionable Russell Square Hotel, near the British Museum, and was taken charge of by Henry Watkin, an older cousin. In one unforgettable afternoon and evening, they went "all the way to Richmond," a suburb where a politician named Winston Churchill was giving an important address on free trade, and back to the elegant Reform Club in the heart of Whitehall. There drinks, dinner, port, and good talk lasted until "about three or four a.m."

His English relatives and hosts paid Watkin a high compliment. Some of them asked him to change his plans and go with them to Normandy for two weeks. He did not, however, and always regretted this decision after discovering later how delightful Normandy and the French coastal areas could be. "Had I known," he wrote Aunt Hepsie, "I would have canceled my tour of notable English cathedrals, churches, and monasteries with University of Pennsylvania classmates." This may have been a bit overdrawn for Aunt Hepsie's benefit. That trip with his classmates became the basis of his thesis, and final qualification for a degree in architecture, as well as a principal means of entering employment with the firm of Cram, Goodhue & Ferguson.

There were other highlights of the 1908 journey to England. He had the good fortune to travel to Leeds, Yorkshire's historic city, during the royal visit of King Edward VII and Queen Alexandra the first week in July. The prime architectural attraction in the area was

Harewood House, built by the Lascelles family between 1759 and 1770 [13]. William Ward Watkin also made his pilgrimage to Northampton in 1908, to visit the Guildhall of the East Midlands county seat from whence his family had come, as evidenced by a sketch, found among his papers, of the handsome stained-glass windows of the Guildhall.

Eight decades later there would be a firsthand report from Northampton by another highly competent family observer. This was Nolan Barrick, Watkin's son-in-law, former student, and retired chairman of the department of architecture at Texas Technological University. Professor Barrick stayed at a hotel two blocks from John Watkin's residence at 14 St. George's Street. Reading in the local library, he found that Jenny Lind, the "Swedish Nightingale" of extraordinary range and purity of voice, gave a benefit concert in 1862 to help finance the remodeling of the Church of the Holy Sepulchre by John Watkin.

Records at the Church of the Holy Sepulchre showed Nolan Barrick that another John Watkin, a bachelor of divinity from Oxford's Lincoln College, was vicar there from 1776 to 1787. His younger brother George, also an Oxonian bachelor of divinity, succeeded the Reverend John Watkin in 1787, and served until 1803, two generations before John Watkin the builder completed construction of the Town Hall and the restoration of the Church of the Holy Sepulchre. The Watkins, it seemed, had broad as well as long-established ties to Northampton, which celebrated its 800th anniversary in 1989.

Notes

1. The first section of President Lovett's address added William Marsh Rice to the "charmed circle of immortal philanthropists such as Nobel, Rhodes, Rockefeller, Carnegie, Johns Hopkins, Leland Stanford, and Ezra Cornell." It then recounted the early role of the trustees, and recalled Lovett's epic journey in 1908–1909, mentioning by name and discipline the noted scholars participating in the 1912 opening. Tribute was paid to the "constant creative work of the supervising architects," as well as to the dedicated engineers.

    Section two lauded Houston as the Rice Institute's "greatest opportunity," in a nation where the new cry is, "Go South; Stay South." The third section addressed how the new university would pursue "the advancement of letters, science and art . . . by investigation and by instruction." The final section spoke to the "immortal spirit of inquiry or inspiration which has been clearing the pathway of mankind to intellectual and spiritual liberty, to the recognition of law and charm in nature, to the fearless pursuit of truth and the ceaseless worship of beauty."

The eloquent Edgar Odell Lovett continued with a tribute to the original faculty he had recruited with such care, speaking of "A society of scholars in whose company your children, and your children's children and their children, may spend formative years of their aspiring youth under the cultivating influences of humane letters and pure science." Then, Greek scholar that he was (in addition to distinguished mathematician and astronomer), President Lovett concluded by recalling his visit in 1909 to the Parthenon. "It is'" he said, "no long flight of fancy from the Parthenon above the fields of Hellas to these towers that rise on the plains of Texas."

2. Actually, while Goodhue had certainly participated fully in the long discussions and many sketches, drawings and elevations from which the master plan evolved, he would leave Cram, Goodhue & Ferguson in less than a year. He sent his regrets to President Lovett in a cordial note that acknowledged receipt of his invitation to the dedicatory festival, but explained that he would be "hunting moose in a remote area of Canada."

3. The quotation on the "Tablet to Art" is from Plotinus, the third century Egyptian-Roman soldier, mystic and philosopher whose Neoplatonism had an enormous effect upon European as well as Islamic thought and religion for more than a millennium.

4. Sir George Gilbert Scott was the grandfather of Sir Giles Gilbert Scott, who designed the Anglican Cathedral at Liverpool, Oxford's Bodleian Library, and the Waterloo Bridge in London.

5. The very name "Glendower" must have had a unique appeal for William Hancock. Every Staffordshireman worthy of the name knew of Owen Glendower, the fiery rebel and self-ordained Prince of Wales who took control of most of the ancient Welsh kingdom near Staffordshire's western boundaries in the first decade of the fifteenth century. Finally defeated by Prince Harry Percy (later King Henry V of England), Glendower remains the transcendent hero of Welsh separatists today, as he was more than a century ago.

Hancock bought out the other Glendower shareholders in 1858 and operated the mill as sole proprietor for almost a decade. There was a tremendous demand for iron and steel during the four years of the Civil War, ending in 1865. Anticipating the many changes of the post-war economy, Hancock organized the National Iron Company (for which he would serve as chief executive for the remainder of his life) in 1867. The new enterprise incorporated the Glendower Iron Works and related operations.

6. Through the first half of the nineteenth century, even concert pianos were essentially harpsichords, built completely of wood with internal braces bearing all of the stress produced by the strings. As a result, relatively thin strings yielding little of the range, tone, and volume of sound we expect from a modern piano had to be used, amid growing demands for an instrument with louder and more brilliant sound.

   Chickering had been experimenting with a grand piano built upon a one-piece frame of cast iron. As a result, he developed an instrument with tension exerted per string at least six times greater than that possible in earlier pianos (from 25 pounds tension to well above 150 pounds). William Hancock, the consummate ironmaster, was naturally interested in Chickering's research, which essentially made possible the contemporary concert grand. Henry Engelhard Steinway and others later added innovations such as overstringing and felt hammers. Overstringing involved crossing much longer and more resonant bass strings over the treble; felt hammers softened the harsher, louder tone of the new instruments by replacing a leather covering with the sponginess of a thin layer of felt.

   Mary Ann Reay Hancock's Chickering concert grand would end up in the Smithsonian Institution in Washington, D.C., after researchers rediscovered it three generations later in the possession of Ray Watkin Hoagland, and arranged to have the historic piano rebuilt and placed on permanent exhibition with other national treasures of the performing arts.

7. This was true even when there had been strong links to another denomination. Frederick's parents had been married by a Catholic priest, in a faith his mother's family had probably followed for centuries. And his maternal grandmother, Mary Hobson, was the granddaughter of the Reverend Andrew Fuller, doctor of divinity, theologian, and perhaps most prominent Baptist of his generation in England.

   Dr. Fuller (1754–1815) was the chief proponent of a somewhat moderate exegesis of John Calvin's doctrine of predestination that stirred vigorous controversy within the ranks of both Baptists and Presbyterians. He was, nevertheless, a co-founder of the highly influential Baptist Missionary Society, for which he served as charter secretary from its establishment in 1792 until his death. Mary Hobson Watkin began her married life with William Watkin in 1815 as a staunch Baptist, in a family that produced not only the Reverend Andrew Fuller, but other less-well-known Baptist ministers and a host of Fullers, Hobsons, Pickerings, and Osbornes adhering to the same faith. She and William Watkin nevertheless died as Episcopalians, and are buried side by side in the old Church of England churchyard at Pitsford.

8. Boston was named for the town of Boston, England (fifty miles northeast of Northampton in neighboring Lincolnshire), in an area long familiar to the English Watkins. Most of John Winthrop's Puritan immigrants of the

Massachusetts Bay Company had come from Lincolnshire's Boston, then a small port within the Hanseatic League and rich farming area.

The largest city in colonial America until challenged and passed by both New York and Philadelphia, Boston seemed to offer new opportunities in the 1880s. This was especially true in the booming new textile industry, the railroads fanning out down the Atlantic seaboard and westward toward the developing frontier, banking, and finance.

9. Great-uncle Dennis Bright could also spin fascinating yarns of his experiences with the Union forces in what he called the War of the Rebellion—of a wound, for example, suffered in the battle of Cheat Mountain in West Virginia that could have crippled him for life but luckily did not. A Confederate musket ball had gone completely through Captain Bright's ankle while he fought as a junior officer in Major-General George B. McClellan's forces, through the fog-bound valleys near Elk Water in the shadow of Cheat Mountain. McClellan's victories there, in the early summer of 1861, were a key factor in restoring Northern morale after the disastrous defeat at first Bull Run. General Joseph Johnston and the legendary Thomas J. (Stonewall) Jackson had saved the day there for the Confederacy, Bright explained, by holding their ground until they finally turned the Union right flank. Then the Yankees were subjected to both withering artillery fire and a terrifying charge by Southern cavalry brandishing sabers as a Union retreat turned into disorderly flight.

10. In the Danville library, Will found that the last two dozen of the proud Susquehanna, reduced from an estimated 5,000 by smallpox and other diseases brought in by European settlers, had been killed in 1763 by colonists hearing reports of Indian attacks on the Pennsylvania frontier. He also learned of another tribe that had lived along the ancient Susquehanna and its tributaries: the Shawnee, a mysterious clan that spoke the Algonquin dialect and finally settled in the Oklahoma Territory as part of the Cherokee Nation. He wondered if some of the quite different arrowheads that he dug up were fashioned by the Shawnee.

11. Paul Phillipe Cret, a graduate of the distinguished Institute of Fine Arts in his own city of Lyons, rose quickly to the height of his profession by winning the competition for the design of the Pan-American Union Building in Washington, D.C. and then collaborating with the noted Polish engineer Ralph Modjeski on some of the longest, highest, and most innovative bridges in the United States, including the Benjamin Franklin Bridge in Philadelphia. (In 1972, the maintenance of this bridge came under the direct supervision of Brigadier General William Ward Watkin, Jr., as Port Director of the Delaware Port Authority.) Meanwhile, Cret also established himself among the foremost educators in the field of architecture.

12. In Lyons, at the crossroads of centuries-old trade routes to the Mediterranean and across the nearby Alps, there arose what was arguably the cultural as well as the economic heart of France, in the High Renaissance. For Lyons became both the center of the silk industry, with its significant commercial fairs and banking operations, as well as the home of noted writers, publishers, architects, and politicians during much of the fifteenth and sixteenth centuries. The resulting prosperity was little diminished until the desperate years of the French Revolution, which placed the manufacture and marketing of silk into temporary eclipse.

    Napoleon had added important luster to Lyons by remodeling and expanding an elegant old convent into a Museum of Fine Arts, perhaps the most significant of several established in the provinces as repositories for remarkable paintings rivaling those in Paris' Louvre. The new emperor sent to Lyons what the *New York Times* has described as a "dazzling" collection of works by Rembrandt, Tiepolo, Corot, Rubens, Delacroix, and other masters.

13. Harewood House was built at the then enormous cost of 100,000 English pounds. This huge structure was built in the ornate Corinthian style, most ornate of the three varieties of classical Greek architecture. The adjacent gardens, park, and "ornamental waters" were designed by the renowned horticulturist, Capability Brown.

    What might have interested young Watkin even more was Leeds Castle, 200 miles southeast in Maidstone, Kent. His great-uncle, John Watkin, as mentioned, had worked with Sir George Gilbert Scott, the prominent English architect and authority on the Eleanor Crosses, on the restoration of the twelfth-century Church of the Holy Sepulchre. Edward I, grieving for his dead queen, Eleanor of Castile, ordered memorial crosses at the two towns in Northamptonshire where her burial procession had stopped en route to Westminster Abbey in 1290.

    Edward I acquired Leeds Castle in 1278 and made it almost impregnable to attack and far more comfortable as a favorite retreat for the royal family. A daily Mass would be celebrated there for centuries for the repose of the soul of Queen Eleanor. She has a memorial today, in the very heart of London: King Edward spoke French to Eleanor, and called her "Chere Reine," or "Dear Queen." Thus, the final Eleanor Cross, before her remains arrived at Westminster Abbey, became "Chere Reine Croix" or Charing Cross, hub of the London subway system.

CHAPTER FOUR

Talent, teaching, and camaraderie in Cram, Goodhue &
Ferguson's Boston office in 1908 . . . William Ward
Watkin is given added responsibilities as a complex
master plan evolves . . . Gentlemanly but firmly stated
differences of opinion between Ralph Adams Cram and
President Lovett . . . In 1910, Watkin arrives in growing
Houston to confront flooding, material shortages, and
intricacies of design and workmanship . . . Watkin
determines that he will make his life and career half a
continent away from Boston . . . Enter a slim, vivacious,
red-haired, and beautiful debutante from San Antonio
. . . William Ward Watkin is not only a faculty member,
but a key administrator, soon involved in civic projects
. . . The move to Texas . . . The intricate Physics
Building . . . An original faculty of distinction is
appointed . . . Formation of the Department of
Architecture in 1912 . . . William Ward Watkin marries
Annie Ray Townsend . . . The birth of their first child
and death of Texas Senator Marcus H. Townsend

I.

Much as a talented and ambitious young Italian might have made his way to sixteenth-century Florence to work under painter-sculptor-architect Michelangelo Buonarroti, William Ward Watkin went to Boston late in 1908. There, in the city where European traditions had been imported very early and transformed into the patterns of America's own culture, young Watkin began his career with Cram, Goodhue & Ferguson, a unique architectural firm just emerging into national prominence. Its principals, Ralph Adams Cram and Bertram Grosvenor Goodhue, would have been at home in Renaissance Florence or medieval Ravenna.

Chester Anderson Brown, who joined the firm as a draftsman soon after William Ward Watkin, provided valuable insight into Cram, Goodhue & Ferguson in its early days. In 1971, he published *My Best*

Years In Architecture, With Ralph Adams Cram, FAIA. This memoir clearly shows the warm ambience and camaraderie that must have marked the firm's operations during the period Watkin worked in Cram's Boston office.

More significantly, Brown describes the manifest abilities and exacting professionalism exhibited by Cram, Goodhue & Ferguson partners. His recollections, especially through anecdotes, demonstrate how Cram was an instinctively gifted teacher, imparting his skill, knowledge, and experience with patience to even the most junior apprentice draftsman. Similarly, the more outgoing Goodhue passed along his remarkable ability as an innovative designer, creative artist, and master of detailed drawing to the draftsmen.

It is quite possible that the seed of William Ward Watkin's decision to establish, build, and administer the Department of Architecture at Rice Institute was planted at 15 Beacon Street as he watched the senior partners teach the various requirements of the profession.

Chester Brown had hoped to join Cram, Goodhue & Ferguson while he was apprenticed to a smaller firm of considerably less distinction. His opportunity to join the firm came with the Rice Institute commission. This commission, atop the ongoing projects at West Point, not only necessitated larger quarters for the firm but also the addition of more draftsmen. Six decades later, Brown wrote of the staff parties in 1910, both at Cram's home on Chestnut Street and later at the family's summer retreat in Sudbury, several miles west of Cambridge. Alexander Hoyle, another partner, was often host for informal beer parties at the Hoyle home on Acorn Street.

And there were the long days of summer, with baseball games in which the athletic Brown participated against other architectural firms, tickets to the Red Sox games, and outings at Hingham Bay. The Red Sox had moved to Boston from Buffalo in 1901 with the formation of the American League. Often, the close-knit members of the architectural firm met informally after work at the bar of the adjoining Bellevue Hotel. Cocktails there were two for a quarter, accompanied by free appetizers of tiny sandwiches and bits of salted Boston cod, which the Cram, Goodhue & Ferguson staffers enjoyed while they discussed important design problems or the latest bit of Back Bay gossip.

The highlight of the year was the annual staff Christmas party. All work stopped early on Christmas Eve morning. Tables were arranged in a "U," with the partners at the head and Ralph Adams Cram installed as master of ceremonies. A magician once performed, and specially composed poems were recited and songs were sung as the senior partner presided with his inimitable wit and presence. A fine catered lunch and the distribution of gifts followed. The liquid refreshments, which flowed on, included excellent wine and "malt liquors."

Watkin himself often spoke of the interesting experience of working for Cram. There is a picture of the 1908 Christmas party in the Watkin files that shows new employee Watkin in the midst of the celebration. He probably heard one of Cram's favorite stories. It tells of the wife of an important client who expressed concern that their project "would not be Gothic enough." "When I am done with this design," Cram assured his listeners, "it will be so convincingly Gothic that she will not be able to sleep nights after seeing it." [1]

With that strong inclination, little wonder that Cram, Goodhue & Ferguson was soon given the assignment of taking over perhaps the largest commission in modern church architecture. This was to design the remaining portions of the gigantic Church of St. John the Divine in New York in the Gothic style, and to convert existing construction wherever possible to the Gothic form and tradition.

Chester Brown's keenest memories of Cram, Goodhue & Ferguson, however, were of Ralph Cram the teacher: "Each morning," he wrote, "if not traveling to confer with office clients, [Mr. Cram] would visit each man's drafting board, examine the progress made since his previous visit, and approve or make such changes as were required. If there was an unusual element of planning or design which was of some significant importance, a group of us might congregate and listen to his remarks. This unconventional attitude was very stimulating, and tended to spur each man to work industriously to improve his work, thus hopefully to be praised by Mr. Cram."

II.

William Ward Watkin was fortunate not only to begin his career at Cram, Goodhue & Ferguson at an auspicious time, but in his choice of a place to live. He moved into the Technology Chambers, an apartment hotel where members of the faculty at the Massachusetts Institute of Technology resided. This was only a short distance from the MIT classrooms on Boylston Street near Copley Square. The small hotel had been recommended both by Ralph Cram and by Frank Cleveland, an associate at Cram, Goodhue & Ferguson and an MIT alumnus. Cram himself taught at MIT, and would later become chairman of the Department of Architecture there.

The Technology Chambers, demolished long ago to make room for a turnpike, was near the heart of Old Boston and Copley Square, the Public Library, the Commons, Boston Gardens, and Old South Church. The Cram, Goodhue & Ferguson office could be reached in a long but pleasant walk across Copley Square and the Gardens.

Almost immediately after his arrival at the architectural firm, young Watkin was put to work on a considerable number of college and university commissions that had followed Cram's contract with the United States Military Academy at West Point. He was given various assignments involving the University of Richmond; Williams College; Sweet Briar, the well-known women's college in Virginia; and, when needed, on the West Point job and on the new St. Thomas Church on New York City's Fifth Avenue.

Then, late in the summer of 1909, Cram assigned Watkin an intriguing new project that was to shape his entire life and career. This, of course, was the commission for the Rice Institute, a new university to be built in Houston. Watkin was the junior member of the team developing a master (general) plan for Rice, and the design of the initial structures. He would assume more and more responsibility as the plan emerged amid growing complexities, beginning with a unique building site, Cram's differences of opinion with the client, and varying designs proposed by the two brilliant senior partners, Ralph Adams Cram and Bertram Grosvenor Goodhue.

First thought had to be given to the style of architecture for the Rice Institute. Ralph Adams Cram had pointed out that the "collegiate Gothic" projects Cram, Goodhue & Ferguson had designed for West Point and for Princeton were "totally inappropriate" in Houston's climate. "Colonial" architecture, as seen in the older buildings at the University of Virginia, had seemed a second possibility. Cram's opinion, however, was that "colonial" was too closely related to "classical or Renaissance" architecture. Cram felt that these styles, evolving well after the "purity" of the medieval, were "part of a pagan civilization."

The third proposal was Spanish Renaissance, thought to be out of the "pagan" tradition, and possibly acceptable in a state and region with strong ties to the history and traditions of Spain. When the Rice trustees showed no enthusiasm whatsoever for Spanish Renaissance, Cram's "refreshing and creative stubbornness" offered a fourth approach: "[Since] Gothic architecture never developed successfully in Italy, and the great monuments of medieval art in Italy are those of the Romanesque," why not turn to that style for the master plan? Thus the Italian Romanesque style as seen in Lombardy was chosen for the Rice Institute, uncontaminated by the Gothic and Renaissance. If Cram, the apostle of the Gothic, could not use the Gothic style in Houston's heat and humidity, he would turn to something aesthetically and philosophically pleasing, as well as uniquely suitable to the climate.

The trustees quickly approved the fourth option, and progress was resumed on the master plan. Many differing aspects of the plan still had to be resolved.

Stephen Fox, a talented architectural historian, has covered the development and execution of the general plan in masterful fashion in his scholarly *Monograph 29*, published in 1980. Some of his detailed findings regarding the earliest stages of developing the plan are briefly summarized here.

The Boston and New York City offices of Cram, Goodhue & Ferguson had a laudable custom of having the two offices engage in an internal "architectural competition among members for the benefit of the client," according to Watkin [2]. The Boston solution, very much Cram's own, consisted of Plans A, B, and C, developed in sequence. These began with quite rough pencil sketches that reflected Cram's fervid imagination and helped to consolidate his thoughts in a meaningful way. He then proceeded to very detailed perspective drawings indicating proportion, scale, mass, and volume. In a third stage, Cram, Goodhue & Ferguson partners joined the process by preparing and criticizing alternate, full-scale perspectives.

The New York office's proposal for the Rice Institute, which contained Goodhue's views almost entirely, was for a campus twice as wide as the Boston concept, and considerably longer. Spacing between buildings and areas was much larger. There were, however, many similarities between the two designs. Cram's Plan C, which soon gained ascendancy over his Plans A and B, and Goodhue's solution were in accord on major points. As Stephen Fox points out: ". . . [both had] a long east-west axis crossed by a shorter north-south axis about which most of the buildings gravitated . . . . [buildings] were set in symmetrical groupings and arranged according to use and [academic] discipline."

However, both Cram's Plan C and the Goodhue plan had some fanciful and thoroughly impractical elements due to their lack of knowledge concerning Houston's semitropical heat, sudden and sometimes torrential rainfall, and ferocious infestations of mosquitoes.

Cram included an outdoor theater in the classic style of ancient Greece, with an adjoining lake later shown as a reflecting basin. Goodhue proposed a Persian garden, complete with pools of water between an amphitheater and huge auditorium. The latter structure was to have been larger and more important in the general plan than the Administration Building. These elements of the general plan were quietly jettisoned, probably very soon after Cram, Goodhue & Ferguson became aware of the realities of Houston's climate. One counterproposal from a local wag was to stock lake, basin, and pools with alligator gar, a particularly voracious fish noted for its consumption of mosquitoes and their larvae.

The difficulties between Cram, Goodhue & Ferguson's thoroughly competent but sometime temperamental senior partners and their new client in Houston could have been predicted. Neither Cram nor Goodhue were particularly known for being overly influenced by clients, or for timidity in putting forward their own convictions. Edgar Odell Lovett, while a thorough gentleman considerate of the views of others, had his own definite views on academic architecture, and specifically on how to develop—overall and in specific detail— the 300 acres selected for the Rice Institute. The six other trustees, primarily mature and well-experienced businessmen, bankers, and attorneys, had little experience in dealing with architects. However, they were quite accustomed to expressing their own opinions, and to having them heeded.

There was also an underlying problem of communication between architect and client. Cram, Goodhue & Ferguson was staffed from top to bottom with men of a different profession, area, culture, and even accent. In 1909, there was neither air transportation nor FAX machines. Direct dialing was a full half-century away, and long distance telephone calls were apt to be delayed and unreliable. Travel between Boston and Houston involved a 56-hour train ride. The fastest and most reliable communication was via Western Union.

In spite of the difference of opinions, which centered upon adoption of a general plan for the Rice Institute campus and the design of the original buildings, a considerable degree of consensus between Cram, Goodhue & Ferguson and client was reached in the final weeks of 1909. Ralph Cram's Plan C, with some revisions, was approved. An important factor was Cram, Goodhue & Ferguson's agreement to reduce the firm's professional fee from the usual 6% to 5%.

Another difference of opinion appeared in 1910, when President Lovett insisted that the Administration Building be placed in a more pivotal location, considerably nearer Main Street and the principal entrance to the campus. This was strongly opposed by Cram, Goodhue & Ferguson, in a letter signed only "Cram, Goodhue & Ferguson," but probably written by Cram himself. A handwritten postscript signed "RAC" would sometimes indicate which portions of a significant letter should or should not be communicated to the other trustees. Such communications came directly to President Lovett at the Rice Institute office in the Scanlan Building, Houston's first downtown "skyscraper."

President Lovett prevailed in his polite, but unequivocal, manner regarding the placement of the Administration Building. He also won out in a related demand for the maximum "free circulation of air so essential in a climate like this . . . removing all obstructions to the gulf breeze." The first Cram, Goodhue & Ferguson reply to relocating the Administration Building was the expressed hope that ". . . this arrangement is only for the purpose of convincing yourself that it is not a good one."

Lovett and the entire governing board were reconciled with their architects before Houston's brief winter of 1910 spun into spring, but not before more classic communications between 15 Beacon Street and 1110 Scanlan Building. Cram, Goodhue & Ferguson was understandably concerned by delays in receiving a signed contract or any payments whatsoever from their newest client. The trustees had indicated their approval orally in a meeting at Houston on December 1, 1909, with Cram and Goodhue. However, there were no payments pending the resolution of ongoing differences and a more formal agreement.

Cram pointed out late in January 1910 that "The Building Committee of St. Thomas' Church in New York . . . made up of some of the shrewdest and richest bankers, lawyers and business men in the City . . . paid us 3% on an estimated contract of $1,000,000 . . . more than six months ago [although] at this writing no contracts have been let." He added that "The United States Government, which is notoriously the hardest taskmaster architects have to contend with . . . had paid 2 1/2% on the very large West Point contract with Cram, Goodhue & Ferguson, before the signing of a binding agreement."

There were some shaky moments in this earliest phase of the Rice Institute-Cram, Goodhue & Ferguson relationship. Just as virtually all remaining differences had been resolved, Dr. Lovett made another request, apparently at the behest of one or more of the trustees: Could Cram, Goodhue & Ferguson prepare a new perspective of the Administration Building with the loggias (roofed galleries open to the courtyard below) omitted?

The loggias were impressive parts of a design on which many weeks had been spent. Further, Cram had indicated recently that his firm was spending "$275 a week right along on draftsmen" and tying up the entire Boston office on Rice Institute plans. He therefore asked by return post: "Now can you not place some reliance on us as your chosen architects . . . on a matter almost wholly [one] of design?"

It may have been one of the frankest questions ever put to a major client by a leading architect. Perhaps its obvious frankness proceeded from the fact that Rice Institute had finally signed a contract with Cram, Goodhue & Ferguson little more than two weeks earlier. This agreement, dated March 1, 1910, covered the general plan, the first buildings (including the power plant), and certain landscaping. Cram may have thought that they wanted to renegotiate from the unexpected inquiry involving a design component as important as the loggias.

Cram's candid, even bold, inquiry seems to have had the desired effect. His letter emphasizing the need to put some trust in "your chosen architects," was received by President Lovett on March 21. Dr. Lovett replied that same evening with a night letter. Cram's enthusiastic response was: "Your night letter of March 21 [was] satisfactory in the extreme . . . . In approving in principle the last scheme of all for the General Plan, you are acting with the broadest view . . . . You are also doing what will justify itself in the end . . ." The loggias would remain, and things were finally going more smoothly.

III.

Meanwhile, in the Boston office, Watkin had been assigned full time to the increasingly important Rice Institute commission. From its beginning, helping with preliminary design sketches and drafting later variations, he had worked exclusively on the new project, often directly with Cram. He produced, to quote Stephen Fox, ". . . two alternative presentation plans . . . elaborate watercolor washes on stiff board . . ." The plans were sent to Edgar Odell Lovett on October 9, 1909. In November, after additional work on the Rice job, Watkin started a series of drawings on the first changes to the general plan. These went to President Lovett two weeks before Christmas. The hope was that approval, at least in principle, could be obtained in Houston quite early in January 1910. This would still allow construction to commence soon after New Year's Day.

Further delays were in the offing, even though President Lovett had hoped to begin classes in September 1911. The delays resulted in young Watkin becoming more and more active in the preparation of plans for the Rice Institute, and increasingly knowledgeable about the institution. At the same time, he moved steadily into position as the logical candidate for Cram's personal representative on the Rice project. By August 1910, Watkin would be sent to be on his own in Houston, 1,500 miles from Boston. Little did he realize that Cram would not be in Houston again until October 10–12, 1912. Or that Goodhue, extremely busy again with West Point and with the Church of St. Thomas, could devote little additional time to Cram, Goodhue & Ferguson's problems at Rice Institute.

Letters from Cram to President Lovett became quite positive after the resolved crisis late in March 1910. This followed a request from Lovett that must have caused some final anxious moments. He wanted copies of all six earlier versions of the general plan. Fortunately, the copies were returned promptly by Lovett, with only minor changes noted. Watkin started almost immediately on a large "presentation drawing." Cram wrote that he ". . . [took] no exception whatsoever to [your] final ideas regarding development of the General Plan . . . . working plans for the Administration Building are developing admirably . . . . Mr. Watkin [is busy with] a tracing showing precisely how the whole thing works out." And there was further good news: Frank Ferguson, in Houston for some on-site studies and a survey of the possible availability of construction materials in the city or area, had discovered a "distinctly promising, quite pink" local brick at the Sherman Brady Brickyard.

April 30, 1910, brought disturbing news from Boston. Cram reported to Dr. Lovett that, "On Monday, Mr. Watkin, who as you know has more than any other outside the firm had charge of the [Rice Institute] work, was taken down by scarlet fever and is now in the hospital, from which he cannot emerge for at least five weeks." There was an epidemic of scarlet fever in Boston at the time.

A following letter pointed out that this would delay not only the "vital plans for the Administration Building, but the cycle of specifications, estimates, bids, selection of contractor, changes, obtaining specific materials, etc. . . . ." It also postponed Watkin's first trip to Houston. Cram had asked him to go there with the new tracing of the overall plan. The younger architect had been requested to study the complex problems of color and contrast of brick, tile, stone, and masonry on the building site. He had demonstrated an obviously marked ability in color and design, reflected in his watercolor renderings.

Fortunately, the situation soon improved. Watkin recovered fully and was back at work in less than a month. Cram reported that the office was "[still] in a state of chaos amid a lot of new work," but promised Lovett to have detailed plans and specifications for the

Administration Building in Houston by June 1. Watkin's new assignment was a $5^{1/2}$- by $3^{1/2}$-foot rendering that became the official, approved plan for the Rice Institute. This was sent to President Lovett on July 25, 1910.

Cram soon wrote Lovett that he was "used up," and would be off to Europe for the summer on June 15. Another communication, signed only "Cram, Goodhue & Ferguson," stated that "Mr. Cram regrets . . . the necessity that compels him to go abroad [but] is convinced it is unavoidable on the score of his health, as the complications, annoyances and overwork of the past winter have been distinctly too much for him."

The conscientious Mr. Cram, however, finished a vital task before settling down with wife and children in their suite aboard a transatlantic liner departing Boston Harbor for Southampton. In spite of a heavy pre-vacation calendar, he completed "blocking out" plans and elevations for both the power plant and mechanical laboratories. This would allow ongoing progress on two of the smaller, but highly important, original buildings at Rice Institute during his absence in England and northern France.

IV.

"We expect," the letter of August 4, 1910, from Cram, Goodhue & Ferguson to President Lovett stated, "that Mr. Watkin will start for Houston on the eleventh of this month to enter upon his duties as our representative there."

Watkin's being sent south as the personal representative of Ralph Adams Cram had been decided well before Cram's departure for Europe. However, this was the first indication of the exact date of his arrival in Houston and it was incorrect. Watkin actually left for Houston after a brief vacation with his mother and the Brights in Danville, and arrived on August 17. The change in date was, of course, communicated to Edgar Odell Lovett by Watkin in a letter mentioning that "two cases of books and supplies" had been forwarded to the Rice Institute office in the Scanlan Building from the Cram, Goodhue & Ferguson office in Boston.

Watkin soon discovered the enormous differences between his new city and Boston. But he adapted to the differing situations. The previous decade had seen significant changes in Houston. The city was an amalgam of Old South and bustling, brash, energetic West. It had already emerged as the major railroad center south of St. Louis. Timber and cotton were giving way to petroleum, manufacturing, banking, retailing, and the prospect of a deep-water port. The remarkable growth in population would mushroom again from 1910 to 1920 by 75.5%, from 78,790 to 138,276, according to U.S. census figures. The Chamber of Commerce claimed that these robust statistics did not include tens of thousands of people residing in areas near the expanding city limits.

Only weeks before Watkin's arrival in Houston, President William Howard Taft had signed the appropriations bill containing $1.25 million to help finance the construction of a 51-foot-wide, 25-foot-deep Ship Channel providing access to Galveston Bay and the Gulf of Mexico. It was an appropriate response to a humorous article in the *Galveston Daily News.* This had reported, amid the first attempts to provide a waterway from Buffalo Bayou to the open seas, "Houston Now A Salt Water Port." The story accompanying this headline told how a barge carrying a cargo of huge bags of salt had recently capsized in the upper reaches of Buffalo Bayou.

The Port of Houston, opened in 1914 after completion of the Ship Channel, was to have an enormous impact on Watkin's new home-town. Jesse Holman Jones, a 36-year-old immigrant from Tennessee who had become, and would remain for another half century, one of Houston's leading citizens, was a principal backer of the new channel and port. He provided much of the financing for the additional $4.25 million required [3]. Widely copied, this early example of federal-local cooperation on major public projects became known as the Houston Plan.

Houston, as was common in the deep South, had many excellent boarding houses early in the century. Apartments had not yet become commonplace. The best of these boarding houses were usually owned and operated by women of good family well known in the community. They chose boarders carefully, depending a great deal upon written recommendations and personal introductions. Watkin took accommodations at "The Gables," located at 1218 McKinney near the corner of Caroline. It was only eight blocks from his Rice Institute office in the Scanlan Building, located at 405 Main Street between Preston and Prairie.

Watkin took his meals for a time at another popular and well-recommended boarding house, that of Mrs. Jack Bryan. There the tall, slender architect, with his shock of wavy brown hair, met many prominent citizens, as well as new arrivals to prospering Houston. Among them were Birdsall Briscoe, grandson of Colonel Andrew H. Briscoe, a signer of the Texas Declaration of Independence and Harris County's first judge back in 1841; and State Senator and Mrs. McDonald Meachum. He later worked with Birdsall Briscoe, a prominent Houston architect, in organizing the first local chapter of the American Institute of Architects.

Later Watkin decided he would take both room and board at The Gables. Watkin remained at The Gables for almost four years; his mother would come from Danville each winter to stay with him, thus avoiding Pennsylvania's harshest weather.

Among the interesting Houstonians he had met earlier at Mrs. Bryan's, however, were the Reverend James T. Power, assistant rector at nearby Christ Church; and the legendary millionaire-philanthropist, Robert Alonzo Welch [4].

The Reverend Mr. Power was a cousin of William Stamps Farish, who had come from Mississippi via Spindletop to Houston, there to become a founder and president of Humble Oil & Refining Company. Watkin, a devout Episcopalian, would see the young minister regularly at Christ Church, only a five-minute walk from The Gables.

Houston had several other elegant places to dine, however, during Watkin's first years there. Colby's restaurant featured a good game dinner for fifty cents. One dollar, including the tip, provided a ten-course meal at the Bender Hotel. This more-than-adequate repast started with a choice of several soups or gumbo, and continued with either oysters or shrimp, according to the season. The diner then proceeded through steamed crabs, stuffed flounder, roast beef, larded quail, ham, salad, various vegetables, and dessert. Wines or mineral waters were extra. Also, the new Houston Country Club on Wayside Drive was already setting high standards in cuisine and service, including the use of fine table linens and exceptional china and silver.

In the Houston Watkin found when he arrived in 1910, Houstonians had their choice of four theaters, the newest and largest being the Majestic on the current site of the *Chronicle* Building. There were occasional stage plays, but the main fare was vaudeville and movies. The Sweeney and Coombs Opera House offered performances by a number of touring opera companies, and rare appearances by symphonies such as the New York Philharmonic, as well as individual stars of the caliber of Enrico Caruso, Sarah Bernhardt, and Ignace Jan Paderewski, the eminent pianist who later became prime minister of his native Poland. The earlier Pillot Opera House had presented everything from a sparring exhibition by John L. Sullivan to Edwin Booth in *Hamlet*.

Miss Ima Hogg, epitome of gentility and daughter of the memorable Governor James Stephen Hogg, was already a demure but pivotal force in cultural and civic betterment circles. She had launched a campaign to establish the Houston Symphony Orchestra, working quietly but effectively with close friends including young Maurice Hirsch and his sister Rosetta. General-to-be Hirsch was a student at the University of Virginia. Rosetta was a talented violinist. The HSO made its debut at a 5 p.m. concert in the Majestic Theatre on June 21, 1913. Admission ran from a quarter in the balcony to a dollar in the few box seats. Miss Hogg bought an ad in the morning Houston *Post* urging attendance. Her keen interest in music, art, architecture, fine antiques, landscaping, education, and literature enriched Houston for the next six decades.

The *Post,* dating from April 5, 1885, was clearly the dominant Houston newspaper in 1913, as it had been virtually from its founding [5]. Even so, the afternoon *Chronicle* was gaining acceptance steadily under its president and editor, Marcellus E. ("Mefo") Foster. Foster had used some of his modest fortune from speculating in the great 1901 oil strike at Spindletop to establish the new daily (originally the *Chronicle and Herald*) on July 3, 1902.

"Mefo" faced strong competition from the beginning, although it was apparent from the time Watkin arrived in Houston that his *Chronicle* was a sound enterprise capable of continuing growth and expansion. The *Post,* in business for a quarter-century, had an able, experienced staff. Foster himself had been a senior reporter there.

Foster and his *Chronicle* were to become important to the Rice Institute in its early years. He quickly developed a growing interest in the new institution, and especially in Rice's probable impact on Houston. The result was a friendship and occasional correspondence with Edgar Odell Lovett, personal visits to the developing campus, and regular articles on the phases of progress there. Foster and members of his staff naturally became acquainted with Watkin, who kept a meticulous record of every step in the construction by daily photographs and detailed written reports.

These relationships, in addition to those with other media, became important in the weeks before, as well as during and after, the academic festival formally opening Rice Institute on October 10–12, 1912. One fortuitous result was the beautifully illustrated sections in both *Chronicle* and *Post,* reprints of which were widely distributed.

V.

William Ward Watkin had not realized how all-encompassing his position as personal representative of Ralph Adams Cram at Rice would be. To assist him, Cram sent Watkin an experienced clerk of the works, or overseer, Albert C. Perry, a Cram, Goodhue & Ferguson employee who had recently served in the same capacity on the USMA contract at West Point. He had been reassigned to Houston three weeks before Watkin's own arrival. Perry, an architect, provided major assistance in superintending the large number of laborers and craftsmen on the job, the flow of materials, and quality of work. However, he remained in Houston only one year before returning east in mid-1911 to serve as clerk of the works for the new Graduate College at Princeton. He was replaced by Joseph Northrup, newly employed by Cram in Boston, and a recent graduate of MIT.

Watkin was responsible for Perry's performance in addition to a wide range of other duties. Chief among these was interaction with Lovett and, to an increasing degree, with Captain James A. Baker and the other trustees. In the earlier stages, if President Lovett had a question regarding construction, materials, or details of design, he contacted Cram himself by telegram or letter. After the award of a contract on the Administration Building (for the sum of $319,471, on July 2, 1910) and Watkin's arrival, Lovett turned more and more frequently to the young architect, who was usually immediately available in an adjoining office in the Scanlan Building.

Watkin also found himself in a new and significant relationship with Chairman Baker and the five other trustees, particularly as questions involving the general contractor, William Miller & Sons of Pittsburgh, arose. Members of the governing board discovered early on that Watkin was a reliable source of answers that were best explained right at the construction site. There were mandatory photographs taken for the Boston office each day as the work progressed. Occasionally, these photos showed Watkin on site with the regents of the Rice Institute. On these special occasions, everyone was attired in the dark suit and derby hat that were customary for professionals and business leaders of that day, complete with matching topcoat during the nippier days of Houston's brief winter.

Watkin found himself spending full time on such problems as the selection and timely delivery of specialized materials, including brick, marble, limestone, and tile. Directly related was the responsibility of recruiting and maintaining craftsmen and artisans as specialized (and sometimes temperamental) as brickmasons, stonecutters, tilesetters, and experts on tunnel construction. Though these areas involved responsibilities of the general contractor, Cram, Goodhue & Ferguson monitored them painstakingly. Cram himself took an unusual interest in the work of special artisans, aware that the function of the architect was to assure rigid adherence to quality workmanship.

There were also troublesome, potentially catastrophic, difficulties connected with topography, flooding, drainage, and Harris Gully. And Watkin would have to confront the nightmare of any architect: a general contractor turning a job over to the bonding company, as was the case with the original contracting firm, William Miller & Sons.

Separate problems involved the quality and the supply of brick and marble early in 1911 after the laying of a 6,500-pound cornerstone for the Administration Building on March 2, 1911. Regarding the cornerstone, Edgar Odell Lovett, mathematician, astronomer, and scholar of ancient history, personally selected the inscription in Greek, " 'Rather,' said Democritus, 'would I discover the cause of one fact, than become King of the Persians.' " [6]

There had been considerable enthusiasm at Cram, Goodhue & Ferguson over the color of the original exterior, or face, brick chosen for the Administration Building. A "delicate pink," had been selected, thought to be ideally suited for the Byzantine Lombard style selected for the structure. When samples arrived just after New Year's Day of 1911, however, they were "orange, not pink [and] . . . as soft as if they had been merely sunburned, not baked in a kiln." Many were roughly cut or broken. Dr. Lovett happened to be in Philadelphia at the time this was discovered. He was asked by the architects to go to nearby Enfield, Pennsylvania, to confer with the manufacturer. Although he did so, the problems at the kiln could not be resolved.

Watkin recalled that Frank Ferguson, the Cram, Goodhue & Ferguson partner who specialized in contracts and sources of supply, had mentioned a source of pink brick of acceptable color and quality in Houston. Nothing had been done about purchasing it, because the Enfield product was thought to be quite good and was already under contract. Upon inquiry, Watkin found that the "local pink" was available from Sherman Brady, owner of a Houston brickyard making an inexpensive common brick of excellent quality.

Brady had a clay deposit on Brady's Island near the Ship Channel from which was produced brick of varying tones of pink. He was soon delivering "Brady face" of a pink color that blended perfectly with the gray mortar on the exterior of the Administration Building. Further, his brick was found to be "smooth and true," with a slight rounding that the masons required for the proper effect.

The availability of materials became even more important as construction began on the first building, a combination "power house and mechanical laboratory" linked by a machine shop. Plans for a first dormitory complex were rushed to completion late in the summer of 1910. It was still hoped that classes could begin in September 1911, although this was becoming unrealistic. Watkin prepared a fine rendering of the front elevation of the power house and laboratory. A pen-and-ink drawing was dominated by the handsome campanile, a unique feature of the developing campus. It was an ideal way to disguise a smokestack.

A contract for construction of the new facility was awarded September 29, 1910, to William Miller & Sons, the firm that had also been the low bidder on the Administration Building in July 1910. The amount bid was $182,430, almost 10 percent under estimates, but another shortage became evident as work started on this second project. Marble, needed in large quantities for the Administration Building and to some extent on the entire job, had been arriving from a quarry in the Ozark Mountains. The source was an apparently inexhaustible deposit on the Arkansas and Missouri borders with Oklahoma. Problems involving quarrying and shipping soon developed, however. Miller & Sons, the general contractor, plagued by delays and complexities involving the marble, decided to give this aspect of the Administration Building back to the bonding company.

At this point, Watkin was asked to step in. Although unfamiliar with the remote Ozarks, he went there by train and fortunately found a much more dependable source of supply from another mine in the region. Rice Institute was forced to purchase this entire operation to expedite quarrying and shipping. The problem was resolved as shipments quickly resumed.

The question of opening the Rice Institute for classes in September 1911 remained. With continuing emphasis upon the completion of the Administration Building and the power house-laboratory building, and plans for a President's Home and faculty housing also being given priority, something had to give way. It was late in October 1911 before bids were taken on a simplified dormitory complex (South Hall with an interlinked Commons). Since classes could not start without an element of living and dining facilities for out-of-town students, the opening had to be moved to Fall 1912.

The President's Home was delayed, however, for four decades, and it would not be until the post-World War II period that the masters of residential colleges, along with their families, would be provided faculty housing. In 1915, President Lovett and his family moved to the Rice Hotel, after a massive 1915 hurricane, rivaling the catastrophic Galveston storm of September 8, 1900, struck Houston full force. Dr. Lovett was in their leased home at 1218 Caroline alone when he discovered just how powerful and terrifying a major hurricane can be. The storm blew away much of the roof while the president was trying to close a window in a corner of the attic. For the rest of his life, he preferred living in a hotel.

Meanwhile, heavy spring rains and the perennial periodic flooding from Harris Gully made it doubtful, for a time, that classes could be under way even by September 1912. Wilmer Waldo, engineer and member of a prominent Houston family, had been retained to prepare a topographical survey and report on drainage and flood conditions on the Rice campus. A graduate of Princeton, Waldo had established a successful consulting practice in Houston after an earlier career as resident engineer for the Southern Pacific Railroad, and as a developer of Westmoreland, a fine subdivision adjoining the elegance of Courtlandt Place.

The heavy rains, continuing from mid-April 1911 through much of May, made Waldo's report to President Lovett on drainage and flooding very timely. When some of the multi-inch downpours reached the level of what native Houstonians termed "frog-stranglers," the water became a source of construction delays and added expense. Many campus roads (for which Waldo was responsible) had flooded and excavations for the tunnel system he had designed had to be pumped out frequently. The 1,600 feet of reinforced concrete tunnels were a vital link in the construction program, since they furnished electricity, water, and steam heat from the power house to the rest of the campus.

Wilmer Waldo had become accustomed to rounding up the stray, trespassing cattle during the earlier phases of his survey of the site for the new Rice Institute. However, this new development of abnormal spring rains proved to be providential. These rains pointed out the true source of the recurring drainage problems and temporary flooding on the campus. It was found that a county road crossing Harris Bayou, Waldo reported, was "acting as a dam which holds the water in 'flood' on our property." The gully, a channel of Harris Bayou, came through the western portion of the Rice acreage.

This was aggravated by a new ditch along the west side of the streetcar track from Eagle Avenue south to the campus. Waldo recommended that Harris County be asked to widen and straighten the channel of Harris Bayou, which would greatly increase its capacity. His diagnosis was correct, and the problem was eventually solved as Waldo suggested, but not before other property owners (including George Hermann) joined in a petition to Commissioners' Court.

Flooding caused major concern again almost a year later on April 16, 1912, as the contractors and Watkin came closer every day to the reality of two immovable deadlines: Classes were to begin on September 23, 1912, and the formal dedicatory ceremonies, with dozens of distinguished participants and guests, would open three weeks later on October 10. But the rains continued, bringing Harris Gully again to flood stage.

Wilmer Waldo relieved the most immediate problems with a drainage ditch along the northern perimeter of the campus. The trustees ordered a special meeting with Watkin and the contractors every two weeks to review the progress of the three buildings being rushed to completion. The degree of concern over the rapidly approaching deadlines was such that Watkin also had to respond personally to many inquiries from the trustees and President Lovett between the scheduled meetings.

During the construction stage, the Princeton graduate, Waldo, also an expert in railroading, was invaluable as a consultant in the installation and continuing operation of a campus spur of the SA&AP (San Antonio & Aransas Pass, or "the Sap") Railroad. The spur brought extremely heavy shipments of marble, brick, steel, concrete, lumber, tile, and other materials directly to a central receiving point at the power house. And its advantages were manifold, in an era when modern cranes, hoists, trucks, and other equipment were still unknown. Much of the power available in constructing the first buildings at the Rice Institute, as numerous photographs attest, was mule power.

Upon completing the Administration Building, the William Miller & Sons construction firm retired from the Rice job. A new firm was chosen by Cram to finish the remaining buildings. This was the well-known national and international firm, James Stewart & Company, founded in Scotland in 1844, and active in the United States and Canada since 1865. A family organization, Stewart & Company had a well-deserved reputation [7].

In the United States, Stewart & Company had pioneered new techniques involving the construction of railroads (Missouri Pacific and the Santa Fe); had built state capitols (Oklahoma, Idaho, and Utah); and had been the contractor for New York City's Grand Central Station. Their work included factories in Pittsburgh, textile and paper mills, hydroelectric power plants, and huge grain elevators. They had also built many fine hotels, including the Chateau Frontenac in Quebec, the Savoy in London, and the Broadmoor in Colorado Springs.

Ralph Adams Cram was familiar with James Stewart & Company's excellent work. Having built the Royal Naval College in England, James Stewart had also been the successful bidder on Cram, Goodhue & Ferguson's major additions to West Point. For this reason, Stewart was asked to bid on the South Hall and Commons at Rice Institute. Though the project was small in relation to their usual contracts, the Stewart firm won the job at $202,000, and a grateful William Ward Watkin saw the firm carry out their traditionally excellent work on schedule.

The deadlines on the three original buildings were finally met, though finishing touches would be under way for months to come. Classes started on September 23, 1912 (the twelfth anniversary of the death of William Marsh Rice). There was an initial enrollment of fifty-nine students. This grew later to seventy-seven (fifty-two men and twenty-five women), although there was to be an attrition rate of almost half the original class. The splendid dedicatory ceremonies were also held on schedule on October 10, 1912.

Watkin had many people to thank, as he looked back on the twenty-six months since his arrival in Houston. President Lovett, Captain Baker, and the five other trustees had been most supportive of him over this difficult and busy period. His growing friendship with Dr. Lovett had continued to broaden and deepen. He also expressed special gratitude to John A. Roberts, superintendent of construction for William Miller & Sons, and to the clerk of the works, Albert C. Perry, who had gone on to a next assignment at Princeton, as well as to Perry's replacement, Joseph W. Northrup.

Roberts was in a position somewhat similar to that of Watkin, in that the home office of William Miller & Sons, for whom he worked, was also a half-continent away, in Pittsburgh. His wide experience had proven to be invaluable, given the sometimes new and different procedures called for in constructing the Administration Building, as well as the power house and laboratory. Roberts worked well with the various laborers, craftsmen, and artisans, including the stonecutter-sculptor chosen by Cram, Oswald J. Lassig. Lassig, a sculptor from Austria, had carved in place the ornate passageway columns of Texas granite on the Administration Building.

John Roberts, among other jobs, had been superintendent for the additions to the USMA at West Point, and for a new wing of the Metropolitan Museum of Art in New York City, financed by J.P. Morgan. "The Administration Building of the Rice Institute," he told reporters, "is my star piece of work . . . . Few people realize the difficulties in constructing a building like this . . . there is not a building in the whole world that is more artistic, more substantial. It is truly a work classical."

Joseph W. Northrup was a 1910 architectural graduate of the Massachusetts Institute of Technology. Hired by Cram, he had worked on plans for the Rice Institute as his first assignment at Cram, Goodhue & Ferguson in Boston. Arriving in Houston in the summer of 1911, he followed Albert Perry as clerk of the works on the Rice job until the completion of the Physics Building in 1915. Northrup quickly became a close friend of his colleague Watkin and, in 1914, he was best man at Watkin's wedding.

The young clerk of the works soon knew all of the members of the original faculty at Rice, many of whom were also bachelors. After his own wedding in 1915, Northrup opened an architectural office in Houston. One of his first projects was a home for four young bachelors on the Rice faculty, near the campus at 1318 Oakdale [8]. Northrup would remain in Houston for the remainder of his successful life and career.

VI.

Paul Philippe Cret had remained in touch with many of his former students at the University of Pennsylvania. His very successful private practice ranged from his commission for the Pan American Union in Washington, D.C. to his various assignments for spectacular bridges, designed in collaboration with the gifted Polish engineer, Ralph Modjeski. Cret particularly remembered the quiet and exceptionally able William Ward Watkin, who had taken a degree with high distinction in one of his first graduating classes. Professor Cret also remembered that Watkin had followed his advice in consulting Ralph Adams Cram on the matter of his post-graduate tour of noted English churches and monasteries in 1908.

Early in 1912, Cret wrote Watkin advising him that, should his former student wish to pursue a career in academic architecture, there was a promising opening at the University of Illinois in Champaign. In a gracious reply, Watkin stated, in effect, that unless there were extraordinary advantages or opportunities in the Illinois position, he thought that he would remain where he was.

William Ward Watkin was a native of Cambridge, Massachusetts, raised and educated in Pennsylvania. The traditions of the East, a half-continent distant from Houston, were deeply ingrained in the young architect. Yet he had already decided to continue his new life in a brash, booming, strikingly different city in Texas. It was a momentous decision, yet one that was not surprising when some of the many factors involved were considered.

On the one hand, Watkin undoubtedly felt strong ties to Cram, Goodhue & Ferguson, and especially to its charismatic leader, Ralph Adams Cram. There was little doubt that he could return to Boston with the invaluable experience gained at Rice Institute, to what promised to be a rewarding career in a firm of growing national repute.

However, there was his inherited instinct to seize a perceived opportunity, as had both his Watkin and Hancock forebears, in a new setting. Houston was not only a prosperous and exciting city, but one of marked friendliness, seemingly poised for ongoing growth and expansion. Watkin liked opportunity, and he liked Houston.

There were also increasing ties to Edgar Odell Lovett, and a desire to continue to participate in President Lovett's great educational project, now rapidly taking form.

There was growing recognition of the excellent caliber of the faculty being recruited by Dr. Lovett, who had returned from another trip to the East and to England seeking men of high talent and potential. Many of those casting their lot with the new Rice Institute became Watkin's close and lasting friends as they established their own ties to Houston.

For Watkin, there were already increasing community, professional, social, and religious links to his adopted city. Once Rice had opened, he had begun to give occasional public lectures, and to be involved in areas such as local city planning, as well as the planning of parks and carefully designed subdivisions. Captain Baker had sponsored him as a new member of the elite Houston Country Club, with its elegant new clubhouse and excellent golf course. Watkin greatly enjoyed golf during the rare times he was away from work. He looked forward to the prospects of a fine private practice, as new and old Houstonians sought well-planned new homes. As a devout Episcopalian, he had been active in Christ Church since his arrival from Boston. The beautiful and historic old structure, to be named, in time, a cathedral, was only minutes from the boarding house where he lived.

Finally, there was to be a new factor in William Ward Watkin's decision to make his life and career in Houston. At the 1912 Coronation Ball of No-Tsu-Oh in the City Auditorium, Watkin was the invited guest of President and Mrs. Lovett. That particular year, Lovett was chosen to reign over the event as King Nottoc XIII. The ball had stood at the apex of Houston's social calendar since 1899. The Queen of the Carnival was Miss Annie Vieve Carter, daughter of S.F. Carter, the lumber magnate. The ball marked the end of festive days and nights of celebrating as it honored Houston's flourishing businesses, greatly strengthened by new growth in petroleum, banking, and transportation.

There had been a series of parades and flotillas, with early automobiles festooned in gorgeous autumn flowers and occupied by the city's beautifully attired young matrons, and lavishly decorated floats drawn down Main Street between marching bands. Flares lit Allen's Landing for the night arrival of flotillas of ornate launches.

The leading families of the city were assembled at the Auditorium for Dr. Lovett's coronation as King Nottoc XIII. Seated in orderly rows were the Andrews, Ayars, Bakers, Baldwins, Berings, Blaffers, Bryans, Carters, Cullinans, Clevelands, Farishes, Hutchesons, Malones, Parkers, Reds, Rices, Torreys, Weems, Whartons, and many other families prominent in Houston's 1911 society. H. Malcolm Lovett and Ben Rice, Jr., were pages to Queen Annie Vieve.

The following year, 1912, Watkin again attended the colorful No-Tsu-Oh Ball, but on this occasion his invited guest was a vivacious young redhead from San Antonio, Miss Annie Ray Townsend, who was making her debut that winter. She was accompanied at the Houston ball by her brother's recent bride, Mrs. Foard Townsend. A souvenir still marks the occasion of this memorable evening: William Ward Watkin's dance card and ball program, an elaborately designed, beautiful little memento with a long gold cord and tassel. Obviously Watkin only had eyes for the slim, smiling young lady from San Antonio. Her name was written down for the first and third dances (the second went to her sister-in-law, Mrs. Foard Townsend) and for all the waltzes on the remainder of the program. Watkin apparently felt safer with a waltz than a foxtrot.

Watkin had met Annie Ray Townsend, the daughter of a prominent lawyer and state senator from an early Texas family, earlier in the year at a social gathering in Houston. The debutantes of the season in San Antonio were invited to the prime social events in Houston and Galveston. Several of the No-Tsu-Oh debutantes in town would be guests of the Order of the Alamo at the San Antonio presentation and at the traditional events of the season in Galveston.

Miss Louise Ayars (later Mrs. Louis Stevenson), a childhood friend of Annie Ray's from Columbus, was one of the Houston debutantes presented at the No-Tsu-Oh Ball of 1912. The queen of the ball was Miss Garland Bonner, who later, as Mrs. George Howard, became one of Annie Ray's close friends.

As their courtship developed, Annie Ray Townsend told Watkin that she would never consider leaving Texas. This may well have been the factor that tipped the scales in favor of Houston. Watkin had earlier asked President Lovett to consider permitting him to establish a Department of Architecture at the infant Rice Institute. This would be a small but initial commitment to ensure that art would be included along with letters and science, as had been specified in the charter of the Institute. Dr. Lovett agreed enthusiastically, and his newest faculty member soon started to work on the curriculum for the academic year 1912–1913.

Watkin could hardly have been busier than he was during the months preceding the opening of classes at the Rice Institute. There were innumerable details to be completed on the Administration Building, as well as on the power house and laboratory, now already called the Mechanical Engineering Building, and on South Hall and the Commons. Meanwhile, planning went ahead full tilt on the Physics Building, which was to be divided into facilities for physics, biology, and chemistry. The final Rice building to be designed before World War I under the aegis of Cram, Goodhue & Ferguson (East Hall, now part of James A. Baker College) was also begun.

It was about this time that the name of Ralph Adam Cram's firm was changed. Cram, Goodhue & Ferguson became Cram & Ferguson on January 1, 1914. Bertram Grosvenor Goodhue had formally withdrawn to establish his own firm in New York.

As Watkin began making plans for his new Department of Architecture, there was the problem of recruiting an additional faculty member for the 1913–1914 academic year. Both enrollment and curriculum would expand in the second year, and would continue to do so until the first fifth-year class was graduated in May 1917.

When President Lovett prepared to launch the first academic year at Rice, he began the formation of various key committees within the institution. Watkin, after almost two years in Houston, had grown closer to President Lovett as both friend and colleague. It was thus inevitable that young Watkin would receive his share of committee assignments.

First, Watkin was named chairman of the Committee on Buildings and Grounds, which meant that he was to be curator of grounds. Second, he was named chairman of the Committee on Outdoor Sports, attesting to President Lovett's confidence in Watkin's diversified capabilities and interests.

He would serve in the first post for the remainder of his life. Both his professional training and experience obviously suited him admirably for matters involving the buildings. Further, Cram, Goodhue & Ferguson had always emphasized the total setting for its projects, including the selection of plantings, roads, walks, and general landscaping. It was thus natural to include both disciplines within the total scope of the Committee on Buildings and Grounds.

Watkin would prove to be a fortunate selection to head the Committee on Outdoor Sports as well. The chairman of this group was to serve as faculty adviser on athletics. As it developed, Watkin would see the Rice Institute through sixteen years of intercollegiate athletics. He would finally relinquish the chairmanship of this committee in 1928, before leaving for a well-deserved sabbatical year in Europe. It was then given to his good friend and colleague, John T. McCants.

But of vital importance in 1912 and 1913 to the busy William Ward Watkin, there was the pleasant matter of Miss Annie Ray Townsend. She had continued to occupy more and more of his thoughts since the No-Tsu-Oh ball of November 1912.

Annie Ray Townsend was born in Columbus, Texas, of a family with deep southern roots. Townsends had been in America since the early seventeenth century [9]. The family, known more usually in England as Townshend, probably originated in Norfolk from Saxon and Norman forebears. The ancestral home of Raynham Hall, designed by the famed architect Inigo Jones in 1625 for Sir Roger, first baronet Townshend, still stands near Norfolk.

There were Townsends in all thirteen U.S. colonies, but Annie Ray's family lived in Marlboro (then Marlborough) County, South Carolina, as well as in Pittsylvania County, Virginia. They later migrated to Bullard, Liberty, and McIntosh counties in Georgia, and then to Jefferson and Madison counties in Florida, and from there to Texas.

Benedictus Townsend, who probably came to Marlboro County, South Carolina, from Virginia soon before issuance to him of a royal grant of January 27, 1764, left his plantation to his sons, Light and John. Light Townsend, who came to South Carolina with his father, is known as "Light of the Revolution" because of his service under Captain Robert Lide in a company of sixty men organized in 1775. He was also one of the many South Carolinians to campaign with General Francis Marion, the "Swamp Fox," during the Revolution.

Light's son, Thomas, and his wife, Elizabeth Stapleton, had eight sons and a daughter. They left McIntosh County, Georgia, in 1822 for Florida, which had become a territory of the U.S. that year. Joining them there in what were to become Jefferson and Madison counties were uncles, aunts, and cousins from Marlboro County, South Carolina. The Townsends soon owned major grants of Florida land, but the family had become quite large. Learning of the generous land grants available in what was then the Mexican state of Coahuila y Tejas, in 1826 they decided to send two of Thomas' seven sons to investigate. The emissaries chosen for the long and hazardous journey were Thomas Roderick and his younger bother, Spencer Burton.

The reports from Coahuila y Tejas were positive. Over the next decade, the Townsends sold their Florida land and headed west for what had become the Republic of Texas. They settled together in the northeast corner of fertile, historic Fayette County, which was then part of Bastrop and Colorado counties. Their town, which was first called Townsend, Texas, was later known as Round Top. Three of the Townsends fought at the Battle of San Jacinto on April 21, 1836. Members of the family prayed for their safe return at their little chapel, which they named the Florida Chapel for their former home in that state.

Asa Townsend and his wife, Rebecca Harper, Annie Ray Townsend's great-grandparents, had remained in Florida until 1836, until their fourteen children were old enough to travel. They decided to settle in Columbus, Texas, a dozen miles east of the Fayette County line. Asa, the oldest of the seven Townsend brothers who came to Texas, received a land grant of 640 acres about ten miles northwest of Columbus. The grant, dated 1838 and signed by Anson Jones, president of the Republic of Texas, was near the hamlet of Borden, along Havens Creek. There he raised cattle and horses.

Soon after the grant was confirmed and a proper title issued, Asa Townsend sold a portion of the land to his good friend and neighbor, Gail Borden. Borden, editor, patriot, and inventor of a process to condense milk, wanted to add to his adjoining acreage. At that time, he was the publisher of the *Telegraph and Texas Register*, the official newspaper of the Texas Revolution and Republic, at nearby San Felipe de Austin.

Asa and Rebecca Townsend became prominent citizens of Colorado County, and are buried together in the little cemetery at Borden. Asa maintained his friendship with Gail Borden, who received U.S. and British patents on his condensed milk process in 1856 and founded the present-day Borden, Inc., a giant of the food industry. He would have wanted to be remembered as much, however, for his part in writing the first Texas constitution; for founding the state's oldest newspaper, the *Galveston News*; and for publishing the first map of Texas' varied topography [10].

Moses Solon Townsend, Annie Ray's grandfather, was born October 23, 1830, in Jefferson County, Florida. He came to Texas with the family as a child, and served as a lieutenant in the Confederate Army. Two years after returning home from the war with one of the many volunteer regiments from Texas, he drowned in Rocky Creek near Columbus when crossing the creek on horseback.

Marcus Harvey Townsend, Annie Ray's father, was born March 26, 1859. His father died when Marcus was 8 years old. His widowed mother, born Annie Beth Harvey, was left with four small sons and did not remarry until Marcus was twenty, in 1879, but he was raised amid a large and caring family on a farm near Columbus. Marcus read for the law, in the Columbus office of Major Robert Foard, from the time he was a teenager. He attended a series of lectures at the Baylor College law school at nearby Independence, Texas.

Only two years after being admitted to the bar in 1882, he was elected to the state House of Representatives from Columbus at the age of 23. As the representative for the Eleventh District, he introduced and guided to final passage the bill for the purchase of the Alamo by the state of Texas. Legislator Townsend then served as chairman of the committee that negotiated the acquisition of the historic monument by the state.

Marcus Townsend was elected to the State Senate in 1888. Noted for his detailed knowledge of the legislative process and wide influence, he served as chairman of two key Senate committees, and as a member of thirteen other committees in the senior chamber.

After retiring from the Legislature, Senator Townsend became one of the state's best-known attorneys. He moved to San Antonio in 1906, opened a new firm with his son, Foard, and T.F. Mangum, and began amassing a comfortable fortune in land, ranching, banking, and other business interests. He was a director of the City National Bank of San Antonio, and prominent in many civic, professional, and business organizations.

The family was active in San Antonio's social clubs and especially in the Order of the Alamo, which presented Annie Ray Townsend as one of the debutantes at the Battle of Flowers ball in 1913. Her escort for the occasion was, not surprisingly, the rising young architect and member of the Rice Institute faculty, William Ward Watkin.

Meanwhile, Watkin's commitment to the ongoing construction program at the Rice Institute had not lessened, in spite of his concurrent academic demands. He was soon working again with Cram on the construction of the complex new Physics Building. There are few university facilities that compare with the Physics Building in design detail. Watkin wrote of this unique structure in an article entitled "Architectural Traditions Appearing in the Earlier Buildings of the Rice Institute" (*Slide Rule*, volume 13, number 7, July 1953, published after his death). The Physics Building consisted of a long, thin, rectangular block facing south, and an amphitheater parallel to the block. In its location parallel to the Administration Building, Cram, Goodhue & Ferguson followed the layout of the master plan.

Originally, the entire structure would have been wholly within the "engineering and science court" further to the west, and therefore reasonably plain, with brick or limestone trim. Because the rectangular block adjacent to the ornate Administration Building was clearly within the academic court, it had to be embellished accordingly. This meant colored tile, carved heraldic owls, "and Venetian ornaments" for the building.

Watkin explained such sophisticated treatment as ". . . reflect[ing] more . . . ornament than would have been appropriate to a simple science building, but its proximity to the Administration Building seemed to justify this treatment." Stephen Fox mentions such detailing as ". . . Marble lunettes . . . twin tabernacles . . . simplified versions of those atop St. Mark's Church in Venice . . . tesselated paving and a Guastavino tile vault . . . [an] exo-narthex motif from St. Luke's of Stiris . . ." Cram, Goodhue & Ferguson was clearly setting a pace for a Physics Building unmatched in 1914, if indeed ever. It remains a jewel of design and of execution.

The James Stewart Company, successful in completing the South Hall and Commons project on time, although under considerable pressure, had also won the contract, at $285,903, for the more complex Physics Building. They finished this job on schedule in September 1914, only to face a delay in the delivery of the laboratory equipment until early December. The Stewart organization, in the meantime, was awarded a contract on East Hall, the second dormitory, for $103,800. This was completed in the summer of 1915, with some overtones of medieval Italian architecture in the design. Cram and Ferguson then initiated plans for West Hall, a third dormitory, as enrollment continued to increase in the fourth academic year.

VII.

As was expected of the Rice Institute's high standards, architectural training at the Rice Institute was to be thorough and demanding. It involved a "full course extending over five years, leading to a bachelor of arts degree at the end of the fourth year, and to the degree of bachelor of science in architecture at the end of the fifth year."

The objective was to lead students to a "comprehensive understanding of the art of building, to acquaint them with the history of architecture from early civilization to the present age, and to develop within them an understanding and appreciation of those concepts of beauty and utility which are fundamental to the cultivation of ability in the art of design."

Students were given access to campus buildings under construction "[in] the inspiring environment of a gradually expanding group [of structures] of great beauty." There were also visits and inspections of the "many building activities throughout the rapidly growing city of Houston." As architects-to-be, the students were told to observe that "Of the more strictly architectural subjects, design is given by far the larger place." Further, along with architectural, engineering, and technical subjects, "certain indispensable elements of a liberal education" were also included.

The first class in the Department of Architecture, consisting of six freshmen, was received with the other members of the Class of 1916 at a historic ceremony attended by the trustees, faculty, and "representative citizens." On September 26, 1912 in this meeting in the Faculty Chamber, President Lovett began his long tradition of an annual address to the entering freshmen and other new students.

These first architecture majors faced a rigorous class schedule plus the traditional laboratories and assigned problems. The class requirements included Mathematics 100 (stumbling block for many a freshman), English, French, physics, architecture, freehand drawing, and the first of two required years of military training. Watkin himself taught a freshmen class in architecture and freehand drawing. He was already seeking another instructor for the 1913–1914 academic year, when architectural design, architectural history, and "antique" drawing would be added to the curriculum.

The Department of Architecture had been assigned space on the second floor of the mechanical laboratory. The space included a large, modern, well-lighted "draughting" room, plus a spacious studio for freehand drawing and watercolor. An adjoining library contained the start of what was to become a fine collection of books, periodicals, and other publications, plus art reproductions, photographs, and slides.

Late in the spring of 1912, a list of the original faculty was drawn up by Edgar Odell Lovett for distribution to the press. Many of the hand-picked faculty were among the most distinguished in terms of academic honors and accomplishments in their fields. A pattern of distinction at Rice had clearly been set.

The list is reproduced here as it first appeared in the bulletin:

Philip Heckman Arbuckle, B. A. (Chicago), of Georgetown, Texas; Director of Athletics in Southwestern University; to be Instructor in Athletics.

Percy John Daniell, M. A. (Cambridge), of Liverpool, England; Senior Wrangler and Rayleigh Prizeman of the University of Cambridge; Lecturer in Mathematics at the University of Liverpool; to be Research Associate in Applied Mathematics.

William Franklin Edwards, B. Sc. (Michigan), of Houston, Texas; formerly Instructor in the University of Michigan, and later President of the University of Washington; to be Lecturer in Chemistry.

Griffith Conrad Evans, Ph. D. (Harvard), of Rome, Italy; Sheldon Fellow of Harvard University; to be Assistant Professor of Pure Mathematics.

Julian Sorrell Huxley, M. A. (Oxford), of Oxford, England; Newdigate Prizeman of the University of Oxford; Lecturer in Biology at Balliol College, and Inter-collegiate Lecturer in Oxford University; to be Research Associate in Biology.

Francis Ellis Johnson, B. A., E. E. (Wisconsin), of Houston, Texas; recently with the British Columbia Electric Railway Company; to be Instructor in Electrical Engineering.

Edgar Odell Lovett, Ph. D. (Virginia and Leipzig), LL. D. (Drake and Tulane), of Houston, Texas; formerly Professor of Mathematics in Princeton University, and later Head of the Department of Astronomy in the same institution; President of the Institute; to be Professor of Mathematics.

William Ward Watkin, B. Sc. (Pennsylvania), Architect, of Houston, Texas; to be Instructor in Architectural Engineering.

Harold Albert Wilson, F. R. S., D. Sc. (Cambridge), of Montreal, Canada; Fellow of Trinity College, Cambridge University; formerly Professor in King's College, London; Research Professor in McGill University; to be Professor of Physics.

Foremost among those with established professional reputations were President Lovett (whose achievements at Virginia and Leipzig, as well as at Princeton University have been mentioned), and Dr. Harold A. Wilson. The latter's imposing accomplishments are worthy of special note.

Wilson, only thirty-seven when he arrived at the Rice Institute in 1912, was already a fellow of the Royal Society (of London for the Improvement of Natural Knowledge), and thereby in the company and tradition of Great Britain's greatest scientists. Having received his doctorate in science from Cambridge University, Wilson was named F.R.S. in 1906 at thirty-one. He accepted a lectureship at Kings College of the University of London, only to discover that research facilities there were somewhat marginal.

By 1907, Wilson had become interested in an appointment in the United States or Canada. Much of this was because his sister Lillian had married O.W. Richardson, a fellow physicist with a leading role in a potent new research program at Princeton University. Through Richardson, he learned of a vacancy at McGill University in Montreal, applied for, and was soon offered a professorship there. There were some misgivings about Montreal's climate ("harsh in winter, hot and humid in summer"), but he accepted the post and was soon a busy and contented member of the McGill community.

In the fall of 1911, a charming Canadian girl, Marjorie Paterson Smyth, enrolled in one of Harold Wilson's graduate classes. She was an honor graduate of McGill in mathematics and physics. In the summer of 1912, soon after she was awarded the master of science degree, she and Harold were married.

Meanwhile, Edgar Odell Lovett had been on another recruiting trip. He stopped by Princeton, as he often did when in the East, and learned from Professor Richardson of Dr. Wilson's impressive record both in research and in graduate instruction. He then went to Montreal to offer Wilson the professorship of physics at Rice.

Harold Wilson recalled a half-century later how "the idea of helping to start a new university, and especially a new physics department," had appealed to him a great deal as "an exciting adventure." Always conscious of the importance of well-planned facilities and the most modern equipment, the McGill professor was obviously much impressed by what President Lovett told him. The well-endowed Rice Institute was to be a small university with high standards, a graduate school, and a carefully chosen faculty given the best possible physical plant and equipment. He was shown a small copy of the master plan by Cram, Goodhue & Ferguson, by this time well recognized as perhaps the leading firm in academic architecture. The plan, most importantly, included a new physics building.

Further, if he came to Houston, Professor Wilson would have a key role in planning the new building, selecting equipment, and in recommending faculty appointments, since the new facility was in a second wave of construction and would not open until at least 1914.

After consulting with his fiancee, who agreed to the "exciting adventure," the Wilsons came to Houston as newlyweds in the summer of 1912. The bridegroom always kept a clipping from the Houston *Post,* which told of ". . . the first Rice Institute professor arriving . . . with his pink-cheeked bride from the Canadian North." He and Marjorie would recall five decades later driving from their home at the Savoy Apartments to Rice in their new Ford. If their car stuck in the mud beyond Eagle Avenue, there was almost always a farmer around to pull them out with a team of mules, unless they had slid into "the great mudhole by the second gate." [11]

Each of the remaining members of the original faculty (several of them, including William Ward Watkin, still in their mid-twenties) had significant early accomplishments that clearly indicated their marked ability.

Griffith Conrad Evans won the coveted Sheldon Fellowship in pure mathematics at Harvard while earning his doctorate. He went on to the University of Rome to pursue post-doctoral research under Professor Vito Volterra [12]. Volterra, a member of the Italian Senate, was an authority on mathematical physics and celestial mechanics, both specialties of great interest to Edgar Odell Lovett. The Italian mathematician and physicist had recommended Evans to Dr. Lovett during the latter's visit to Rome en route to Moscow.

Julian Sorrell Huxley, later Sir Julian, was the grandson of Thomas Henry Huxley. The grandfather was a self-educated biologist who, much as Charles Darwin, took a four-year trip in the Pacific as a naval officer. Thomas Henry became a fellow of the Royal Society and turned down offers from Oxford, Edinburgh, and Harvard to remain at London's tiny School of Mines. By the end of his life (in 1895), he had transformed the little institution into the prestigious Royal College of Science. The elder Huxley defended the controversial theories of Charles Darwin against strident criticism from prominent theologians. He himself hypothesized that life had originated from a series of chemical reactions.

Following in this tradition, young Julian Huxley had come to Rice with a sparkling record in biology at Oxford. He was fascinated with Houston and its new Institute, as indicated in his marvelous account of the opening ceremonies (*Cornhill Magazine*, July 1918, as quoted in Chapter I). Huxley made lasting contributions to Rice in planning both curriculum and physical facilities for the Department of Biology, working in conjunction with William Ward Watkin on the facilities. Huxley was an extremely effective teacher and researcher, and a central figure among the younger members of the faculty. Unfortunately for Rice, he chose to return to England in 1914 to volunteer for service at the outbreak of the first World War [13].

Joseph Iliot Davies, who had come from England with Huxley as a laboratory assistant, and who took the first Ph.D in biology awarded by the Institute, was to remain on the faculty for five decades. He taught two generations of premedical students and biology majors, and taught them well.

One of the most fortunate additions to both faculty and staff was John Thomas McCants, although not listed in the 1912 announcement of the original faculty at Rice because he was regarded primarily as an administrator. He was appointed secretary to President Lovett on December 1, 1910, replacing F. Carrington Weems. Dr. Lovett announced this change in a handwritten statement praising the "value of [Mr. Weems'] service to the Institute," and noting McCants' accomplishments.

J.T. McCants would remain at the Rice Institute for forty-one years before retiring in 1951. A "Georgian reared in Alabama," he held master of arts degrees from both Virginia and Yale. McCants had served as an instructor in English at the former institute, and as a fellow in English literature at Yale. When appointed to Rice, he was assistant superintendent and professor of English at the Marion Institute, then a well-known college at Marion, Alabama.

McCants became bursar (or treasurer) of Rice, and a close friend and colleague of both President Lovett and Watkin. The McCants and Watkin families would be neighbors from 1915 until Watkin's death in 1952. Upon his retirement in 1951, McCants wrote a detailed and invaluable history of Rice (modestly entitled "Some Information Concerning The Rice Institute"). It was published only as a mimeographed, single-spaced typescript. The text was "lost" for some time, but fortunately turned up in the McCants' garage.

Philip Heckman Arbuckle, a graduate of the University of Chicago, came to the Rice Institute in 1912 from Southwestern University, a small but well-established institution at Georgetown, Texas, near Austin. His only title was instructor in athletics. It was intended from the start, however, that Arbuckle would serve as director of athletics (the rank he had held at Southwestern), football coach, and chairman of a military training program that evolved into a Department of Physical Education. A full year of physical education was required for a degree from the Institute, regardless of the area of specialization.

Percy John Daniell had the singular distinction of having been senior wrangler (first of all those taking first-class honors) at Cambridge, where he was awarded the coveted Rayleigh Prize upon graduation in 1909. A specialist in mathematical physics, Daniell came to Rice from the University of Liverpool. He was named research associate in applied physics.

William Edwards, a noted chemist who had left the University of Michigan to become president of the University of Washington, became a lecturer in chemistry. He would be first in a succession of eminent scientists who were also administrators to head the Chemistry Department at the Rice Institute.

William Ward Watkin had already proved himself academically at the University of Pennsylvania. By 1912, he had added invaluable experience and accomplishments in his professional field. Now he fitted well into an original faculty of distinction, many of them men his own age, with common interests. They became friends as well as professional colleagues. Of particular note, one early faculty member who became a very close friend and neighbor of the Watkin family was Albert Leon Guerard, French scholar and writer. Although not listed on the original roster, he joined the Rice faculty soon after its opening. Guerard, professor of French, was a graduate of the University of France and had formerly taught at Williams College in Massachusetts, as well as at Stanford University.

VIII.

As busy as he was with the final details of the first wave of buildings constructed at Rice, the new Physics Building, and his administrative assignments at Rice, young Watkin found time for three other areas of vital importance. These included the growth of his private practice in the prosperous city of Houston, his basic and growing responsibilities as head of the Department of Architecture, and his personal life.

The young architect and professor continued to meet and to interact with many leading Houstonians. He was increasingly interested in such matters such as city planning and the need for a museum of fine arts. He saw the need for an active local chapter of the American Institute of Architects, and was successful in getting this started with the cooperation of Houston architects Birdsall Briscoe and Olle J.

Lorehn. Another interest for him, as a devout Episcopalian, was his membership in Christ Church and later in Trinity Church.

Every faculty member at the new Rice Institute was firmly committed to Edgar Odell Lovett's insistence upon rigorous academic standards. It was soon obvious, even in 1912, that there would be a considerable number of students who had the requisite number of credits for admission, but had not been adequately prepared in high school. About half of the first entering class did not pass the examinations administered before the middle of the term, two weeks after Thanksgiving.

Watkin's response in the Department of Architecture was to work patiently with his first group of six enrollees, and to screen applications for the next entering class even more carefully.

In his personal life, Watkin continued to be absorbed by his abiding new interest: the cheerful, intelligent, and beautiful Annie Ray Townsend. Their courtship proceeded through 1912 and 1913 with a constant stream of letters and frequent trips to San Antonio by young Watkin. He was seen on the westbound Southern Pacific train headed for San Antonio whenever he could spare the time. Watkin was spotted traveling in style in the club car when he went to visit Annie Ray, and was attired in a well-cut suit, complete with spats, gray homburg, and gloves.

William Ward Watkin and Annie Ray Townsend were married on June 1, 1914, in the Travis Park Methodist Church in the center of San Antonio, with their many friends in the Alamo City in attendance. The couple spent their honeymoon in the beautiful resort town of Asheville, North Carolina at the new Grove Park Inn, and returned to their first home, an apartment on Main Street near the Savoy.

Their first child, Annie Ray, was born May 11, 1915, just after the Watkins moved into their new home at 5009 Caroline. It had been designed with exacting care by the prospective father. Their joy was dimmed, however, by the death of Annie Ray's father, Marcus Harvey Townsend in June 1915. He succumbed to a long illness only weeks after the birth of Annie Ray's first child.

Notes

1. Ralph Adams Cram was already quite involved in Boston's cultural life, and this would increase. There was to be growing identification with the city's rich activities in literature, music, and art. He and Mrs. Cram are believed to have organized with their neighbors the tradition of the Christmas Eve bell-ringers of Beacon Hill. The bells are still heard in Louisberg Square and on adjoining Beacon and Chestnut Streets at Christmas.

   A music critic, correspondent, and author from his twenties, Cram wrote significant volumes of architectural criticism and history, as well as his autobiography. With his partner, Goodhue, he published a literary quarterly (*The Knight Errant*) for a brief time. Both Cram and Goodhue were among the organizers of the White Rose Society, a literary group whose members met regularly to read or recite their own articles, stories, and poems.

   Cram was also the author of *Excalibur,* a medieval drama that reflected his lifelong interest in that period of history and its Arthurian legends. In 1912, he autographed a special copy of this work to William Ward Watkin, expressing his appreciation for Watkin's central role and many accomplishments in carrying out the Rice Institute commission.

2. This internal competition in the Cram, Goodhue & Ferguson offices was also described by the Boston critic Douglass Shand Tucci in his book on Cram.

3. Jesse Jones was not unfamiliar with imaginative, yet sound, financing arrangements. As early as 1902, he borrowed $500 from a Houston bank, locked it safely away, and repaid principal and interest just before the due date. After repeating the cycle several times at increasingly higher levels of principal and lower rates of interest, he established strong lines of credit. The time had come. He borrowed $10,000 that enabled him to organize the South Texas Lumber Company, and was on his way. From this beginning, in 1904, Jones built an enormous fortune in real estate, banking, and other highly successful business ventures, in addition to a career in politics and national affairs that made him at one time a well-regarded candidate for the White House.

4. Robert Alonzo Welch, a South Carolinian, arrived in Houston as a penniless teenager. From a lowly job in a drug store, he learned first merchandising then banking, and in time rose from clerk to owner of the James Bute Company, paint manufacturers. A timely investment at Spindletop turned his attention to oil and to sulphur. Welch studied petroleum and mining journals and knew, soon after its discovery, of Herman Frasch's process to extract sulphur with superheated water. He was soon a major shareholder in Freeport Sulphur and other corporations, finally amassing a fortune of more than fifty million dollars. As James A. Clark has recounted in his biography of Welch, he left a sixth of this to his thirty employees, and placed the remainder in the Robert A. Welch Foundation. The foundation, closely allied with Rice Institute over the years,

has become a leading international force in the support of highly sophisticated research in chemistry.

However, Clark also tells of how Welch lived most of his life in relative penury. He once took E.A. Peden to lunch, insisting that Peden be his guest as a business discussion continued. They went to Colby's, even though Peden, founder of Peden Iron & Steel, was more accustomed to the fashionable Thalian Club. Colby's featured one meat dish and one vegetable dish for a total bill of ten cents. When served, Welch split the two orders between them.

5. The morning newspaper often had the jump on important news breaks. It also had advantages such as the first linotype machine west of the Mississippi River, and the fact that it still charged only a penny a copy, versus two cents for the *Chronicle.* Its reporters had included the great O. Henry, as a columnist writing under his real name, Sidney Porter. Some collections of Houstoniana include original copies of prized columns that O. Henry wrote for the *Post.* One of the rarest of these details O. Henry's recollection of standing on the new bridge over Buffalo Bayou at San Jacinto Street one cloudy spring night:

". . . Half of a May moon swam in a sea of buttermilky clouds high in the east. Below, the bayou gleamed darkly in the semi-darkness, merging into inky blackness farther down. A steam tug glided noiselessly down the sluggish waters, leaving a shattered trail of molten silver . . . . A mellow voice, with . . . too much dramatic inflection, murmured at [my] elbow, and quoted incorrectly from Byron: 'Oh, moon, and darkening river, ye are wondrous strong . . .' "

6. Stephen Fox explains the care with which Cram, Goodhue & Ferguson selected the style of lettering cut into the stone. The inscription, although in Greek, was from the fourth-century Bishop Eusebius of Caesarea, a noted Roman chronicler of the first four centuries of Christianity. Ralph Adams Cram himself, noting that ancient Greek lettering would be "chronologically incorrect" for Eusebius, chose a Byzantine Renaissance style from the Church of St. Luke at Stiris. He had seen the church while on a cruise with friends in the eastern Mediterranean. Cram described it as "perfectly articulated."

7. James C. Stewart himself, namesake of the founder, was still remembered in England and Scotland for huge military bases and port installations completed on time, but also for an anecdote involving the elegant Hotel Savoy, a landmark Stewart project in London's Strand. Learning that brick work was falling behind in spite of double shifts, Stewart showed up at the job in white tie and tails one twilight. He was en route to the opera at nearby Covent Garden. After watching a mason for a time, James Christian announced that he himself could lay brick faster.

"Show me," said the craftsman he was criticizing. Stewart promptly peeled off his coat, rolled up his sleeves, and showed the dumbfounded brickmason how well he had learned his trade as an apprentice long ago.

8. The house that Joseph W. Northrup designed was built for four very interesting young bachelors on the faculty, including Julian Huxley, Griffith Evans, Arthur Hughes, and the youngest professor at the Rice Institute—a mathematical genius named William Sidis, only sixteen years old.

9. Thomas Townsend came from London to Lynn, Massachusetts, in 1637 to join relatives who had already settled there. Three Townsend brothers, John, Henry, and Richard, joined a group of colonists settled at Oyster Bay on Long Island before 1645; however, it is unproven that these Townsends were related to Annie Ray Townsend Watkin.

10. After Gail Borden's death in Borden, on January 11, 1874, the State Legislature honored him by creating huge, sparsely-settled Borden County, with its county seat of Gail and present population of only 781. On the Caprock Escarpment under Muchakooga Peak in far West Texas, it is an appropriate memorial to a surveyor and topographer who began life surveying Covington, Kentucky, and who completed laying out Galveston late in 1836, thus launching what would be the state's largest city on into the next century.

11. Harold Wilson's experience was after the days of getting to the campus by horse and buggy or via the "Institute Toonerville Trolley": the latter ran from Eagle Avenue to tiny sheds at the three entrances to the new university. The trolley was supposedly on a half-hour schedule from 7:00 a.m. until midnight, but this schedule was subject to severe disruption from students walking down the track, as well as from trespassing cows.

12. A colleague and close friend of Henri Poincare, the world-famed French mathematician and astronomer, Vito Volterra replaced Poincare as a featured lecturer at the October 10–12, 1912, opening of the Rice Institute. The French scientist had died only weeks before the dedicatory ceremonies after having prepared three papers on his specialty: new models and theories in astronomy. Adapted versions were delivered by Volterra in English, having been translated from the original French by Dr. Evans, who was also an accomplished linguist.

13. Julian Huxley would not return to Houston, although he continued to correspond with Dr. Lovett and with his friend Watkin on the details of building and equipping facilities for the Department of Biology. After the war, he resumed a career in teaching, research, and administration. Huxley became a world authority on ecology, the philosophy of science, and developmental processes. First a professor of zoology at King's College of the University of London, he later served as secretary of the Zoological Society of London, and as the first director general of UNESCO, the United Nations Educational, Scientific and Cultural Organization. His papers are in the Fondren Library at Rice, due to the efforts and generous donations of Chalmers M. and Demaris DeLange Hudspeth and other alumni.

CHAPTER FIVE

*A full and happy life at 5009 Caroline near other faculty
families . . . The Watkin children enroll at the Kinkaid
School . . . Vacations at the Grove Park Inn, and
summer camp for the girls . . . Expanding the
Department of Architecture . . . World War I brings
changes to the Rice Institute . . . Lasting emphasis
upon both professional and personal development of
students . . . The first Archi-Arts Ball is held . . .
Watkin's private practice is successfully launched . . . A
very busy chairman of Buildings and Grounds and of the
Committee on Outdoor Sports . . . The one and only
Salvatore (Tony) Martino . . . Watkin helps organize the
Southwest Conference and recruits the legendary
football coach, John W. Heisman*

I.

In the years to come, William Ward Watkin would increasingly realize how significant the decade and a half between 1914 and 1929 was in his life, as well as in the unfolding history of the young university with which he had cast his lot. It was a time of meaningful developments in areas of special consequence to Watkin. These included his personal life; his expanding career as architect, professor, and administrator; his private practice; and his growing involvement in community and professional matters.

It was a full and happy life for the Watkin family in their home at 5009 Caroline Boulevard, located in the pleasant and attractive Southmore subdivision less than a mile from the Rice campus. Their firstborn child, named Annie Ray for her mother, was followed by another daughter, Rosemary, born February 12, 1917. Then, on October 27, 1919, William Ward, Jr., "Sonny," the "heir apparent" of the Watkins, was born and was dearly loved by both parents and sisters. He was very special to his father, for William Ward, Sr., was the only son of Frederick Watkin, who had died at age 28. This left their Watkin line in America represented by only one very young boy.

A number of the original Rice Institute faculty and staff, plus new additions arriving as early as 1913, lived in close proximity to the Watkins. John T. and Julia McCants were across the street at 4910 Caroline, and the Harold Wilsons were nearby on Chenevert. On Oakdale, a few blocks to the south, Joseph Northrup had designed a home for four young faculty bachelors, Julian Huxley, Griffith Evans, Arthur Hughes, and William James Sidis.

Several of the distinguished new faculty members also had their homes in this area. They included Albert Leon Guerard, French scholar and writer; Radoslav Andrea Tsanoff, the Cornell-trained philosopher; Harry Boyer Weiser, a renowned chemist; Robert G. Caldwell, noted historian; and Claude W. Heaps, who had won honors as a research fellow at Princeton. Most of these men had children who were and remained close friends of Ray, Rosemary, and Sonny (soon renamed Billy) Watkin.

One of their neighbors was the William Lockhart Clayton family. Mr. Clayton was a founder of Anderson Clayton Company. As one of Houston's truly notable citizens, he would later accept and carry out assignments of international impact under several U.S. presidents, and would serve as assistant secretary of state in Washington, D.C. He and Mrs. Clayton, the former Susan Vaughan, lived down the street at 5300 Caroline in a beautiful mansion that later was given by the family to house one of the nation's finest genealogical libraries. Julia, youngest of the Clayton daughters, was Rosemary Watkin's age. They were classmates at Kinkaid School and close friends.

Annie Ray Townsend Watkin fitted well into her new life in the small but growing academic community at Rice Institute, and in the larger sphere of the city of Houston. A slender, vivacious young woman, her natural beauty was reinforced by titian-red hair, green eyes, and clear, translucent skin. Mrs. William Ward Watkin had a warm, outgoing personality, natural wit, and a contagious smile, reflecting her happy childhood and marriage. She enjoyed riding horses, a favorite sport learned as a girl in Columbus. Her mother had also provided her with lessons in piano and violin, which gave her a lasting interest and ability in music.

One quickly apparent characteristic of Annie Ray Townsend Watkin was her love for and enjoyment of her children. From their early childhood, she always enjoyed participating in their activities.

There had been many new friends for Annie Ray at every stage of her life. This had been true when, as a girl, she moved with the Townsend family from Columbus to San Antonio, in 1906; then at finishing school at Belcourt Seminary in Washington, D.C.; and again as a debutante in her new hometown of San Antonio. In 1913, she was "Duchess of the Lily Pond" in the court of San Antonio's spectacular Battle of Flowers, staged annually by the Order of the Alamo. One of her closest friends from her childhood days in Columbus was Louise Ayars.

Louise, the daughter of Lee C. Ayars, state senator and former law partner of Marcus Townsend, had moved from Columbus to Houston with her family soon after the Townsends moved to San Antonio. A No-Tsu-Oh debutante of 1912 in Houston, Louise later became godmother to Annie Ray Townsend Watkin's firstborn: her daughter, Ray. In 1912, the *San Antonio Express* reported the popularity of both Annie Ray and Louise Ayars, in an era when debutantes from Texas' largest cities attended traditional presentations around the state, including in Houston, San Antonio, and Galveston:

> "The Artillery Ball last Tuesday evening at the Hotel Galvez in Galveston, was one of that city's leading social events of the season. Among the beautifully gowned out-of-town girls there was Miss Annie Ray Townsend of San Antonio, wearing a white brocaded charmeuse with chiffon draperies and princess lace trimmings. Miss Louise Ayars of Houston wore an empire robe of white charmeuse with trimmings of cloth of gold."

This friendship between Annie Ray and Louise was to continue through their married years in Houston.

The Watkin home was an attractive residence, occupying three-fourths of a city block on Caroline Street. It had been well designed by Watkin himself, well built, and attractively furnished. The garden, also a Watkin design, was admirably suited to the delightful outdoor birthday parties that Annie Ray loved to plan and to give for her

The Town Hall, Northampton, England, built by William Ward Watkin's great-uncle, John Watkin, in 1864. From the Northamptonshire Libraries Local Studies Collection.

Engraving given away with 'The Northampton Mercury' dated May 21st 1864 to commemorate the opening of the new town hall.
Northamptonshire Libraries Local Studies Collection

John Watkin of Northampton, England, 1864.

The Town Hall, Northampton, as it looked in 1890.

119

Frederick Ward Watkin in his twenties, husband of Mary Hancock Watkin and father of William Ward.

William Ward Watkin at about age eight with his mother, Mary Hancock Watkin, in Danville, Pennsylvania.

Childhood home of William Ward Watkin in Danville, Pennsylvania, circa 1880. The house belonged to Lucy and Dennis Bright, his aunt and uncle, with whom he and his mother lived after his father's untimely death.

The staff of the Danville High School Yearbook, 1903. William Ward Watkin, shown here in the center of the front row, was the editor.

Watkin home from the University of Pennsylvania for a break in Danville, Pennsylvania, circa 1906.

*Watkin as a senior at the University of Pennsylvania. From the 1908
yearbook of the University of Pennsylvania.*

*The Architectural Society at the University of Pennsylvania, 1908. Watkin
is shown in the 4th row, to the left.*

*The cast of "The Brain Trust" at the University of Pennsylvania in 1908.
Watkin is second from right in the front row on stage, standing.*

A group of architectural students in the dormitory at the University of Pennsylvania in 1908. William Ward Watkin is in the center.

William Ward Watkin in 1908, age 22, soon to embark on his lifelong career of architecture.

One of the festive Christmas parties given at Cram, Goodhue & Ferguson, this one in 1909. William Ward Watkin is the second from right. Photo by Ralph Adams Cram.

Christmas in the offices of Cram, Goodhue & Ferguson, Boston, 1909. Ralph Adams Cram is on the far left; William Ward Watkin is the third from right.

The Watkin home at 5009 Caroline Blvd. in Houston, designed by William Ward Watkin and completed April 1915, one month before the birth of Annie Ray, their first child.

Little Annie Ray Watkin posing for her father's camera in front of their home at 5009 Caroline in 1917 or 1918.

William Ward Watkin and wife, Annie Ray, with their firstborn child, Annie Ray, 1915.

The Watkin children, 1920. Left to right: Rosemary, William Ward Watkin, Jr., and Annie Ray.

Mrs. William Ward (Annie Ray Townsend) Watkin gracing the society page of a Houston newspaper in 1921, following her sister Florabel's wedding.

The Watkin family before their 1925 trip to Europe. Left to right: Watkin, William, Jr., Annie Ray, Rosemary, Mrs. Watkin.

William Ward Watkin enjoying himself in Granada, Spain, during the 1925 European trip. Here he is posing with the George Howard family, also from Houston. Left to right: George Howard, Frank Bonner Howard (seated below), William Ward Watkin, Garland Howard.

Rice faculty daughters, April 1925. Back row, left to right: Katherine Tsanoff, Virginia Walker, Annie Ray Watkin, Nevenna Tsanoff, Rosemary Watkin. Front row, left to right: Marjorie Weiser, Alice Caldwell, Molly Tidden, and Dorothy Weiser. Not shown: Kathleen and Joan Wilson. No pictures are available of faculty sons Donald, Malcolm, and Robert McCants; Neal and Stanley Heaps; Albert Joseph Guerard; Robert Caldwell; and Jack and Stephen Wilson.

The Watkin home at 5009 Caroline Blvd. in 1950. The front columns were added to the house in 1926.

The Watkin family's 1928 Christmas card, drawn by William Ward Watkin, shows the house he designed for his family at 5009 Caroline.

Mrs. Watkin's passport for the 1928 sabbatical to Europe. Note that her place of birth should have been Columbus, Texas, *not* Ohio.

128

Watkin in golf knickers, Vichy, France, 1928. Golf was one of Watkin's favorite pastimes; he sponsored the first golf team at Rice Institute in 1926.

The Villa Lalo, St. Jean de Luz, France, Fall 1928, where the Watkin family stayed while Mrs. Watkin convalesced.

Another view of the Villa Lalo, St. Jean de Luz, France, November 1928.

William Ward Watkin at the Villa Lalo in November 1928.

Claude Hooton, architectural graduate student from Rice, with "Sonny" Watkin, whom he tutored, in front of the Hotel Argencon in Neuilly, France, 1928.

Mrs. Albert L. Guerard, wife of Professor Albert Guerard of Stanford University and one of the original Rice faculty members, shown in 1928 visiting the Watkins in Neuilly.

Professor William Ward Watkin in costume at an Archi-Arts Ball in the early 1930s, sketched by one of his architectural students.

A sketch of Frank Lloyd Wright and William Ward Watkin in the early 1930s by Francis Vesey, Class of 1929. Wright did not approve of Houston's architecture.

Watkin and his daughter, Annie Ray, in Houston, 1930.

Ray Watkin's graduation from Rice in 1936. Left to right: John Yeager, Nevenna Tsanoff, Margaret Polk, Ray Watkin, Paul Blair.

Bronze bust of William Ward Watkin by sculptor William McVey, done about 1938 in appreciation for the help Watkin had given him in obtaining key sculpting commissions. McVey, Class of 1926, was one of Watkin's former architectural students.

The bridal party at Rosemary Watkin's wedding to Nolan Barrick, which was celebrated at the Trinity Episcopal Church (designed by her father) on October 27, 1938. Left to right: Lucille Meachum, Marjorie Dudley, Mary Greenwood, Rosemary Watkin, Ray Watkin, Margaret Turner, Barbara Madden (flower girl).

*Rosemary Watkin Barrick,
circa 1942.*

*The graduation of William Ward Watkin, Jr.,
from West Point, June 1942. William Ward
Watkin, Sr., is standing to the right of his son.*

*Rice graduation ceremonies,
1962. Second row (in the black
hat), Josephine Cockrell
Watkin, William Ward Watkin's
second wife, and next to her,
Ray Watkin Hoagland. It was at
this time that Ray began to
collect the "Watkin papers" for
the Rice Library.*

133

Ray Watkin Hoagland at the Rice University Homecoming in November 1990. She is wearing a "Golden R" ribbon, which indicates that she has passed her 50th class reunion.

Brigadier General William Ward Watkin, Jr., U.S. Army Corps of Engineers, 1971. This photo was taken upon his return from his second tour of duty in Vietnam, where he had served on General Creighton Abrams' staff just before his retirement.

The tradition continues: Cadet William Ward Watkin III graduating from the U.S. Military Academy at West Point, 1976. At the time of publication, he was a major in the Corps of Engineers stationed in Heidelberg, Germany.

children. These were long remembered by the three Watkin children and their many guests.

Daughter Ray still happily recalls her seventh birthday in May 1922. The garden was turned into a children's carnival, with clowns, fortune tellers, a gaily decorated carousel, rides around the block in a pony cart, countless balloons, and ice cream and cake.

Professor and Mrs. Albert Leon Guerard arrived on the faculty in 1914 and built a home on the corner of Oakdale and Austin. Professor Guerard was from Paris. Their second child and only son, Albert Joseph, was born in Houston in 1914.

Albert Joseph Guerard was a good friend of the Watkin children. Many years later as a prominent professor at Stanford University, he would recall the neighborhood in a beautiful and nostalgic piece in a 1972 issue of the *Southern Review*. This memoir describes "the experience of going back to the good green places of one's childhood . . . an impulse . . . deep in our bones." There are cheerful recollections by Guerard of Caroline Boulevard and its median of lush green grass "which belonged to the rich"; of the "pillared mansion of . . . the architect William Ward Watkin, whose daughters I had loved centuries ago . . ."; of a ride in "Will Clayton's brown Pierce-Arrow touring car"; and another ride in 1924, "down Buffalo Bayou in Miss Ima Hogg's yacht," en route to a picnic near the San Jacinto battleground [1].

The beautiful and personable Mrs. Watkin had many friends among the faculty wives. Her nearest neighbor was Julia McCants, a dear friend and the first chairman of the Faculty Women's Club at Rice. A native of Selma, Alabama, who would live in Houston for more than six decades, Mrs. (John T.) McCants had a "green thumb." She enjoyed raising plants and flowers, and frequently gave them to her neighbors. One of her principal interests was the Southmore Garden Club, in which she soon enlisted Annie Ray Watkin. Another close friend of Mrs. Watkin's and a faculty wife was Margaret (Mrs. J.W.) Slaughter, who lived on West Eleventh Place in the Bissonnet area. Mrs. Slaughter was a renowned horticulturalist.

Belle (Mrs. Claude W.) Heaps was an interesting young faculty wife who also became a good friend of Mrs. Watkin. A charter member of the Art League of Houston, she played an important role with Mary Ellen (Mrs. Edgar Odell) Lovett and others in founding that League, which led to the building of the Houston Museum of Fine Arts, designed by William Ward Watkin. Belle Heaps had studied at the Art Institute of Chicago. In Houston, she became a student of Frederic Browne, a well-known painter who was later a member of the Rice Institute architectural faculty. Mrs. Heaps was active in the formation of the Pan American Round Table and the Houston Symphony Society. She succeeded Julia McCants as president of the Faculty Women's Club.

Other faculty wives included Marjorie (Mrs. Harold A.) Wilson, herself a master of science in physics and mathematics from McGill University, and Isabelle (Mrs. Griffith) Evans. Isabelle John Evans, a direct descendant of Sam Houston, had entered Rice in 1913 and graduated in 1917. She married Dr. Evans, one of several bachelor members of the 1912–1913 faculty, soon after graduating. Griffith and Isabelle lived on Caroline near the Watkins, and she (much like Annie Ray) gave delightful parties. These were often held at the summer home that the Evans maintained at the bay near La Porte.

There were other good friends for the Watkins and their children. In addition to the Guerards, three other couples joined the original faculty of nine in 1913 and 1914. Harry Boyer and Hazel Weiser and Robert G. and Edith Caldwell lived next to each other on Bayard Lane, just north of Bissonnet. Their homes were each designed by Watkin. Radoslav and Corinne Tsanoff were among their many friends who also lived in Southmore. Their home was on Austin Street, one block east of Caroline.

The Weisers became close friends of the Watkin family early on. In 1914, Harry was quickly involved in the planning of the Physics Building, which contained temporary facilities for his specialty, chemistry. Hazel, also the mother of two daughters, Marjorie and Dorothy, had much in common with Annie Ray and her daughters, Ray and Rosemary. Both young mothers were active members of the Southmore Garden Club. Edith Caldwell, a very attractive woman, took a key role in organizing the Faculty Women's Club. Radoslav and Corinne Tsanoff had two daughters, Nevenna and Katherine, just as did the Watkins and Weisers.

Radoslav Tsanoff soon became a central figure on the faculty, with growing ties to the overall community. Mrs. Tsanoff served for many years on important social agencies such as the Rusk Settlement House, Ripley House, and the Community Chest. Both she and Radoslav were very active in the Houston Symphony Society as it continued to expand. Marjorie (Mrs. Harold) Wilson was also a leading faculty wife who had two daughters, Kathleen and Joan, and two sons, Jack and Stephen.

William Ward Watkin was always the head of his family, providing its support with a modest but increasing salary, soon augmented by his developing private architectural practice. However, the settlement of Marcus Townsend's estate late in 1915 had a considerable effect upon the total funds available to the young Watkins, as Annie Ray inherited a comfortable income from her father.

Marcus Townsend left substantial holdings in San Antonio. This included stock in a leading Alamo City bank and proceeds from a prosperous law practice. A shrewd and skilled investor, he had seen well before 1910 the potential for another exclusive residential area in his new hometown. San Antonio proved Marcus Townsend correct: It became the largest city in Texas during a population surge between 1910 and 1930, before yielding leadership to booming Houston.

Soon after moving to San Antonio in 1906, Senator Townsend started to acquire acreage in what was to become Alamo Heights, an attractive subdivision just northeast of the city's downtown business district. He then laid out and developed the site for many of San Antonio's finer homes, which included a Townsend Street in the original plot.

For the Watkins, their first emphasis was on the best education possible for their children, and then a comfortable and well-furnished home. Maggie had already been hired as a cook; now her sister Mittie served as a maid. There was additional help, including a laundress and a gardener. This left Annie Ray more time with the children— valuable time in their formative years. It also provided additional hours in which she and her husband could more actively participate in their expanding social, professional, and community life.

Annie Ray chose to teach daughter Ray at home through the equivalent of the second grade. She was then entered in the third grade at the Kinkaid School on San Jacinto at Elgin. Founded in 1904 by Margaret (Mrs. William J.) Kinkaid, the school was soon well regarded as a substitute for William Fairfax Gray's Grammar School at Christ Cathedral, a good thirty blocks and more from the new residential areas. Kinkaid was quickly and favorably known both for its curriculum and level of instruction, and for the deportment taught to and demanded of its students. It was soon recognized as well for the number of its students admitted to leading prep schools, colleges, and universities.

The firstborn Watkin daughter was soon joined at Kinkaid by her siblings, Rosemary and Billy. There they were well prepared for excellent scholarship later in college, while forming lifelong friendships. Early in 1924, a committee consisting of Captain James A. Baker, his daughter Alice Graham Baker, and Robert Lee Blaffer met with Margaret Kinkaid. Representing a group of parents and students, they suggested to Mrs. Kinkaid that she consider building a larger facility on a new and expanded campus.

Mrs. Kinkaid agreed. The original school at Elgin and San Jacinto was clearly overcrowded, with more students applying for admission each year. Fund-raising was quickly under way, with the help of many other parents including the W.L. Claytons, W.S. Farishes, and Kenneth Womacks. William Ward Watkin's contribution was a major gift: a handsome and thoroughly functional architectural design, in Spanish Renaissance style, for the new, $85,000 Kinkaid School to be located at Richmond Road and Graustark. His fee for the project was $600, which probably did not even cover drafting, blueprints, and other out-of-pocket expenses.

The larger school and campus, which opened in the fall of 1924, served Kinkaid and an entire generation of students until 1957, exactly one-third of a century.

Aside from the sine qua non of the best possible education for the children, the additional income from Marcus Townsend's estate permitted other things that added quietly, yet significantly, to the quality of life for the young Watkin family. Soon after the Watkin's marriage in 1914, there would be a Model T Ford at 5009 Caroline. It was a reliable automobile—once Watkin had mastered its mysteries, which included the interaction of spark, speed, clutch, and brake, which could be quite complex. In the early 1920s, the Ford was replaced by a Franklin, unique with its air-cooled engine. There was no need for the usual radiator, which controlled engine temperature with circulating water.

Watkin never mastered the advancing technology of the automobile from this point on. The cook's husband, Tom, drove the Franklin. He also helped with many tasks in the home and around 5009 Caroline's garden and grounds.

The Franklin, comfortable though it was, failed in elegance by comparison to the electric automobile of Annie Ray's mother in San Antonio. That had featured velvet upholstery, imported cut-glass vases holding fresh flowers, and many other attractions. Passengers sat in a circle, on high seats. The roomy, quiet-running vehicle was one of young Ray's vivid childhood memories.

Automobiles had completely replaced the horse-drawn carriages in which earlier generations of Houstonians had paid their formal, yet brief, calls on visiting days. The Watkin's Franklin paled in comparison to the Pierce-Arrow of the neighboring W.L. Claytons, or Mrs. Samuel Fain Carter's Lincoln. Mrs. Carter would arrive in considerable style at meetings of the Blue Bird Circle, which she had organized as a project of the First Methodist Church. The Circle, which Annie Ray Watkin joined at Mrs. Carter's invitation, now operates the widely praised Children's Clinic of the Methodist Hospital, and many other charitable projects. Mrs. Carter's daughter, Annie Vieve, who had married E. L. Crain, was one of Annie Ray's closest friends.

As Watkin's private practice grew, the boon of summer vacations away from Houston's dreaded heat and humidity was attainable. This was very important, especially to a Pennsylvanian such as Watkin. In the early 1920s, Annie Ray and the children were often en route by the end of June to the cool mountain resort of Asheville, North Carolina. When classes ended at Rice, Watkin would join the family at Asheville as soon as he could leave his administrative duties and private practice. There they would rent a house adjoining the splendid Grove Park Inn, in the shadow of the Blue Ridge. The Watkins had spent their honeymoon at the then new Inn in 1914.

As the children grew older, there were other memorable vacations. Annie Ray had come to know Adele Waggaman, a Rice graduate of the Class of 1917. Miss Waggaman, from a well-known Houston family, would organize and chaperone a group of girls who went to Camp Quinibeck on Lake Fairlee near Ely, Vermont, each summer. Many of the campers were Kinkaid students who went together on the long train ride from Texas to the beautiful mountain lake in Vermont's cool summer. Annie Ray stayed at an adjoining resort, Shanty Shane, with young Billy and her good friends Annie (Mrs. W.S.) Cochran and her son Billy, and Lucile (Mrs. McDonald) Meachum and her daughter, Lucile.

As had become the custom, Watkin would come up from Houston during part of the summer vacation. Much as he enjoyed the quiet and beauty of Vermont, and the marked contrast with the heat and humidity at home, he was already looking forward to a much longer journey with his beloved Annie Ray and the children. They had long been planning a trip to Europe. It was to combine pleasure and relaxation from a decade of increasingly hard (although satisfying and fulfilling) work. For Mr. Watkin it would provide the opportunity to study the Continent's architectural treasures, with the advantage of far more knowledge and experience than he had had in 1908. The opportunity to do so would not arrive until 1925.

During this time, Annie Ray Townsend Watkin continued her strong ties to her family in San Antonio. She was devoted to her mother Annie, sister Floribel, and brother Robert Foard. After her father's death in 1915, she made frequent trips to San Antonio by train to visit her mother, sister, and brother. Mrs. Townsend died in 1920 after an illness that placed a great deal of strain on Annie Ray.

She felt even closer to Floribel and Robert Foard after the shock of her mother's death. Her sister, seven years younger, visited the Watkins in Houston often, and Annie Ray continued to go to San Antonio. Floribel married in San Antonio in 1921; both her older sister Annie Ray and her young niece Ray (as flower girl) were in the wedding. Then, tragically, Floribel was stricken with cancer and died only a year after her marriage.

This tragedy, so soon after the loss of her mother, was especially difficult for Annie Ray. She bore the dual catastrophe as best she could, while strengthening ties to her brother Robert Foard, his wife, and their three small children, Eleanor, Bettie, and Robert Foard, Jr.

William Ward and her children were, of course, her continuing source of comfort.

Then in 1925, after time and happiness with her own little family had begun to heal Annie Ray's sorrow, Robert Foard, her sole remaining close relative in the Townsend line, died. He was only thirty-nine, the same age as his brother-in-law, William Ward Watkin. Annie Ray had now lost her mother, sister, and brother in four short years. She mourned them all deeply. A busy and active life revolving around husband and children of ten, eight, and six, however, helped her recover. She was a caring person, sensitive to sorrow and to the problems of others, but she was also, by nature, a happy woman.

As the children continued to mature, there seemed to be almost endless trips around Houston involving their activities. The pace could be quite tiring, but Annie Ray was well aware of the value of these pursuits. There were the many extracurricular programs at Kinkaid and birthday parties or other festive gatherings. Fortunately for Annie Ray, there was also Tom, the chauffeur, who by now drove the new 1926 Lincoln.

Afternoons were often devoted to piano and dancing classes for Ray and Rosemary, Billy's Cub Scout meetings, and frequent visits to the downtown office of Dr. E. B. Arnold, the orthodontist. The able and popular dentist had a large practice fitting braces on many of the Watkin children's classmates.

Rosemary also enjoyed riding and elocution lessons. The *Houston Gargoyle* reported on her riding "Spider" at the popular Horse Show: "Little Rosemary Watkin, her long curls falling about the shoulders of her smart red coat, posed for her picture . . . [saying] 'please don't put an "s" on the end of my name.' "

During the early 1920s, the Watkin family often took drives with friends on pleasant Sundays. The destination was sometimes the San Jacinto Battleground or the nearby San Jacinto Inn. It would become, and long remain, one of the most popular places to dine in the Houston area. On occasion, Tom might also drive the family to Columbus. This allowed Annie Ray and the family to visit Townsend and Burford relatives there. The trip via the Southern Pacific railroad was the alternative.

While at Columbus, the Watkins might drive to nearby Round Top, originally named Townsend, Texas. The first Texas Townsends had settled there in the late 1820s. Annie Ray's forebear cousins had originally built and operated the historic Stagecoach Inn at Winedale (two miles northeast of Townsend/Round Top) before the Texas Revolution. In 1961, Miss Ima Hogg purchased the Inn from her friend Hazel Ledbetter, who also engaged in preserving important landmarks from Texas' past. Miss Hogg then restored the traditional 19th-century stopping place and established the Winedale Museum.

Soon after the birth of his first child, Assistant Professor Watkin (he had been promoted from instructor after the 1916–1917 academic year) was busier than ever with his evolving career at the Rice Institute. He had found it necessary to devote the major part of his time through 1915 to supervising the completion of the Physics Building, and readying it for occupancy. A surprising number of details to finish on the original campus buildings also remained.

This limited the hours available to instruct the expanding number of students in the Department of Architecture, to plan new curricula, and select the first additional faculty members for the new department. Watkin taught the first two classes through May 1913 himself, while proceeding with care to choose a new instructor. Though tall, thin Mr. Watkin was reserved and seemingly very formal, he could also be warm and understanding with his students, with an unusual ability to perceive instinctively the problems confronting them. He was very helpful in resolving their difficulties.

In his search for new teaching personnel in architecture, Watkin again turned to his former mentor, Paul Philippe Cret, and the University of Pennsylvania's School of Architecture. He concentrated upon finding an instructor well trained in drawing, watercolors, and painting. Watkin had been able to teach alone the architectural drawing component of Architecture 100, a separate course in freehand drawing, and the fundamental courses in design and history.

For 1914–1915, a third (and larger) matriculating class would be added to the department. Further, the third-year curriculum would include both antique and watercolor drawing. It was clear that Watkin needed to concentrate on the more significant instruction in design and history. He set out to find a new person to take over architectural, antique, and freehand drawing. It would be well if the addition to the faculty could also assist with the formation and activities of a Student Architectural Society. Watkin had planned from the beginning to have this type of organization under way after the completion of the department's first two years.

Watkin found his man, with Professor Cret's assistance, at the Pennsylvania Academy of Fine Arts. This was John Clark (Jack) Tidden, a graduate, fellow, and traveling scholar of the Academy. In addition to his high academic achievements and recommendations, Jack Tidden had other accomplishments and clear potential for the future. He was an artist of considerable talent, as was his wife, Agnes Lilienberg Tidden.

Jack Tidden was an excellent teacher. He was also an extrovert, actor, and set designer who became a key figure in many Architectural Society projects, including student dramatics and the legendary Archi-Arts Ball. The latter event, for students, alumni, and faculty alike, developed into an important link between the Department of Architecture, the Rice student body, and the community. It was also thoroughly enjoyed by all.

Tidden, who had first been appointed for the 1914–1915 year as an instructor in architectural drawing, quickly became a valuable member of the department and a popular member of the Rice faculty. Within a few months, colleagues were buying his oil paintings. Mrs. Edgar Odell Lovett soon commissioned a Tidden portrait of her father, Major Henry M. Hale of Mayfield, Kentucky.

The enrollment within the Department of Architecture continued to grow, and in anticipation of fourth- and fifth-year courses being initiated during 1915 and 1916, Watkin soon went recruiting once more. Again, the search was centered upon his alma mater, the University of Pennsylvania. This time, he found Francis Xavier Keally.

Keally had earned the baccalaureate in fine arts at the Carnegie Institute of Technology in Pittsburgh, and the master of science degree in architecture under Paul Philippe Cret. He came to Rice in the fall of 1915 as a highly recommended instructor in architectural drawing. The new professor taught freshman and sophomore classes in design, thus freeing Watkin to concentrate upon advanced design and the history of architecture. He also instructed some of the drawing classes, especially those in pen-and-ink rendering. This allowed Jack Tidden to add fifth-year courses in painting to his own assignments. Planning for the final year of the bachelor of science degree in architecture was under way.

The new instructor, Keally, a bachelor, lived on campus in South Hall as did several of the unmarried faculty members in the early years of the Institute. It was suspected that Keally's decision to return north after only one year at Rice might have been at least partly influenced by an outbreak of target practice in the corridors of his dormitory one Saturday night. Some of the South Hall residents had brought their pistols and smaller rifles with them to college. However, the prime reason for Keally's leaving was Houston's infamous heat and humidity, relieved only by "northers" from November until early spring.

Return north he did, first to accept a position on the faculty of the University of Minnesota, and then to establish a successful practice of architecture in New York City. He remained a good friend of Watkin throughout the remainder of Watkin's life.

This vacancy led next to the appointment of James Henry Chillman, Jr., in 1916. A Philadelphian, Chillman had earned his master of science degree in architecture under Cret at the University of Pennsylvania, where he had also won a coveted Alumni Fellowship. He had been named to an instructorship in freehand drawing at Penn in 1914. Watkin felt very fortunate to have Chillman join his architectural faculty at Rice in 1916. "Jimmy" Chillman had a long and distinguished career at the Rice Institute, and in the Houston community. He remained a close personal friend and a most valued colleague of Watkin throughout the latter's life.

II.

The First World War would have a tremendous effect on Rice, which was less than halfway through its first decade when the U.S. Congress formally declared war on Germany on April 6, 1917. Mobilization proceeded so rapidly that the United States had more than a million troops, trained and equipped, in Europe in little more than a year [2].

At the Rice Institute, students, faculty, and administrators alike were subject to draft registration in that war depending upon age, physical condition, marital status, number of dependents, and occupation. Watkin, married, with two daughters still in their cribs, and serving in a critical position, was exempt—along with many of his faculty colleagues and students. He was also busier than ever before, with new college responsibilities related directly to the war, and filling in for his faculty colleagues absent because of the conflict.

The male students on campus formed an informal military group very soon after the April 6, 1917, declaration of war against Germany. Beginning with the 1917–1918 academic year, all Rice students were required to wear unattractive and uncomfortable uniforms. Professor (and Coach) Philip Arbuckle's mandatory classes in physical education had already been transformed into sessions in military training.

The early stages of World War I, the so-called "years of stalemate" through mid-1916, had aroused relatively little interest at Rice. Considerably more attention was paid to the developing program in intercollegiate athletics, which often dominated the pages of the *Thresher,* the student newspaper established by the campus literary societies. The interest in athletics at Rice evident at the start of World War I was largely attributable to Watkin's success as chairman of the Committee on Outdoor Sports. By 1916, it was clear that Watkin was doing an excellent job in an area far removed from architecture. Credit for success and growing interest in the athletic program Watkin would have attributed to the excellent coaches, the many talented athletes at Rice, and support from President Lovett. The war's marked effects would await late 1916 and April 6, 1917.

Watkin and his colleagues on the faculty saw the first student enlistments as the effects of war grew ever closer. It was soon obvious that U.S. entanglement was quite possible. A few faculty members were already considering assignments with the armed forces or elsewhere in government service. It would be more and more difficult for Watkin and those remaining at Rice to keep the academic ship afloat.

As the threat of war grew apace, the first Commencement address of the Rice Institute, delivered by David Starr Jordan on June 12, 1916, could not have been more timely, or correct in its predictions.

Jordan, trained as a physician, naturalist, and philosopher, had completed a brilliant 22-year term as president of Stanford University. He had attracted deserved attention at the West Coast institution, founded by a former governor of California and railroad magnate as a memorial to his deceased young son and namesake, Leland Stanford, Jr.

In a new career, David Starr Jordan had been appointed executive director of the World Peace Federation. The title of his Commencement address at Rice was "Is War Eternal?" It was reported in detail in both the local and national press, as well as in a special issue of the *Thresher.*

In his speech, Jordan made the prediction that the First World War would not be the last of such conflicts, and was unfortunately quite correct, although he died in 1931 before he could see his prediction come true. His June 12, 1916, commencement speech at Rice did, however, seem to have an effect both upon the student body and the Houston community overall. In combination with the grim news of truly catastrophic losses on both sides during the summer and early fall of 1916, there was inevitable and steadily growing emphasis on the war as the U.S. moved inexorably toward direct involvement.

Football would still be in the *Thresher* headlines as the 1916–1917 academic year began at Rice. Understandably, because the Owls had won an unprecedented six games, tied two and lost one in the 1916 season. Texas A&M was defeated 20–0 in a victory that Coach Philip Arbuckle particularly relished. A game with Southern Methodist, correctly described as a "track meet," ended with the score Rice 146, SMU 3.

But before the Christmas holidays, there was a definite new and nonathletic program emphasis in the *Thresher.* Less than fifty students, by far the lowest percentage yet, had failed the dreaded tests required of all incoming freshmen before midterm examinations. Rice was obviously attracting a better prepared class of students. It was decided that caps and gowns would be worn by graduating seniors only during Commencement Week, rather than during the entire final semester. There was prominent coverage of "The Brain Trust," the Architectural Society's intriguing and handsomely-produced satirical play, as it went into rehearsal. A laudatory review of the play by the *Thresher*'s critic appeared in the student paper.

However, news directly related to what turned out to be preparation for war soon dominated both in the student newspaper and the campus: President Lovett, with the unanimous approval of the other trustees, applied to the War Department for a unit of Reserve Officers Training Corps, U.S. Army. There were regular stories on the growing number of students entering, or applying for, the armed forces. Cadet uniforms were ordered from the Quartermaster Corps, with a handmade version available downtown at Shotwell's for $16.50.

Congress had voted to go to war only hours before a regular edition of the *Thresher* was due on campus. The staff responded with a well-written editorial entitled "The Nation Is At War." It began:

"Early this morning, Congress declared war on the German Empire. In spite of our great desire for peace [and] great patience under numberless wrongs inflicted . . . we can no longer remain idle . . . . There is no peace, there can be no peace, while Prussian militarism exists in the world . . . . [It is] autocracy versus democracy, a war to the death.

"What will Rice students be called upon to do? [It is] too early, but very likely that Congress will pass a selective conscription law. This is certainly to be hoped for. Let the classes of service be outlined by law and men be selected for each. If it is a man's duty to be in the front rank, let him do this. If [his duty and better opportunity to serve is] at home, let him serve here. And very often, the latter requirement will be harder than the first."

The "selective conscription law" would not be long delayed. It was passed by Congress, viva voce, before the end of April. The *Thresher* had correctly predicted "that the men of Rice, yea, and the women too, will do their full duty . . . . No one who knows them dares to question [this] . . ."

Almost fifty male students were already en route to Leon Springs, Texas, a U.S. Army reserve training center near San Antonio. The Rice administration had ruled that anyone joining the armed forces with a passing grade in a course would be given full credit. Remaining classes, laboratory work, term papers, and final examinations were waived. In addition to those at Leon Springs, the rest of the men in the graduating class of 1917 soon showed up en masse at the downtown recruiting center, and many more were sent to join the burgeoning Rice Institute contingent at Leon Springs.

Then, on May 12, 1917, the application for an ROTC unit on campus was approved by the War Department. Special Order 110 also detailed Major Joseph Frazier, USA (retired), to report to President Lovett immediately as professor of military science and tactics. The major, a veteran of such historic campaigns as the Philippine revolt against Spain and the Boxer Rebellion in China, lost little time in taking up his duties. Dr. Lovett introduced him to the male student body in the Physics Amphitheater on May 25, less than a week after Special Order 110. His audience, almost entirely undergraduates, was told to report to the athletic field three days later "for military instruction."

The Rice campus responded more and more to the reality of war. From the status only weeks before of a private educational institution, the university became, to a considerable extent, a military installation. All of the seniors had departed, with a number of undergraduate students. The male members remaining now drilled twice a day in uniform, to marches raggedly performed by a cadet band. Women also wore uniforms, but had fewer drills.

Students finally reacted, in predictable manner, to what many thought the unnecessarily severe change on campus. They requested, and were granted late in January 1918, a meeting with Chairman James A. Baker, President Lovett, and the other trustees. At the meeting, a spokesman explained that he and other student petitioners understood the need for drastic change while the nation remained at war. They acknowledged the need for some military training while continuing their studies, but they wanted what had become "a military regime" to revert to "the Rice of old, with an ROTC added because of necessity."

The trustees, all reasonable men, listened carefully. They asked questions, made some statements of their own, and agreed to respond to the students. The response came two weeks later, after consultations with Frazier and long discussions within the governing board. Some parents were also consulted.

The students scored heavily on a number of their complaints: Morning drill for the male cadets, as well as the hated 5:30 a.m. reveille and various calls to quarters, were abolished. There was to be no more guard duty, or roll call during meals. Women students also won some important points: Drill for them was replaced by mandatory physical training sessions once a week, plus participation in Red Cross projects. Their "highly unattractive" uniforms would be worn only for physical training. Coeds, moreover, were to have a voice in deciding upon suggested changes in the hated uniforms of heavy khaki.

The men also had to accept some new regulations: Carefully maintained uniforms must be worn at all times to the reduced number of drills. No overnight absences were allowed without written permission. Monitors were to be posted to maintain better order in the residence halls, where women were forbidden to enter "without adequate chaperonage." Throwing food in the Commons was strictly forbidden.

Special courses, including wireless telegraphy and the maintenance of Army trucks, would be added to an already demanding wartime curriculum. The changes, which included a decision by the trustees to expedite the formation of a Student Association, were all beneficial.

Other problems, especially concerning the number of faculty on leave in the armed forces or other government service, became more and more significant. Watkin was confronted by a range of shortages in attempting to keep buildings in good order and the grounds in reasonable condition. Even such basics as student drawing instruments were virtually unobtainable. He faced both the threat and the reality of losing faculty members. What he did not realize was that he was receiving valuable training for the far more extensive problems that would arise years later during a much longer World War II, at a larger and more complex Rice Institute.

For a time, just before Armistice Day on November 18, 1918, it appeared that Watkin might well be the only member of the architecture faculty during the 1918–1919 academic year. Jack Tidden, in Philadelphia for the summer, had sent President Lovett a telegram on August 24, 1918. This announced, only two weeks before the opening of the fall semester, that he had enlisted in the Army, and requested a leave of absence from Rice. A letter explaining this decision followed.

Dr. Lovett responded with a gracious letter commending Tidden for his patriotism, and stating the belief that the leave of absence could be arranged. This was soon confirmed, along with news that the Institute would make up the difference between Tidden's Army pay and his salary at Rice. About the same time, it became necessary for President Lovett to file a formal request for deferment for James H. Chillman, who had a temporary summer job with the U.S. Food Administration at Germantown, Pennsylvania. The basis for the petition was that Chillman would be teaching enrollees of the Student Army Training Corps unit at Rice, as one of the remaining members of a faculty decimated by the departure of twenty-six men on various military or government assignments. The request for deferment was granted.

With Chillman back on campus, he and Watkin were able to cover the classes, studio work, and project assignments within the Department of Architecture. Enrollment had dropped because of the war, but it was still a formidable task to provide instruction ranging over a five-year curriculum. Thus there was the relief when Jack Tidden telegraphed on December 6, 1918, that he had been released by the Army and would be resuming his teaching at Rice immediately after the approaching Christmas holiday.

Professor Watkin's faculty problems in the Department of Architecture were not over, however. Just as the war ended in 1918 and things seemed to be proceeding smoothly, with Jimmy Chillman increasingly valuable and Tidden handling a heavy teaching and extracurricular load, a new development arose: Chillman won a coveted fellowship in architecture at the prestigious American Academy in Rome. He would not return to Rice Institute until late December 1922.

Watkin had always taken a long-range view toward the development of his department. James H. Chillman was not only a good friend. His obvious professional abilities would be broadened by the new fellowship abroad. Therefore, Watkin arranged that Chillman's job would be waiting and that he would be promoted to assistant professor upon his return. He would be brought back to Rice for what would become a long and notable career.

As a temporary replacement for the 1919–1920 academic year in the Department of Architecture, Professor Watkin added a Houston architect to the staff, Alvin C. Bieber. This appointment lasted for only a year, however. Bieber was replaced by Charles L. Brown, a recent graduate of Paris' elite Ecole des Beaux-Arts. Brown would remain for many years on the architectural faculty at Rice as a great asset to the department.

The early post-World War I years at Rice Institute, especially those of 1919–1920 and 1920–1921, were a time of adjustment. Students returning from the Great War were added to those they had left behind, pushing enrollments considerably higher. In addition, some of the twenty-six faculty members absent on active duty or in other wartime service either did not return or were delayed getting back to the campus.

Julian Huxley, one of the most notable postwar faculty losses, remained in England, where he had returned late in 1914 to volunteer for the armed forces. He had been much impressed with the potential of the Rice Institute, however, and retained his many friendships and professional contacts there. The brilliant young scientist was soon a full professor of zoology at the University of London's Kings College, and well into a lifetime career in teaching, research, and administration. Mr. Watkin was one of the Rice faculty who maintained his friendship with Huxley into the next decade.

Seven members of Rice's early senior faculty had exceptionally notable assignments during World War I. Stockton Axson, the widely acclaimed Shakespearian scholar from Princeton, served as national secretary of the American Red Cross. He did not return to Rice until 1920, having been busy carrying out his duties connected with the postwar organization of the International Red Cross in Geneva.

Harold A. Wilson, a former associate of three Nobel laureates in physics at Cambridge University, had directed a team of several hundred scientists for the U.S. Navy. He had been working in a secret center on the vital problem of antisubmarine detection equipment. He was personally credited with having developed an effective deep-water listening device called the "Sea Tube." This deadly weapon was used against the marauding German submarines that had sunk so much of the English merchant marine fleet between 1915 and 1917.

Griffith Evans had been commissioned a captain in the U.S. Army's Aviation Corps (the forerunner of today's separate Air Corps). Utilizing his dual abilities as both mathematician and linguist, Evans was sent to Rome, where he had studied a decade earlier. Dr. Evans served as scientific attache to the U.S. Embassy and liaison to the Italian Air Corps. He also conducted mathematical research of use to Air Corps operations on the Western front.

Others of Watkin's faculty friends in the Southmore area had also covered interesting assignments in the war. Albert Leon Guerard had been commissioned with other members of the Rice faculty at Leon Springs. At this Army installation near San Antonio, reserve commissions were issued after three months of intensive training. President Lovett had gone there for a ceremony at the beginning of the war to personally present diplomas to graduates of the Class of 1917 who could not attend the campus commencement.

Dr. Guerard was transferred overseas almost immediately, and attached to a liaison group working with high officials in the French government. He was decorated for exemplary service, in the tradition that had earlier won him the honor of being the first-ranking student at the University of Paris.

Harry Boyer Weiser took temporary wartime leave to be commissioned by the U.S. Army. He headed a key research group of sixty men within the Chemical Warfare Corps. They had been assigned the difficult task of discovering means of protecting Allied troops against the wide and terrifying use of poison gas by the Germans. Captain Weiser's performance in this unique and significant project advanced his growing reputation among leading U.S. research chemists and at the Rice Institute.

A. Llewelyn Hughes, physicist, known more often now by his first name of Arthur, spent the war working on the same problem that Dr. H.A. Wilson had studied so successfully for the U.S. Navy: the detection of enemy submarines. He headed a unit of thirty men from the British Navy whose studies were somewhat different. Stationed off the coast of England, Hughes' command was active in highly secret experimentation involving the use of detection equipment on dirigibles and specially equipped ships of the Royal Navy.

The multilingual Thomas Lindsey Blayney (the Rice Institute professor of languages skilled in German and French) served his war years with the famed "Blue Devils" division of the French regular Army. He was decorated with the Croix de Guerre for this tour of duty. Major Blayney also served as liaison officer to the British general staff at Ypres, to a French division in the advance on Amiens, and to the U.S. Army at Chateau-Thierry. It was there, on the River Marne north and northeast of Paris, that combined French and American forces stemmed the tide of German invasion and turned the initiative toward Allied victory in November 1918. Professor Blayney then completed his tour by serving with a post-war Allied mission to Germany.

Clearly, then, many of the senior teaching staff of the Rice Institute had made substantial contributions to the war effort. But, in their own way, so had President Lovett and the trustees, as well as Watkin and his colleagues who remained on campus. They kept the institution alive and under way during a trying time by covering other faculty duties in addition to their own.

Maintaining faculty strength was a problem, extending on through the 1920–1921 academic year. However, the opening of the second post-war year in September 1921 signaled a welcome return to normalcy.

Within the Department of Architecture, the curriculum had been kept intact through June 1917. Three of the original students from 1912 had been awarded the bachelor of arts degree in 1916, as well as the fifth-year bachelor of science degree in architecture a year later. These three men were W.P. Clyce, Leonard Gabert, and Rollin Montfort Rolfe. They, together with Francis T. Fendley, L.A. Hodges, J.T. Rather, C.M. Sanford, S.M. Sanford, T. Shirley Simons, Lloyd Y. White, and L.J. Woodruff, had organized the Rice Institute Architectural Society in the fall of 1916.

Fendley, the first president of the Society, and Rather would both serve as members of the Rice Board of Governors a generation later. They were both active in the Architectural Society's opening project. The Society put on a play entitled "The Brain Trust," set in Panama. It was presented March 22, 23, and 24 of 1917 in a room temporarily renamed the Blue Drawing Room Theatre. This new center of the dramatic arts was actually the drafting room for the Department of

Architecture, located at that time on the second floor of the Mechanical Engineering Building.

Produced by two "supervising artists" (John Clark Tidden and James H. Chillman, Jr.), the satirical "Brain Trust," a mixture of comedy and drama, had a marked resemblance to a similar production by architectural students at the University of Pennsylvania in 1908, in which Watkin had played a leading role. "Brain Trust" was an important step in the growing sense of camaraderie within the Department of Architecture. Chairman Watkin was quietly and effectively encouraging the comradeship and good will he had known as a student at Penn.

The Architectural Society was barely under way in 1916 before the growing threat of war rendered it inactive. The minutes of the final meeting of 1917 stated that many students in the architecture department "threw down their T-squares and took up the sword." However, with the returned Jack Tidden playing a central role and with Watkin's strong support, the Society was reorganized in 1919.

The first post-war meeting of the architectural group was convened on November 7, 1919. A constitution had been drafted by J.T. Rather, who was elected president after the constitution was adopted and new members sworn in. They agreed to support the programs of the Society, together with its principles and objectives, with their right hand resting upon a copy of Kidder's *Manual of Construction*. There were regular meetings every other Monday evening, as post-war programs and activities resumed slowly but steadily.

An important moment came on February 21, 1921, when William Ward Watkin introduced Ralph Adams Cram to a joint meeting of the student group and the local chapter of the American Institute of Architects [3]. At the meeting, Ralph Adams Cram emphasized the traditions, opportunities, and potential rewards of the architectural profession most eloquently. His lecture seemed to stimulate a new level of activity for Rice's student Architectural Society. That same year, Professor Albert Guerard followed Cram with a lecture on the architecture of Paris. Soon thereafter, a record class of initiates joined the Architectural Society, to be honored with a dinner-dance. Then it was suggested that planning should begin for what would become an annual tradition of the Rice Institute architects: the annual Archi-Arts Ball.

Both Watkin and Tidden had encouraged and hoped for a project that would increase campuswide "interest in art and architecture." Now the project was under way, as planning began for the first Archi-Arts Ball. A costume ball was suggested and approved. A. Stayton Nunn was named chairman of the first Ball Committee. Months of imaginative thinking, plans, and hard work would go into a "Baile Español," to be held February 3, 1922, at Autry House, the new center for extracurricular activities at Rice. Students, faculty, and alumni were busy for months on decorations, costumes, a program of authentic Spanish music and dances, and the more prosaic but vital matters of a band, food, and ticket sales.

The "Baile Español" was a huge success, and even made money for the tiny Architectural Society. Of far more importance, it seemed to have clearly achieved its objective of building campus as well as citywide interest in art and architecture at Rice. At the same time, the ball strengthened a sense of togetherness among students, their teachers, and the small but growing band of architectural alumni. In the next several years, the Archi-Arts Balls would draw increasing attention and attendance with a variety of themes, including the motif of the streets of Paris, Old New Orleans, the civilization of Mexico's Aztec chieftains, and many more.

III.

The lack of building projects at Rice between 1916 (completion of the West Hall dormitory) and 1920 (the Field House) was of major importance to William Ward Watkin. It signalled the end of almost a decade of dedicated service as Ralph Adams Cram's personal representative at the Rice Institute. There were to be other significant associations with Cram, however, and the extension of a long friendship that meant a great deal to both men.

Cram, Goodhue & Ferguson (Cram & Ferguson since 1914) closed its Houston office in the Scanlan Building after almost ten years, on November 15, 1919. This, plus the completion of a few final details at West Hall in 1917, left Watkin free, for the first time, to concentrate more upon his promising private practice. His own practice had begun as early as 1915 with the completion of the Watkin home at 5009 Caroline and a rectory for St. Mark's Episcopal Church in Beaumont.

Watkin now also found more time to give his committee posts at Rice. He had received an indirect commendation from Edgar Odell Lovett in 1912 when Lovett appointed him as chairman of the Committee of Buildings and Grounds.

The chairmanship also carried with it the title of Curator of Grounds. He learned to value his related knowledge of landscaping. As the number of campus buildings grew, care of the grounds also grew in importance. The number and extent of trees, central to the architects' original landscaping plan, began to grow almost geometrically. Handsome plantings of rose bushes, cape jasmines, hedges, and trees began to appear. The staff to maintain the grounds was expanded, with accompanying budgets for plants as well as fertilizer, tools, wages, and even feed for a team of mules.

In 1912 as has been noted, Lovett had also appointed Watkin to head another post: the Committee on Outdoor Sports, with the added title of faculty adviser on athletics. This job had expanded steadily from the beginning. Even before World War I, there was great interest at Rice in a program of intercollegiate athletics. A Field House and improved playing fields for the major competitive sports were now immediate priorities. Coaches had to be found, placed under contract, and supervised. The Southwest Conference was being organized, at which Watkin represented Rice during the complex negotiations. Finding solutions to problems such as eligibility rules, team schedules, contracts, and traveling arrangements suddenly emerged as part of the duties of the busy chairman.

After a decade or so, Watkin began, in his own gentlemanly manner, a campaign for relief from his responsibilities for the buildings and grounds. He had been conscientious in carrying out his manifold duties. However, in the busy 1920s he was finding conflicts in the time available to him for administrative assignments, the Department of Architecture, and his private practice. Watkin's quiet campaign consisted of appropriate remarks in meetings, suggestions in committee reports, telephone calls, and a few personal conferences with President Lovett. But all to no avail. Dr. Lovett would not budge. Watkin was to continue as chairman of the Committee on Buildings and Grounds.

Edgar Odell Lovett had indeed given him an indirect tribute, by refusing to replace him for what was to become a record term of forty years. Professor Watkin remained in full chairmanship of the committee, as he would for the remainder of his life.

The campus benefitted from Watkin's attention. Apart from the satisfaction of an aesthetically pleasing physical plant, the buildings were enhanced in their settings amidst an increasingly appealing background of trees, shrubbery, flowers, and lawns.

The growing beauty of the landscaping was largely attributable from the beginning to the dedicated care of the Institute's master gardener, Salvatore (Tony) Martino. Martino was a trained horticulturist, as well as a fine and colorful person. Watkin ("Mr. Wat" to Martino) was Tony's supervisor for almost four decades. Towering over the little Italian gardener by a good ten inches, Watkin soon came to understand and to appreciate the gardener's many admirable qualities. At the same time, Watkin learned that Martino's loyalty could be balanced with stubbornness, his innate kindness with quick-flaring temper and lasting vendettas (although never, of course, against "Mr. Wat") [4].

Fortunately for the Rice Institute, Watkin, and Tony Martino himself, the young Italian had first been employed as a gardener by Captain James A. Baker. Baker and his family had a handsome home and garden on most of a city block, at 2305 Helena, just west of Smith and Louisiana Streets. Still far from downtown Houston in the early 1900s, the property would in time be quite near the heart of the city. In addition to the elegant main house, the Baker estate included a carriage house, stables, servants' quarters, and extensive lawns and gardens. The latter gave Martino an opportunity to apply his Italian training and experience to Houston's climate and plants.

As noted, Watkin took over his marathon chairmanship of the Committee on Buildings and Grounds in 1912, while still completing the final details of the original campus buildings throughout 1912. It was not until the spring of 1913 that Watkin and President Lovett met to discuss a landscaping program for the campus.

Progress was understandably slow. The Physics Building and additional dormitories were at the working-drawing stage, and completion of these projects was a good two years away. The 1909 general plan by Cram, Goodhue & Ferguson had included tentative landscaping designs for various structures. Some of these, such as a huge auditorium, graduate college, and professional schools of medicine and law were never built. Nothing had been done, however, to produce final and approved plans for landscaping, or to transform them into reality.

In 1913, it was decided that Watkin should start work on the grounds. The opening move was to borrow Captain Baker's gardener for a time. The young Italian could report on the few trees that were on campus, and make plans for new plantings of trees and gardens under Watkin's direction [5]. Martino was also skilled in laying down the gravel walks and drives planned by the architects.

Watkin had been impressed by Martino from the first time he arrived at Rice "on loan" from Captain Baker. Martino was obviously well trained, with a real love for the plants he so carefully tended. After several months, Watkin decided to put him in permanent charge of a grounds staff, if he should become available. There were some problems in communication, as Martino's stay in a special night class for immigrants had been unfortunately short and unproductive. When excited, Tony spoke in an incomprehensible mixture of English and Sicilian, which he never overcame.

The few trees on the Rice Institute campus originally were severely damaged in the devastating August 1915 hurricane, the same hurricane that had blown the roof off President Lovett's leased home and caused great damage in Houston. Watkin had to borrow Martino from Captain Baker again. Tony once more proved his value, both in saving trees and in greatly extending and improving the system of campus walks and driveways. Flooding from the hurricane had emphasized the need to fill in many low areas.

Late in 1916, Watkin came to a decision. The building program at Rice had been temporarily halted due to the war. It was time to move ahead with an ongoing, permanent plan for improving and maintaining the campus grounds. As early as 1909, while in charge of the renderings for the original Rice Institute buildings, he had been instructed by Cram to include a master plan for landscaping, as well as campus roads and walks. It would not be difficult now to update the plan in terms of present and future needs.

Martino was still on loan from Captain Baker. It was clear to Watkin that Tony was needed in the new program. In his usual careful manner, Watkin first went to Dr. Lovett. With the president's approval, he requested permission from Captain Baker to hire Martino on a permanent basis and permission was fortunately granted [6].

Tony asked his new boss to accompany him on a campus tour the very day he was transferred from an "on loan" status to the official Rice Institute payroll. They marched first along Main Street, all the way from Sunset Boulevard to Harris Gully. They returned to Sunset and next came a fast walk due west up the main entrance drive to the Administration Building. The deliberately striding Watkin could barely keep up with the little gardener. The result was that Martino, his brother, and two helpers, soon planted truckloads of live oaks ("li-VOKA," in Martino's colorful accent) that are such a part of the Rice campus today. Set out along the line of their initial walk, each of the small trees was placed in enriched soil, braced against prevailing winds, and carefully tended.

There were also plantings of hedges of cape jasmine ("capa da jazz") [7], hundreds of crepe myrtles and azalea bushes, plus what finally totalled five miles of privet hedges. Other ornamental trees such as magnolias, cedars, and camphors were added later. In accordance with Watkin's original watercolor rendering of the campus, a double row of 44 elegant Italian cypress trees reminiscent of the Vatican gardens were soon added as a striking feature of the landscaping of the Academic Quadrangle.

Tony Martino quickly became a favorite of the student body. The students saw the cheerful, energetic gardener often. He was ever-present on the Rice campus, and they soon related his presence to their ever more beautiful surroundings. Gertrude Boxley (Mrs. Hubert Evelyn) Bray reported this revealing anecdote many years later: She was going out on her first date with Dr. Bray, an honor graduate of both Tufts and Harvard. He was a doctoral candidate and teaching fellow in mathematics, and they would marry after her graduation with the Class of 1921. She realized that Hubert was on a limited budget that would probably not provide even a small version of the then customary bouquet for a first date or prom.

Miss Boxley and her classmates had been admiring the pansies blooming on either side of the main entrance drive. On her way home after her classes on the day of the date, she went to one of the beds of small, multicolored flowers and began carefully gathering a tiny bouquet. Gertrude was absorbed in this when she looked up to see Martino watching her. Anticipating a reprimand, she stood up. Martino smiled, and indicated that he would show her a better way to pick the pansies. He did this quickly and, with another gracious smile, handed Miss Boxley a most attractive bouquet.

Over the years, Tony Martino became a universally beloved campus figure at Rice. His traditional appearances at student pep rallies during each football season were a vital part of the Rice ''spirit.''

IV.

Had someone told William Ward Watkin when he first arrived in Houston in 1910 that he would make significant and lasting contributions to intercollegiate athletics at the Rice Institute and, indeed, throughout the Southwest, he might well have claimed mistaken identity. He played and enjoyed golf and tennis when time permitted, and had a normal interest in the broad range of intercollegiate sports that continued throughout his life. The administration of a sports program, however, was hardly an assignment to be expected.

Watkin's first major move as chairman of the Committee on Outdoor Sports was one that bore dividends through the next decade. In 1912, with President Lovett's help, he recruited and brought Philip Heckman Arbuckle, a graduate of the University of Chicago and disciple of Coach Amos Alonzo Stagg, from Southwestern University to Rice. Arbuckle was appointed instructor in athletics on the original faculty. He also served as director of athletics and football coach from 1912 through the 1920–1921 academic year, although absent on military leave for the abbreviated 1918–1919 season.

Coach Arbuckle's first football team at Rice in the fall of 1913 had only fourteen men on the entire squad. The turnout was actually remarkable, from a total of one hundred freshmen and sophomore men. The Owls won four games and lost none, outscoring the opposition in their beginning season 81 to 14.

At this time, a new football conference was about to be formed, and Watkin was invited to represent Rice at the meeting. At the end of the 1913–1914 academic year, L.T. Bellmont, director of athletics at the University of Texas, had invited representatives of Texas A&M, Baylor, Texas Christian, Austin College, Southwestern, Louisiana State, and Oklahoma to meet with representatives of his own institution to discuss the formation of the Southwest Conference. When Louisiana State decided not to join the new organization, Rice was invited to fill out the slate of eight original members, and accepted provisionally at a second meeting, held in Houston in December 1914. Following the brief disruption of World War I, the Institute rejoined the Conference late in 1918. Active as Rice's representative in the SWC from its beginning in 1914, Watkin was named vice-president of the organization for 1918–1919, and president in 1920–1921.

Philip Arbuckle remained as football coach through 1921. His overall record was 43 wins, 10 losses, and 6 ties, including memorable first victories over Texas, Texas A&M, Baylor, and Southern Methodist and defeating the University of Arizona and the Haskell Indians. As early as 1915, overall competition in sports at Rice had been broadened by the addition of baseball, track and field, tennis, and a quite successful pre-World War I program in basketball. Through 1918, Owl teams in basketball often had less than 10 men on the entire squad, yet won 44 games against 19 losses [8].

By 1921, Chairman Watkin saw the need to replace Arbuckle as football coach, in spite of his excellent record. Phil, as he was known, simply had too much to do. He was in charge of a new one-year course in physical training required of all male students, as well as football and a full program of intercollegiate athletics. Watkin had little difficulty recognizing Arbuckle's plight, which was resolved by narrowing his responsibilities to professor and director of athletics.

Between 1921 and 1923, two promising younger men attempted to replace Arbuckle, after he stepped down as football coach. The result was an unhappy one: a succession of losing seasons after the Owls had begun so promisingly. Late in 1923, Watkin sought and obtained the necessary permission to recruit an outstanding replacement for

Arbuckle, who had obligingly resigned as director of athletics to coach the football team temporarily during the disastrous 1923 season.

Chairman Watkin decided to aim for the top. He sought John W. Heisman of Washington & Jefferson College, a small but distinguished institution at Washington, Pennsylvania. Heisman had been coaching, since 1892, successively at Auburn, Clemson, Georgia, Georgia Tech, and Pennsylvania. His team at Georgia Tech had been undefeated in 25 games between 1915 and 1917. Often compared to Alonzo Stagg of Chicago, and later to Notre Dame's Knute Rockne, Heisman changed the game of football forever by originating the snap from center. He was even better known for pleading successfully before the Rules Commission in 1906 for the approval of the forward pass, and for his innovative "Heisman shift."

Washington & Jefferson was only 20 miles southwest of Pittsburgh, on the West Virginia border. Founded in 1781, the institution was sound academically, with a student body about the size of that at Rice Institute. Apparently, an alumni group had underwritten an extraordinary contract of $10,000 a year to bring Heisman to W&J as football coach and director of athletics, in the hope of achieving the success he had enjoyed elsewhere. Then fifty-five years of age (although he appeared to be a decade younger), Coach Heisman had left the extreme competitiveness of his Ivy League position at Pennsylvania. He had established a sporting goods distributorship in New York City, which he combined with his coaching at W&J. From W&J, he could reach Manhattan by train in a few hours, and still enjoy a comfortable income through his lofty standing in the coaching profession.

Heisman was not entirely happy at W&J, however. The difficulty was that he found it all but impossible to recruit the caliber of players to which he had become accustomed. W&J was definitely not in Penn's class. Watkin was generally aware of John Heisman's having left Pennsylvania, and of rumors of his dissatisfaction at W&J. What he apparently did not know was the size of the eminent coach's salary, which was well above that of anyone on the Rice faculty other than President Lovett.

Following several discussions with Dr. Lovett, Watkin arranged to meet with Coach Heisman in New York City early in February 1924. Heisman had done his own homework regarding Rice Institute and

Houston, and he was interested, but on his own terms. He would come to the Rice Institute as football coach and director of athletics on a five-year contract through 1929, at an annual salary of $9,000. Since this was less than he had made at W&J and due to the pressures of his relatively new and continuing sporting goods business in New York City, he wanted to be in Houston only from September 1 until the beginning of the Christmas vacation in mid-December, and again from March 1 until the start of final examinations late in May.

Watkin, of course, had to have such an unusual proposal studied and discussed at length in Houston by President Lovett and the governing board. Lovett and the trustees, ever preferring quality, had been impressed by Coach Heisman's record from the time that Watkin first brought him to their attention. His chronological age, the $9,000 salary, and the proposed long absences from Houston were definite negatives. However, on balance, the formidable reputation of Heisman prevailed. The decision was for Dr. Lovett and Watkin to meet with the candidate, and to accept his proposition with the request that he reconsider being away from Rice half the time [9].

It had obviously occurred to everyone involved that a football championship for the Owls was overdue, and that the renowned John W. Heisman might be the man to bring this distinct honor to the Rice Institute.

Arrangements had been made for Lovett and Watkin to meet with Heisman in New Orleans in mid-February 1924. A day or two before their departure, Dr. Lovett came down with influenza, and Watkin went on to New Orleans alone. As authorized by the trustees, Watkin offered the candidate the posts of football coach and director of athletics through 1929 at the requested $9,000 annually. He felt better about the $9,000 after stopping by to see Alonzo Stagg in Chicago, who pointed out that the going price for coaches of far less renown was reaching the $7,500 range. Watkin did express to Heisman the hope that the coach would be staying longer in Houston each year, and then gave the new colleague his congratulations and assurance of full cooperation.

The Houston newspapers produced prominent stories about Rice's new coach and director of athletics, and there was substantial coverage in sports sections over the state and nation. Locally, there were various predictions that Heisman would bring the Institute and the city a coveted and long delayed SWC football championship. Some emphasized that this could well come in the first season of 1924, since many senior lettermen were returning to the practice field out on South Main. At the least, one sports editor hoped, Heisman might be able to defeat the University of Texas, and to greatly improve upon the two preceding disastrous seasons.

The highly personable new coach gained immediate and continuing attention after joining the Rice faculty in late summer 1924. He frequently spoke on campus, and before various business clubs and organizations. Also a columnist for the *Thresher,* he was at all pre-game pep rallies, notably at the ''Slime Parade'' opening the football season [10].

Heisman and his Owls defeated the Texas Longhorns 19–6 in that first season of 1924, but the year ended at 4 wins and 4 losses, far from a conference championship. When the new coach announced to the trustees the following spring that he would stay on duty straight through the academic year of 1925–1926 if given a salary increase of $2,500, Captain James A. Baker did not bother to respond for the governing board to this outrageous request. Heisman was more in evidence, however, as his win-loss record began to go downhill.

By the end of the 1927 season, Coach Heisman's record in football at Rice was a losing 14 wins, 18 losses, 3 ties, and no conference championships. The Owls won only a single SWC game in 1925, and none in 1926. Heisman's resignation was accepted by the trustees on December 1, 1927. He had accepted a position as the first athletic director of the Downtown Athletic Club of New York City, and would remain there for the rest of his life. After his death on October 3, 1936, the DAC Trophy awarded each December to the nation's outstanding football player was renamed the Heisman Memorial Trophy. ''The Heisman'' has gained dramatically in prestige in the intervening more than half-century.

In retrospect, John Heisman was probably hampered at Rice Institute by eligibility problems and the inability to recruit outstanding players in the area. He and Watkin remained on friendly terms. Watkin, as completely honest as ever, made it clear to Heisman that they held utterly different views on certain policies regarding inter-collegiate athletics. The coach believed in energetic recruiting of players, with generous scholarships and less demanding academic courses for them, plus minimum faculty control over the intercollegiate program. Chairman Watkin was strongly opposed to all of this.

V.

As John W. Heisman departed the scene, Watkin now realized that he had served a full fifteen years as chairman of the Committee on Outdoor Sports, with an unusually heavy investment of his time since the recruitment of Coach Heisman in 1924. Coupled with his steadily augmented duties in his post as head of Buildings and Grounds, there were too many conflicts for his available time.

He decided to resign from the Committee on Outdoor Sports, within days after Heisman's departure for New York City. This followed several informal meetings and diplomatic hints as to the length and recent intensity of his service as chairman of the Committee. To his gratification, the resignation was accepted, with a gracious note of appreciation from President Lovett for his long and effective service. It was none too soon, in view of the many demands upon Watkin by January 1928.

By 1927, Watkin's family was demanding more of his time. Annie Ray, the firstborn Watkin daughter, was now almost a teenager. Rosemary and Sonny were ten and eight. Also by 1927, there had been eleven graduating classes at the Department of Architecture. Professor Watkin had a larger and ever expanding group of students at all levels. He wanted to give more personal attention to his department. He had also decided to institute certain collateral programs, including the new Rice Traveling Scholarship in Architecture, all of which continued to keep him busy.

Notes

1. On a return trip to the city many years later, Albert Joseph, in his reminiscences of Houston in the 1920s, also recalled, with regret and lingering sadness, the Brazos Hotel with its elegant Palm Court (''redolent of the Old South''), which had long since been torn down. It was there that the Watkin and Guerard families had enjoyed ample Sunday dinners, as a string quartet played and ''courtly black waiters'' walked a spotless black-and-white

marble floor. Albert also regretted to find the Majestic Theatre half-demolished, the wrecking ball poised to resume its noisome destruction. Doomed as well, he discovered, was the old City Auditorium, where he had seen the immortal Anna Pavlova dance, and heard Ignace Jan Paderewski weave the entrancing melodies of his countryman, Frederic Chopin, on the piano.

The demise of the Majestic Theatre and the Brazos Hotel, however, also reminded Guerard of the "banshee wail," so strangely sad, of the northbound Katy Limited. This was the train that left at precisely one minute after midnight, bound from Houston's old Central Depot to St. Louis. Young Albert would hear it often in the summer, after Houston's sultry heat had once again awakened him on the family sleeping porch. (It was still more than a full generation before residential air conditioning.)

2. There had been "preparedness" parades in Houston as early as June 1916. The Army, Navy, and Marine Corps shared busy recruiting offices in the remodeled old Federal Building on Fannin at Franklin Avenue. The city adjusted steadily to the possibility of war, which seemed ever nearer as Germany stepped up its submarine warfare early in 1917. Then, only weeks after the declaration of hostilities, facilities were prepared for more than 30,000 troops in what would later become Memorial Park, the Hogg family's magnificent gift to Houston. Training soon began for national guard units ordered to Camp Logan, on the western borders of the city, from all over the nation.

World War I had a lasting economic impact upon Houston, and thereby on the Rice Institute's ability to attract and retain superior students and faculty alike. The conflict accelerated the ongoing development of the petroleum industry, which had slackened somewhat since the booming decade after Spindletop's 1901 gushers. A prolific new field had been discovered at Goose Creek, just as the demand for oil increased sharply.

The importance of the city as a railroad center also escalated. Soon the Chamber of Commerce adopted a slogan in use for many years: "Where [a steadily growing number of] railroads meet the sea." Shipments of cotton, rice, timber, and manufactured goods, as well as petroleum products, increased steadily as the war intensified.

3. There had not been local AIA affiliates in Texas when Watkin arrived in Houston in 1910. He had considered joining the nearest chapter, in New Orleans, but decided to wait. In 1919, he and Birdsall Briscoe, together with Olle Lorehn, were in the forefront of a successful campaign to establish the first Houston Chapter of the AIA.

The Houston chapter of the AIA is now one of the largest and most active in the nation, and was host to the national AIA convention in 1990. It has a tradition of providing leadership for the organization, and of carrying out significant projects while maintaining professional standards at the highest level.

4. Salvatore Martino was a native of the hamlet of Alia, near Sicily's ancient capital of Palermo on the Tyrrhenian Sea. Born August 21, 1885, into a family of trained horticulturists, young Salvatore was sent away to school at eleven. He attended a botanical institute in Italy's cultural center of Florence for four years, earning a certificate in agriculture and horticulture.

An older brother who headed a monastic order in Rome (reputed to have been named a cardinal later by Pope Pius XI) had Salvatore appointed a second gardener at the Vatican in 1901. In the world-famed papal gardens, he added substantially to the knowledge of plant propagation, floriculture, pruning, pest control, fertilization, and other aspects of horticulture he had acquired in Florence.

Young Martino, however, kept hearing of the opportunities and advantages of life in the United States, from two other brothers who had emigrated there. He joined them in 1903. However, in 1904, Salvatore returned to Italy for military service, and did not return to America until 1908. He went to Houston, which had a climate similar to that of southern Italy and Sicily he knew so well, and somewhat comparable plant life.

5. Martino had toured the Rice campus soon after entering Captain Baker's employ, in the spring of 1909. He found only a small grove of pin oaks near the principal entrance on Main Street, a clump of what were called "volunteer" pines along the Sunset Boulevard border, and small thickets of undergrowth along Harris Gully. The remainder was barren Harris County prairie, with an occasional thin cover of ragged native weeds or grasses overgrazed by trespassing cattle.

A convert later to the longer-lived live oak, Martino did plant a tiny stand of pin oaks to complement those at the main entrance. They were placed just to the left and slightly east of the future site of the Administration Building. The trees, little more than saplings, were probably obtained from Edward Teas Nursery. In business since 1894 as Houston's pioneer nurseryman, Teas was already acquainted with President Lovett.

6. When making the decision to employ Tony Martino full-time at the Rice Institute, Watkin had asked for any appraisal of Martino that Baker might be willing to provide. Baker wrote: "I have a very good opinion of Tony Martini (sic) . . . his services were generally satisfactory. He is an indefatigable worker, and I am inclined to believe he will render you satisfactory service. Mrs. Baker always thought that he paid more attention to large matters than to details. She had occasion frequently to correct him in this particular. Otherwise, I have heard no complaint of him."

This fell somewhat short of an enthusiastic recommendation, but it served, nevertheless, and Martino was soon officially a key figure of those reporting to Watkin, as he would be until his retirement thirty-two years later.

7. A generation and more of Rice graduates would recall the fragrance of Tony's "capa da jazz." These fragrant plants filled the Quadrangle, and their blooms were timed to appear in late May during commencement week. Luxuriant azaleas, planted between the live oaks lining the main entrance, also had a controlled blooming season. Their flowers appeared at the time of the May Fete, and were long remembered by faculty children including the Watkin, Weiser, and Tsanoff daughters. At a young age, they were flower girls in one of the first of these annual spring ceremonies.

   Apart from "li-VOKAs," Tony Martino's obsession was rose bushes. "The rose," he explained, "she da queen of flowers." "Mr. Wat" was soon accustomed to hearing pleas for more trees, hedges, and ornamentals on campus, but especially for more rose bushes. Tony also wanted extra mules, to keep the lawns and peripheral fields properly mowed. Watkin heeded many of his head gardener's requests, in spite of tight budgets, but it was never possible to fund the greenhouse that Martino had always wanted. Tony's roses, many of them a special variety from Nebraska that thrived in Houston's relatively temperate winters, began to appear frequently at faculty teas and in administrative and faculty offices on the campus.

8. It was not until around 1926 that Rice organized its first golf team. This was a sport close to Watkin's heart, and one he personally enjoyed. Watkin sponsored the golf team and arranged for the team to play on his membership at the Houston Country Club. Hermann Park only had 9 holes at the time. The first captain of the team was James Greenwood, Jr., Class of 1927, later a prominent neurosurgeon in Houston. His brother Joe, Class of 1930, was also a captain of the team. Their sister, Mary Greenwood Anderson, Class of 1938, has written a history of this first Rice golf team, which is now in the Fondren Library at Rice.

9. An overriding factor in the decision to hire Heisman might well have been the mushrooming, almost obsessive, desire on campus and throughout Houston for the Rice Institute to win the football championship of the Southwest Conference against much larger and longer established opponents. Heisman was seen as a possible answer to this.

   The Texas Intercollegiate Athletic Association, sometimes described as a "loose knit and informal" organization, had been formed by Southwest institutions as early as 1909. Rice joined the Association in 1913 for a brief time, with Watkin representing Rice in the meetings. The two dominant members, Texas and Texas A&M, had quickly developed an annual football game, played each November in Houston as a feature of the No-Tsu-Oh Carnival. At the 1911 game, there was a near riot when students cheering on the opposing teams clashed. This was before the No-Tsu-Oh Ball at which Edgar Odell Lovett reigned as King Nottoc XIII, and which William Ward Watkin attended as his guest.

The near-riot had several negative consequences. President W.T. Mather of the University of Texas canceled the game with A&M until further notice. Houston lost a very popular athletic spectacle, always preceded by a colorful parade of Aggie cadets and marching band as well as Longhorn students and their band. Further, the organization of the Southwest Conference was delayed until the very end of 1914.

There was a positive result for the Rice Institute, however. Between 1912 and late 1914, Coach Philip Arbuckle was able to launch a program of intercollegiate athletics at Rice with considerable success. This made the Institute a viable candidate to accept charter membership in the Southwest Conference.

10. In the Slime Parade, a traditional event, male freshmen marched from the campus to the Rice Hotel in pajamas. There Coach Heisman shared a makeshift podium with Tony Martino, who had become a beloved symbol of school spirit. Martino made one of his brief, highly enthusiastic and largely unintelligible speeches. The gist of this was always "Owlsa gonna win," followed by tremendous applause from the assembled students, faculty, alumni, other backers and curious onlookers.

Tony always wore his best suit to these pregame pep rallies. It was the one probably purchased for a special highlight of his long career at Rice: the February 5, 1920, visit of General John J. Pershing to the campus on "Pershing Day." On that great occasion, the head gardener superintended the planting of a handsome pecan tree donated by the World War I hero.

CHAPTER SIX

A 1925 trip to Europe for the Watkin family . . . Rice's Chemistry Building, in handsome "Brady pink" brick, becomes a most important commission . . . Impressive residential assignments for Watkin in Montrose, Shadyside, and nearby areas . . . Broadacres, a "lush urban park". . . . Planning new institutions of higher education for Texas' expanding system . . . A series of notable commissions further establishing Watkin's reputation as an architect: Autry House, Miller Memorial Theater, Museum of Fine Arts, Houston Public Library, Palmer Memorial Chapel, and the Houston Independent School System . . . A traveling scholarship in architecture is established . . . Preparations for a 1928–1929 sabbatical in Europe for the Watkin family

I.

William Ward Watkin's private practice had grown rapidly. The number and variety of commissions were a tribute to his excellent work on the Rice Institute project. They reflected his increasing stature as an architect in general practice, and especially in the field of campus and church design. Watkin's participation in community organizations and his friendships among Houston's business and professional leaders were also factors. Many of these businessmen were building elegant homes in the city's best subdivisions, and Watkin was to receive his good share of these commissions.

Due to Watkin's heavy workload in the early 1920s, he was forced to postpone a long-planned vacation in Europe during the summer of 1922. Instead, the Watkins went for their customary July respite from Houston heat to the Grove Park Inn in Asheville, North Carolina. There, while Houston sweltered, there were sometimes logs ablaze in the two splendid lobby fireplaces, each 12 feet wide. The elegant resort hotel was built of granite boulders from the Blue Ridge mountains. Watkin, as usual, sent the family on ahead. He would join them later, after clearing his desk of the details of another busy year.

The postponed journey to Europe was finally possible for the Watkin family in the summer of 1925. Watkin and Annie Ray toured France while the children remained at a summer camp for American children on the Normandy beach at Houlgate. The camp, located in a French beach villa and run by Mrs. Charlotte Wiggin of New York City, offered the valuable opportunity for Watkin's children to learn French from the French children on the beach. To their pleasant surprise, Ray, Rosemary, and Billy found three of their Kinkaid friends at the same resort for a brief time: Jane, John, and Cecil Amelia ("Titi"), the children of Mr. and Mrs. Robert Lee Blaffer of Houston [1].

The plan had been for the Watkin parents to continue on together to Spain, after an automobile tour of Normandy and a brief stay at the Hotel Crillon in Paris. The Paris and Normandy tours were accomplished. Mrs. Watkin, however, who had not been well on the ship over from the States, became ill in Paris and had to remain in the American Hospital to recuperate. A friend from Houston, Mrs. Ralf Graves, had come over to be with her. At Mrs. Watkin's insistence, Watkin went on to Spain. He was accompanied by good friends from Houston, Mr. and Mrs. George Howard, who had already planned to join the Watkins on this part of the trip.

On July 23, 1925, Watkin wrote President Lovett from the Grand Hotel in Seville: "Seville in July! But the breeze has been from the mountains, and it is as cool as Houston in April." He described Northern Spain as reminiscent of "the plains and hills of West Texas." Amid some of Europe's most illustrious architecture, Watkin was understandably more concerned about his beloved wife's health. Again to Lovett from Spain: "I hope she will be ready [early in August] for our trip into Italy." There had been elaborate preparations for this journey, with detailed advice on interesting highlights and local accommodations from Jimmy Chillman, who so recently had been a resident of Rome as a fellow of the American Academy.

Fortunately, Mrs. Watkin recovered quickly in Paris. She was able to accompany Mr. Watkin on his long-awaited tour of Italy. From Venice on August 21, 1925, Watkin wrote President Lovett regarding the famed cloister of the Doge's Palace: "I have made a detailed study of the lower order [of the cloister].'' A reproduction had guided him as early as 1909 in following this element of the Doge's Palace, ''for my detailing of the lower order of the Administration Building.'' Sixteen years later, with this component of one of the jewels of Venetian architecture actually before him, Watkin proudly reported to Dr. Lovett that ''We have kept color [in the Administration Building at Rice Institute] equal to Venice.''

The Watkins went on from Italy to England via France (where they picked up their children). The town of Oxford would be their headquarters for a month. Mr. Watkin had remained in touch with Julian Huxley, who was well into his successful career as a scientist and administrator. On September 14, 1925, Watkin wrote President Lovett from Oxford: ''Have been here a week. As cold as Houston in December. If [only] English hotels had a little more generous provision for heating.

''I have seen Huxley a number of times, and he has driven Mrs. Watkin and me to adjoining towns for sightseeing. We are having dinner together tonight. As you know, he is moving very shortly to London, having accepted the professorship [in biology] at King's College. He is enthusiastic over the chance and likes the chance to live in London, as well as the work.''

Back in Houston in the fall of 1925, Watkin was again busy with his private practice and the myriad details of a new academic year at Rice. He returned to what would prove to be another disappointing season for John Heisman and the Owl football team.

Watkin was in the midst of the final stage of completing what is still considered one of the most handsome and functional structures on the Rice Institute campus: the Chemistry Building. This project, for which Cram and Ferguson acted as associated architects, can be regarded as one of Watkin's most significant commissions.

Watkin described the original concept of the Chemistry Building, dating back to the Cram, Goodhue & Ferguson General Plan of 1910, as a ''simple rectangular mass.'' More than a dozen years later, with planning advice from Harry B. Weiser, Watkin could see that a different approach was needed. A colleague and friend since before World War I, Dr. Weiser was also a chemist of international renown.

He had provided Watkin with invaluable counsel regarding the design and construction of the Chemistry Building.

It was obvious that emphasis had to be put on the specific number of both large and small laboratories, and the proper venting of fumes and gases generated in experiments. Even details such as storage areas for certain chemicals posed special problems. Cram, Goodhue & Ferguson's "simple rectangular mass" quickly took on a very different configuration. As early as January 1923, Watkin wrote President Lovett about ". . . sketches of the Chemistry Laboratory which have been carefully studied by Mr. Weiser and myself . . . over a period of many months." From this point, Watkin's role shifted steadily to that of principal architect. It is properly listed among his own designs.

As the Chemistry Building design continued to depart from the original concept, the quiet Watkin gave a diplomatic explanation. "Early plans," he pointed out, could often be seen as "the foundation for more complete solutions as experience [is] gained from . . . actual buildings." His new Chemistry Building, which was finished by the fall of 1925, was indeed a "more complete solution." Further, it was not merely functional. The structure blended exceedingly well into Rice's expanding campus, with its overall design, brick, arches, cloisters, amphitheater, limestone banding, and handsome tower.

The brick might well have been a problem instead of an asset. While preparing specifications for the Chemistry Building, Watkin discovered that the "Brady pink" brick used in the original structures at Rice was no longer available. Sherman Brady had died in a racing car accident. His kiln had shut down and the Brady Company was in receivership.

Watkin was anxious to find a new supply of "Brady pink" brick, if at all possible. He was helped by Tom Tellepsen, who had been awarded the contract for the Chemistry Building. Tellepsen, long a Houston general contractor, knew members of the Brady family, who assisted him in locating a one-time foreman of their brickyard, now in his eighties.

The Bradys had been well known in the Houston area for generations. Sherman Brady's father, Colonel J.T. Brady, had been a state senator and leading businessman for many years. Sherman's mother Lucy was the daughter of General Sidney Sherman, who commanded the left flank of Sam Houston's army at San Jacinto. Colonel Brady operated a large brickyard on Hill Street bridge near present-day Navigation Boulevard. The clay for Brady bricks came from a deposit on Brady Island, formed by redirecting a portion of the Ship Channel. Kilns were operated both on the island and at Navigation Boulevard locations.

With help from Sherman Brady's sister Lucy (Mrs. W. Sperry Hunt), his widow, Chaille Jones, and others, a new supply of Brady pink was finally made available [2]. Construction on the Chemistry Building was delayed several months because of the problems involved, but Watkin's recommendation to wait on the exterior brickwork was accepted. The wait was kept to a minimum by his skill at rescheduling work at the site, and the cooperation of Tellepsen.

II.

Watkin had commenced his private practice of architecture in 1913 with Lovett's approval, not long after the opening of the Rice Institute in September 1912. In 1915, he formed a partnership with George Endress of Austin, and the firm was known as Endress & Watkin. Offices were in Houston's Scanlan Building, where Watkin had been working with such intensity from 1910 to 1912 on the original buildings at Rice. Mr. Endress kept his offices in the Littlefield Building in Austin. The first commissions were remodeling projects in Beaumont, San Antonio, and Galveston, but they later received commissions for several new state colleges: West Texas State at Canyon, Texas; Sul Ross Junior College at Alpine, and others.

But Watkin was soon to begin work on his first important church commission. A new Trinity Episcopal Church in Houston was being contemplated. In 1917, Watkin was to share his first church commission with Cram for a new church and parish house for Trinity Church at Main and Holman. Trinity had become a major new Episcopal parish serving expanding residential areas near Rice Institute.

The Watkin family later transferred their membership to the new Trinity Church, which was some two miles closer to their home than the downtown Christ Church. The rector of Trinity Church, the Reverend Robert E. Lee Craig, had completed the drive for a new church and rectory when he died suddenly in 1916. Father Craig was replaced in January 1917 by a 34-year-old priest, Clinton Simon Quin, who had left careers as a pitcher in professional baseball and as an attorney to enter the priesthood. Clinton Quin was later Episcopal Bishop of Texas during a period of extraordinary growth and progress for his denomination in the diocese.

Within a year, the Reverend Mr. Quin was named bishop coadjutor of the diocese. He was soon administering the diocese for his superior, Bishop George Herbert Kinsolving. Bishop Kinsolving died in 1928, at which time Bishop Quin succeeded him.

Watkin was fortunate to be able to deal directly with the dynamic Quin during the critical phases of the design and construction of Trinity Church in 1917 and 1918. Watkin had obtained the commission himself for the Cram & Ferguson firm, with Watkin as "associated architect." He also became the key figure during all the succeeding stages of building the church, from the early planning through the dedication of the church and parish house in 1919.

The Cram & Ferguson office in Boston prepared the initial drawings, with Ralph Adams Cram in a vital role as critic and adviser. Watkin, however, was responsible for the finished product, as well as for an impressive tower added in 1921. He also provided the plans and supervision for the details of interior embellishment, which continued during much of the 1920s. The style of architecture can be described as Norman Gothic, reflecting the 11th-century architecture of northern France. This was close in form to the French Romanesque tradition, later brought into England and especially admired by Watkin. He would later write of "The marvels of the French Gothic [style, which] cause it to stand apart, alone in its splendor." Watkin also wrote that church architecture must again "be understood as a problem, major and meaningful, in which a dignity of emotion is to be expressed and an atmosphere of quiet contemplation, and consolation is to be achieved in terms and with materials consistent with our own days."

Trinity Church still dominates its surroundings at Main and Holman, and has now been listed in the National Register of Historic Places. Watkin always considered this one of his most important and satisfactory commissions.

It was a matter of understandable pride and sense of achievement to have had such a major role in the handsome and inspiring church. Further, the well-executed commission for Trinity parish brought favorable attention to Watkin in other consequential groups within the city. This may well have led to the volume of residential commissions and civic projects awarded him in the early and mid-1920s.

The fact that Watkin was the principal architect for the new Trinity Church and parish house also had lasting results in the relationship between Cram & Ferguson and Watkin. As indicated, Cram & Ferguson closed its Houston office late in November 1919, soon after the dedication of the new Episcopal church. There was an understanding that Watkin was to share fully in the design and supervision of any future commissions awarded the firm in Houston.

Within months the trustees at Rice had Watkin under contract as architect for the first post-World War I structure on campus. The contract covered a Field House, tucked away in a remote area near Harris Gully along Main Street. It was intended to be a temporary structure. The Field House, which opened in time for the 1920–1921 academic year, included offices, facilities for physical training, and a two-story basketball court. Outside the Field House, to the west, were bleachers and an athletics field for football, baseball, and track.

The entire project was completed for less than $55,000. As a temporary facility, it was built with reasonably attractive and serviceable materials, but Watkin concentrated on usefulness and economy. The result was a boxlike structure of inexpensive brick and stucco, with ready-made windows and doors, and a minimum of decorative effects. The Field House had no cost overruns, and was ready on schedule despite remaining postwar shortages. It was what President Lovett and the other trustees had wanted: a minimum facility that would serve a purpose for more than a decade, and then be replaced. The success of the Field House may also have had a considerable effect upon the decision to have Watkin assume a more central role in designing the tremendously more complex Chemistry Building.

In 1917, Watkin received the first of many residential commissions from prominent Houstonians, a commission to build a new home for Howard R. Hughes, founder of the company bearing his name. The Hughes Tool Company had already established dominance in the relatively new industry of oil field equipment. Hughes had acquired one of the best lots in Montrose Place, which was a new 165-acre development a mile northeast of the Rice Institute campus. John Wiley Link had launched the addition, much larger than either Southmore, Westmoreland, or Courtlandt Place, and had built his own mansion there at the intersection of Montrose Boulevard and Alabama.

The Howard Hughes property was located at 3921 Yoakum Boulevard, one block from the Link mansion, now the administrative center for the University of St. Thomas. Watkin designed an imposing two-story residence of brick, with rooms of generous dimension and careful architectural detailing. He could hardly have selected a client with more influential ties to 1917 Houston. Hughes, the classic entrepreneur, had left his prosperous law practice in Keokuk, Iowa within months after learning of the great oil strike at Spindletop. He soon made wide contacts in petroleum, industrial, and legal circles of booming Houston [3].

A few years later, looking back on his work at Rice with its Italian Romanesque architecture, Watkin was to incorporate the Mediterranean style into the design and decor of two large commissions in Shadyside. The first, in 1919, was the residence of Harry C. Wiess at 2 Sunset Boulevard, which faced Main Street directly across from the main entrance to Rice. This two-story home of stucco, tile, multiple windows, and interior elegance had many of the elements of an Italian villa. The building had a sense of openness, emphasized by four tall casement windows at either side of the front of the long, rectangular house. The scale of the home was large and grand. Many years later, upon the death of both Mr. and Mrs. Wiess, this home was generously left to Rice University.

The second Shadyside residence designed by Watkin was immediately next to the Wiess home and also faced Main Street, which was already flanked by an avenue of live oak trees. This was the commission for the home of Mr. and Mrs. Frederick A. Heitmann. Heitmann's father had arrived in Houston from Germany in the mid-19th century. He had dominated Houston's freight forwarding business in the late 1850s, and opened the city's largest hardware store in 1865. The Heitmann residence, built at 1 Longfellow Lane in 1922–1923, was even more reminiscent of some elements of the

Italian buildings at Rice Institute. It, too, like the adjacent Wiess home at 2 Sunset, would not have been out of place in some exclusive enclave along the Mediterranean shore.

Graceful arches framed the south terrace entrance, with five tall, narrow windows and iron grillwork immediately above on the second floor. Beautiful tessera tile, flooring, and other special materials were used throughout the handsome interior. A gently curving stairway and paneled stair hall, with a striking sun room, were among the other features of the Heitmann home. The sun room was similar to some of the attractive interiors at Rice. Watkin had provided a vaulted ceiling, hand-carved mantel for the stone fireplace, and tall casement windows set in arches of white plaster.

Ernest Shult, a 1923 graduate in architecture from the Rice Institute, recalls working for Professor Watkin both during the summer of 1923 and after graduation in 1924. He still remembers a unique feature of the Heitmann home that would draw attention during many a dinner party. The ceiling of the dining room was decorated using the "sgraffito" technique (translated literally, "having been scratched"). It involves scratching through a surface layer of plaster to a colored layer below, a technique originated in Bologna that gained popularity in Italy in the early 16th century.

Watkin's commissions in Shadyside had a positive effect upon his expanding career as a residential architect. He was also to receive several assignments in urban subdivision planning during the busy decade and a half from 1913 through the 1920s.

Soon after Watkin had started work on the residence of Howard Hughes in Montrose in 1917, Watkin had contacted Joseph S. Cullinan to solicit the commission to design Cullinan's projected home in Shadyside, a new subdivision on Main Street near Rice. Cullinan, who was already a legendary oilman, had left the Texas Company in 1913, amid a dispute over moving the corporate headquarters from Houston to New York City. Plans for the development of the new Shadyside subdivision were being made by Cullinan. Its proximity to the Rice Institute made consultation with Rice authorities inevitable. Number 2 Remington Lane was the choice oversized lot that Cullinan had selected as the site for his own home.

Shadyside brought Watkin into contact with George E. Kessler. Kessler was a national authority on landscape architecture and city planning who had moved his practice to St. Louis after a highly successful career in Kansas City. After Kessler was hired by Houston's park commissioners to design Hermann Park and to landscape Main Street, turning it into a wide boulevard framed by oak trees, J.S. Cullinan retained him to assist with Shadyside. This may well have cost Watkin a contract on the Cullinan residence at 2 Remington. Kessler apparently convinced Cullinan that he should bring in for consultation Kessler's good friend, James P. Jamieson, a St. Louis architect who specialized in residential architecture.

Jamieson designed a 17th-century English manor house. It was two years in design and construction and was one of the largest homes in Houston at the time. The huge residence included stables for matched trotting horses and several blooded riding horses, plus an adjacent carriage house, which were later converted to garages and storage areas. In the days before automobiles took over, the carriage house had sheltered everything from a pony cart to a fine imported surrey. The house was purchased in the 1940s by Governor and Mrs. William Pettus Hobby, who enjoyed it for many years. It was demolished in 1972.

Eclecticism had begun to defeat any hope for an Italianate Shadyside, from the moment the J.S. Cullinan residence was completed in 1919. The addition included architectural styles ranging from Watkin's Mediterranean villas through Tudor, Regency, Georgian, Jacobean, and Spanish and French farm houses to "Latin Colonial." The central emphasis among the old-line Houstonians drawn to Shadyside was obvious quality and good taste, regardless of the architectural style chosen [4].

Ten years after Rice opened, Watkin had received another subdivision commission: that of laying out Southampton, a development directly north and west of the Rice campus. The many English names for streets in the subdivision were selected by Watkin. The assignment included the difficult problem of removing Wilmer Waldo's railroad spur coming across from Blodgett Street to the campus power plant. The spur, so necessary during Rice's construction, had become a major obstacle to developing Southampton.

Meanwhile, Watkin had additional assignments in areas adjacent to Shadyside. The widening and paving of West Eleventh Street, renamed Bissonnet, had stimulated other offshoots of Bissonnet just west of Montrose Boulevard, such as the development of John H. Crooker's new Shadowlawn Circle and of the N.P. Turner addition. Watkin designed six homes in this immediate neighborhood between 1922 and 1925. Among the owners were his Rice colleagues Harry B. Weiser at 5201 Bayard Lane (later the office of Howard Barnstone, FAIA) and Robert Caldwell at 5203 Bayard Lane, as well as homes for John Virgil Scott at 1122 Bissonnet, E.M. Armstrong, M.D., at 1128 Bissonnet, and M.L. Graves, M.D., at 11 Shadowlawn.

Joseph W. Northrup, Jr., as was noted, had come from Boston in 1911 to succeed A.C. Perry as clerk of the works at the Rice Institute. After launching a successful practice of his own, Northrup had purchased a small tract perpendicular to Bissonnet, and turned it into West Eleventh Place, a tiny development of eight homes. At 1 West Eleventh Place, Watkin designed a French provincial-style residence for E.A. Hail, which was later owned by the Ben Thompsons.

Only three blocks to the west, Watkin was asked to lay out a fine new development called Broadacres [5]. Broadacres was described as the ". . . last and grandest [of the] Bissonnet private places . . . [with] consistent architectural quality [as well as] exceptional landscaping and planning." Broadacres was a project of James A. Baker, Jr., son of the chairman of the Rice Institute board and father of the U.S. secretary of state under President George Bush.

Now the small, 34-acre Broadacres gave Watkin the opportunity to plan and landscape a bare section of prairie land. His solution was simple, yet appealing: three streets in a U-shaped configuration, set apart by broad esplanades. The esplanades were planted with allées of live oaks on either side of patterned brick walkways. Almost seventy years later, the effect was described as that of "an amazingly lush urban park."

At 1318 North Boulevard in Broadacres, Watkin designed what some critics identify as one of his finest residences. This was a Spanish villa for B.B. Gilmer. The perfectionist Watkin, knowing that he would be in Spain during the summer of 1925, postponed the project until he could check colors, materials, and ornament in that country firsthand. He studied these details in Seville and in northern Spain, to the obvious benefit of his client.

Other significant residential commissions soon followed for Watkin, as Houston moved into the prosperous mid-1920s. Among these were homes for the developer E.L. Crain on North Calumet in MacGregor Place and for W. T. Eldridge, Jr. in Sugar Land.

III.

By 1926, William Ward Watkin had completed almost two dozen homes, most of them in the relatively small and exclusive area encompassing Montrose, Shadyside, and the upper reaches of Bissonnet.

Stephen J. Fox has pointed out how the architect, barely in his thirties in 1917, had joined in an especially meaningful campaign for Houston that year. A high-level crusade was begun for "urban improvements in the South End by those [determined] to maintain the standards of planning and design introduced by the Rice Institute."

In addition to Cullinan, the planner Kessler, and Watkin, the nucleus group for this campaign included Edwin B. Parker and Will C. Hogg. Parker was a senior law partner of Captain James A. Baker, often entrusted with civic projects of special importance to their firm. Will Hogg, brother of Mike and Miss Ima, was a son of the storied Governor James Stephen Hogg. He and his siblings had a major effect upon what was then still called the South End.

These men, according to Stephen Fox, had a vision of Houston. It was ". . . largely one of significant institutions dispersed in sylvan verdure surrounded by the artistically designed residences of gracious and cultivated families." The other four in the group were soon more aware of Watkin's steady rise as an architect. They became a positive factor in a number of highly significant commissions awarded him in the period from 1921 to 1927.

Watkin was interested in a broadening range of civic activities, including the fine arts, city planning, zoning, and Houston's mushrooming public school system. There were opportunities for new commissions for him in which he was clearly qualified as a candidate, but to obtain them he might also benefit from appropriate endorsement or intercession.

These new civic commissions included his design for the original Miller Memorial (Outdoor) Theater in Hermann Park (1921), the Museum of Fine Arts (1924–1926), the Houston Public Library (as an associate with Cram & Ferguson and Louis Glover of Houston, 1926), the new Kinkaid School on Richmond Road and Graustark (1925), and the architectural supervision of nine new Houston public schools built during Mayor Oscar F. Holcombe's administration (1925–1927).

As the interest in the new buildings at Rice grew, Watkin began to receive inquiries and contracts for other buildings of higher education. As early as 1915, Endress & Watkin were asked to design "Old Main," the administration center for a new campus at West Texas Normal College at Canyon. In 1919, a commission followed for the design of Sul Ross Normal at Alpine, a teachers' college in Big Bend County. Both of these jobs necessitated long train rides to the far corners of West Texas for Watkin.

Then, in 1924–1925, Watkin received a major commission to design a new college in Lubbock, Texas, this time as associated architect with Wyatt C. Hedrick of Fort Worth. It involved the design of a campus plan and the first five buildings for the Texas Technological College at Lubbock, which had been recently authorized by the Texas Legislature. The members of the board of the new college were influenced in their selection of Watkin as architect because of his experience with Cram & Ferguson in the design of the Rice Institute campus. At that time, Lubbock was poised for greater growth as a center of the cotton industry and of "agribusiness" in Texas.

As had the Canyon and Alpine jobs, this project, on the South Plains of Northwest Texas, posed transportation problems. A generation before air travel and air conditioning, train schedules to these towns were not as convenient as those available to major cities. To break the monotony of the long train trips during the summer months, Watkin sometimes took one of his children with him. Both Rosemary and Billy remembered the trips they took with their father as children. Nevertheless, Lubbock offered Watkin a rare opportunity to design the general plan and original buildings for a large Texas university and he was delighted to have the chance. He was sketching preliminary designs late in November 1923, even before formal contracts were approved.

Interestingly, to a considerable extent, Watkin followed the alternate general plan for the Rice Institute, proposed in 1909 by Bertram Grosvenor Goodhue. The Goodhue plan was, as Stephen J. Fox has pointed out, ". . . nearly one-third longer and twice as wide" as Ralph Adams Cram's compromise that was finally approved.

Having a large campus area to work with on the outskirts of Lubbock, Watkin adopted the concept of a much larger scale as proposed by Goodhue. This provided considerably more space between buildings. The buildings were arranged along two axes, again as Goodhue had planned for Rice. The style selected was Spanish Renaissance, featuring an open plaza and extended academic quadrangle, and a "great square" at the intersection of the basic axes.

Conscious of the importance of landscaping, Watkin included a unique tree-bordered watercourse centered in the quadrangle. Overall, he sought the effect of small, open parks between buildings. "As at Rice," Stephen Fox has summarized, "cloisters were distributed to interconnect building groups, and trees, planted in file, defined the principal routes of circulation."

The successful commissions at Texas Technological College, Canyon, and Alpine were soon followed by another. In 1925, Watkin and one of his former students, Shirley Simons, were engaged to design a large dormitory for the College of Industrial Arts at Denton, 50 miles northwest of Dallas. This was another institution in Texas' currently expanding system of public higher education.

As early as 1921, Watkin was being recognized on and off the Rice campus as an architect in his own right, rather than in his original capacity as Ralph Adams Cram's representative. Two projects he was involved with were immediately adjacent to Rice, both "off campus," but both of great importance to the university. They were the Autry House, built in 1921, and the Palmer Memorial Chapel, built in 1927.

The Autry House, a formal student union building, had long been overdue at Rice. Few institutions of higher education had been launched with scantier facilities for non-resident students than the

Rice Institute. In the beginning years, students arrived and departed via streetcars boarded at Eagle Avenue or at the third entrance to the campus. In bad weather, the only place to eat home-packed lunches was in the temporary library in the Administration Building. The accommodations were even more minimal for female students. They were required to be off campus by 5 p.m., and were not allowed to "hitch" rides with still-rare automobiles on Main Street, as the men had begun to do.

Fortunately, Bishop Clinton Quin had sent the Reverend Harris Masterson, Jr., to the Rice campus. Masterson was an Episcopal priest assigned to special ministries who had just returned from service as a World War I chaplain. He was greatly concerned at the almost total lack of student facilities. The only thing available close by was a little shack across from the streetcar stop where students could buy snacks and Coca-Cola. This was "The Owl," operated by the enterprising Ernest Shult in the time he could spare from his architecture courses.

Masterson managed to get two surplus mess halls from Camp Logan. The training facility, which had been located in today's Memorial Park, was in the process of being dismantled. As the 1919–1920 academic year began, the rough wooden structures were placed just southeast of the campus. The Episcopal Diocese of Texas had acquired a piece of property there, in an exchange with the City of Houston for land nearby. Together, the two mess halls became a "community house," providing lounges, a cafeteria, and facilities for student meetings, dances, and plays—as well as serving as an all-important gathering place between or after classes.

The community house served an even more important function. It increased the Reverend Mr. Masterson's interest in replacing it with something better, and it also drew the attention of prominent Episcopalian families who felt the same way. Within the year, he had commissioned Watkin and Cram & Ferguson's Boston office to design a master plan for the Episcopal property to include a chapel, a proper community house and rectory, and a dormitory for nurses at the proposed Hermann Hospital just to the south.

The master plan was forthcoming, with major input from Watkin, but financing was not available. At this point, Masterson and the

Reverend Peter Gray Sears, the well-known rector of Christ Church, went to Mrs. James L. Autry seeking a contribution for the community house portion of the project. Her husband, J.S. Cullinan's attorney, had recently died. Just as had Cullinan, he had been quite interested in Rice. Autry had even more reason to be interested as both the Autry children, Allie May and James L., Jr., were students there.

Mrs. Autry gave $50,000 for what became Autry House. This was a two-story building of stucco and brick, with minimum ornamentation other than a handsome red tile roof. It was designed in a modified Mediterranean style. The soul of the new facility was a huge common room with a high ceiling of thick exposed beams stained a dark brown, a fireplace, and a small stage. It opened for the fall term of 1921, and would remain the center of student life at Rice Institute for almost thirty years. Watkin, who became the principal architect for the project, had included lounges, a kitchen and cafeteria, offices, meeting rooms, and even a barber shop.

As the Rice community continued to grow, Autry House fulfilled a unique function. It brought students, alumni, and faculty members and their families together, thus answering needs of real importance in an institution without its own student center, faculty club, or alumni hall. As a result, the facility became known as "Rice's fireside." Students could have coffee, soft drinks, or a modest lunch there; join in the incessant bridge games; have a meeting of campus organizations or alumni groups; or even watch the plays that faculty members staged by and for their children. In addition to its being the headquarters of the Reverend Mr. Masterson's Episcopal ministry, Autry House was always a place in which to just sit around and talk.

As the 1920s progressed, there was a revival of interest in a nearby campus chapel, the first element of the master building plan envisioned by the Diocese of Texas for their property on Main Street next to the Autry House. On June 16, 1927, it was announced that Daphne Palmer Neville had donated $100,000 for the Edward Albert Palmer Chapel as a memorial to her deceased brother. The architect for the project would be William Ward Watkin.

The chapel offered a fortunate opportunity to Watkin to express certain ideas on chapel design. He described this project as one incorporating modern elements combined with a quite traditional interior. The exterior was a striking mixture of what Stephen Fox terms a "tall, slender bell tower, articulating the juncture of the connecting cloister with the chapel." Fox emphasized that the interior seemed to be closely akin to that of the Church of Santa Maria dei Miracoli in Venice. Watkin had drawn this in great detail in a sketchbook while in Italy. Mrs. Neville had observed the church in Italy and had admired it. In 1897, Ralph Adams Cram had written that the Church of Santa Maria dei Miracoli was "almost the last piece of good work done before the catastrophe of the Renaissance."

Bishop Clinton Quin must have also admired Watkin's choice of a model for the Palmer Memorial Chapel's interior and his execution of the overall project. After being elevated in 1928 from bishop coadjutor to bishop of the Diocese of Texas, one of his earliest decisions was to establish the chapel across from Rice as a separate Episcopal parish. The final steps to accomplish this were taken in 1930, when the details of the redesignation were completed.

Watkin had already been working on another project, a project he knew had long been needed at Rice (before the formal contract signing for the Palmer Chapel). This new project so important to Rice was a prospective faculty club. George S. Cohen, a Houston merchant, had expanded the original Foley Brothers into what would become one of the largest department stores in the state. He was in a position to make a sizable gift to Rice. He had proposed informally to members of the governing board that he be allowed to contribute $125,000 to build, furnish, and maintain a faculty club to be named for him.

The Rice Institute had a long-established policy prohibiting the naming of any campus facilities for living donors, but a compromise was made in this case. The building was named for Cohen's parents, Robert I. and Agnes Lord Cohen. The senior Cohens were distinguished citizens and civic leaders of Galveston. George Cohen, who was a friend of Watkin's, was happy that Watkin was named principal architect for the club. Watkin must have been anticipating this project, because less than a month after George Cohen's gift was formally accepted at the March 1927 meeting of the trustees, he had completed both preliminary plans and elevations. These were quickly endorsed by Ralph Adams Cram, whose firm had been appointed as consultants rather than as associated architects.

The Cohen House was the first Rice building on which Watkin was the sole principal architect. It was finally clear, both at Rice and in Boston, that Watkin was now on his own, fully qualified, and separate from the Cram dominance.

The architecture of the Cohen House has been analyzed with his usual depth by the architectural critic Stephen J. Fox. He describes Watkin's skill at combining seemingly disparate elements of Europe's emerging new modernism with Rice's Italian Romanesque style, with exterior details recalling the medieval Greek monastery, St. Luke of Stiris.

Fox pointed out that Cohen House ". . . exhibited a . . . studied resemblance to the earlier campus buildings," specifically in the "tower and terrace configuration first used in Commons and South Hall." He found the lounge of the three-story structure of concrete and brick-and-hollow tile to be "one of the most impressive interiors on campus." The ". . . polychromed wood ceiling . . . and large hearth overhung by a stone hood" are still most striking and appealing in a building that remains a nucleus facility at Rice. The open patio, "enriched by cloisonne piers and an iron railing," also drew Fox's special attention, as did "the likenesses of faculty members on pier capitals." Watkin was depicted in one of these carvings of the original faculty, designed by Edward Arrants, a graduate architectural student, and executed by Oswald J. Lassig, the Austrian master carver of the capitals of the Administration Building.

Cohen House was dedicated on Thanksgiving Day 1927 and added substantially to faculty cohesion, pleasure, and effectiveness from the very beginning. Long before Cohen House was built, the teaching faculty had shown strong interest in a faculty club, holding frequent meetings of the "Committee on Organization of the Faculty Club of the Rice Institute." Robert G. Caldwell, by then the dean of the Institute, was chairman of this group, which included William Ward Watkin, Griffith C. Evans, J.T. McCants, John Willis Slaughter [6], Harry Boyer Weiser, and Harold A. Wilson. The first and many subsequent meetings were held at the Watkin home, usually with no absentees. George Cohen was a special guest on several occasions.

IV.

The Museum of Fine Arts, one of Watkin's most significant commissions, was a distinct outgrowth of the Houston (Public School) Art League, founded in 1900 to encourage "art culture" in the city's public school system. One of their first projects was to purchase and install reproductions of notable art in classrooms. The scope of the organization expanded quickly. As early as 1902, there were sponsored lectures on art and musical concerts for members and their guests. In 1913, only months after the opening of the Rice Institute, a new charter emphasizing art exhibitions and lectures had been issued to the renamed Houston Art League. In that same year, a persistent effort was begun to find a suitable piece of land on which to construct an art museum.

A tract donated by the City of Houston, at Holman and Austin, was found to be unacceptable. In 1914, Art League officials then negotiated a free lease on land owned by George Hermann, across from Rice Institute, but the aged philanthropist died before the papers could be signed. The problem was solved when J.S. Cullinan generously gave the League a triangular parcel of land directly east of Shadyside at the intersection of Main, Bissonnet, and Montrose, late in 1916.

Watkin had naturally been interested in art, so integrally a part of architecture, since his student days at the University of Pennsylvania. Art had been studied in Professor Paul Phillipe Cret's "Beaux-Arts" School. In Houston, Watkin had often visited the Art League offices in the Scanlan Building, as well as some of the League's earliest exhibitions. The League had located in that building temporarily in 1913, soon after Watkin had opened the offices of the firm of Endress & Watkin in the same location.

Watkin's involvement in the city's art circles grew steadily. He now appeared often before various community organizations including the Art League. He was frequently a speaker at the popular Sunday afternoon lecture series at Rice. He wrote President Lovett regarding the subject of one of his specific lectures: "I shall be glad to accept the assignment of Sunday lecture series on the value of Michelangelo's sculpture and painting, from the point of view of being architectural monuments."

It was quite natural that Watkin was a prime candidate to design the Museum of Fine Arts. However, there was to be a gap of almost four years between the Art League's acquisition of the site and the issuance of a commission to Watkin, with Ralph Adams Cram in the secondary role of consulting architect. Much of the intervening time was consumed in changing the structure of the governing board of the League. Additional trustees were named in preparation for a $200,000 fund-raising campaign. The museum was to be the key element of an ''Art Center'' in the South End.

A new Houston civic project, also located in the South End, very close to the Art Museum, had recently been awarded to Watkin. It was the Jesse Wright Miller Memorial Theater in Hermann Park.

Jesse Wright Miller was a Houston pioneer and very successful cotton broker in the days when cotton was still king. A friend of George Hermann and organizer of the Houston Cotton Exchange, he left approximately $100,000 for the enhancement of Hermann Park, specifically for facilities that would make it more enjoyable for the public. The park commissioners, quite conscious of the ongoing program to develop a South End Art Center, decided that an appropriate memorial for Miller would be a handsomely designed outdoor center for public meetings, concerts, plays, and other events in the park.

Stephen J. Fox accurately termed the Miller memorial the ''Greek theater'' (in the original master plan) ''which Rice was never to acquire.'' The $50,000 project of Indiana limestone was described by the *Houston Post* as a beautiful structure, with two long, covered colonnades flanking the central stage. Fox characterized the classic theater as a ''monumental Doric proscenium bordered by Doric peristyles which terminated in blocky pavilions.'' [7]

By late 1921, it was apparent that the Art League campaign goal of $200,000 to construct a Museum of Fine Arts would not be reached. About $70,000 was in hand, however. The decision was made to award the commission to the architect and build the project in stages.

In his design, Watkin turned to neoclassicism, in consonance with a post-World War I revival of scientific interest in archaeological research in Greece and Italy. His Rice colleague, Stockton Axson, Shakespearian scholar turned critic, described the design as a mixture: ''. . . pure Greek facade, [but] including reminiscences of Spanish civilization once indigenous here.'' Watkin's first plan essentially involved a classic rectangular structure of three stories around an open courtyard. It was the courtyard in which several Spanish touches such as stucco walls, arches, and a clay roof had been incorporated.

Financing difficulties continued, along with the problems of design involved in the triangular location. It was obvious that the first rectangular plan did not fit the site. Watkin then redesigned the central block, with divergent wings running parallel to Main Street and to Montrose Boulevard. When available funds would not yet cover this scheme, the wings were temporarily omitted. Will Hogg undertook an emergency fund-raising campaign in early 1924 that allowed completion of the initial phase, which was dedicated on April 12, 1924.

In the intervening two years, the Art League had celebrated its twenty-fifth anniversary (on March 24, 1925) by merging its charter with the charter of the Museum of Fine Arts. The silver anniversary was marked with an afternoon lawn party in front of Watkin's classic facade. Nine young girls from Mrs. Stuart Poor's ballet class represented the muses of Greek mythology. They performed the ''Dance of the Nymphs'' to the music of ''Moment Musicale.'' Rice Institute was overwhelmingly represented in this winsome group, with their filmy Grecian veils. All nine dancers were faculty daughters, most of them nine or ten years old. They were Annie Ray (Polyhymnia) and Rosemary (Euterpe) Watkin, Alice Caldwell (Clio), Nevenna (Calliope) and Katherine (Terpsichore) Tsanoff, Mary Stuart Tidden (Thalia), Virginia Walker (Urania), Dorothy Weiser (Melpomene), and Katherine Ander (Erato).

With the opening of the museum in 1924 came the announcement of the appointment of the Museum of Fine Arts' first director, James Henry Chillman, Jr., distinguished graduate of the University of Pennsylvania and of the American Academy in Rome, and the newly promoted associate professor of architecture at the Rice Institute. Technically, he would be part-time director at the museum at the modest salary of $200 a month, which was all the minimal MFA budget could provide. Chillman, at the same time, did not shirk his expanding responsibilities at Rice. He met his classes there in the morning, and directed the museum in the afternoon. Chillman became more and more valuable to both institutions, and to the community as a whole. He remained, through his long career, an important link between the university and the museum. Watkin and his fellow alumnus from Pennsylvania remained close friends and colleagues all their lives.

A series of significant commissions in Houston and elsewhere now followed in Watkin's office. In 1925, again as an associate architect with Wyatt C. Hedrick, Watkin was asked to design the First Methodist Church in Wichita Falls. He was invited by officials of Humble Oil & Refinery Company to design a number of homes for employees near the huge new refinery at Baytown. He was commissioned in 1923–25 to design a handsome new YWCA center in Galveston. One job disappointment was lack of financing for a proposed grand plan for a new Cotton Exchange building to replace the historic structure at Travis and Franklin. The old building, dating from 1884, would remain. The proposed design for the 15-story replacement remains in the Watkin files at Rice University.

But one of the most important contracts awarded Watkin in Houston during this time, of which he was most proud, was the new Houston Public Library, at Smith and McKinney (later named the Julia Ideson Building).

The particularly challenging library commission was shared by Watkin, as an associate architect, with Ralph Adams Cram and with Louis Glover, a local designer. Watkin had been strongly recommended for this job by the Reverend Harris Masterson, Jr., who was so well acquainted with Watkin's abilities. The Reverend Mr. Masterson was chairman of the municipal Library Board.

The new downtown center for the library gave both Watkin and his former employer, Cram, an opportunity to work in the Spanish Renaissance style, one of several styles that Cram & Ferguson had once proposed for the master plan at Rice Institute. Both Watkin and Cram knew Spain; both understood and appreciated the classic Spanish Renaissance architecture, which had been so ably expressed in the palace of Charles V at the heart of the Alhambra in Granada. The mid-16th-century palace of the Spanish king and Holy Roman emperor also reflected strong Italian influence, and many elements of design that were applauded by Watkin and Cram.

The Julia Ideson Building was designed essentially as a deep rectangle with a single wing. The entrance, of brick and stone, featured elegant arches and loggias, reflected in a library designed by Cram & Ferguson for the University of Southern California. The extravagant interior use of tile, dark woods, ornamented ceilings, columns, and stonework was strongly Spanish.

Between 1925 and 1928, Mayor R.H. Fonville, who had come to know Watkin as an authority and writer on city planning, had named Watkin to the position of supervising architect for the Houston Independent School District. In this period, nine new public high schools were designed and built for the HISD under his supervision [8].

During this surge level of activity in Watkin's office, one of the mainstays in the office for more than 10 years had been one of his own graduate students. C.M. Sanford of the Class of 1917 began to work part-time in the Endress & Watkin office in the Scanlan Building when it was opened in 1915. He remained with Watkin for more than a decade before moving on to establish his own practice in the early 1930s.

By 1927, as William Ward Watkin began to look forward to a long-planned sabbatical, A. (Addison) Stayton Nunn had become a key factor in the commission for HISD schools. Several years later, Nunn would be appointed supervising architect for Houston's public school system, when Watkin retired from that position.

Also in 1927, Watkin, though busy as never before with a record level of activity in both his private practice and at Rice, began to plan the innumerable details to clear his schedule for a 1928–1929 sabbatical in Europe. This trip would involve the absence of Mr. and Mrs. Watkin and the three children from Houston for an entire year.

One important project remained to be completed, one dear to his heart. He began to give the highest priority to this new matter, discussing it with Nunn, other architectural alumni, his faculty colleagues, and potential candidates. The project was the establishment of a traveling scholarship in the Department of Architecture at Rice.

Watkin, remembering his own experience traveling in Europe in 1908 as a Pennsylvania graduate, and his 1925 trip to England, France, Italy, and Spain, was convinced of the value of such travel and study abroad for advanced architectural students. He personally undertook to raise the necessary funding from a group of some ten wealthy Houstonians. Their private contributions would finance the cost for the candidate chosen by an architectural competition among the fifth-year students of the Department. 1927 had been a prosperous year for Houston, and Watkin had no trouble in raising the money from among his immediate friends and clients.

After solving the problem of financing the scholarship, Watkin saw that the project was well under way before leaving for his own sabbatical to Europe in the summer of 1928. For Watkin, the approaching sabbatical year (1928–29) would shape his remaining career and entire life, as well as that of his family.

Notes

1. Blaffer, who had founded Humble Oil & Refinery Company with Stephen Power and William Stamps Farish and other pioneer oilmen, was to become an active member of the governing board of the Rice Institute. His wife, Sarah Campbell Blaffer, was the daughter of a founder of the Texas Company and leader of Houston society. She became an internationally known collector and donor of art masterpieces. Several of her gifts are in the permanent collection of the Museum of Fine Arts.

2. After Sherman Brady's death, Chaille Jones Brady had married Benjamin Botts Rice, the nephew of the founder who replaced his uncle on the Rice Institute board of trustees. The Ben Rices lived just down the street from the Watkin family, at 5303 Caroline. They were a positive factor both in the search for Brady pink, and in maintaining additional support and contact within the governing board.

   The key to the brick problem was John P. Williams, the retired one-time foreman of the Brady brickyard. Although quite old, Williams was mentally alert and able to recall even minute details of his former responsibilities. He located a remaining deposit of the exact clay required on Brady Island, and listed from memory the minute particulars of exact temperatures and time in the baking kilns. Watkin then had to convince President Lovett and the trustees of the need to finance reopening long dormant Brady clay deposits and kilns. This he did. The result was the highly attractive match between Brady-pink brick in the new Chemistry Building and pre-World War I structures.

3. Hughes had married Allene Gano, one of three sisters of a prominent family. His brothers-in-law were Frederick Rice Lummis, M.D., and J.P. Houstoun. Several years after the death of the Hugheses, Dr. Lummis, a leading

physician, and his wife acquired the Hughes' home at 3921 Yoakum. Dr. Lummis was a cousin of Benjamin Botts Rice whose son would become administrator in the 1980s of the vast industrial and real estate empire of Howard Hughes, Jr. Houstoun and his partner Louis A. Stevenson were general partners for the Hartford Insurance Company throughout South Texas.

The Hughes family had moved to 3921 Yoakum when Howard Hughes, Jr. was 12. Young Howard was already demonstrating some of the myriad and unusual abilities that would bring him success in everything from the petroleum industry to the manufacture of aircraft, moviemaking, and huge real estate developments. During the summers between preparatory schools in Boston and Ojai, California, he assembled and operated one of Houston's first amateur radio stations. While a student at Rice, he set up an amateur radio station that operated out of the Mechanical Engineering Building. The Campanile tower served as an aerial support, according to E. Finley Carter, Class of 1922, who was there at the time. Many years later, when the tower of the Campanile was remodeled, the antenna was found, but its purpose was a mystery until finally explained by Carter.

4. Much of this emphasis upon eclecticism resulted from Harrie T. Lindeberg, New York City's guru of residential architecture in the 1920s. Lindeberg had been commissioned by Hugo V. Neuhaus, the "baron" who had married a Rice, to design a home for him at 9 Remington Lane. At a single dinner party given by Neuhaus in Houston in 1921, Lindeberg had come away with two additional contracts for residences in Shadyside. One was with W.S. Farish, a founder of Humble Oil; the other was with Kenneth E. Womack, a leading cotton broker.

Harrie Lindeberg was according to some critics an "architectural chameleon," wary of monotony and "free from formula." He preferred differing styles, based upon client, site, or situation, or even a mixture of styles. To supervise his commissions in Shadyside, Lindeberg sent a highly competent young architect, John Fanz Staub, a one-time student of Ralph Adams Cram at MIT. He quite agreed with Lindeberg's eclecticism, so long as the end product fulfilled the client's specific needs and reflected the refinements of good taste and quality materials. And soon there were five Lindeberg-designed homes in Shadyside, each of a different style.

5. The discerning Birdsall Briscoe, Watkin's tablemate at Mrs. Jack Bryan's rooming house in 1910, was quick to recognize the beauty of Broadacres. He was commissioned to design seven residences in the new subdivision. They ranged in style from a Spanish country house to a Tuscan villa, including Georgian, Regency, French, and Norman manor houses. Many of these were enhanced by formal gardens created by C.C. (Pat) Fleming.

6. Professor Slaughter, who had already become one of the most popular members of the faculty, also had a considerable role in encouraging Cohen to

provide the new and long-needed faculty facility. A brilliant sociologist from the University of London's School of Economics, he was a frequent speaker on campus and before community organizations. His writing and lectures on the value of philanthropy in society had attracted George Cohen's attention, as well as that of the eminent Rabbi Henry Cohen, leader of the large and influential Jewish community in Galveston.

The Slaughters would remain close friends of the Watkins, as both men enjoyed long and successful careers at Rice Institute and in the Houston community. The Slaughter home was in West Eleventh Place, across Bissonnet Street from residences Watkin had designed for Weiser and Caldwell on Bayard Lane. Mrs. Slaughter was a close friend of both the first and second Mrs. William Ward Watkin.

7. Houston is indebted to Henry Rockwell, who, along with his brother Jim and their parents, preserved a major portion of the first Miller Outdoor Theater. When a new and far larger memorial to Jesse Wright Miller was built in Hermann Park in the 1980s, the Rockwell Endowment moved the Doric peristyles of the original memorial to the intersection of Hermann Drive and San Jacinto. There they have been rearranged in an elegant circle around a graceful and complementary fountain. The core of Watkin's handsome design lives on.

8. Among the nine schools built under Watkin for HISD were: John H. Reagan Senior High School (John F. Staub and Louis A. Glover, architects); Jefferson Davis Senior High School (Briscoe & Dixon and Maurice Sullivan, architects); Jack Yates Colored High School (Briscoe & Dixon and Maurice Sullivan, architects); James S. Hogg Junior High School (Briscoe & Dixon and Maurice Sullivan, architects); Albert Sidney Johnson Junior High School (Sanguinet, Staats, Hedrick & Gottlieb, architects); George Washington Junior High School (Endress & Cato and Joseph Finger, architects); Sidney Lanier Junior High School (R.D. Steele and Henry F. Jonas & Tabor, architects); and Stonewall Jackson Junior High.

CHAPTER SEVEN

*Houston in a time of exceptional expansion . . . William
Ward Watkin establishes the Rice Institute Traveling
Scholarship in Architecture . . . A long-anticipated
sabbatical in Europe . . . Tante Marie and the Forest of
Compiegne . . . The "Villa Lalo" and St. Jean de Luz
. . . A memorable tour of the chateaux country . . . Annie
Ray becomes ill . . . Help from friends in Paris . . .
A remarkable letter from mother to daughter . . . Tragedy
strikes . . . The sad return over an icy Atlantic
. . . Convalescence from a dangerous bout with
pneumonia . . . Watkin reorients his life . . . Rice Institute
in the Great Depression . . . Personal help and guidance
for students . . . A second marriage brings new happiness*

I.

Houston was midway through a year of remarkable growth and
international visibility as the Rice Institute celebrated its thirteenth
commencement in 1928. Jesse H. Jones had half completed the
37-story Gulf Building, originally named for Jones himself before
Gulf Oil became the principal tenant. Built on the site of the 1845
home of Augustus C. Allen (founder of Houston with his brother
John K. Allen) and Charlotte Baldwin Allen on Rusk at Main and
Travis, it was, at the time, the tallest structure west of Chicago. It was
also the most costly, at $6.5 million, of any of the buildings under
construction in Houston in 1928. A record $35 million was spent on
construction in Houston that year. From twilight until sunrise, an
8,000-candlepower beam atop the skyscraper pointed to the new
Municipal Airport, opened March 2, 1928, off Telephone Road.

Jesse Jones had become a national figure in politics, banking, and
real estate. He was instrumental in bringing the 1928 Democratic
National Convention to Houston, and was, at one point, a major
candidate for the presidency. Supporters of Governor Alfred E. Smith
of New York had, however, quickly solidified their overwhelming
strength in delegates, and Smith, nominated by Franklin D. Roose-

velt, won the nomination on the first ballot. Smith ultimately lost the presidential election to Herbert Hoover in a Republican landslide. Texas went for Hoover in the November election.

The Watkin family attended the Democratic National Convention in June 1928, as guests of John Carpenter. A business, civic, and political leader from Dallas, Carpenter was a regent of Texas Technological College. Watkin had met him in 1925 when he began to design the new campus for the Lubbock institution. The convention was one of the last large functions attended by the Watkin family before they left for Europe in July. Ray still remembers being overawed by the enormous size of the crowd, the banners, and the music.

William Ward Watkin could look back now on almost two decades in Houston. When Watkin arrived in 1910, Houston's population had been only 78,800 according to the census. The Chamber of Commerce was predicting a total as high as 300,000 for 1930; the final count was 292,352, or a phenomenal 271% population increase in 20 years. This was a city clearly marked for greatness.

Watkin was 42 years old in 1928. He had accomplished much since arriving in Houston, so sharply different from his native Boston or his home in Pennsylvania. He had adapted well to the difference. Now Watkin had only a few fully occupied months until he and the family left on a sabbatical in Europe that he expected would involve an entire year's absence from Houston. The whole Watkin family had looked forward to this opportunity. The Watkins were anticipating relaxing and enjoying a foreign setting for a longer time than on their previous vacation there in 1925.

Watkin's European vacation three years before had reemphasized the significance of studying firsthand the architecture of France, Italy, and Spain. For some time, Watkin had wanted to write a book on the Gothic churches of those countries. It would examine the imagination, dignity, and beauty of sixth- to sixteenth-century church architecture, and its message for church architecture of the future. His book was to be titled "The Church of Tomorrow," but it would not to be written until his return from Europe.

Before his departure, Watkin had found time to complete details of the new Rice Institute Traveling Fellowship in Architecture. Seeing the fellowship actually under way represented an important step in the development of the department. The project clearly involved the realization of one of Professor Watkin's remaining goals: providing a means for graduates of marked accomplishment and potential to complete their training by travel. A year in Europe would offer the opportunity to observe the actual structures that they had studied in their Rice classes.

Watkin met his deadlines and, by coincidence, Milton McGinty, first winner of the traveling scholarship in architecture, was en route to Europe on a freighter shortly before the Watkin family departed New York City for Paris on the *S.S. Berengaria* in the third week of July 1928. Professor Watkin had carefully provided McGinty in advance with detailed information and suggestions for his nine-month stay in England, France, Spain, and Italy [1].

McGinty sailed for Liverpool on the *S.S. Cripple Creek*, at the leisurely pace of 10 knots an hour. After disembarking in Liverpool, McGinty stayed in England for the first two weeks of his trip, going from Liverpool to Oxford and London. He spent 10 days visiting notable cathedrals and monasteries at Liverpool, York, Manchester, Nottingham, Worcester, and Gloucester. He spent four days in Oxford, enthralled by the beauty of its ancient colleges, before continuing on to London for a week.

In the great English capital, young McGinty studied the illustrious examples of the best work of Britain's master architects. He went, of course, to Sir Christopher Wren's masterpiece, St. Paul's, as well as to Westminster, the Houses of Parliament, and the British Museum, but he also left time for Wren's Hampton Court, the Royal Gallery, the historic bridges over the Thames, St. Martin's in the Fields, and the Church of St. Bartholomew the Great. The latter was a remnant of a priory built by Augustinian monks in 1123 in north London's Smithfield District. Watkin had visited that priory in 1908 at the suggestion of Ralph Adams Cram, and Watkin, in turn, recommended it to McGinty.

After stopping at storied Canterbury, McGinty took the Channel ferry from Dover and arrived in Paris on August 9, 1928. While in Paris, he dined with the Watkin family, who were staying at the Hotel Crillon. McGinty and Watkin enjoyed seeing several Rice architec-

William Ward Watkin at the Rice Institute, mid-1912.

The first Rice Institute Board of Trustees, circa 1910. Captain James A. Baker, first Chairman of the Board, is shown on the far right.

Ralph Adams Cram,
William Ward Watkin's
first architectural mentor,
circa mid-1930.

Dr. Edgar Odell Lovett, first
president of the Rice Institute,
as he looked as he began his
presidency in 1912.

200

"The Gables" boarding house, Houston, 1910. Watkin and his mother stayed here on their arrival from Boston in 1910. Located on the south side of McKinney between Caroline and Austin Street, it was considered one of the finest boarding houses in Houston at the time. Photo from the collection of Max Roy, Rice Institute Class of 1930.

A group of boarders in front of The Gables, 1911. Mary Hancock Watkin, William Ward Watkin's mother, is shown in the lower right-hand corner of this photo.

Mary Hancock Watkin (in large hat) and Mrs. John T. (Julia) McCants on the boarding house porch, Houston, 1911.

Mrs. John T. (Julia) McCants, right, wife of one of the earliest faculty members at Rice, and Mary Hancock Watkin, left, Watkin's mother, in Houston, 1911.

The flooding encountered by Watkin when he arrived in Houston was much like this. Looking north on Main Street from the Harris Bayou bridge, April 16, 1912.

The first construction office for the Rice Institute, August 1910. Courtesy of the Rice University Archives.

*A gasoline tank is put into place for the Power Plant
in 1910, using one of the means available at that
time—manpower. Courtesy of the Rice
University Archives.*

*Excavation for the Mechanical Engineering
Building was begun in 1910 or early 1911.
Courtesy of the Rice University Archives.*

*In 1910, mules provided the
needed muscle to excavate
the foundations for the
Administration Building.
Courtesy of the Rice
University Archives.*

Conducting a test on the cloister slab,
south wing of the Administration Building,
May 6, 1911. William Ward Watkin is in
the coat and hat in the foreground.

Putting the marble columns of the
Administration Building in place, 1911.
Here you can see the first floor arcades.
Courtesy of the Rice University Archives.

Raising the marble columns of the Administration Building to
the second-floor level using a winch, 1911.

The marble capitals, finally in place at the third-floor level of the Administration Building, 1911. Courtesy of the Rice University Archives.

Watkin (in bowler hat) supervising the setting of the cornerstone of one of the original buildings. Courtesy of the Rice University Archives.

The construction site of one of the original Rice buildings being inspected by the meticulous Mr. Watkin, circa 1911.

*Watkin towering over Captain James A. Baker (at center), President
Lovett (to the right of Baker), and other members of the first board of
trustees as he supervises the laying of the cornerstone of the
Administration Building, March 2, 1911. Courtesy of the Rice
University Archives.*

*Watkin inspecting the construction of the
Residential Halls in early 1912. Note the
Campanile in the distance.*

The Administration Building, close to completion, in July 1912. Photo courtesy of the Rice University Library.

Several of the first trustees and faculty members of the Rice Institute standing in front of the new Administration Building, September 1912, just before the Institute officially opened. Left to right: W.F. Edwards, F.E. Johnson, T.L. Blayney, P.H. Arbuckle, E.O. Lovett, B.B. Rice, W.W. Watkin, E. Raphael, G.C. Evans, J.E. McAshan, J.T. McCants, J.A. Baker, H.A. Wilson. Photo courtesy of the Rice University Archives.

The Administration Building completed, October 1912. Courtesy of the Rice University Archives.

The main entrance gate of the Rice Institute as it looked on October 10, 1912, the day of the opening ceremonies for the Institute. The culvert on Main Street can be seen in the foreground. Courtesy of Rice University Library.

The Residential Hall completed, October 1912.

Opening day ceremonies, October 10, 1912.
Both of the main Houston newspapers carried
special supplements celebrating the opening of
the great, new institute. Captain Baker is seated
to the left of President Lovett, who is speaking.

Part of the Houston Chronicle's *Sunday, October 7,*
1912 special "Rice University [sic] supplement,"
celebrating the opening of this grand new Institute.

William Ward Watkin at his desk in his architectural office in the Scanlan Building, Houston, probably the early 1920s.

The Rice Institute in the 1920s. Oak trees have already been planted all around campus by Tony Martino.

The Administration and Physics buildings completed and the landscaping in place, circa 1919.

Another view of the Administration and Physics buildings, circa 1920.

Autry House, designed by Watkin in 1921, was the first formal student union building for Rice students. From The Campanile, *Vol. 36, 1949/50. Courtesy of the Rice University Archives.*

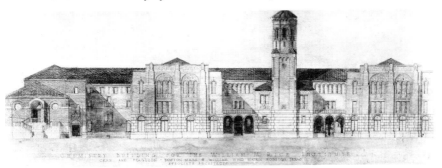

The elevation for the Chemistry Building, drawn by Watkin in 1923 or 1924. Watkin was able to locate "Brady-pink" brick to match the Administration Building.

The new Chemistry Building can be seen in the background of this photo of the Rice campus in 1925.

A stone carving of William Ward Watkin on one of the capitals of the Chemistry Building. The carving shows the long-legged Watkin with a T square, accepting the homage of his students.

Laying the cornerstone for Cohen House, 1927. Left to right: William Ward Watkin, George Cohen, Mrs. George Cohen, Mrs. Robert I. Cohen, B. B. Rice, Edgar Odell Lovett, unidentified, Robert I. Cohen, unidentified.

The Cohen House of the Rice Institute, designed by William Ward Watkin, opened in 1927.

Dr. Edgar Odell Lovett, first president of the Rice Institute, circa mid-1930. He would stay at Rice as president until 1946.

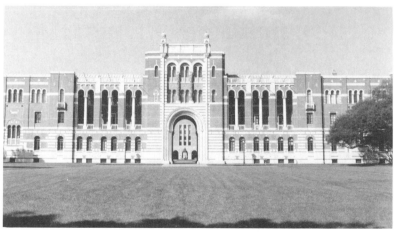

Rice University's Lovett Hall (formerly the Administration Building), in 1972. The library can now be seen through the sally port; there was originally an unobstructed view of the flat land beyond the Administration Building. Photo by Thomas C. LaVergne.

tural alumni in Paris that summer. Bill McVey was studying sculpture there at the time, and would remain in Paris until his return to Houston in the early 1930s. Other Rice architects abroad that summer included Francis Vesey and Claude Hooton, and the Rice group arranged to have a lively reunion in Paris.

II.

By July 1928, the months of preparation for the trip that Watkin had looked forward to for so long were finally at an end. The Rice Institute's first traveling scholar in architecture was on the high seas. The family residence at 5009 Caroline, completely remodeled in 1926, had been leased for a year to good friends, the DeWitt Dunns, with their daughters Bessie and Dorothy. The original New England front of the residence had been restyled, with graceful Southern Colonial columns added. The new design was reminiscent of a home in New Orleans (on St. Charles Avenue in the Garden District) that Mrs. Watkin had seen and admired. The antebellum style reflected her strong ties to the Old South.

Clarence Sanford and Stayton Nunn would be in charge of Watkin's private practice at the office in the Scanlan Building while Watkin was abroad. Jimmy Chillman had been approved by President Lovett as acting departmental chairman for the interim. John T. McCants was the new head of the Committee on Outdoor Sports. The Committee on Buildings and Grounds, which Dr. Lovett had decided to keep under Watkin's care indefinitely, would operate for a year under the supervision of the other committee members.

By July 1928, passports were in order, detailed travel arrangements and accommodations were confirmed, and the many bags were packed. Six trunks had been sent ahead, filled with enough clothes for an entire year. The sabbatical, so carefully planned and so long anticipated, began with the trip to the old Southern Pacific Depot in Houston, and then on to New York City and the *S.S. Berengaria.*

But what began in happiness was to end in tragedy.

From the busy port of Cherbourg, crowded with arriving and departing transatlantic liners, the Watkins went directly to Paris for a brief stay at the Hotel Crillon. Watkin had arranged for the children to stay with a Mademoiselle Marie Oelker, who opened her summer home to children for the summer. Her home was located in the Forest of Compiegne, about 40 miles northeast of Paris. They stayed in the little village of Vieux Moulin, population 300, near the restored castle of Pierrefonds and only 10 miles from the town of Compiegne. It was also near the battlefields of World War I. "Tante Marie" had taken in French children during the summer months for some time, but Ray, Rosemary, and Billy were the only American children she had taken into her home. Consequently, and by deliberate plan of their parents, the young Watkins were forced to learn to speak French in order to communicate with Mlle. Oelker's other guests.

For their entertainment, Watkin had also arranged to make it possible for his daughters, then 13 and 11, to rent horses from a stable in nearby Compiegne. Billy, still only eight, had not had riding lessons. The girls would ride through the Forest of Compiegne, through the imposing "allees," or formal avenues cut through the woods. The avenues had been cleared by French royalty, who had enjoyed hunting with horses and hounds there for centuries. One special day, Ray and Rosemary, accompanied by Tante Marie's nephew, had ridden from Compiegne to Vieux Moulin and back, a round-trip of 20 miles through the forest. It was a long-remembered and beautiful experience for the two young Texas girls.

For the Watkin children, the cool, dark Forest of Compiegne was their playground. Every afternoon they enjoyed "gouter" (a snack of bread and chocolate) in the woods. A favorite excursion for them was a brief train ride from Vieux Moulin to Compiegne, where they found wonderful patisserie shops filled with delicacies. It was a glorious summer, as they quickly learned French and formed close friendships with Tante Marie Oelker's other children.

Meanwhile, their parents were enjoying an extensive tour of France and Italy. Annie Ray did seem to tire easily, as she had on the 1925 trip when she had been forced to remain in Paris to regain her strength. Meanwhile, she now had some concern over the children, though she knew that they were safe with Mlle. Oelker and there was every indication that they were happy at Vieux Moulin. Nonetheless, she missed them. For one of the few times in her life, Annie Ray's children were not with her.

Watkin was happy to be at last beginning his long-awaited tour of Europe. He had written his good friend Edgar Odell Lovett the week before the departure from Houston, "to thank you for the kindness and enthusiasm with which you make it possible for me to take a sabbatical year."

In the letter, he shared his plans and ideas with Lovett. He felt there was a need for a further understanding of the "romance of medieval architecture," of its detail and symbolism and architectural quality. "Modern work in a medieval style," Watkin maintained, "has remained medieval—it has not been modern." He told Dr. Lovett in conclusion: "I feel that if the romance of medieval composition could be clearly understood, it is one of the most directly suggestive fields in which the modern imagination can create new and excellent buildings."

This thesis was central to Watkin's 1936 book, *The Church of Tomorrow*. He also wrote to President Lovett about a continuing fascination with the monastery of St. Luke's in Greece, which related to the design of the original buildings at Rice, and which he hoped to visit. This isolated complex of buildings in the prehistoric district of Phocis dated from the 10th century. A striking example of medieval architecture, it had been described in detail in 1901 in a treatise published in London under the sponsorship of Oxford University's Bodleian Library.

Watkin had used a copy of the treatise, replete with drawings, in preparing the presentation sketches of the general plan for Rice. Ralph Adams Cram and Bertram Grosvenor Goodhue had taken the sketches, his first major assignment at Cram, Goodhue & Ferguson, to Houston for a crucial meeting with the trustees on November 30, 1909. The meeting was instrumental in the granting of a contract to Cram, Goodhue & Ferguson.

The detailed study of St. Luke's had remained in Cram's personal library long after its drawings had influenced the architectural plan for the Rice Institute. Before leaving for his 1928–1929 sabbatical, Watkin wrote President Lovett of requesting Cram to send him the treatise on the Greek monastery—". . . the work . . . which I used to such a considerable extent in the first drawings of the Institute." Watkin felt that the monastic center at Stiris, near

Mount Parnassus and the Gulf of Corinth, ". . . still suggests an infinite freshness of further design possibilities in architecture on the Institute campus. We have not reached the maximum color and texture possibilities in this architecture."

What Watkin had in mind in 1928 was the possibility of a personal inspection of the remote St. Luke of Stiris while he was in Europe. This emerges at the end of the letter to Dr. Lovett:

"I am not anxious to try to get to that rather inaccessible portion of Greece . . . where the monastery of St. Luke lies, but I feel one of us ought to go there for first hand information concerning that remarkable piece of work, which is the direct background of the style in which the Institute buildings have been studied.

"If my confidence grows as to remote travel in rather uninviting foreign countries, I would like to try to get to this monastery at Stiris in Phocia. [In that event] it might be necessary for you to get either the American consul or some-body in Athens to arrange for safe and comfortable travel in that section of Greece for me."

Watkin would not be able to make the difficult journey to Stiris to study St. Luke's firsthand. In an excellent treatise (*Monograph 29*), Stephen Fox has pointed out the overall influence of the medieval Greek monastery on Rice's architecture, as well as specific instances of its style appearing on campus. For example, the arched openings in the cloister of the Physics Building were filled with marble lunettes "of plate tracery [stone open-work] adapted from . . . St. Luke of Stiris." Fox, a knowledgeable architectural critic, has written more generally on architecture at Rice of "a variety of ornamental bands and marble panels, column shafts and carved bands" in Rice buildings that "were appropriated" from drawings of the monastery.

Watkin was considerably influenced by St. Luke's in designing the striking ornamental patterns of the exterior of Cohen House, one of his favorite designs in 1927. Fox cites the multicolored cloisonné enamel base, the "bands and fields of ornamented masonry," and the voussoirs of brick and stone forming a wedge-shaped arch on the north elevation of the faculty club. These and other elements of the exterior were derived, according to the critic, from the medieval Greek monastery at Stiris.

The influence of St. Luke's lives on in another location at the Rice Institute, in the Byzantine style of lettering on the cornerstone of the Administration Building. Watkin was the only nontrustee present when President Lovett and the other six members of the governing board formally sealed the cornerstone in place on March 2, 1911.

III.

With the children safely entrusted to Mlle. Marie Oelker in the little village of Vieux Moulin, Mr. and Mrs. Watkin had the remainder of the summer and early fall to tour France and Italy. There were postcards to President Lovett from Avignon, deep in southern France near Marseille; from the "chateaux country" along the River Loire in north central France; and from St. Jean de Luz, in the ancient region of the Basques on the southwest border with Spain. It was a carefully planned itinerary that would combine relaxation and viewing some of France's most pleasant and interesting areas with the opportunity for Watkin to study timeless examples of the very best of European architecture.

Avignon, the seat of seven popes during a troubled era for the papacy, was a historic nucleus of memorable architecture and art. Watkin examined the 14th-century Palace of the Popes [2] and a 12th-century cathedral (Notre Dame des Doms) in detail, together with late medieval churches and chapels richly adorned with ancient frescoes.

Along the Loire, in an area centering upon Tours and nearby Blois, the Watkins enjoyed the masterworks of the chateaux country. There they saw the beautiful chateaux of Blois and Chambord. These two national treasures were especially interesting to Watkin. They illustrated the historic transition from the late Gothic at Blois to the French Renaissance style at Chambord [3].

Late in the summer of 1928, Mr. and Mrs. Watkin went on to St. Jean de Luz. Here they made the final arrangements to lease "Villa Lalo," a delightful residence overlooking the harbor and lovely beach of the little French town just south of Biarritz and a few miles from the Spanish border. The plan was for the entire family to return there, after Tante Marie, who would accompany them, had closed her home in the Forest of Compiegne for the winter. In the interim, the parents would complete their tour of France and go on to Italy. Christmas was to be spent in St. Moritz.

Unfortunately their plans were changed. Mrs. Watkin had become quite tired during the trip through France. In September, she suffered what seemed to be an inflammation of the liver or gall bladder. This improved somewhat, but it was decided to forego Italy for the time being. Mlle. Oelker came to St. Jean de Luz with the children from Vieux Moulin, and would remain with them until late November.

Watkin wrote Edgar Odell Lovett soon after they had settled in at "Villa Lalo":

"We are here in a charming villa, with good weather and beautiful surroundings. However, Mrs. Watkin continues to suffer from the liver attack of September and does not improve satisfactorily.

"I had hoped to avoid winter [by remaining] here, and to read and write, which I have found to be quite possible. But I also want to use this as headquarters for several Spanish journeys. As yet, I have not found Mrs. Watkin well enough to warrant my going. We are still hoping her strength will return, and after our winter here to go in February to Florence and back to France for early spring before coming home. The children all speak French constantly in the household.

"Should Mrs. Watkin continue depressed by failure to recover her strength, I feel I will be back by mid-year [of 1929]."

President Lovett was of course distressed to hear of Mrs. Watkin's illness. Earlier, he had sent news of the campus: "Chillman says you need have no anxiety about the conduct of the department. We are making preparations for the installation of our Phi Beta Kappa chapter with appropriate ceremonies." There was other news of colleagues, and of campus happenings. It was quite characteristic of Dr. Lovett that he said little about the chapter of Phi Beta Kappa, with his typical modesty [4].

Watkin continued to hope that his wife would regain her health in the beautiful surroundings of St. Jean de Luz. As the signs of autumn deepened in the nearby Pyrenees, however, her condition became an increasing concern. Watkin had written Dr. Lovett earlier of "trying to cover my Italian and Spanish journeys—[even if] hurriedly." Soon Mrs. Watkin's health overshadowed everything, although both parents continued to look forward to her recovery and to emphasize the well-being and happiness of the children.

Early in December 1928, as the first snow of the usually mild winter appeared atop the "Pic du Midi d'Ossau" (the 10,300-foot peak dominating the Basque region), he decided to take Annie Ray by overnight train to the American Hospital in the Paris suburb of Neuilly-sur-Seine. The hospital was recognized as among the best in Europe, with a staff of France's leading specialists.

Watkin then returned to the children in St. Jean de Luz. "I have come from Paris," Watkin wrote President Lovett from St. Jean de Luz on December 19, 1928, "where I left Mrs. Watkin at the American Hospital with excellent care—but with little progressing recovery." He mentioned again the "most charming" Villa Lalo, a "delightful house with abundance of room . . . a certain charming quiet and restfulness amid beautiful scenery and Old World life, where we had hoped to continue until March. I am here only for four days now to close the house, discharge the servants and pack up to go back to Paris with the children.

"We shall stay at the [Trianon Palace] Hotel in Versailles for some weeks, depending on Mrs. Watkin's progress—and in all likelihood be on our way home across the Atlantic in the month of January."

These were obviously difficult times. Annie Ray seemed to improve on occasion, only to "fall back further on succeeding days." She was comforted, of course, by the love and attention of husband and children, and by the presence of the dependable Tante Marie Oelker. Mlle. Oelker had become virtually indispensable, looking after the children, as a companion and interpreter, and always as a trusted friend.

Fortunately, Mrs. Albert Guerard, a close friend of the Watkin family, was in Paris at the time with her son, Albert Joseph, age 14. Her husband, Albert Leon Guerard, had been a distinguished member of the Rice faculty from 1913 until 1924, when he returned to Stanford University to continue a notable career as a French professor, scholar, writer, critic, and speaker. The Watkins and Guerards had lived as neighbors for almost a decade in Southmore, with lasting friendships developing between parents and children alike [5].

In the summer of 1928, Albert Leon Guerard, his wife, their son, Albert Joseph, and daughter, Therina, came to Paris, where Guerard was working on his book *L'Avenir de Paris*, a study of city planning that put him in contact with the leading architects and planners in the city. Professor Guerard had returned to Stanford when classes resumed in the fall of 1928, but Mrs. Guerard and Albert Joseph remained in Paris at the Victoria Palace Hotel. Her daughter Therina had been diagnosed as tubercular, and had been taken to a sanatorium in Davos, Switzerland [6]. They would visit her there on holidays, while Albert Joseph attended a French elysee in Paris. The three had a joyful reunion during the 1928 Christmas season.

Both Guerard and his wife had many friends and important connections in Paris. Mrs. Guerard and her son Albert Joseph (a friend and playmate of the Watkin children during his years in Houston) were naturally distressed to learn of Annie Ray's hospitalization, and anxious to do whatever they could to help their friends. A letter to Guerard at Stanford advised him of the situation, and his reply to Madame Guerard expressed not only his sympathy and concern, but included a number of suggestions as to introductions to Parisians who might be helpful. His wife already had a number of these under way as she did more and more to help.

Through the Guerards, an introduction to the mayor (prefect) of Paris, Monsieur Bouju, was quickly arranged, and an invitation to tea with Prefect and Mrs. Bouju in their private apartments at the Hotel-de-Ville (City Hall) followed. Watkin and his children, along with Tante Marie, Mrs. Guerard, and young Albert, attended. The Watkin children were much impressed, not only by the pomp and circumstance of the liveried guards at the prefect's door, but by Madame Bouju's elegant salons, complete with cages of ornamental singing canaries.

Watkin was granted access to several rare library collections soon after being received at the Hotel-de-Ville, collections he hoped to have time to concentrate on. Tickets to the Opera Comique, which Ray, Rosemary, and Billy particularly enjoyed, were sent to their hotel. Arrangements were made for their father to meet some of the leaders of French architecture.

On December 19, 1928, Watkin wrote President Lovett: ''I have just had sufficient start in getting notes together and in finding the open welcome in Paris which I would eventually need, to long to stay till next August. But as it is, I can only see three or four more weeks here, with all the daylight hours occupied in trips to the hospital and care of the children. I will simply have to hope for a later chance.''

Watkin did not want the children to know how critically ill their mother had become, in order that the more and more frequent visits to the hospital would be made in an aura of cheerfulness. Christmas had been spent in Versailles at the Trianon Palace Hotel. But in January, Watkin had rented a large apartment on the Avenue de Neuilly, in a private hotel only a few blocks from the American Hospital. Mrs. Watkin, quite homesick, talked constantly of wanting to return to Texas; this would not be possible unless she showed substantial improvement.

The children, obviously much distressed by their mother's illness, tried to remain cheerful during their frequent visits to the hospital. One of the best means of doing this was to tell Annie Ray of their various excursions around Paris with Madame Guerard, Albert Joseph, and Tante Marie. The Opera Comique combined enchanting music and drama. There they saw Bizet's *Carmen,* their first opera, and Maurice Ravel's *L'Enfant et les Sortileges* (described as ''an edifying and hilarious fantasy of a child''). The box seats, those of Mayor Bouju himself, were the best in the house, high above the orchestra. They also allowed whispered translations from Mrs. Guerard, explaining pantomime when necessary, without disturbing other viewers. At other times, there was skating for the children on the frozen ponds in the Bois de Boulogne while wearing snug winter coats from the Old England store. Yet what the young Watkins enjoyed most of all, never to forget, was seeing their first snow drifting down upon the gardens and rooftops of Paris.

Many years later, Albert Joseph Guerard wrote of his winter in Paris, recalling his romantic fantasies at age 14:

"The sacred love for me, against the terrible and tempting profane, was the girl [Rosemary Watkin] whose mother was dying in the American Hospital, gentle and lovely, perhaps twelve, with the soft Houston voice I had begun to forget. From the turmoil and guilt and excitement of Paris I would go to their apartment in Neuilly for tea, a green and placid district near the hospital. There was an older sister, she beautiful too, and a younger brother. We had excursions to the Bois de Boulogne: a row on the lake, and a ride on the little train with its open cars threading the woods from the Porte Maillot to the zoo. We saw a few last horse-drawn carriages and footmen on the Avenue du Bois and Avenue des Acacias whose vanishing Proust lamented.

"The distraught father, a rather austere personage for me, was not much in evidence."

During those months in Paris, the Watkins were grateful for the presence of Claude Hooton, one of Watkin's 1927 graduates in architecture who was working on his master's degree. Hooton would succeed Milton McGinty as the second traveling scholar the next year. This personable young architect would later join the faculty at Rice. While in Paris, he was helpful to Professor Watkin in arranging appointments, and also in library research. He also served as a tutor of young Billy Watkin, aged 9. It was decided that he would be tutored in order to not drop behind his class at Kinkaid.

On the other hand, Ray and Rosemary were somewhat advanced academically for their age group at Kinkaid, and so it was decided that they would simply not attempt to keep up their normal school-work for the year.

Annie Ray Watkin continued to have the very best in medical attention and care. Edgar Odell Lovett, who had many friends at Johns Hopkins in Baltimore, had been in contact with specialists at that renowned medical and training center. President Lovett suggested that, if feasible, Mrs. Watkin be brought to Johns Hopkins Hospital for consultation and treatment.

It so happened that Dr. Massod, the French specialist in charge of Mrs. Watkin's case, was scheduled to sail for Baltimore in mid-January, to deliver a series of lectures at Johns Hopkins. Watkin replied to President Lovett that "if no further improvement occurs, I am tempted to sail on [the same] boat [in order] to have his service amid the trials of [a] midwinter Atlantic passage." But this was not possible.

Watkin continued to leave no stone unturned in the hope of getting his wife on the road to recovery. At the American embassy in Paris, he sought the help of the U.S. ambassador, Myron T. Herrick. Herrick was able to obtain the services of Dr. Charles de Martel, one of France's outstanding surgeons, well known internationally.

Watkin wrote President Lovett on January 16, 1929, of later developments in the case. Another specialist had concluded after a series of X-rays that Mrs. Watkin did not, as feared, require surgery for the removal of gallstones. The specialist "feels [that] in one month's time he can have her quite well enough to travel home in safety and comfort. I hope we are not too optimistic and we can all be safely back in February. I will be most glad to be there."

As January turned into Paris' typical gray and overcast February, it became apparent that Watkin's optimism had indeed been misplaced. Annie Ray had become steadily weaker, in spite of the very best medical attention available. An English nurse, devoted to her patient, had continued to provide excellent care in the tradition of the American Hospital.

Dr. de Martel saw that the only resort was major surgery, on a patient with little remaining strength. In an era when modern techniques of blood transfusion had not yet been developed, there were no really effective emergency procedures to counter weakness during surgery. Annie Ray Watkin knew that the operation had little chance of success. She wanted that chance, nevertheless, and the opportunity to return home—to be back in Texas with her dear husband and children.

The surgery was scheduled for the very end of February 1929. A few days before, Annie Ray wrote a very special letter to Ray, her firstborn:

THE AMERICAN HOSPITAL OF PARIS 63 Boulevard Victor Hugo Neuilly Sur-Seine Telephone: Adresse Telegraphique CARNOT 51-32, AMHOSPMA 51-32-33-34-35-36, Neuilly-Sue-Seine

My dear little girl:

I am sick and may not get well so I want to write you a note. The hardest part of leaving is in the thought of being separated from Daddy and my dear children. But we must have faith in God's promises and know we will meet again.

You have always been dear and sweet as well as conscientious in your studies. I hope you will continue to be interested in your school work as a good education means so much to a woman. If you have the physical strength I hope you will go to college. Always remember that your health comes first, as there is not much in life without it. While you are not sick, you are not very strong, and can't do the foolish things lots of stronger girls can.

Be a good Christian woman, kind and thoughtful of others— always be modest and never do anything you would not want to tell Mother. Take good care of Daddy and remember he is your best friend. You can ask him anything and tell him anything. And dear do help with your brother and sister as much as you can. Be patient with them and set them a good example. They both have sweet lovable dispositions and can be managed only with kindness and reason. Closeness too and great love for your brother and sister will give you much happiness in life which you would not get otherwise. My sister was so much pleasure to me and I always regretted I could not get closer to my brother. He always seemed so much older than I.

Be kind and considerate of your grandmother and remember old people are set in their ways. Always try to do what is right in the very best way you can and you will be a wonderful woman, as you have a fine mind. Daddy is the finest of men and try to do what he says even if you don't always understand the reason. I love you very, very much, dear, and remember if you ever have any children and it seems hard, how much they will mean to you afterward. You will be repaid for your suffering a hundredfold. My children mean everything to me. They make

life very happy indeed. Again I want to tell you much I love you
my baby.

(P.S.): I will write Sis and Sonny soon.

Mother

Dr. de Martel found what he had feared, soon after the operation
began at the American Hospital: a malignant tumor of the pancreas.
Mrs. Watkin died less than a week later, on March 2, 1929, Texas
Independence Day.

One of the first messages of sympathy came from Edgar Odell
Lovett, who received the sad news by cable: "Trustees, faculty and
students join in sincerest sympathy. Please cable plans." A small
private funeral was held for Annie Ray in the chapel of Paris'
beautiful Episcopalian American Cathedral. Mrs. Guerard and Albert Joseph were there with Claude Hooton and Mlle. Oelker.
Representatives of Ambassador Herrick and doctors and nurses of the
American Hospital also attended. Friends also included the elderly
Mr. and Mrs. Harvey Twining of the British tea firm, who had been
fellow guests at the Hotel Argencon; as well as the Wormser family,
a Paris banking family who had a summer home in Compiegne.
There the Watkin children had become good friends of the son Oliver,
16, and daughter Nanette, 12.

The Guerards moved into the Hotel Argencon with the Watkins for
the week required to make the necessary arrangements to return
home to Texas. There was plenty of room at the Argencon, with its
spacious apartments. The only other guests in the hotel were Mr. and
Mrs. Harvey Twining.

Stunned with grief, and the realization that he now had the sole
responsibility for three children of ages 13, 11, and 9 thousands of
miles from home, Watkin was near exhaustion. He asked Mlle. Oelker
if she would come to Houston for a time to help with the children.
Tante Marie wanted to go. She had become very fond of the girls and
of Billy, and knew that she could help their father. The children liked
her, and Mrs. Guerard had recommended faraway Houston without
endorsing the climate. But at her age, Mlle. Oelker explained, it would
be too difficult to be "transplanted." She would either return to the

Forest of Compiegne, with her French youngsters for the summer, or she would return to Italy to live with her sister in Arona [7].

When it was clear that Mlle. Oelker would not return with the Watkins to Houston, Watkin next turned to the British nurse who had attended Annie Ray in the hospital. She also saw the need for someone to help with the children during the difficult passage across the Atlantic in late winter. They were likable youngsters, and had suffered a tragic loss. Further, the nurse had developed an intense curiosity to see Texas. She agreed to go to Houston with the family. Claude Hooton also agreed to return on the ship with them.

They sailed from Le Havre, the busy port on the Bay of the Seine, with hastily arranged accommodations on the *S.S. Paris*. Mrs. Watkin's body was aboard. The Atlantic in early March was cold, icy, and racked with storms, which meant a rough and uncomfortable voyage. Watkin, heartbroken and totally exhausted, fell seriously ill with pneumonia during the voyage. The family felt that the English nurse probably saved his life with her skillful care and 24-hour attention.

On arrival in New York City, Watkin was taken from the ship to the Lincoln Hotel in a wheelchair. An attending physician ruled against the idea of his continuing to Texas until he had regained his strength. Convalescence would be a slow process of several weeks. It would be well into April before he and the children, the nurse, and Claude Hooton could continue on to Houston.

Annie Ray Watkin's funeral in Houston was held March 16, without her husband and children, with interment in the family vault at Forest Park Mausoleum. President Lovett sent this telegram to the Lincoln Hotel after the final ceremony: "We have just come from Forest Park. Mrs. Lovett, Adelaide, Captain Baker and I thought everything most appropriate and impressive. I told your mother that I shall be seeing you Monday [in New York City]. Many friends and practically all the trustees and faculty present. Flowers altogether beautiful and weather perfect."

IV.

In mid-April 1929, William Ward Watkin was finally able to return to 5009 Caroline. He was still convalescing, but was steadily regaining his strength. Nine months had gone by since he and Annie Ray and children boarded the train for New York City with such anticipation.

As soon as possible, Watkin took the children to the Forest Park Cemetery to visit Annie Ray's last resting place. They would return often, on days that had meant much to her and to the family. Watkin now confronted his many new responsibilities, first of all Ray, Rosemary, and Billy. Their mother would have wanted her beloved husband and children to get on with their lives. And she would have approved completely of one of her husband's very first decisions: that his mother, Grandmother Watkin, would come to live with the Watkins at 5009 Caroline. She enjoyed her son and grandchildren, and they enjoyed her. She gave a sense of stability to the family.

The new term at Kinkaid would not begin until fall, but the three children began to review the textbooks and outside reading assignments that they had missed while away. The two girls had missed an entire academic year while in Europe. Billy, however, tutored by Claude Hooton, remained in normal progression. All three of the young Watkins quickly picked up again with their friendships. There was so much to tell their classmates of their travels, from their rides through the Forest of Compiegne to having high tea with the mayor of Paris. Billy told of adding to his stamp collection at the Marche des Timbres in the Champs d' Elysee, and of seeing his first snow in Paris.

President Lovett knew that Watkin, anxious to return to his responsibilities at Rice, might be slow in recovering fully from his bout with pneumonia. He urged moderation, and a gradual return to his duties. However, by September, Watkin was back at his office in the Department of Architecture, reviewing the 1928–1929 academic year with Jimmy Chillman and his other colleagues, asking about individual students, and planning for the year ahead.

Watkin brought back to the architectural faculty and students a firsthand report on Milton McGinty and his travels in Europe. McGinty was now en route to Paris from Florence, where he had been from December through mid-March of 1929 [8]. Professor Watkin had referred to Florence as the center of "new architectural expression that led the world in the 15th century."

Picking up again as chairman of the Committee on Buildings and Grounds, Watkin arranged a meeting with Dr. Lovett, primarily to pursue a recommendation for a formal plan of maintenance of all campus buildings. He had sent Dr. Lovett such a plan, with accompanying budget, before leaving for Europe. He pointed out the need now for regularly scheduled maintenance of the original physical plant as it neared its twentieth anniversary. Watkin also arranged for a conference on the grounds with Tony Martino, the head gardener who had just returned from Europe himself, on a vacation in Sicily and Italy followed by a tour of France.

Understandably, Martino and his longtime boss "Mr. Wat" found problems needing attention. The omnipresent John T. McCants, Watkin's dependable friend and colleague, and Martino's hard-working crew had continued the excellent care of the grounds during the interim. Nevertheless, the head gardener's expert eye spotted things to be done.

The huge azalea bushes that burst into bloom for the annual May Fete required extra feeding. Martino's fragrant cape jasmine hedges also needed attention. There were limbs to be pruned from the live oaks, coming into their dominant grace and beauty after twenty years.

Chairman Watkin had kept in touch with his department during his nine-month absence through correspondence with President Lovett and with capable Jimmy Chillman. Soon after returning to the campus he had several conferences with Chillman. Watkin found that most minor problems had resolved themselves. There had been complaints about architectural students singing and "carrying on" ("loudly, most of these times") during chemistry lectures in adjoining areas of the Chemistry Building. The cross-complaint was that "noxious fumes" from the chemistry laboratories were often a problem in much of the second-floor area allotted to the Department of Architecture. The matter was satisfactorily resolved by a friendly discussion between Watkin and his good friend Harry Boyer Weiser, chairman of the Chemistry Department, who was also the newly appointed dean of the Rice Institute.

Watkin now returned to teaching his fourth- and fifth-year students. As the department continued to mature, a record total of eleven were awarded the fifth-year degree of bachelor of science in architecture. A new matter arose involving Charles L. Browne, a key member of the Rice Institute architectural faculty and a young graduate of Paris' Ecole des Beaux Arts who had been in poor health for more than a year. His condition had been aggravated by injuries sustained in an automobile accident during Watkin's absence in Europe.

Browne, an instructor in construction techniques, had joined the faculty in 1920. An experienced and effective teacher, Browne, however, had suffered from illness which he blamed on the Houston climate.

Complicating the situation further, Browne had been offered a post at Clemson in South Carolina, which had an excellent architectural program. Watkin dealt with this problem promptly. After several meetings with Browne, he began a quiet canvass of available replacements, while marshalling other facts for a report to President Lovett.

Fortunately, the situation changed somewhat in the late summer of 1929. With a new academic year rapidly approaching, Browne decided not to go to Clemson, after discovering that the climate there was similar to Houston's. But, reflecting a department accustomed to openness and frankness, he told Watkin that he would continue to seek another position, this at a university "in a higher and cooler climate."

Chairman Watkin duly reported the entire matter, including several related recommendations, to President Lovett in a letter of August 15, 1929. "The problem of [finding] a thoroughly fitted man in construction with a real sense of its modern significance toward design," he wrote, "is a difficult and costly one. The only man I have located as being more able than Browne is at Ann Arbor [University of Michigan], and wants $4800 [for a nine-month academic year]." This was well above Charles Browne's salary, at a time when Rice was beginning to face the reality of the depression and of a reduction in teaching budgets.

Watkin proposed a resolution that would be fair to everyone concerned, including Rice Institute and its architectural students. Two earlier graduates in architecture at Rice would be benefited.

First of all, Charles Browne would be given a modest salary increase in recognition of the market for specialists in construction techniques. Further, Stayton Nunn would be added to faculty and awarded a fellowship as a teaching assistant, assigned to teaching one of the classes in construction. Nunn, a fifth-year graduate at Rice in 1922, was a personable young architect who had spent most of his seven years in practice in Watkin's private office in the Scanlan Building. As noted, he and Clarence Sanford, of the Rice Institute class of 1919, had been in charge of the office during Watkin's absence in Europe.

Stayton Nunn had decided to open his own practice. He was also interested in teaching—his aptitude for it had impressed Watkin—and he could use the $750 stipend given teaching fellows at Rice. In addition to Nunn's many other qualities, Watkin was quick to note his ". . . most unusually complete construction experience." He felt that the young architect ". . . needs only . . . adjustment of his practical experience to sound preparation of the required lecture(s) . . ."

Charles L. Browne remained and was now content as a result of his increase in salary and the help from Stayton Nunn. Watkin was correct in his assessment of Nunn's potential as a teacher. In spite of the growth of his private practice, Stayton joined the regular Rice faculty in the early 1930s, and taught construction there for the next two decades.

Watkin, always looking for opportunities for his graduates, concluded the Browne dilemma by alerting C.A. Johnson, a 1927 graduate, to the vacancy at Clemson. Johnson had been an able student who had also shown an interest in teaching. Recommended by Watkin, C.A. was named to a beginning position at Clemson. However, he greatly missed Texas, and soon returned from Clemson for an appointment at Texas A&M.

As the 1929–1930 academic year began, Watkin gained steadily in health and energy and turned to other matters. In a long and thoughtful letter to President Lovett, Watkin renewed his proposal from the Committee on Buildings and Grounds for a permanent campuswide plan of maintenance and depreciation, adequately financed. Watkin had told Lovett that he had been greatly impressed with the policies of the Ministry of Art of the French Government, as applied to the careful preservation of the historic French buildings for active daily use and ". . . not as antiques preserved for tourists." Fortunately, portions of Watkin's proposal were finally adopted at Rice to protect the "architectural quality, soundness and usefulness for effective service" of a splendid physical plant.

Watkin next became busy with the project to commission and install an appropriate statue of William Marsh Rice in a central location on campus, as a memorial to the founder. As early as 1926, the other trustees had asked Dr. Lovett to begin the search for a sculptor who could bring forth from stone the unique characteristics of William Marsh Rice. Lovett consulted Ralph Adams Cram after preliminary discussions with Watkin. Both were well aware of Cram's knowledge of the work of many leading American sculptors.

Cram had retained the English master sculptor, John Angel, for the great, still-unfinished Cathedral of St. John the Divine in New York City. Cram had written Dr. Lovett on December 15, 1926, of Angel's eight figures in the baptistery of St. John the Divine: ". . . in these he demonstrates not only brilliant artistic ability, but also an absolutely unique power of characterization. I know of no man who puts so much vitality and personality into his work . . ."

John Angel was born in 1811, a native of Newton Abbot, the large town just northeast of Torquay on Devonshire's Lyme Bay. He entered art school at age fifteen, graduating from Lambeth School, a center for instruction in the arts near London's great galleries. The gold medal of the Royal Academy won Angel his first wide recognition in 1911. Commissions for memorials in Exeter to the British who fell in World War I brought him increasing attention. Soon other commissions, many in the United States, followed.

Within weeks after being consulted in the matter, Cram had decided to recommend John Angel for the statue of William Marsh Rice. He wrote President Lovett again on January 10, 1927:

"I have been considering with extreme care the question of the sculptor for the proposed statue of the founder at Rice Institute. I need hardly remind you that this is a very important matter, almost focal in the whole campus. In order to obtain something that will be not only significant, but noble and dignified, it is necessary to have a sculptor with peculiar ability, and one who has demonstrated his ability through work he already has done. . . . We have, therefore, been carefully scrutinizing the whole field. . . . As a result . . . I am prepared definitely to recommend to you as first choice, Mr. John Angel. . . . I am entirely persuaded, through the experience that we have had with Mr. Angel.''

Early in 1927, it was understood that the commission would be awarded to John Angel. However, there were understandable delays in negotiating a number of important details. These included the size and dimensions of the sculpture and of the pedestal on which it was to be installed, the exact materials to be used, the precise location on campus, whether the subject should be shown standing or seated, and the amount of Angel's fee. Other questions were to arise, most of them less significant.

One meaningful matter had been decided as early as 1922. The governing board had appointed a committee of the founder's two trustee-nephews (William Marsh Rice II and Benjamin Botts Rice) and President Lovett. They were charged with recommending an appropriate repository for the founder's ashes, kept in the trustees' vault since his death in 1900. The committee decision was to place the ashes in a campus monument surmounted by an appropriate statue of William Marsh Rice.

Six years had passed before William Marsh Rice II, after several meetings with Angel in New York City, told the sculptor to ''go ahead with it.'' A formal letter of authorization was issued July 26, 1928. Now what Cram correctly described as the ''focal point'' of that campus was to be the site of a new installation. This had to fit well into the master plan on which he and Watkin had worked for years to bring to reality.

The firm of Cram & Ferguson, with Watkin as their representative, was retained to work with John Angel on the memorial to the founder, and through Watkin with President Lovett and the governing board. Cram & Ferguson was specifically assigned the task of designing a rectangular pedestal seven feet in height, with appropriate shields and inscriptions. The four- to five-foot bronze statue of the founder would be placed on the pedestal, with his ashes in a repository inside the structure.

One of Watkin's first assignments was to help obtain the specially quarried Texas granite for the seven-foot base. It was chosen to blend with the pink granite bought for the columns of the Administration Building almost two decades earlier. After discussion, it was decided to place the monument in the exact middle of the academic quadrangle, facing the sally port of what is now Lovett Hall. The location pleased both Cram and Watkin, who had recommended it to President Lovett.

William Marsh Rice II, his brother Benjamin Botts Rice, and Dr. Lovett, comprising the original committee dating back to 1922, desired a seated rather than a standing figure for the statue. The recommendation was unanimously approved by the trustees, and by Angel. There is no record of the exact fee paid John Angel. It is thought to have ranged between $60,000 and $75,000. Four years would elapse between 1926, when the governing board asked President Lovett to begin the search for a distinguished sculptor, and the date of dedication of the memorial at Commencement on June 8, 1930. During the intervening time, Watkin and John Angel had become good friends.

Soon after signing the contract with Rice Institute, Angel asked Ralph Adams Cram for help in finding as much information as possible concerning William Marsh Rice. Cram referred him to Watkin. The sculptor explained to Watkin his need to understand his subject—to comprehend his essential traits, motivational patterns, and basic personality. Watkin was soon assembling copies of available letters, publications, records, and other information concerning the founder, with the approval and assistance of his nephews and President Lovett. The material was sent on to John Angel.

John Angel continued his friendship with Watkin. As late as 1951, the last Christmas before Watkin's death, Angel was still sending him his distinctive Christmas cards, featuring beautifully engraved pictures of his latest works. Among these sculptures were that of Mary and the Christ Child, for the chapel of Chatham Hall School in Virginia; a quite different St. Joan of Arc and a striking angel, both for St. John the Divine Cathedral; and one of St. Anne, mother of the Blessed Virgin, "made for the joy of doing it, for myself." There was always a personal note, and often a longer letter, included with the cards.

Ralph Adams Cram would look back on the project of William Marsh Rice's memorial with particular pleasure. The long-deserved tribute to the founder had further reinforced the master plan of the Rice Institute, with its very long vistas and emphasis upon the original academic quadrangle. The seven-foot base designed by Cram placed the shield of the Rice Institute on the front facing the Administration Building, with the dates of the founder's recorded birth and death, and a slightly edited line from Virgil: "Salve aeternum, aeternumque salve" (Hail forever and forever hail).

The shield and motto of Massachusetts (William Marsh Rice's native state) was placed on the left side of the base. On the right side was the shield of Texas, and a curious Latin expression once chosen as the motto of the founder's adopted state: "Imperium in imperio" (An empire within an empire).

President Lovett and the other trustees were so pleased with the project that they invited Ralph Adams Cram to deliver the commencement address on June 9, 1930, at the time of the memorial's dedication. The internationally renowned architect spoke eloquently of the interrelationships between universities and his own profession, and of the need to protect and advance cultural values and tradition. He was handsomely attired in his honorary doctoral robes from the Massachusetts Institute of Technology. Watkin was delighted to have a chance to entertain and visit with his former mentor again in Houston after so many years.

As Watkin joined his colleagues for the seventeenth commencement procession winding its way through Tony Martino's fragrant cape jasmine blooms, he was struck by the major changes in the faculty during the past decade. The faculty had grown in size to seventy-five, a tremendous increase from the original nine (including President Lovett) who began instruction on September 23, 1912.

Four members of that 1912 faculty remained: Dr. Lovett, the original professor of mathematics whose presidential duties understandably left him no time for teaching; Harold Albert Wilson, the eminent physicist from Cambridge University's Cavendish Laboratory; Griffith Conrad Evans, the Harvard-trained mathematician who would soon become a legendary departmental chairman at the University of California in Berkeley; and Watkin himself.

Dr. Wilson had from the first been one of Rice's most eminent professors. He had temporarily left Rice in 1924, to President Lovett's deep dismay, to accept the Kelvin Professorship at the University of Glasgow. Once established in Glasgow, however, Dr. Wilson discovered some major problems. There was a great deal of equipment in the laboratories, but much of it was clearly outdated, with minimum budgets for new purchases. The pension he would receive upon retirement was "absurdly small."

Word of this came back soon to President Lovett, especially grieved to have lost Dr. Wilson. Lovett had also recently lost Percy John Daniell, another faculty member and a gifted mathematician who had led his class at Cambridge as "senior wrangler." Daniell had returned to England to accept a professorship at the University of Sheffield. Dr. Lovett scheduled a trip to Europe early in 1925, and went to Glasgow to visit with Mr. and Mrs. Wilson. He found that his former colleague was indeed dissatisfied at his new post in Scotland.

President Lovett had already worked out a new offer for Dr. Wilson. This included a substantial salary increase, and arrangements for a part-time consultantship at Humble Oil & Refining. Both of these positions included pensions well above the retirement plan available at the University of Glasgow. The happy result of this offer was that the Harold Albert Wilsons and their four children were back in Houston when the 1925–1926 academic year began at Rice Institute in late September.

There had been a number of other distinguished appointments to the faculty made during the earliest years, and virtually all of these men were still at the Institute in 1930. Among them were Harry Boyer Weiser, a distinguished colloid chemist with marked ability as an administrator; Robert G. Caldwell, historian and dean of the faculty; Stockton Axson, President Woodrow Wilson's brother-in-law and world authority on Shakespeare; Radoslav Andrea Tsanoff, the philosopher from Cornell; Edgar Altenburg, geneticist, and Asa Chandler, parasitologist, in biology; Joseph H. Pound, in engineering; and William C. Graustein, a mathematician who would leave the Institute to become chairman of the department at Harvard.

Asa Chandler, some of whose all-encompassing courses in parasitology were said to exempt Rice pre-medical students from similar instruction at a number of medical schools, had left the campus for several years, but returned in 1926. He had been in Calcutta, as head of the only research institute devoted solely to helminthology (the study of intestinal parasites), one of the major problems in tropical medicine. Another ascending star of the Rice faculty in the 1920s had not returned after leaving. This was Lindsey Blayney, the language expert. He had come back to Rice after a distinguished record as a senior liaison officer in World War I, but was later named president of what is now Texas Women's University, in Denton. As mentioned, Albert Leon Guerard, the noted French scholar and writer, had left Rice in 1924 to return to Stanford University.

V.

After a full academic year of 1929–1930, Watkin had regained his physical health. He wrote Edgar Odell Lovett in revealing words, as the first academic year of the 1930s began: "My recent bereavement together with my illness have led me to reduce and concentrate my work. I desire simply to devote my time to the inspiring work with my students, and to a very limited but selective practice which will emphasize creative opportunity, and in this manner afford me a much larger portion of my time to devote to my children." Watkin knew instinctively the basic importance of his own presence and participation in the daily lives of children.

As co-executor of his wife's estate with the Second National Bank, Watkin was in regular contact with his good friend, Hudson Ellis, trust officer of the bank. Annie Ray's estate had been invested in stocks, Houston real estate, and land elsewhere in Texas. Unfortunately, Ellis died in the summer of 1929, four months after Mrs. Watkin's death, complicating matters. Then came, on October 29, 1929, the devastating crash of the New York stock market.

The unprecedented prosperity of the 1920s soon began to fade. Building permits, both residential and commercial, were in eclipse. Watkin closed his office in the Scanlan Building, although he would continue to practice as associate architect or consultant. The historic crash of the New York Stock Exchange wiped out the then astronomical sum of $50 billion in stocks and bonds in the United States, and triggered the Great Depression.

Yet not a single Houston bank would fail. This was largely due to heroic efforts of Jesse Jones extending over one long historic weekend. A series of almost nonstop meetings in his downtown office resulted in what the financial tycoon later described as "the strong helping the weak, plus some necessary mergers and emergency loans."

There were concomitant changes in the Watkin household. By 1931, it was no longer possible to keep Tom, the faithful chauffeur, or Mittie the maid. The cook, Maggie, remained, and Ray and Rosemary learned to prepare meals under her tutelage. They also became adept at sewing, at housekeeping tasks, and, most importantly, at driving the car.

Grandmother Mary Matilda Hancock Watkin was a great asset to her son and the family. The petite, quiet, but ever-alert little woman was seemingly more a part of the Victorian England of her forebears than of 1930 Houston, content to watch over her son and grandchildren and their busy lives. It was clear that she was happiest at home, simply being there with her family. She often entertained her granddaughter, Ray, with stories of the quite different and far more sheltered existence of her childhood in Danville.

Her life in a small Pennsylvania city almost 1,500 miles away and two generations ago was more like life on distant Mars to the grandchildren. Ray later realized that her lifelong interest in the family genealogy and history was heightened by the stories and recollections of her Grandmother Watkin.

As the oldest of the Watkin children, Ray was the first to learn to drive. She was soon driving the family Lincoln, which had not yet been replaced by a smaller car [9]. Her father had given up driving after failing to master the changes of the Model T Ford a decade earlier. Grandmother Watkin had never learned to drive a car.

A frequent topic for discussion at 5609 Caroline was the subject of education, which Watkin continued to spell with a capital "E." He made it perfectly clear to the children that education should be their first priority until they had graduated from college. This meant to Watkin a preference for private schools, which, in his judgment, provided the best education.

This emphasis on education meant that their report cards were analyzed in detail and discussed with their father. If one of the children began falling behind in a specific subject, Watkin saw to it that coaching was readily available to them.

In September 1929, Ray, Rosemary, and Billy had returned to Kinkaid. The private school was already enlarging its relatively new physical plant on Richmond Avenue. Enrollment and academic standing had grown steadily under Margaret Hunter Kinkaid's firm yet visionary leadership, strengthened by a small governing board of community leaders. Among the nucleus of this group had been R.L. Blaffer of Humble Oil & Refining, James A. Baker of Baker & Botts, Captain Baker's daughter, Alice Baker Jones, and Palmer Hutcheson.

Ray graduated from Kinkaid in the tenth grade in June 1930 and in September entered Chatham Hall, an Episcopal preparatory school in Chatham, Virginia, near the North Carolina border. Rosemary and Billy, two and four years behind their older sister, remained at Kinkaid until their graduations in 1932 and 1934. Ray, who was the first Houston girl to attend Chatham Hall, majored in American history, which at Chatham Hall meant largely the history of Virginia.

VI.

Watkin now returned to the challenges at the Rice Institute. Enrollment in the Department of Architecture had continued to grow steadily in the 1920s, but the class of 1929–1930 was definitely smaller in number as a direct result of the economic downturn. In Houston, there was a marked reduction in new construction. As a result, there were only two fifth-year graduates in 1934: T.B. Douty and Lavone Dickensheets (Mrs. Mark Edwin Andrews).

However, due in part to Professor Watkin's close attention to the economic problems of his students, enrollment began to rebound strongly by the fall of 1930. The next two classes in due course produced a new record of nine fifth-year graduates. Among them were architects who would later attain the higher levels of their profession: Nolan Barrick '35, Robroy Carroll '34, Frank Dill '34, C.G. Elliott, Jr., '35, Graham Jackson '35, Seth I. Morris '35, and Talbott Wilson '34.

Looking back over that decade, there had been many instances of Watkin's concern for helping his students secure financial aid when necessary. Milton McGinty, now age 84 after a successful career in Houston, was a prototype of two generations of architects who received aid and personal counseling from Watkin while at Rice. McGinty relates his own experience during the 1927–1928 academic year. He had received a low grade in a fundamental course in the methods of construction from Charles L. Browne, the junior member of the faculty. This placed him on academic probation. Quite discouraged, McGinty sought the advice of Professor Watkin, who was aware of McGinty's overall ability, including his "ability to express conceptions of architectural form." The fifth-year student was a "townie," residing at home and on a limited budget. He and his nondormitory classmates sometimes found it expedient to sleep in the drafting room three or four nights in a row in order to complete a complicated "charette" (assigned problem) on time. They lived on sandwiches from "The Gables," Gaylord Johnson's drugstore on Main Street. But McGinty's solutions were always on time.

Just as had many students, McGinty had perceived "Mr. Watkin" as a dignified, highly competent but rather austere and aloof teacher. However, once he managed to overcome his reluctance to request Watkin's advice, he found that his professor was a warm, understanding, and helpful person.

Professor Watkin was a good listener. Over the years, he had made it his business to know his students, especially as they advanced to the fourth and fifth years of their curriculum. He understood Milton McGinty's concern over his poor grade in construction, as well as his problem of a lack of income. Watkin listened carefully as McGinty explained his difficulties and asked for help. He then told McGinty he had faith in him and in his ability, and that he would help.

Watkin recommended a course in either history, literature, or a foreign language to relieve Milton's heavy emphasis upon construction and laboratory projects, and for financial aid offered him a part-time job at $50 a month as librarian for the Department of Architecture. Finally, he encouraged McGinty to enter the first competition for the new traveling scholarship, which had just been announced.

McGinty still remembers, more than 60 years later, how pleased he was that the "man we all looked up to so much had said that he had *faith in me*." He responded by completing the fifth-year program without difficulty, winning the traveling scholarship, and going on to an auspicious career in architecture. This would later include working in practice together with his former professor.

Another instance of the quiet and seemingly austere Watkin's concern for his students was the case of C.A. Johnson, Class of 1925. Today C.A. is an active octogenarian and architectural alumnus living in Houston. He tells the story of how he worked his way through college by part-time campus jobs secured for him by Professor Watkin, while carrying a heavy classroom load. He remembers working with Stayton Nunn, Class of 1922, on the committee for the first Archi-Arts Ball at the Autry House in 1922 as a freshman. He also took an active interest in campuswide activities, as did many of the architectural students.

When Johnson needed a $250 advance from the student loan fund to see him through his fifth year, he applied to Bursar John T. McCants. The ever-cautious McCants usually made loans of no more than $25 to $50, but this time a loan of $250 was approved for Johnson after a positive word from Watkin. Watkin recommended C.A. as a hard-working, able, and deserving young man. He had recently sent one of Johnson's drawings to an international competition at the School of Fine Arts in Buenos Aires, where it had won second prize and a handsome medal. After graduation, as noted, C.A. became an instructor in architecture at Texas A&M, on Watkin's recommendation.

Across the intervening years, Johnson still remembers how hard he had to work to pay back the $250 student loan, and Watkin's kindness. Later, as their friendship grew, there were also the rounds of golf with his former mentor during summer vacations ("he had a good short game around the greens with that favorite 'mashie' of his"). C.A. also remembers the many rubbers of bridge they later enjoyed together.

Francis Vesey of the Class of 1929 also told many interesting stories about the wide variety of part-time campus jobs Mr. Watkin had found for him as he worked his way through college in architecture. One job he embarrassingly confessed he found for himself was serving as a model for a life class at the Art Museum. Both C.A. Johnson and Francis Vesey had been elected presidents of the student association at different times while at Rice. In 1930, Vesey was a winner of the Mary Alice Elliott loan fund award for a year of foreign travel and study in Europe.

Ernest Shult, Class of 1923, also remembers that he found it difficult to complete the fifth-year bachelor of science degree on a very limited budget. His problems were complicated by having fallen in love with Cathryn Thompson, and they were anxious to be married. She was studying art at Kidd-Key College in Dallas, which meant that frequent train fares to and from North Texas were added to Ernest's already strained financial situation.

Shult had decided that in order to marry, he would have to be content with four years of architecture, and would withdraw from the fifth-year class. He came to Watkin to tell him of his decision. Watkin, however, soon convinced Ernest of the importance of completing the fifth year. There could, he explained, be more problems inherent in returning later, than in the difficulties of the moment. Watkin asked Shult to please send his bride-to-be to Watkin's office for a chat. After listening to Mr. Watkin's argument for the importance of the fifth year to Ernest, Cathryn herself agreed to postpone their marriage for one year.

Watkin then gave young Shult part-time work as a draftsman in Watkin's office, working on the Chemistry Building, the Frederick A. Heitmann home project in Shadyside, and on additions to Ye Olde College Inn. When Ernest received the bachelor of science in architecture, Watkin recommended him for a position with Joseph Finger, who had been awarded the commission for the Plaza Hotel on Montrose Boulevard. This elegant new hotel was soon to become the residence of President and Mrs. Edgar Odell Lovett.

Robroy Carroll, Class of 1934, was another especially promising student who had to drop out of the department for financial reasons. Watkin learned Robroy had taken a job in a local ladies shoe store. Watkin arranged to stop by to see him at the shoe store, and promised him part-time employment on campus if he would return to his studies. Carroll, startled to see Professor Watkin in the ladies' store, accepted the offer promptly. A year later he had earned his bachelor of science degree with considerable distinction. Fortunately, at the time of Carroll's graduation, William Farrington (developer of Tanglewood and other major projects in Houston during the '40s, '50s and '60s) was seeking a young architect to join his staff. He hired Carroll the day before his graduation.

There were many more such cases of financial aid to Watkin's architectural students through the 1930s.

The problems of the economic depression became severe in the 1930s for Rice Institute, itself a university that charged no tuition. The income from endowment funds dropped ever lower as bonds regarded as perfectly safe stopped interest payments. Dividends on even blue-chip stocks were sharply reduced or simply omitted. Some of the Institute's best real estate no longer produced income, as lessees faced bankruptcy.

The Rice faculty was directly affected. The trustees were forced to announce a 10% cut in all salaries in 1932 (5% for married men paid less than $325 a month). A.B. Cohn, Rice's financial wizard, predicted the first budget deficit and a possible invasion of capital. From a high of nearly seventy-five members in 1930, the total faculty had declined more than 20% by 1938. It was decided, with considerable reluctance, to hold the student body at approximately 1,300, virtually all of whom were undergraduates.

The Department of Architecture was hit especially hard in 1934, though Watkin had done everything possible, including many conferences with a sympathetic President Lovett, to protect his teaching staff. Charles L. Browne, who had decided to remain at Rice in 1929, and who had taught construction since 1920, received his last contract for the 1933–1934 academic year.

Frederic Browne (no relation to Charles L.), instructor in freehand drawing since 1926, could not be retained on the faculty. Chairman Watkin did all he could under the circumstances, shifting and increasing assignments for Jimmy Chillman, Claude Hooton, Stayton Nunn, and the teaching fellows, and instructing additional classes himself. He himself spent even more time with students at the drawing boards, resolving their design problems.

Watkin was happy that he was able to help obtain another position for Frederic Browne at the University of Houston. Charles L. Browne, still uncomfortable with the heat and humidity of Houston, left permanently for the East after fourteen years at Rice.

VII.

The life-style changes due to the Great Depression at the Watkin home meant that there were no longer leisurely summer vacations in Vermont, or the Blue Ridge Mountains of the Carolinas, or the West Coast, or in Europe. Now Galveston or San Antonio had to suffice. Young Ray Watkin, however, later described Houston in the Depression during her college days as "not a 'sad' place, but one where people cheerfully pitched in and enjoyed simple pleasures." The atmosphere at 5009 Caroline was one of family closeness and progress toward goals.

"We quickly learned," according to Ray, "that the best way we could help our father through those difficult years was to show our love and appreciation for his sacrifices by bringing home good grades." And this they did.

During 1931, Watkin was able to move definitely ahead on the book he had planned to write since his sabbatical year of 1928–1929. His modus operandi was to work late into the night, often well after midnight, outlining, writing, and reviewing his notes. This usually followed a long day on campus, and dinner hour with the family.

Watkin had long ago selected the subject of his book. It would relate to the history of church architecture. He would explore in terms of past, present, and future, the lasting beauty and impact of the medieval and Gothic cathedrals he had studied with such interest and appreciation. The title, as has been noted, would be *The Church of Tomorrow*.

As he began the vital project of his book in 1931, Watkin also was working on a series of three significant articles, entitled "Impressions of Modern Architecture" for the architectural magazine *Pencil Point*. The articles discussed the many new influences on American architecture, including those emanating from such strong new sources as the German *Bauhaus* movement.

Sometime in 1932, Watkin met Josephine Cockrell Watkin, the person who would share the remainder of his life with him. Josephine, by coincidence, was the widow of another man (not related) named Watkin. She was the daughter of the late Judge E. Cockrell, a member of a pioneer Dallas family. Her father, a leading Dallas attorney, had served as chairman of the governing board of Southern Methodist

University. A 1913 graduate of Bryn Mawr College, Josephine was five years younger than Watkin and had many similar interests.

Their friendship developed after the two met at the home of John Willis Slaughter, professor of sociology and social studies and one of the newer stars on the Rice faculty. John and Margaret Slaughter had been close friends and colleagues of Professor Watkin's in the Institute community. Mrs. Slaughter had been a childhood friend of Josephine Cockrell in Dallas. Their many common interests included gardening. Margaret Slaughter had created an especially attractive garden at their home just west of the Museum of Fine Arts. She was already an active member of the Garden Club of Houston, and soon sponsored Josephine for membership. Dr. Slaughter was a popular speaker before a host of civic organizations and a consultant on community studies.

Watkin found himself quickly attracted to Josephine and he soon introduced her to his children. He began escorting her to social and cultural events in Dallas and in Houston, whenever she returned for visits with the Slaughters.

Watkin and Josephine found that they had many interests in common. She had entered Bryn Mawr college in Philadelphia the year after Watkin completed his studies at the University of Pennsylvania's School of Architecture. Their friendship deepened, and they were married in Dallas on October 26, 1933.

The ceremony, with Dr. Umphrey Lee, pastor of the Highland Park Methodist Church and longtime friend of the Cockrell family officiating, was held at the home of the bride's sister. Watkin's best man was his Rice colleague of many years, Harry B. Weiser. The guests included close Houston friends and another friend of the groom, L.W. (Chip) Roberts of Atlanta, assistant secretary of the treasury, with whom Watkin would soon be associated on an important project in the nation's capital.

The bride and groom returned to Houston in mid-November, following a trip to the East that included visits to Philadelphia and New York City.

After four-and-a-half years as a widower, William Ward Watkin had entered upon another phase of his life, and a happy and rewarding marriage that would extend over the remaining two decades of his life.

Notes

1. Watkin's instructions to McGinty began with how to book passage in steerage on a slow freighter from Houston to Liverpool. The traveling scholar left June 30 on the *S.S. Cripple Creek*, of the United States Shipping Board's cargo fleet. He paid $63, or $3.00 a day including meals, for the 21-day voyage to England. McGinty was also provided guidance on such other vital matters as itineraries in Europe, architectural highlights, how to live comfortably at minimum rates *en pension,* and the need for extreme accuracy in drawing and coloring.

2. The papal palace was actually two structures: the unadorned Palais Vieux and the Palais Nouvelle, the latter rich in frescoes and architectural embellishment. Perched on a 200-foot rock overlooking Avignon, the eight-towered palace was one of the last of the chateaux-forts, which served both as a residence and as a fort. Notre Dame des Doms and the town's many churches and chapels were important repositories of works by artists of the Avignon School. They had produced late Gothic paintings incorporating Italian and Flemish characteristics so prevalent in other 14th-century French art. The resulting works influenced French painting for much of the next two centuries.

3. A first wing of Louis XII's chateau at Blois, dating from 1503, was clearly late Gothic. Pointed arches and high roofs were featured in its asymmetrical design. The second wing, completed in 1524, was still recognizably Gothic. It had, however, many elements of the Renaissance architecture being imported into France from northern Italy: open loggias, pilasters of differing proportions, and classic ornamentation.

   The great 440-room chateau at Chambord, a few miles east of Blois, was regarded as the finest example of early Renaissance architecture in France. Almost 500 feet long, it was based on a novel concept differing from traditional chateaux. This was the Italian idea of a main core, quite symmetrically organized on crossing axes, with round towers in each of the four corners. The towers contained large, multi-story apartments. Ornamentation at Chambord was clearly early Renaissance.

4. Actually, establishing a chapter of the Phi Beta Kappa, the nation's preeminent honor society, at the Rice Institute in 1928 was a most unusual tribute that had drawn attention throughout university circles. Rice was still a very small institution. It had granted its first degree only a dozen years before. Far older, larger, and more prestigious colleges and universities had been turned down by Phi Beta Kappa, or stood patiently in line hoping for admission to the academic society that brought distinction to institution, faculty, and graduates alike.

The answer to the early selection of the young Rice Institute for a Phi Beta Kappa chapter had to relate considerably to Lovett's prestige and to the quality of the faculty he had brought to Houston. There were other factors: worldwide recognition of the academic festival of October 10–12, 1912; distribution of the impressive *Book of the Opening*; ongoing accomplishments of the faculty; and the growing attainments of the still-small Rice alumni body. The *Book of the Opening*, dedicated to Woodrow Wilson, had been sent to the leading institutions of higher education, both in the United States and abroad. It was a remarkable publication of which any university could be proud.

A number of the members of the Phi Beta Kappa Senate had also been to the Rice Institute by 1928. Others were in touch with faculty members at the Institute, through shared interests in research and other scholarly pursuits or as fellow members of various academic organizations. There was exposure both to the beauty of the campus, with its core of original buildings in place amid handsome landscaping, and to the level of scholarly activity there.

When the application for a chapter of Phi Beta Kappa at Rice Institute came to a vote in the organization's Senate, there was another unusual and positive factor considered. Rice was one of the few universities with a student honor system, the concept that originated at the College of William & Mary. Phi Beta Kappa had begun there in 1776, when the small Virginia institution, founded in 1693, was approaching its first centennial. President Lovett was familiar with the honor system, which was administered by students themselves through an elected Honor Council. It was in effect both at the University of Virginia and at Princeton during his years at those institutions. He had proposed it, and seen it installed during the earliest years of the Rice Institute.

5. Albert Leon Guerard had joined the Rice Institute faculty early in 1913, coming from Stanford to establish the French Department. He arrived at the same time as another eminent full professor, Stockton Axson. Axson, President Woodrow Wilson's brother-in-law, had come from Princeton to head the English Department.

   In the fall of 1913, Guerard, Axson, and Julian Huxley had joined Professor Harold A. Wilson on a curriculum committee, the first organized faculty group at Rice. Always popular with students, Guerard was chairman of a committee on student affairs. He appeared more than three dozen times on the University Extension Lecture Series.

   Professor Guerard once wrote President Lovett of the need to remain small in departments, professors, students, and physical facilities, but to be ". . . the best." When the Guerards returned to Stanford in 1924, it was a major loss for Dr. Lovett, his other colleagues, students, many friends in the community, and especially for the Watkin family. A major consideration in the move was the hot and humid Houston climate.

6. During one particularly difficult Christmas in Houston in the early 1920s, all the members of the Guerard family had been hospitalized at the same time,

with the father increasingly disturbed over the mounting cost of the hospital care. Professor Guerard was enormously touched and relieved when Captain James A. Baker called on him at the hospital after learning of the situation. The chairman of the Rice board assured the distraught professor that the trustees would cover all hospital charges, which were substantial. Professor Guerard and his family never forgot this kindness.

7. Ray, Rosemary, and Billy would long remember Tante Marie and Vieux Moulin. They would recall bicycling trips through the forest or the road from Vieux Moulin to the nearby Chateau de Pierrefonds, a medieval chateau-fort with its moat, drawbridge, and 20-foot-thick walls. Completely restored by the great architect, Viollet-le-Duc, it sat on a rocky cliff overlooking the countryside.

    Ray would see Tante Marie again 23 years later in Arona, Italy, while traveling in Europe in 1952. Mlle. had aged, but was overjoyed to see her and to get news of the Watkin family. She was sad to learn of Mr. Watkin's death, and asked for detailed news of Rosemary and Billy and of their life during the intervening years. Tante Marie died a few years later at Arona.

8. Milton McGinty had completed the major study required under the terms of his scholarship in the Tuscan city of Medici. His project was a measured drawing of the sacristy of the Church of the Holy Spirit, built in the period between 1475 and 1490, and described as "one of the truly fine interiors of the Florentine Renaissance in which Gothic structure and classic forms happily blend."

9. Shopping errands for groceries were often made to Joe Jett's store on Montrose, where the family had traded since Ray's childhood. When Ray was a child, Joe Jett had served the Southmore and Montrose areas with his traveling grocery store, which had first been from a wagon pulled by one horse, and then a small, open, motorized truck. Every day he came by with a large selection of fresh fruits and vegetables. Several plump, live chickens in crates hung on the back of Jett's wagon. The cook came out to the wagon after hearing Joe's bell and picked out fresh fruits and vegetables, and looked over the chickens. When she made her choice, Jett took the chicken out of the crate and wrung its neck in front of her eyes. She would then have plucked it, cleaned it, and put it in the oven in time for dinner. There was no doubt that Joe Jett's chickens were fresh!

By the 1930s, Jett had moved to his highly successful neighborhood store on Montrose Boulevard. Orders were placed by telephone and filled by a fine panelled delivery truck.

CHAPTER EIGHT

William Ward Watkin places new emphasis upon teaching and a selective practice . . . The Great Depression and its effects at Rice Institute . . . A new policy brings marked success for the Owls in intercollegiate sports . . . Professor Watkin is appointed to the National Architectural Advisory Board . . . His book, "The Church of Tomorrow," wins critical acclaim . . . New commissions "emphasizing creative opportunity". . . Graduation from Rice with honors and marriage for daughters Ray and Rosemary . . . World War II at the Institute . . . William Ward Watkin, Jr., at West Point and in the South Pacific . . . An AIA fellowship, and honor to Frank Lloyd Wright . . . Significant new consultantships . . . A memorable exchange of letters with President Lovett . . . The birth of Watkin's first grandson, William Ward Watkin III . . . Death comes for William Ward Watkin, but Houston is left his memorable legacy

I.

William Ward Watkin's thoughtful letter to Edgar Odell Lovett at the beginning of the 1930–1931 academic year, writing of his intent to "reduce and concentrate" his work, proved to be prophetic. His concentration was to be upon Rice Institute, and "the inspiring work with my students;" and upon a "very limited but selective practice . . . emphasizing creative opportunity." This would "afford me a much larger portion of my time to devote to my children."

Watkin definitely followed this plan, and in a reasonable, intelligent manner by balancing many factors. As a result, he found more time for his primary responsibilities as professor, practitioner, and parent, as well as for writing his book on a new concept of church architecture. As has been noted, he had hoped to get the book well under way during his sabbatical of 1928–1929 in Europe, when personal tragedy intervened.

Watkin discovered that his work at the university and his civic role in Houston continued to involve a substantial amount of time. There was still his long-standing appointment as chairman of the Committee on Buildings and Grounds, complicated by budgetary restrictions. He had accepted other assignments, often of a temporary nature, as a senior member of the university faculty. These included maintaining "town and gown" relationships dating back to 1913, and participating in the ongoing Sunday afternoon lecture series. They included taking part in the numerous activities of the nearby Museum of Fine Arts, the Houston Chapter of the American Institute of Architects, and the related Texas Society of Architects.

As an architect, Watkin limited his practice. However, he welcomed his assignments to regional and national boards or committees, as well as the matter of continuing participation in the Houston Chapter of the American Institute of Architects (AIA). He and Birdsall Briscoe, together with Olle J. Lorehn, had taken major roles as early as 1921 in the rechartering of the local affiliate. The original charter of the Houston Chapter (then not yet affiliated with the AIA), established in 1913 by Briscoe and Lorehn and in which Watkin had also been active, had lapsed during the first World War.

With the new charter, granted in 1924 by the AIA, the Houston affiliate soon expanded substantially in membership, commissions, community activities, and impact. The Houston Chapter was finally moving toward a position of leadership within the national organization of architects. Watkin would remain an active member, both as an architect and professor, for the remainder of his life.

Watkin had, of course, added a new dimension to his life through his marriage to Josephine Cockrell in October 1933. Josephine adapted well to her new life in Houston, though she continued to stay in close touch with her family in Dallas. She enjoyed her new friends among the Rice faculty wives and the wives of Houston architects. She also became active in the DAR, the Colonial Dames, and the Garden Club of Houston. Flower arranging was one of her absorbing hobbies, a hobby that she shared with her close friend Margaret Slaughter, also a Rice faculty wife.

After Watkin's remarriage, his mother, Mary Matilda Watkin, moved to New Orleans to live with Mrs. Ernest Charles Churchill, her son's beloved Aunt Hepsie and her own sister-in-law and friend over so many years. Mary Matilda died in New Orleans in January 1936 at age 72.

Watkin's Aunt Hepsie was the family historian and genealogist. Aunt and nephew had shared Watkin's ambition for a career in architecture as early as 1902. It was then, at age, sixteen, that he wrote Mrs. Churchill during a summer job with the Danville architect J.H. Brugler. The letter reflected remarkable maturity for a teenager: "Architecture," William stated, "not only presents fascination and variety, but offers a broad field for . . . individuality and advancement."

It was Hepsibah Watkin Churchill who wrote Josephine Watkin after Mary Matilda's death in New Orleans. "Aunt" Hepsie recalled, in a letter of November 12, 1936, how the two girls (Mary Watkin and Hepsie) had been "young together" a half-century before in Danville, Pennsylvania. After their marriages, only five months apart, they exchanged baby clothes for their firstborn sons: "She sent me Willie's long baby clothes for our Neil, and I made her some of Willie's short ones in return . . . . All the years since, we understood and loved each other yet were entirely different. We both loved Fred [Watkin, Aunt Hepsie's brother and Watkin's father], and that tie bound us long ago."

II.

The severe effects of the economic depression upon Rice had begun to improve somewhat by 1936. This was in spite of the fact that the face value of the bonds and notes constituting a major portion of Rice's investment portfolio had fallen almost $1 million during earlier defaults on interest payments. Overall endowment income had revived somewhat after reaching a record annual low of less than $700,000, and by now there were no further defaults on interest payments. Income from the Institute's sizable holdings in Houston real estate was also on the increase.

Encouraged by these developments, the members of the governing board rescinded the 10% cut in faculty salaries that had been reluctantly adopted early in 1932. It was thought that the reduction, necessary though it was, had definitely played a role in the loss of two stellar members of the faculty, as well as others of the teaching staff. Griffith Conrad Evans, an outstanding mathematician from Harvard, had been recruited at the University of Rome by President Lovett himself. He had gone to the Italian capital to study with Vito Volterra, one of the giants in the development of modern calculus theory. Evans left Rice in 1933 to become chairman of the mathematics department at the University of California, where he remained for the rest of his distinguished career. A member of the original faculty at the Institute, his resignation came at an unfortunate time. It followed the earlier departure of Percy John Daniell of Cambridge University, another member of the outstanding mathematics team Lovett had hired for Rice.

Another notable departure was that of Robert G. Caldwell, a renowned historian also serving as dean of the Institute, in 1933, although quite special circumstances were involved. An eminent authority on Iberia and the connections between Spain, Portugal, Latin America, and the United States, Dr. Caldwell resigned to accept a major diplomatic post. He became the ambassador to Portugal in the new administration of Franklin Delano Roosevelt. The post of dean of the Institute, as noted, then went to Robert Caldwell's colleague, close friend, and neighbor on Bayard Lane, Harry Boyer Weiser.

There were other effects of the Great Depression that were to have a lasting although indirect impact on the future development of the Rice Institute. Among these were enrollment policies, and the beginnings of a gradual evolvement from a virtually cost-free institution to students (especially those not residing in the dormitories) to one with relatively modest tuition and fees. Without some fortunate developments of the 1940s, tuition and fees would likely have become far more costly, and enrollment even more limited.

As the financial situation at Rice became progressively worse in 1931, the trustees had adopted relatively severe restrictions on the number of students. All freshmen and other first-time enrollees were held to 400, with a maximum of 25 out-of-state students. The object was to keep overall enrollment under 1,500, since there were clear indications of even more drastic cuts in faculty if the budgetary crisis continued.

There were also slight increases in student fees, which had been traditionally quite low. In 1932, the registration fee jumped 150%, but only from $10 to $25. A "blanket tax," covering student publications, admission to athletic events, operation of the Student Association's modest functions, and other small costs, was levied. The cost was $8.40, or less than four cents per day.

Laboratory fees also went up slightly, although they would never approach the actual cost of materials and supplies in many courses. Students in organic chemistry, for example, used high-temperature crucibles of pure platinum, costing almost $100 each. The physics laboratories were also extremely well equipped, especially with the instruments required for complex experimentation. This had apparently become quite manifest to Harold A. Wilson. The distinguished physicist had returned to Rice in 1924 and to the "state-of-the-art" apparatus he had been allowed to purchase for the laboratories there, after less than a year in his position at the University of Glasgow.

A.B. Cohn, business manager and assistant secretary to the trustees, had raised the first alarm about the worsening financial situation as early as 1931. He predicted, quite accurately, a reduction in annual income from endowment to below $700,000. At the same time, Cohn was studying preliminary budget proposals from departmental heads and other sources that totalled almost $650,000 for 1932–1933.

$650,000 represented an increase of almost 10%, at a time when the economic storm signals were already fluttering in shifting winds. Further, $650,000 in outgo was perilously close to the predicted drop under $700,000 for endowment income. To the conservative business manager, whose judgment was highly regarded by the governing board, the course of action was obvious. Budgets had to be prudently trimmed until the gathering fiscal storm abated. After long meetings of the trustees aimed at minimizing potential damage to faculty, staff, student body, and institution overall, Arthur Cohn's recommendations for reduced expenditures in virtually all areas were adopted and followed.

The result was three years of not only holding the fiscal line, but of successive budgetary reductions without ongoing damage to overall operations. The actual costs of running the Rice Institute fell from the proposed $650,000 for 1932–1933 to a sum barely above $450,000 four years later.

A. B. Cohn played a key role in guiding William Marsh Rice's institution through the worst of the Depression. He combined long experience in finance with detailed knowledge of the founder's plans and hopes for his Institute that predated the appointment of the original trustees and the granting of Rice's state charter in 1891. Cohn's contributions, including almost five decades of working closely with the trustees, continued after his death late in 1936. He generously included a $100,000 bequest to Rice in his will.

Predictably, Watkin had set the pattern required for the Department of Architecture during the difficult years from which the Rice Institute began to emerge late in 1936. The pattern, so necessary in a time of stringent budgets, was based upon his experience as a teacher and administrator during the past quarter-century. It drew heavily as well upon the obvious competence and versatility of the other members of the departmental faculty. The emphasis was twofold. He continued to provide excellent theoretical as well as practical instruction in the classroom and at the drawing boards, sometimes accepting an additional course himself after the loss of two instructors in 1934. And he continued to be sensitive to the financial and personal difficulties confronting his students.

For his faculty, Watkin had carefully selected James Chillman, Stayton Nunn, and Claude Hooton. He found that, with him, they were a successful quartet, combining their varied backgrounds and abilities. Chillman, a member of the Rice faculty since 1917, had added the coveted Burnham Fellowship at the American Academy in Rome to his two degrees at the University of Pennsylvania. As an associate professor responsible for key courses in freehand drawing, the fine arts, and design, he had served as acting chairman during Watkin's sabbatical in 1928–1929. A longtime colleague once said of Chillman, ". . . [the] most immediate quality that impressed itself on all who came to know him was an irresistible friendliness. It was not an accident that before long he was known to both colleagues and students as Jimmy. . . . To command both deep respect and genuine personal affection expressed capacities of a very high order."

The ties between Rice and Watkin with the prospective new Houston Art Museum had begun in 1913. Both Lovett and Watkin had been early members of the Art League of Houston, the pioneer group that had obtained a charter for the Museum of Fine Arts that year.

In a widely publicized speech before the League on April 12, 1919, Lovett told the audience that the determination to have a museum was "a high resolve." He urged that it be built as soon as possible after the conclusion of what was then termed the "Great War." [1]

James Chillman had been active in the artistic community's activities since his arrival at Rice. Thus it was not surprising that,with his excellent qualifications, he was chosen to be the first director of the new Houston Museum of Fine Arts in 1924. He was able to work on a part-time basis, while continuing his teaching at Rice. In the days of the mid-1920s, and certainly during the Depression, MFA budgets were necessarily minimal. Being able to have Jimmy Chillman as part-time director at a modest salary undoubtedly helped the young institution through difficult formative years. At the same time it helped Chillman, a young husband and father, with his own finances. Meanwhile, the link between the Rice Institute and the Museum of Fine Arts, begun by Watkin and widened over the years by both Watkin and Chillman, continued to grow in strength and mutual benefit to both organizations and to the community as a whole.

By 1936, Watkin and Chillman had been joined on the faculty first by Stayton Nunn and then by Claude Hooton. Both would combine effective instruction and personal assistance to their students with growing prominence as architects. They were chosen with care at a pivotal time in the history of the Department of Architecture, and were the first alumni to receive full-time appointments there. Nunn had arrived as a student in 1917, eight years before Hooton began his studies at Rice.

Stayton Nunn had worked closely with Watkin as his associate in private practice at the Scanlan Building before his selection as a member of the Rice faculty. Nunn remained on the faculty even after developing a substantial private practice, including appointment as consulting architect for the Houston Independent School District. Claude Hooton, Class of 1927, had come to Watkin's attention as a student of unusual potential and talent. He had become a close friend of the Watkin family, as well as an invaluable help during the tragic months of Mrs. Watkin's fatal illness in Paris, the return home, and Watkin's dangerous bout with pneumonia on shipboard.

Hooton joined the faculty in 1931, after spending most of the two years since his graduation from Rice in Europe. He had gone there first in the summer of 1928, spending part of his time with Milton McGinty before remaining with the Watkins in Paris. In 1929, Hooton succeeded McGinty as Traveling Fellow in Architecture, and returned for another year, this time primarily in France and in Finland. His project was the Church of St. Trophime in Arles, the ancient capital of Burgundy in southeastern France. St. Trophime, dating from the 7th century, was regarded as a superb example of 12th-century Romanesque architecture, with important additions made some 300 years later. It includes what some critics term the finest cloister in all of France.

He continued on to Finland, where he studied examples of the modern Finnish and Scandinavian movement in architecture led by Eero Saarinen of Helsinki, before returning home to Houston and his new appointment at Rice Institute. Recognized as a skilled and talented instructor, Hooton gradually developed a practice specializing in residences and small commercial projects. For the next decade, he taught freshman and sophomore design and the history of ornament to a pre-World War II cycle of architects-to-be. In 1931, his pen-and-ink drawings were used to illustrate William Ward Watkin's articles on "Impressions of Modern Architecture" in the architectural magazine *Pencil Point*.

The traditional Archi-Arts Ball of the Architectural Society continued in the 1930s, although the Great Depression deepened. It no longer made enough money to support the Society and departmental projects. However, the Ball remained a gala affair that provided many opportunities for experience in design, decor, and organization for the students. It also reinforced the tradition of closeness within the Department of Architecture.

There were many imaginative themes, or "motifs," for the Archi-Arts Balls during those years of economic downturn, including Aztec, Celtic, and Louisianne keynotes. Stayton Nunn had been chairman of the very first Archi-Arts Ball, the Baile Español in Autry House on February 3, 1922. Nunn and Hooton, as well as Professors

Watkin and Chillman, took special pleasure and satisfaction in the continuance of this colorful gala.

The Traveling Scholarship was suspended between 1933 and 1937 during the early Depression years, and again during World War II. The Scholarship resumed in 1938, as Houston and the nation began to revive economically, and again after World War II.

In 1936, the Archi-Arts Ball, which was held at the usual time preceding the Lenten season, was an especially beautiful and enjoyable affair. The motif of the 1936 Ball at the Junior League was the "Gay Nineties." Both of the Watkin daughters had prominent roles. Ray was queen of the gala, held in an elaborate setting depicting the old New York Opera House. Her sister Rosemary, Class of 1938 in architecture, was also active in the ball, as well as in other departmental projects. She was vibrant and vivacious, with a multitude of friends. In her senior year, she was named one of the campus beauties, whose full-page photographs appeared in the 1938 *Campanile,* the Rice Institute yearbook.

As noted, the departmental scholarship, renamed the Watkin Traveling Scholarship for its founder, was revived in 1938. Funds for the award were solicited from the growing number of Rice's architectural alumni, recently organized in their own association. There would be some support from net proceeds of the Archi-Arts Ball, when and if it turned a profit, but there was an understandable tendency not to cut corners on ball expenses, such as the location, sets, decorations, music, food, or other costs of the event. Unfortunately, the steadily worsening situation in Europe, foreshadowing Hitler's blitzkrieg attacks in the opening days of September 1939, made it impractical at that time for the new Watkin Traveling Scholars to spend their year abroad in the traditional surroundings of France, Italy, Spain, or England. In the late 1930s, they headed instead for Mexico and for Central and Latin America.

The well-established tradition of personal and financial assistance to students in the Department of Architecture was vital in helping to keep enrollment near appropriate levels between 1930 and 1937, in spite of clearly discouraging prospects throughout the construction industry. A new and major source of assistance to students was the temporary campus employment provided by the National Youth Administration (NYA), one of the many New Deal agencies [2].

Rice, as well as the other Texas institutions of higher education participating in the NYA program, received substantial grants. The many part-time jobs involved helped both students and hard-pressed departmental budgets. And, when all the positions for classroom and laboratory assistants, library, clerical and other student workers were filled, Tony Martino could always use part-time help with his landscaping care. In fact, the NYA funds were especially helpful in grounds maintenance, where it had become regrettably necessary to reduce Martino's budget due to money being sorely needed for other areas of the university operation.

III.

By 1928, Watkin had served sixteen years, from 1912 until the summer of 1928, as chairman of the Committee on Outdoor Sports. His enjoyment of college football as a spectator sport had continued to grow.

In 1914, Watkin had represented Rice in the formation of the Southwest Conference, for which he served both as vice president and as president. As noted, in 1924 Watkin had spent a great deal of effort, at the direction of Edgar Odell Lovett and the other trustees, in recruiting the legendary John W. Heisman as football coach and director of athletics.

In 1928, before Watkin turned the chairmanship of the Committee on Outdoor Sports over to his good friend and colleague, John T. McCants, he made the important decision to bring in the first business manager for Rice athletics, Gaylord Johnson [3].

Watkin's decision had been approved, and Johnson, a Rice Ph.D. in chemistry, was hired for the new position. An astute businessman and investor, Johnson owned The Gables, a popular drug store and hangout for Rice students on Main Street at Rosalie. He was active in the new alumni association, well acquainted in the city, and keenly interested in the expanding field of intercollegiate athletics.

In the mid-1920s, John Heisman had recruited widely outside Texas, as he had few contacts with high school coaches in Texas.

Unfortunately, he had recruited his best player, a fullback, from New Jersey. The departure of this fullback had caused considerable concern in New Jersey, as well as some questions regarding the player's eligibility and Heisman's procedures. It had been expected that recruitment would be mainly in Texas.

In 1929, however, Watkin was drawn quite naturally into a controversy regarding a new system undergirding intercollegiate athletics at Rice. This related to a surprising interest in competitive intercollegiate sports, initially largely football, for such a relatively small institution. The interest was clearly strong in Houston, a young city that wanted championship teams. Watkin continued to be interested in spite of the fact that he had yielded the chairmanship of the COOS to John T. McCants.

At the heart of a proposed controversial new system was the establishment of an academic Department of Physical Education. Male athletes, limited to an annual maximum of 40 students (above the maximum limit of 400 incoming students), were to be carefully recruited for the new department. The selection criteria included both athletic accomplishment and potential, and the ability to meet established entrance standards. Candidates, primarily football prospects, would be able to pursue the new degree of bachelor of science in physical education, aiming at a career in coaching in the secondary school systems.

The curriculum included business administration, biology, English, government, or other liberal arts, in addition to enough courses in education to qualify for a state teaching certificate. The infamous Mathematics 100 was not required for the proposed new degree. A description and endorsement of Mathematics 100, written by Edgar Odell Lovett, still opened the Rice catalog. This freshman course of year-long duration was required for graduation for all Rice students, and had gradually been broadened to include a calculus component. It proved to be a nightmare for many students, sometimes being repeated each of four or five academic years in pursuit of the four minus (D) minimum passing grade that would complete the requirements for their degree.

Watkin was clearly a supporter of intercollegiate athletics. He had backed tutoring for athletes, closer relationships with Houston and

Texas high school coaches for recruiting, and had even suggested a preparatory school to help prepare future Owl athletes for the Rice curriculum. Watkin had also strongly opposed John Heisman's recruiting in the East, especially after it raised problems with the National Collegiate Athletic Association. But he was concerned, as were others among his colleagues, in maintaining strict academic standards within intercollegiate competition. To some, including Watkin, a different curriculum for the athlete seemed to be a possible first move away from the purity of college athletics.

Nevertheless, the matter was explored by not one, but three academic committees. The faculty vote clearly favored the new Department of Physical Education, and the degree of bachelor of science in this specialty. The decision had been reached. William Ward Watkin, with the others who had joined him in gentlemanly opposition, accepted it. Watkin wrote Lovett explaining his reasons for opposing the new approach to intercollegiate athletics at Rice. Regardless, a new era in intercollegiate athletics had begun.

Gaylord Johnson was convinced that one of Heisman's central problems during his four years at Rice had been the failure to establish and maintain close ties with high schools in Houston and over the state of Texas. Dr. Johnson received Watkin's warm support for this emphasis on recruiting near the Institute's home base. With the departure of Coach Heisman, Dr. Johnson was given much wider powers within the athletics program. Watkin's good relations with Johnson continued after 1928, and Watkin found himself enjoying Rice's success in a remarkable series of conference championships, and national or world records for Owl athletes. These encompassed not only football, but basketball, track and field, tennis, and golf. The successes, which extended from the mid-1930s, are seldom now recalled more than a half-century later, but it was a golden era for sports at the Rice Institute.

In 1930, a new football coach was sought for the Rice Institute. The committee selected Jack Meagher, a former aide to the legendary Knute Rockne at Notre Dame. Meagher left St. Edward's College in Austin for Rice.

Even before the winning 1932 season was concluded, the three Houston daily newspapers proclaimed that 1933 would be an even greater year. State and then national publications soon took up the cry. There were feature stories on several of Meagher's best players. This probably would have come to pass, had not several of the star Rice athletes been found guilty of cheating by the Student Honor Council and been suspended from athletic competition. Following a losing season, Jack Meagher resigned and became the coach at Auburn University. Fortunately, however, most of the suspended players returned to Rice after their one-year suspension.

Finally, 1934 saw the beginning of success for all sports at Rice. Rice won the Southwest Conference football championship [4]. As a result, Gaylord Johnson would now have his wish for a much enlarged football stadium. The stadium, located on University Boulevard at the southwest limits of the campus, would triple its seating capacity from barely 10,000 to 30,000 seats. Much of the necessary funds came from increased gate receipts. William Ward Watkin was pleased to be awarded the job to design the new brick and steel structure. The new stadium was impressive in appearance, the brick facade harmonizing in color with the existing Rice buildings.

The stadium included expanded parking lots so necessary for the large crowds. It also provided a much larger press box, made necessary by the constant growth in media coverage of football, especially by radio stations and networks. The new stadium opened in 1938, only months after Rice had won a second SWC football championship and had gone on to play in the Cotton Bowl for the first time. Although the handsome brick sections on the west side of the stadium have now been torn down, the east-side bleachers of the facility remain. A half-century later, it is still used for track and field meets.

IV.

Watkin's decision in 1930 to follow a selective and limited architectural practice now allowed time for other opportunities. He began to have time to serve on various state and national boards and commissions in his field.

The first opportunity in this connection was his nomination to membership on the Washington, D.C.-based National Architectural Advisory Board (NAAB), a nine-man commission that met at regular intervals in the national capitol. This appointment, under Franklin D. Roosevelt, came in 1934 through the recommendation of Lawrence Wood ("Chip") Roberts, an architect and engineer from Georgia Tech and Atlanta with whom Watkin had worked closely on the commission of Texas Technological College in Lubbock.

Roberts had remained in touch with Watkin since their collaboration in 1925, both as a friend and as a fellow architect. He was well and favorably known in the Atlanta area, and had strong political connections both in Georgia and nationally. He had come to know President Franklin Delano Roosevelt well through FDR's visits to the famed spa at Warm Springs, Georgia, dating back to his polio attack in 1921. The Little White House at Warm Springs was the scene of many of Georgia's most important political meetings.

Appointed assistant secretary of the Treasury early in the first Roosevelt administration, Roberts had among his many assignments the chairmanship of the National Architectural Advisory Board, an especially interesting board at the time. The board had major input concerning architectural commissions and building contracts under the National Recovery Administration (NRA) and Public Works Administration (PWA). One of the most important of the federal projects of the board was the group of federal "Triangle Buildings" in the heart of Washington, D.C.

The broad base of this triangular complex of interrelated buildings was the Treasury Department Building. The apex of the triangle was the site of a smaller building, the Archive Building. It housed the priceless records, objects, documents, and rare publications underlying the country's history. This building, the final building built in the triangle, was under construction while Watkin was on the Board.

At his first advisory board meeting, held in the Old Treasury Building in February 1934, Watkin found himself among a group of distinguished architects from all over the nation, including the president of the American Institute of Architects. At 48, Watkin was at least ten years younger than any other member of the Board. In a letter to Edgar Odell Lovett from his room in the new Mayflower Hotel, he explained that his appointment was for a term of six years, modestly describing it as "a nice honor to our university." It was indeed an honor to both the Rice Institute and to

Watkin, who had an opportunity to meet regularly and to exchange views with leaders of his profession. The agenda for a typical NAAB meeting included items that directly influenced both major federal building projects and policies, in addition to architectural trends and procedures.

As an NAAB member, Watkin was able to examine firsthand the effect of the National Recovery Administration and the related Public Works Administration on the architectural profession, which had now begun to recover from the worst consequences of the Great Depression. He concluded, in a paper read before the Texas Society of Architects in 1935, that the two agencies had helped to set a new and positive recovery pattern through ". . . buildings planned for basic civic needs . . . for proper housing and cultural advancement . . . and other laudable requirements of a sound, forward-looking recovery."

Watkin's hope was that architecture, a vital part of such progress, would reflect a "new and changed perspective" in the post-Depression era. "Let our cities, towns and villages," he added, ". . . look to a gradual, well-rounded development." He asked for emphasis upon "interesting and practical solutions" in design and construction, without neglecting "plans of larger meaning than are possible of immediate realization." When the . . . desirability [of such plans and ideas] is made clear, they will be brought to fulfillment," Watkin predicted.

It was an interesting and challenging thesis that hearkened back to Watkin's interest in city planning and zoning in Houston in the 1920s. He had enjoyed Albert Guerard's book on city planning for the French capital (*L'Avenir de Paris*) after his visits to Paris. It was a subject that he had probably discussed with his former neighbor and colleague before Guerard left Rice for Stanford in 1924.

Through Professor Guerard, in 1928 Watkin had met certain leading Parisian architects. He was particularly impressed with Robert Mallet-Stevens, the eminent expert on modern architecture and planning. The two were almost exact contemporaries, having been born within a few months of one another in 1886. Both knew Frank Lloyd Wright, the apostle of modern design and technology. Watkin had met Wright in the 1920s, and would bring him to Rice as a lecturer in the early 1930s.

As Texas prepared to celebrate its one-hundredth anniversary as a republic in 1936, Watkin was named, by Governor James V. Allred, to an advisory committee for the design of the Texas centennial monuments. In this connection and conscious of the advancement of his former students, he called upon A.C. Finn, one of Houston's successful architects and a friend of many years, to help one of his former students, William M. (Bill) McVey.

Finn had been awarded the commission for the 570-foot San Jacinto Monument at the site of the April 21, 1836, battle that brought Texas its independence from Mexico. It was known that his design, deliberately 15 feet higher than the Washington Monument, included a bas-relief at the base as a key component. Watkin hoped to help obtain the coveted job of executing the bas-relief for McVey, a highly talented sculptor and a Rice alumnus of the Class of 1927.

McVey had been an excellent student in the Department of Architecture and one of the few who decided to follow a career in sculpture. He was a contemporary of Milton McGinty and C.A. Johnson, as well as of Francis Vesey, three other Rice alumni who had won departmental honors. McVey's campus activities had been many, ranging from All-Southwest Conference recognition in football to class president, to active participation in the Archi-Arts Ball. After graduation in 1927, he continued his studies in Paris for several years before coming back to Houston to launch what was to be a successful national career as a sculptor. The Texas Centennial would make it possible for young McVey to get his life's work under way in the midst of the Depression.

Aware of the competence of Rice architectural graduates, A.C. Finn interviewed McVey and examined his sketches for the bas-relief proposal. McVey received the coveted commission for the monument at the battleground upon Finn's recommendation. It involved a horizontal frieze encircling the monument depicting the historic Texas victory of April 21, 1936.

While the bas-relief was under way, Watkin endorsed Bill McVey for another sculpture project. This was a quite different work sponsored by the advisory committee for centennial monuments, on which Watkin continued to serve. The project was a statue of James (Jim) Bowie, who died with Colonel William Barrett Travis in the gallant defense of the Alamo, symbol of the victorious struggle for Texian independence over Mexico in 1836. When McVey was awarded the Jim Bowie commission, he had won the opportunity to depict one of the most colorful figures in Texas history [5].

Bill McVey was a sensitive and grateful man, and he appreciated the valuable help given him by Watkin. In 1937, he paid a formal call on his former mentor and benefactor. Watkin was pleased to see McVey and to receive his thanks.

The sculptor, however, proposed something both tangible and appropriate to show his appreciation. (McVey's work at the San Jacinto battleground and the statue of Jim Bowie had now been completed, installed, and well received.) He proposed creating a fine head of Watkin, in bronze. He studied and modeled Watkin while the latter was busy working at his desk at Rice at his daily business. Watkin was pleased with the results and delighted to receive this thoughtful gift. The members of Watkin's family greatly appreciate and enjoy the bronze head more than a half-century later. The family agrees that the work bears a close and lifelike resemblance to the real William Ward Watkin. His eyes are cast down as though reading a book.

While Watkin was active on the committee for centennial monuments, he had a role in naming another sculptor to create a statue of a second Texas hero. The committee was asked to choose a sculptor to design a monument to the memory of Lieutenant Richard H. (Dick) Dowling, the victor of Sabine Pass and a man beloved in Houston during the time of the Civil War [6].

For this assignment, Watkin and his fellow advisers selected Herring Coe, an established sculptor from Beaumont, the East Texas city where Watkin had clients and a number of friends. Coe was quite familiar with the 1863 Battle of Sabine Pass, fought less than 30 miles from Beaumont. Coe was also well known in Houston. When Joseph Finger received the commission to design the new Houston City Hall in 1940, he chose Coe to create and execute a series of friezes for the imposing new civic center.

Herring Coe asked William Ward Watkin to design the base for the heroic statue of Dowling, which now dominates the scene of the Confederate victory. That victory prevented Union forces from retaking Galveston and its vital port. Watkin was already familiar with an existing statue of Dowling, which had been in downtown Houston since the statue's completion in 1903, first at the old City Hall and then in Sam Houston Park. A successful campaign was later launched to move the statue to Hermann Park where it stands today, near Watkin's original Miller Outdoor Theater and his Hermann Garden Center.

V.

William Ward Watkin was no doubt outlining portions of his book, *The Church of Tomorrow*, in his mind long before he first set pen to paper in 1931. In fact, the stage may have been set many years before at the University of Pennsylvania, under the tutelage of Paul Philippe Cret, his mentor from 1903 to 1908. The latter had been educated in the classical tradition at the Institute of Fine Arts in Lyons. There in southeast France, where medieval trade routes running down to the Mediterranean crossed those going north to the Alps, a vital center of commerce and culture had arisen during the High Renaissance. Centuries later, Napoleon Bonaparte had reinforced Lyons' long-established recognition for leadership in the arts and professions, as well as in business.

Napoleon founded both a Museum of Fine Arts and the related Institute where Cret had studied. Priceless paintings and pieces of sculpture were sent from Paris' Louvre to Lyons, building up admirable collections. After studying these firsthand, Paul Cret had only to walk to the next city square to examine an excellent example of French Gothic architecture.

Little wonder, then, that Watkin, after four years of intensive study with Professor Cret at the University of Pennsylvania, described French Gothic as a style that "stands alone in its splendor."

In 1908 came the trip to Boston and on to Europe that shaped young Watkin's early years indelibly. Before following Paul Philippe Cret's recommendation for a semester of study abroad, Watkin went to Boston carrying a letter of introduction from Cret to Ralph Adams Cram, recognized as a foremost American advocate of early Gothic architecture. Within weeks after this meeting, Watkin was in England, on an itinerary suggested by Cram. He toured many of

Britain's renowned Norman and Gothic cathedrals during his stay there in the summer of 1908.

At the time young Watkin joined the firm of Cram & Ferguson in 1909, that office was planning the Gothic splendor of St. Thomas Episcopal Church on New York City's Fifth Avenue. Cram's office also had received another important assignment: redesigning the magnificent Cathedral of St. John the Divine in upper Manhattan. It had been originally planned by Christopher La Farge as a Romanesque-Byzantine structure. Ralph Adams Cram's new concept was a thoroughly Gothic design, which included the necessity of training craftsmen in medieval building procedures, and cutting the stone at the site.

Young Watkin was thus certainly influenced by Cram, who believed so fervently that ". . . the thirteenth was the greatest of all centuries . . ." and its architecture preeminent. Watkin thus came to the view that what critics term "classic" (or "radiant") French Gothic design reached its zenith before the outbreak of the Hundred Years War between England and France in 1337 [7].

Many French cathedrals had remained unfinished during the 116 years of controversy and war. Of the return of peace, Watkin wrote, "A long period of decline followed. The splendor of the Gothic vigor was never recovered." A glorious era, the author of *The Church of Tomorrow* recounted, was over. It had begun, he maintained, on June 11, 1144. On that day, a once illiterate peasant had dedicated the Abbey of St. Denis (the patron saint of all France), in the northern suburb of Paris on the right bank of the River Seine. The ceremony was actually a rededication of one of the oldest religious structures in continuous use in 12th-century Europe, after the completion of major additions involving historic new concepts in church architecture.

The peasant had become a Cistercian monk, architect, and Abbot Suger of an ancient Romanesque church and abbey dating back to the 10th century [8]. The Abbot Suger apparently combined some elements of asceticism with remarkable success as an architect-engineer and adviser to King Louis VI of France. In the latter role, there was no question of financial support when he went to the king with a plan to rebuild remaining portions of the Romanesque St. Denis. The French monarchs had been buried in Suger's abbey church for hundreds of years, and were anxious to see it preserved and improved for posterity.

St. Denis was not only preserved and improved, as Watkin points out; it set into motion "the coming of that perfection we call [French] Gothic architecture." Abbot Suger's plan, elements of which were to constitute a new style of church architecture, included both sweeping changes in design, and in engineering, masonry, and lighting. The principal impact upon the layman was a definite impression of much taller and broader interiors. Far larger windows, often filled with stained glass in elaborate design and Biblical retelling, were now possible. Clerestory windows under higher roofs admitted considerably more light to the interior. The changes were largely based upon advances that were remarkable accomplishments for the mid-12th century. Principal among these were the ongoing development of the "flying" buttress, the ribbed vault, and the pointed arch.

The buttress had been in use as a means of adding strength and stability to the side walls and the vaulted roof. At St. Denis, and in later churches and cathedrals drawing upon Suger's masterpiece of design and construction, the flying buttress concept was substantially expanded, lifting the vaulted roof to new heights. The results achieved came from the teamwork of architect, engineer, and artisan. The latter, especially masons and workers in stained glass, contributed to the overall beauty.

"St. Denis," Watkin concluded, "declares the beauty, power, and daring of a system which passes beyond the restraint and quiet of the Romanesque."

The thesis of *The Church of Tomorrow* was the author's continuing emphasis on the Gothic style of architecture, which he felt had reached its zenith in the 13th century. By that time, Notre Dame and Chartres had brought church architecture in France to lasting ascendancy. Simply stated, Watkin's thesis was that ". . . the church of tomorrow must recover the strength and beauty of the great Gothic [period] in France."

His book covered more than 1,500 years of church architecture, from the reign of Constantine the Great (312–337) through the modern era and on to a vision of the churches of the future. It included 16 pages of illustrative photographs. These ranged from the early

Christian basilica of St. Sabina in Rome and Ravenna's St. Vitale; through the stunning cathedrals of Chartres, Amiens, and Segovia; to the soaring spires of England's Lichfield Cathedral.

The Church of Tomorrow was published in October 1936 by Harper & Brothers of New York and London. More than 30 reviews of the book, beginning with a 500-word critique in *The New York Times*, were printed. Reviews appeared in virtually all the leading architectural journals and in publications on religion. Among these were the *Architectural Forum, Christian Science Monitor, Christian Register, Journal of Religion, Christian Century, Church Architecture, Christendom,* the *Christian Leader,* and various French and English newspapers and architectural journals.

The reviews were almost wholly positive, as some of the following excerpts show:

". . . gives us both historical perspective in church architecture as well as prophetic insight into [its] future . . ."

". . . [This is] the first thorough study of church architecture [to be] based upon a knowledge of the past and how its achievements might improve what is to come . . ."

"The emphasis on the interior [of our churches] is a fresh, creative idea."

"We must adapt site, plan, materials, lighting and decoration to the condition and needs of the present and future . . ."

"This book can provide further inspiration to church architecture, [by] never forgetting the past but also being sensitive to new materials, new meanings and new needs."

"For the man who can read just one book [on church architecture], I would recommend *The Church of Tomorrow.* Gothic is Christianity's own creation. There lies all beauty, perfection . . . and proportion; the problem of the modern builder is to adapt it to the functions and requirements of the church of today and tomorrow."

Watkin, of course, read all the reviews with interest, paying particular attention to a critique by Ralph Adams Cram. Cram wrote in the lead front-page article of the *Christian Register,* then an authoritative journal of criticism in Boston, "The opening historical part," he began, "is excellent." He then agreed to a principal tenet of *The Church of Tomorrow*: "Every religious structure [does indeed] grow from within. Even the great Gothic churches began their grandeur with the interior, although the exterior did in time develop a like magnificence."

However, Cram maintained that Watkin should have clarified the differences between "acceptable and unacceptable" modernism more clearly. He also took issue with some essentially minor points in the book. He opposed the detailed uses of color, or designing "hideously ugly" modern parabolic forms, and the omission of mention that Ravenna's architectural triumphs derived from Constantinople and its Hagia Sophia, "the most noble and glorious church man ever built."

The conclusion of Cram's critique was entirely positive, and quite laudatory: "*The Church of Tomorrow* is a very valuable and welcome book. It was written with enthusiasm and conviction . . ." The long review in *The New York Times* was the most significant examination of Watkin's book. The *Times* reviewer wrote, "Gothic architecture, says Professor Watkin, was functional. But modern copies of Gothic are, obviously, not functional at all . . . . We need to return, not by any means to an imitation of Gothic line and ornament, but to a re-creation of the clarity and vigor which marked Gothic building, and to that strength and beauty of feeling in architecture which this author calls 'romance.' "

The author must also have appreciated the conclusion of the critique in the *Times*. It said, ". . . Professor Watkin has emphasized precisely the qualities of all beautiful and enduring structures which are essential to worthy building." This was a lasting tribute to *The Church of Tomorrow* and to its thesis, painstaking research, and recommendations.

Watkin shared this project with his family. They remember the many evenings at home that Watkin, with his research materials and notes at hand, had written until well into the night. The genesis of his book could be traced to memorable visits to the treasures of European architecture in company with his wife and children both in 1925 and in 1928. At Christmas of 1936, soon after the publication of *The*

Church of Tomorrow, he wrote this dedication on the flyleaf of a copy to his firstborn, Ray:

> To my daughter—Annie Ray
> Within the walls of church or home
> Like richness blooms.
> We cannot reach beyond the veil
> which shrouds the future and the past.
> To each we grant that calm repose
> Eternal: telling us always
> of lasting values loved and true
> from sire to son yet ever new.
> Calling, challenging forward, on,
> Hopeful, rightful, to be reached
> Anon —Dad.

VI.

By 1938, William Ward Watkin had turned again to the active practice of architecture, adhering to the "very limited but selective practice . . . emphasizing creative opportunity" he had resolved to pursue. He soon found new commissions, among them, the restoration of Christ Church after its devastating fire (Watkin had been a communicant there very soon after his arrival in Houston in 1910), and a commission for a new St. Mark's Episcopal Church in Beaumont. At about the same time as these projects came a commission for the Garden Center in Hermann Park and the expansion of the Rice football stadium, which has been mentioned. These new projects seemed to reinvigorate him. President Lovett remarked that his "endless optimism had now apparently returned."

Certainly it pleased him that two of the commissions dealt so directly with church architecture.

Christ Episcopal Church (Cathedral since 1949) dated from 1839. It was first located in a small brick building facing Fannin at Texas Avenue, on property that was greatly expanded by additional purchases of adjacent land. Colonel William Fairfax Gray and a group of leading officials of the Republic of Texas were among the 28 men forming a congregation of the Protestant Episcopal Church.

The present Christ Church Cathedral, long a landmark at the original location facing Texas Avenue in downtown Houston, was constructed in 1893. In September 1938 a spectacular fire in the Waddell furniture warehouse, adjacent to the church on the north, roared out of control and threatened the entire church. However, the fire was confined to the chancel (the area containing the altar, pulpit, and organ), and thereby to spaces normally reserved for the choir and the clergy. Firemen had responded quickly and efficiently to the four-alarm blaze. The roof over the altar collapsed after some hours, to the dismay of many parishioners in the crowd attracted by radio reports of the conflagration, but the firefighters prevented far greater damage.

Christ Church had a tradition of ecumenism dating back to the days of the Republic, when there were few churches in Houston. There are records of weddings and funerals for members of various denominations conducted by the first rector, the Reverend Charles Gillett. It was fitting, therefore, that the priceless rood screen separating the chancel from the main portion of the church was saved by a determined Roman Catholic fireman. He continued to pour water on the intricately carved screen, which suffered only minor scorching. The altar, organ, pulpit, and furnishings were unfortunately destroyed.

Carl Mulvey, an architect serving on the vestry of Christ Church, was engaged to oversee the total restoration of the chancel. Watkin was commissioned to design the restored area. His responsibilities extended from replacing the original altar and stained-glass windows, to redesigning the altar rail and reredos (the screen behind the altar), and even to selecting the upholstery on the bishop's chair.

The altar, intricately carved, had been made in England in 1893 to the specifications of the firm of ecclesiastical consultants retained by Bishop George Kinsolving. It was first thought to have been totally destroyed in the fire, but a small portion remained, only discolored by smoke. This was carefully cleaned, and revealed enough of the carving pattern for skilled artisans to duplicate it at a millwork shop in Houston. The salvaged piece was then incorporated into the new altar. Bishop Quin, ever mindful of tradition, had recommended this action.

Watkin enjoyed this commission, involving as it did opportunities of historic research and church design and the procurement of appropriate materials and furnishings. He hewed close to the budget allowed him, but there were welcome additions as contributions toward the restoration project were received from Houstonians of many churches and faiths, in addition to generous gifts from parishioners and other local Episcopalians.

The new furnishings were made to Watkin's detailed designs by a Milwaukee company specializing in ecclesiastical work. The stained-glass windows, however, were made in Houston. In 1939, a splendid new Aeolian-Skinner organ, the final item needed to complete the difficult restoration, was installed for the Easter Week services at Christ Church. The congregation then saw, for the first time, the redesigned and renovated chancel, with the new altar, windows, and furnishings all in place. It had been a project that Watkin thoroughly enjoyed.

However, Watkin was still busy with another project at Christ Church. This was the beautiful Golding Memorial Chapel. With what evolved as a resourceful use of space, Watkin turned storage closets on the first and second floors into a memorial chapel for Charles Dudley Golding, a Houston industrialist, and his son, Dudley Stafford Golding. The chapel, correctly identified as a "magnificent and intimate space," had its own splendid altar, triptych, pews, and other handsomely designed furnishings.

A second church commission he received as the late 1930s moved into the early 1940s was that of St. Mark's Episcopal Church in Beaumont. St. Mark's provided the means for turning some of the key recommendations in *The Church of Tomorrow* from theory to reality. The new center of worship had to fit in architecturally with the adjoining parish house, which Watkin had designed earlier for the rector of St. Mark's in 1915—one of his first commissions after opening his own office in the Scanlan Building in 1914. In 1915, members of the vestry of St. Mark's had decided that they could no longer delay building a parish house, which would also serve as the main church until a church could be built later. (An existing adjacent house had been remodeled into a rectory in 1914.) The parish house, of plaster with brick trim, involved a Romanesque treatment of the windows. Caldwell McFaddin, a member of St. Mark's and one of Watkin's first students, had worked with him on details of the parish house.

In 1939, almost a quarter-century later, Watkin began sketching plans for a new St. Mark's that would follow one of his tenets: emphasis upon the interior rather than the exterior of the church. This substantially larger structure would harmonize with the parish house and adjoining church properties. A plain yet attractive exterior of brick and plaster had a 30-foot belfry to the right of the main entrance. The interior featured a 24-foot ceiling, wide aisles, and a beautiful circular stained-glass window over the main entry. One of the rectors of St. Mark's, the Reverend Charles Wyatt-Brown, later became the rector at Palmer Memorial Church in Houston.

The Garden Center in Hermann Park, built in 1938, was another interesting commission for Watkin. During almost three decades of planning the buildings and grounds at Rice, he had of necessity become knowledgeable about landscaping in Houston. Also, as architect for the nearby Miller Outdoor Theater, he was interested in this latest addition to Hermann Park.

One-third of the money required for the Garden Center and Botanical Gardens project had been raised by the Federation of Garden Clubs of Houston. Located on Hermann Drive northeast of the Miller Theater, the project included a clubhouse for Federation meetings, an auditorium, and storage areas for rare plants. A system of walks circling a central rose garden led to plantings of a wide variety of native flowers and shrubs, as well as new varieties that adapted well to the local climate.

William Ward Watkin designed a one-story frame structure for the Garden Center, in the style of a Southern colonial home. A taller central section was flanked by lower wings left and right. The design was dominated by a graceful portico with four fluted columns in front of the principal entrance. Construction was delayed somewhat while fund-raising reached the required goal, but proceeded rapidly after ground-breaking ceremonies on January 6, 1941.

VII.

When Watkin emphasized that the prime objective of his new policy of "reducing and concentrating his work" would be to afford a "much larger portion of my time to devote to my children," it would have been far more explicit and accurate for him to have written "an even larger portion of my time." The tradition of much attention to activities with Ray, Rosemary, and Billy, established early at 5009 Caroline, was carefully maintained.

Though the Watkin family had taken wonderful summertime vacations in the 1920s to places such as California, New Mexico, Vermont, and Europe, vacations during the 1930s were now spent closer to home, but still in the tradition of family togetherness.

Josephine Watkin explained her new husband's need for closeness within the family in 1934, soon after their marriage. She wrote of Watkin being a man ". . . sensitive, emotional, artistic, loving beauty in spirit as in visual things. [And] loving love and to be loved by his family—with only the great need that a lonely only child could feel—always needing the warmth of companionship."

The family's emphasis on education continued. Ray entered Rice in September 1932, and was elected to membership in Phi Beta Kappa in 1936. She graduated that June with a baccalaureate degree in liberal arts with a major in French. Rosemary followed her older sister to the Institute in 1934 and was awarded the baccalaureate in architecture in 1938. While still a junior, she also won her election to Phi Beta Kappa. Bill chose to follow a professional military career, entering the U.S. Military Academy as a cadet in 1938. After graduating from Kinkaid in 1934, he attended Culver Military Academy, an excellent preparatory for West Point. Congressman Albert Thomas of the Class of 1920 at Rice and a friend of the Watkin family knew Bill to be a qualified candidate for USMA. He did not have an appointment open for 1937 when young Watkin would complete his studies at Culver, but would have one in 1938.

To await the West Point appointment, Bill entered Rice in September 1937 with the Class of 1941. He enrolled as a freshman in the Department of Architecture. Virtually all of the five subjects required for freshmen architects would help prepare him for his "plebe" year at West Point. General Rudolph Kuldell, a 1912 honor graduate of USMA and an executive with Hughes Tool Company who encouraged Bill to go to West Point, confirmed this. Rice's infamous Mathematics 100, along with physics, were clearly of value in what would essentially be an engineering course at "The Point." French and English were also in the beginning USMA curriculum. The fifth course at Rice, "architectural subjects," involved drafting, which was also an engineering requisite. Bill Watkin had an enjoyable year at Rice. He started his "plebe" year at the Point in August 1938, with no idea that his Class of 1942 would be the first class to graduate after Pearl Harbor, the "day of infamy" that would plunge the nation into World War II.

Rosemary had met Nolan E. Barrick, a student in architecture, soon after enrolling for her own architectural studies at Rice in 1934. Barrick, an excellent student, earned his bachelor of arts degree in 1935, bachelor of science in architecture in 1936, and master of arts degree in 1937. He followed this with a trip to Europe in 1938, having been awarded the Mary Alice Elliott loan fund traveling scholarship. Barrick was to have an outstanding career as a talented architect, professor, and university administrator. He and Rosemary continued to date after first meeting on campus, and were married on October 27, 1938.

In 1935, while still an undergraduate at Rice, young Nolan had been offered part-time work as a student draftsman in Watkin's office. Barrick worked for Watkin on many different projects during the next four years. These included an extensive remodeling of the old Foley Brothers store in downtown Houston and also an extensive addition to the Kipling Street home of George Cohen, chairman of Foley Brothers. Cohen had gotten to know Watkin well in 1927 during the building of the Cohen House at Rice. A strong friendship had developed between the two men, which would last for the rest of Watkin's life.

In the mid-1930s, Watkin received an unusual commission in an interesting way. Howard Hughes, Jr., a Rice alumnus and then an industrialist, movie magnate, and inventor, appeared in Watkin's campus office one day, having just arrived from Hollywood [9]. Watkin had known "young Howard," as he had called him, since 1917. Howard Hughes, Jr., was a precocious teenager when Watkin had designed the Hughes' home at 3921 Yoakum in the heart of the then new Montrose Place. In those days, Howard's hobbies had been primarily building early radio sets and adjusting high-performance automobiles in the family garage.

The architect, William Ward Watkin, in Houston, 1926. Photo by Frank J. Schlueter.

William Ward Watkin in his architectural office in the Scanlan Building (11th floor) in the 1920s. One of his former students, Clarence Sanford, can be seen in the background. Courtesy of the Woodson Research Center, Rice University Library, William Ward Watkin Papers.

The Main Building of Sul Ross Normal College in Alpine Texas as it appeared in 1920.

The original Miller Memorial Theater, designed by Watkin, was completed in 1921.

The handsome new Galveston, Texas Y.W.C.A. building that Watkin designed in 1923–24. From Brochure of the Works of William Ward Watkin, *1927.*

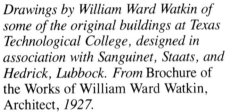

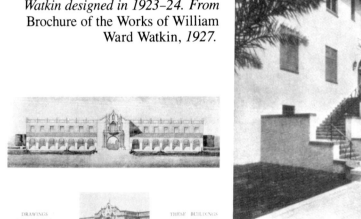

Drawings by William Ward Watkin of some of the original buildings at Texas Technological College, designed in association with Sanguinet, Staats, and Hedrick, Lubbock. From Brochure of the Works of William Ward Watkin, Architect, *1927.*

Sketch by William Ward Watkin of the North Facade of the Administration Building of Texas Tech University in Lubbock, built in 1924–25. From Nolan Barrick: Texas Tech . . . The Unobserved Heritage, *Texas Tech Press, Lubbock, Texas, 1985.*

281

The completed north facade of the Administration Building for Texas Technological University. From Nolan Barrick: Texas Tech . . . The Unobserved Heritage, *Texas Tech Press, Lubbock, Texas, 1985.*

The south facade of the Administration Building at Texas Technological University, undated. From Nolan Barrick: Texas Tech . . . The Unobserved Heritage, *Texas Tech Press, Lubbock, Texas, 1985.*

The Houston Public Library, designed in the Spanish Renaissance style by William Ward Watkin in association with Louis Glover, is located at Smith and McKinney. From Brochure of the Works of William Ward Watkin, *1927.*

Another view of the Houston Public Library. This photo was taken in 1930, eight years after the library was completed.

The Julia Ideson Building of the Houston Public Library as it appears today. Photo by Paul Hester.

Opening day of The Museum of Fine Arts, Houston, April 12, 1924. This was one of Watkin's most significant commissions. Photo by Frank J. Schlueter. Courtesy of the Archives Collection, The Museum of Fine Arts, Houston.

"The Dance of the Nine Muses." In celebration of the 25th Anniversary of the Houston Art League, April 13, 1925, nine Rice faculty daughters danced on the steps of the newly opened museum. They were Ray (Polyhymnia) and Rosemary (Euterpe) Watkin, Virginia Walker (Urania), Alice Caldwell (Clio), Dorothy Weiser (Melpomene), Nevenna (Calliope) and Katherine (Terpsichore) Tsanoff, Katherine Ander (Erato), and Mary Stuart Tidden (Thalia). Photo by Frank J. Schlueter. Courtesy of the Archives Collection, The Museum of Fine Arts, Houston.

The Nine Muses and friends gather around a huge birthday cake celebrating the 25th anniversary of the Art League of Houston. Photo by Frank J. Schlueter. Courtesy of the Archives Collection, The Museum of Fine Arts, Houston.

*James H. Chillman, Jr., Rice
architectural faculty and first director of the
Museum of Fine Arts. From the Archives of
Rice University.*

*The completed Museum of Fine Arts, Houston,
as it appeared in 1926 after the new wings had
been added.*

*Another view of the Museum of Fine Arts in
1926. From* Brochure of the Works of
William Ward Watkin, Architect, *1927.*

Watkin designed a new building for the Kinkaid School at Richmond and Graustark in 1925. All three of his children had earlier graduated from this fine elementary school. From Brochure of the Works of William Ward Watkin, *1927.*

The Methodist Hospital, designed by Watkin, opened its doors to the public in 1951. Watkin passed away there in 1952 after breaking his knee and developing an untreatable staphylococcus infection. From Marilyn McAdams Sibley: History of the Hospital *(brochure), Methodist Hospital, Houston.*

*The residence of Mr. and Mrs. Howard Hughes at 3921 Yoakum Blvd.,
completed in 1917, was one of the first private residences designed by
Watkin. From* Brochure of the Works of William Ward Watkin, *1927.*

*Facing Main Street directly across from the main entrance to
Rice, #2 Sunset Blvd. is the former residence of Mr. and Mrs.
Harry C. Wiess. After their deaths, Mr. and Mrs. Wiess left
their magnificent home, completed in 1920, to Rice
University. From* Brochure of the Works of William Ward
Watkin, *1927.*

The grave marker of Howard Hughes, wealthy and successful industrialist and movie magnate. Watkin was a longtime acquaintance of Hughes and his parents.

The Glenwood Cemetery monument of the Howard Hughes family, designed by Watkin at Howard Hughes' request, was built about 1935. Originally a fifth trumpet stood in the center of the circular monument.

Mr. and Mrs. Neill T. Masterson's home at 5120 Montrose Blvd., one of the many private homes designed by Watkin, was built in 1922. From Brochure of the Works of William Ward Watkin, *1927.*

Frederick A. and Blanche Heitmann built this Watkin-designed home at #1 Longfellow Lane, in Shadyside. The house was completed in 1923. From Brochure of the Works of William Ward Watkin, *1927.*

The home of Dr. and Mrs. E.M. Armstrong at 1128 Bissonnet was completed in 1923. From Brochure of the Works of William Ward Watkin, *1927.*

The B.B. Gilmer home on North Blvd. in Broadacres, an area for which Watkin designed a number of homes, was completed in 1926.

TRINITY EPISCOPAL CHURCH   HOUSTON TEXAS   OCT 27, 1938   FRANK C. DILL

*A drawing of Trinity Episcopal Church, Houston, by Frank C. Dill,
architectural graduate of the Class of 1934. This was one of Watkin's
first major church commissions. Completed in 1919,
Watkin designed it in association with his long-time associates
Cram and Ferguson. Used by permission of the artist.*

*Palmer Memorial Chapel, showing
the bell tower. From the program for
the dedication of the Chapel, 1927.*

*Palmer Memorial Chapel
was built in 1927 as a
memorial to her brother by
Mrs. E. L. Neville, to serve
as a campus chapel for Rice
Institute. Designed by
Watkin, it is located on Main
Street next to the Autry
House, also his design.
Photo by Paul Hester.*

292

The interior of the Palmer Memorial Chapel. Stephen Fox, architectural historian, emphasized that this chapel was closely akin to that of the chancel of Santa Maria dei Miracoli in Venice. Watkin had drawn this chancel in great detail in a sketchbook while he was in Italy in 1925. Photo by Paul Hester.

The parish house of St. Mark's Episcopal Church, Beaumont, Texas, which Watkin designed in 1915.

St. Mark's Episcopal Church, Beaumont, Texas. Designed by Watkin in 1939, this church allowed him to utilize some of the recommendations he made for church design in his book The Church of Tomorrow. Photo by J.C. Morehead, Jr.

The Central Church of Christ, designed in 1939 and located in the 4100 block of Montrose in Houston, again allowed Watkin to put into practice many of his recommendations from The Church of Tomorrow. *Photo by Shoemake-Stiles.*

The Golding Memorial Chapel at Christ Church Cathedral in Houston, was designed by Watkin in the late 1930s. A magnificent yet intimate space, it was designed with its own altar, triptych, pews, and other handsome furnishings. Photo by Nolan E. Barrick.

Young Hughes had attended Rice as an engineering student, enrolling for the 1922-1923 academic year shortly before his sixteenth birthday. He managed to fail Mathematics 100, reportedly for lack of attention to class assignments rather than for lack of ability. His instructor was the memorable Miss Alice Dean, fellow in mathematics and assistant librarian, a post she held for a third of a century. Her freshman math course was the nemesis of most new students.

Howard Hughes, Sr., and his wife, Allene Gano Hughes, had died in the early 1920s and were buried in the old Glenwood Cemetery on Washington Avenue. Their son, Howard, Jr., then withdrew from Rice Institute in order to help run the family-owned Hughes Tool Company, which was already a major manufacturer of equipment for the expanding oil industry. He later attended the California Institute of Technology.

When Howard appeared at Professor Watkin's office, he explained that his purpose in calling on him was to request that the architect design an appropriate memorial for his parents at the family plot at Glenwood. When Watkin asked Howard for his own suggestions regarding such a memorial, young Hughes produced from his pocket a small gold watch fob that his father had worn and treasured. It resembled a small, golden saxophone. He asked if it would suggest an idea to Watkin for the tomb. After deep thought, Watkin came up with a suggestion. The little object could be interpreted as a musical instrument more suitable to a cemetery, Gabriel's horn, the horn that the Archangel Gabriel would sound on Judgment Day. Howard liked the idea.

Watkin then designed a semicircle of four tall, graceful bronze trumpets, slender at the bottom and opening gracefully at the top, arranged around a fifth trumpet. Howard Hughes, Jr., was pleased with the creative, striking, yet appropriate result. He was in Houston soon again to see the memorial horns installed to mark the family plot.

There was a sequel, however, to the story of Gabriel and the horns on the Hughes' graves. All of the trumpets disappeared one night during the late 1930s, only to be discovered by the police on the docks at the Port of Houston in a shipment of scrap metal destined for Japan. They were recovered, repaired and placed again at the Hughes family plot. Howard Robard Hughes, Jr., lies there today with his parents, his grave also watched over by Watkin's graceful trumpets of the Archangel Gabriel, which Hughes himself had commissioned.

VIII.

The very first Rice Institute casualty of World War II had been a German lieutenant who died in Poland, killed in the first lightning-like advances of his panzer division rolling east toward Poznan in 1939. The soldier was Kurt von Johnson, a member of the Rice Class of 1933. The family had apparently Americanized their name before returning to their native Germany in 1931. The death was reported on the front page of the *Thresher,* the campus weekly, with a picture of the lieutenant sent by the official Nazi news agency.

As the Sunday broadcast of the New York Philharmonic was interrupted by news bulletins on the December 7, 1941, the Japanese attack on Pearl Harbor, the first U.S. citizen and alumnus of Rice had already been killed in action. He was Oscar Dean Wyatt, Jr., of the Class of 1939, a pilot shot down at Honolulu's Clark Field while taking off in pursuit of Japanese bombers [10].

The earliest specific indication of war at Rice was the formal opening of a Naval Reserve Officers Training Corps (NROTC) unit on campus in May 1941. Watkin had been assigned by President Lovett to be the faculty supervisor for many war-related affairs on the Rice campus. Thus he was soon taking part in the discussions regarding the new naval ROTC, which involved his good friend, Congressman Albert Thomas of the Class of 1920. Congressman Thomas, well positioned on both Appropriations and Military Affairs Committees, was able to expedite both the establishment and funding of the NROTC branch at Rice. By the time the 1941–1942 academic year opened, Watkin had already met many times with representatives of the Eighth Naval District in New Orleans and Captain Thaddeus Thomson, who would command the reserve training unit at Rice.

Captain Thomson and his staff had been provided temporary offices in the Engineering Laboratories until the NROTC was finally approved. As classes began in mid-September of 1941, a small temporary building near Rice Boulevard, built under Watkin's direction, was ready for occupancy by the more than 100 enrollees in the program. A marked contrast with the Rice Institute of World War I days was soon evident, primarily in the emphasis on preparing students for the growing possibility of active military service right on campus.

In the autumn of 1941, as FDR's "limited national emergency" continued, the *Thresher* stressed the need for trained specialists in the armed forces. Students were urged to hasten to complete their degrees, as the administration planned for year-round classes and earlier commencements short on ceremony. The premedical majors could thus be sent for their M.D. degrees as soon as possible.

The U.S. Navy, with a continuing need for officers (especially those trained in engineering), signed a broader agreement with Rice Institute effective with the 1942–1943 academic year. More than 500 officer candidates, almost 350 of them engineering (or V-12) students, were taught the year around in three four-month terms with no summer break. These men were in uniform and on active duty. The dormitories were modified somewhat to enable them all to be quartered there. The trainees soon constituted a good half of the male student body. There were many problems for them because of the rigorous Institute curriculum, complicated further by shorter terms and longer assignments in class and military studies. But there was no relaxation in established academic standards.

William Ward Watkin would remember the challenges, the excitement, and the accomplishments during World War II at Rice. He was given a series of assignments on the campus, at Dr. Lovett's request, that were directly related to the hundreds of Rice men who would soon go on active duty on many fronts. These ranged from his participation in providing the facilities and related administration for a major U.S. Navy operation, to administering the Civil Defense program at the campus, with numerous "blackouts" and rehearsals for the various contingencies of wartime. The war was a tense and concentrated time for him. His son Bill had graduated at West Point in 1942, and by 1943 had been sent to the South Pacific with the combat engineers, where he would remain for the rest of the war. Many of Watkin's former students were now writing to him from their posts all over the world.

Meanwhile, there had been changes in the faculty of the Department of Architecture as early as 1939, as members of the teaching staff began to depart for active duty with the armed forces. The first departure was James K. Dunaway of the Class of 1936. He had returned to Rice as an instructor after completing a master's degree at Columbia University, but was called to active duty in the U.S. Navy late in 1939. Then, in 1941, Claude Hooton, who had been with the department for a decade, accepted a commission in the merchant marine out of New Orleans. This brought the threatening manpower shortage sharply into focus. Hooton had taught essential courses in sophomore and freshman design as well as in the history of ornament, while accepting his share of extracurricular responsibilities within the Department of Architecture.

The situation grew worse when James (Bud) Morehead, who had come to Rice from Carnegie Tech to assist Stayton Nunn in teaching structures, went on active duty as a U.S. Army reservist in the Pacific in 1940. Then Nunn himself was called up and sent to Randolph Field in San Antonio. This left only William Ward Watkin and James H. Chillman of the regular staff, confronting the additional problem of year-round classes. Watkin had continued to teach fourth- and fifth-year design and architectural history, along with his ongoing administrative duties and a variety of new assignments relating to the national emergency. Jimmy Chillman taught junior design, architectural history, life drawing, watercolor, and art history. He also continued as the part-time director of the Houston Museum of Fine Arts, and had his own responsibilities in counseling and administration on campus.

Watkin had, of course, anticipated the loss of younger teaching staff to the armed forces. To counteract this, he was fortunate to be able to bring Thomas K. FitzPatrick to Rice from the School of Architecture at Clemson in the fall of 1940. A graduate of the Massachusetts Institute of Technology, FitzPatrick was an experienced teacher at what was one of the better schools of architecture in the South. He would teach basic courses in design and history, and was a specialist in structures. FitzPatrick would remain at Rice until 1946 before leaving for Iowa State and later, the chairmanship of the School of Architecture at the University of Virginia.

FitzPatrick, a popular and capable teacher, made many friends at Rice while making a real contribution at a time of stress. He remained in touch with Watkin and his former colleagues for many years after his departure from Rice.

Watkin then asked Milton McGinty to accept a pro tempore appointment teaching city planning and perspective, to which McGinty agreed, rounding out the four-man team that would see the Department of Architecture through World War II. In addition to classroom instruction and the criticism of traditional design problems on a year-round basis, the wartime faculty devoted a considerable amount of time to counseling.

Students were understandably perplexed by the uncertainties of whether they would be called up in the draft or be allowed to continue their studies. But, for Watkin and his staff, there was the satisfaction of keeping the department fully operational during wartime, and the appreciation of letters that came from former students and graduates on duty with the armed forces.

In the months preceding the outbreak of war, Watkin had seen two major changes in the original team that had guided the Rice Institute from its inception. Edgar Odell Lovett had decided, upon reaching his seventieth birthday on May 14, 1941, to retire from the presidency. He offered to remain in office until the naming of a successor, and this was accepted immediately by the other trustees. Then, less than three months later, Captain James A. Baker died on August 2. He was 85, having been a trustee of Rice for 50 years, since May 13, 1891. The original trustees had accepted their election on that date, six days before Secretary of State George W. Smith officially granted the charter of the Institute by signing a certified copy at his office in Austin.

On the Sunday following the announcement of President Lovett's decision to retire, Watkin wrote to his colleague and friend of almost a third of a century. Although relatively brief, his letter expressed well the respect, admiration, and lasting friendship that had developed between two men who had devoted much of their lives together to what Professor Watkin so accurately described as "a noble work faithfully done."

The text of the letter was as follows:

THE RICE INSTITUTE Houston, Texas
Department of Architecture

My Dear President Lovett:

Your decision announced today comes with intense regret to each of us, though with personal understanding that it is a privilege nobly earned.

Out of the marsh and swamp of this campus you have brought beauty and fineness at every step along the way. Into its building you have woven your life with all its clearness and kindliness. All that we see about us is yours in every sense, creating, nurturing and fulfilling toward an enduring meaning. It will ever be yours in each step forward so long as you shall live.

In retrospect you have the right to view with warmth and joy a noble work faithfully done. I pray that for years and into generations to come it may carry on toward the soundness and beauty which your vision for it holds.

With cordial personal regards

I am sincerely Yours

Wm Ward Watkin

Sunday, May 18, 1941

President Lovett replied, on June 4, 1941:

THE RICE INSTITUTE, Houston, Texas
Office of the President
4 June 1941

My dear Mr. Watkin:

On opening your very kind letter about the change in my status at Rice, I was somewhat terrified to recall how long, unbroken, and intimate a line you have on my manifold limitations. So I was all the more gratified to discover how many pleasant things you could write from that background of personal experience. In turn, I know, I think, a great deal better than anyone else the length and breadth and heighth and depth of my obligation to you straight through these years. And I have appreciated more highly than I can tell you your concern in these latter days for my health and comfort on the top floor of the tower. For all that you have been to this institution and for all that you are to us now I shall treasure your letter for the rest of my days.

With all my thanks, please accept also my very best wishes, in which Mrs. Lovett joins, for you and your family, and believe me to remain, as always,

Faithfully yours

Edgar O. Lovett

It was a letter that William Ward Watkin would ". . . treasure for the rest of [his] days." Fortunately President Lovett remained in office until March 1, 1946, allowing for gradual adjustment to a postwar world at Rice.

However, as World War II intensified on all fronts, Watkin's thoughts were dominated by his growing concern for his only son, Bill, and for his two sons-in-law. William Ward Watkin, Jr., was well into his final year at West Point when the Japanese struck their devastating blow at Pearl Harbor. As an honor graduate of the U.S. Military Academy and a combat engineer, he would almost certainly face frontline action in either Europe or the Pacific after his Class of 1942 received their diplomas and commissions.

Lieutenant Watkin's father and his sister Ray attended his graduation at West Point in May of 1942, just six months after Pearl Harbor. General George Catlett Marshall, later chief of staff, secretary of state, secretary of defense, author of the Marshall Plan, and Nobel laureate, gave the commencement address. He announced to the audience and to the world that the first American troops had already landed in Ireland. It was from there that they would later go to North Africa.

After graduating from West Point on May 29, 1942, Second Lieutenant Watkin was assigned to the 2nd Engineer Battalion of the 2nd Infantry Division at Fort Sam Houston, in San Antonio. From there he was sent on maneuvers to provide advanced training for enlisted men who had completed basic training. For months, the newly commissioned officer crisscrossed inaccessible areas of Louisiana and Mississippi, where the battlefield conditions of jungle warfare could be simulated. He was often near the "Piney Woods" area of Mississippi, where his grandfather Frederick William Watkin had gone to seek his fortune in the burgeoning lumber industry of the early 1890s.

There had been a leave, all too brief, for Lieutenant Watkin to come home between graduation and reporting to Fort Sam Houston. While his son had been at West Point, the senior Watkin had enjoyed annual visits with his son. Watkin had been able to combine trips to USMA with meetings of the National Architectural Advisory Board in Washington, D.C. He greatly enjoyed his visits to West Point, the site of Cram & Goodhue's first notable commission, overlooking the Hudson River. Now, in 1943, with the likelihood of a long separation before them, father and son agreed to exchange frequent letters. Since chess had been a favorite game of theirs, it was decided that each letter would contain the next move in a long-continuing chess match. Also, letters from the South Pacific would be understandably brief because of wartime censorship.

Lieutenant Watkin's first move in the new chess game came in a letter via overseas mail from New Guinea. Bill had shipped out from Camp Pickett, Virginia, as a combat engineer with the 106th Engineer Battalion of the 31st ("Dixie") Infantry Division. His outfit was soon in the thick of a campaign devised at the highest level. The U.S. Joint Chiefs of Staff decided upon a so-called "stepping stone" approach leading to a final invasion of Japan itself from the south, as opposed to the original strategy of moving toward Japan from the Aleutian Islands in the North Pacific.

Meanwhile, both of the Watkin sons-in-law were on active duty, and also headed overseas. Rosemary's husband, Nolan Barrick, was an ensign in the U.S. Navy. After intensive training in the specialty of interpreting aerial photographs, he was sent to the South Pacific and to Australia. Ensign Barrick would not return to the States until 1945.

Carl Biehl, who had married Ray in December 1939, had valuable experience as a shipping executive. Ray and Carl went to Washington, D.C., together late in 1941. He had accepted a position there with the War Shipping Administration. A year later, he was commissioned a captain in the Army Transportation Corps and, after a brief duty in New Orleans, was sent overseas to the key port of Bristol, England, on the Bristol Channel. Huge quantities of vital war material were being moved through this major English port, and the ships had to be unloaded with great speed so that they could return to the U.S. On D-Day, June 6, 1944, Biehl landed in the midst of "Operation Overlord" on Omaha Beach in Normandy—his job was to oversee unloading the supply ships on the beach. Promoted to major, he remained in the European theater for the remainder of the war, until October 1945, when he returned home as a lieutenant colonel.

After her husband left for England from New Orleans, Ray returned to her home in Houston. There Rosemary joined her soon after Ensign Barrick's departure for the South Pacific. Rosemary quickly accepted a position as a draftsman for a major oil company. The two sisters took an apartment at the Park Lane, near their father's home, and Ray enrolled for graduate work at the nearby Rice Institute. She pursued her master of arts degree in the history of art, which was awarded in 1944. Her work was done in the School of Architecture and her adviser was James H. Chillman, whose special field was, of course, the history of art. In the 1930s, before the war, Chillman had divided his summers between a lectureship at his alma mater, the University of Pennsylvania, and the guiding of groups on art tours of Italy and France for the well-known Bureau of University Travel. In 1944, Chillman completed his twentieth year as director of the Museum of Fine Arts, and three decades in the Department of Architecture at Rice Institute.

It was a great comfort for William Ward Watkin to have his daughters back in Houston during the war, with Bill, Carl, and Nolan all overseas in combat zones. In Houston, the Watkin family all remained busy and hopeful, but were never unaware of the danger lurking for the other members of their family. The mail was eagerly awaited, and quickly sorted for letters from overseas. They listened daily to the early evening radio broadcasts of Edward R. Murrow and the other commentators, and to scan the Houston press for Ernie Pyle's prize-winning reports from the Pacific and from Normandy.

Two other Houston families, friends of the Watkins, had sons in the 31st (Dixie) Division. Serving there with Bill Watkin were John Harris Meyers and Charles Lykes. Meyers, a 1939 graduate of the University of Texas Law School, was married to Alice Baker Jones, a granddaughter of Captain James A. Baker. Lykes was the son of Mr. and Mrs. James McKay Lykes of the shipping company [11].

Bill Watkin was taking part in some of the most dangerous operations in the South Pacific as the "stepping stone" campaign of the Joint Chiefs of Staff moved U.S. units west across New Guinea and on to the Moluccas, then due north to the Philippines. Late in 1942, he was promoted to the rank of first lieutenant, and then in May 1943, to captain, as commander of Company B of the 106th Engineer Battalion. In 1943, he was promoted to major and battalion operations officer. His unit made assault landings at Aitape, a Japanese stronghold on the coast of northeastern New Guinea, and at nearby Point Sarmi [12].

Major Watkin's 106th Engineer Battalion made two more assault landings as the 31st Infantry Division continued in the exact path of the planned approach toward an invasion of Japan. The first landing was at Morotai, northernmost of the Moluccas (Halmaheras), and only 300 miles from the Philippines. The second landing, even more important strategically, was on Mindanao, the most southern of the Philippine Islands, in an area heavily defended by the enemy. For this operation, Major Watkin's battalion was awarded the coveted Presidential Unit Citation, with its colorful and distinctive patch and ribbon. A few months prior to VJ-Day, Watkin was given command of the 239th Engineer Construction Battalion.

Germany had surrendered as of midnight, May 8, 1945. The U.S. war against Japan had taken a different turn, with mass aerial bombing of Tokyo, Yokohama, Osaka, and other major cities spreading fire storms and tremendous destruction. An invasion of the enemy's homeland, predicted to cost a possible 100,000 or more U.S. casualties, might still be necessary but had become less of a certainty. Then suddenly, the war in the Pacific was also over. Emperor Hirohito agreed to recommended capitulation only days after Captain Kermit Beehan of the Class of 1940 at Rice released the atom bomb from the *Enola Gay* over Hiroshima on the morning of August 6, 1945.

The long-running airmail chess game between William Ward Watkin and his son had only just been concluded with the end of hostilities in the Pacific. From Japan, Lieutenant Colonel Watkin would continue the frequent letters to his father, as he would not return to Houston until December 1946. The 16 months since the end of World War II had seen new assignments that would further his military career. After deactivation of his 239th Engineer Construction Battalion at Leyte in the Philippines, he was named division engineer and commanding officer of the 311th Engineer Battalion, 86th Infantry Division. In July 1946, he joined General MacArthur's headquarters in Tokyo as chief inspector of engineer troop units for the entire Pacific Theater.

Meanwhile, at home during the war, Ray had been serving as secretary to the Houston Chapter of the American Red Cross, a job she held until her husband's return. Her husband, Colonel Carl Biehl, returned to Houston in the fall of 1945 from his final post with the Army Transportation Corps in Belgium. They would soon move to New Orleans, where Carl resumed his position as head of his own shipping firm, with offices in Houston, Galveston, and New Orleans. As had been long planned, Carl had joined his family's firm after graduating from the Harvard Business School in 1934. His father, Carl Biehl, Sr., died soon after this, and the younger Carl took over management of Biehl & Company.

Nolan Barrick also returned to Houston and civilian life late in 1945. He and Rosemary moved to Ames, Iowa, where he joined the architectural faculty of Iowa State University. They returned to Houston in the summers, where Barrick continued to work with his father-in-law on a number of new commissions as the postwar civilian economy revived.

It was a memorable day when Lieutenant Colonel Watkin returned to 5009 Caroline after three and a half years of absence in the South Pacific and Japan. Neither father nor son was demonstrably emotional, but they were both deeply thankful for Bill's safe return. While in Houston, Bill received official orders assigning him as an instructor to the U.S. Military Academy in the Department of Mechanics (Mechanical Engineering). Before reporting to West Point, however, the Army granted him a semester at the Massachusetts Institute of Technology as a graduate student. The four months in Cambridge, his father's birthplace, was a welcome change and an opportunity to prepare for a different phase in his career.

It signaled the beginning of his graduate studies that would, in time, bring him the degrees of master of science (California Institute of Technology, 1951) and doctor of philosophy (Columbia, 1964) as well as the later distinction of graduating first in a class of 528 officers at the Army's Command and General Staff College in Fort Leavenworth, Kansas.

IX.

A new postwar era had begun at Rice Institute as the 1946–1947 academic year opened. The faculty and administrative staffs, worn in mind and body by the 12-month operation, shortages, absence of colleagues, personal difficulties, and other problems of the war, gradually returned to normal.

In 1945, William Vermillion Houston, the distinguished physicist who had left the California Institute of Technology to become the long-sought successor to President Lovett, was settling in on the top floor of the Administration Building as the new president of the Rice Institute. He had an agreement with the trustees to raise salaries, establish a retirement fund, and to bring the number of faculty members to 100 from the wartime total of barely 60. The long-established policies of high quality in teaching and research, along with a low ratio of students to faculty, would be maintained. This was to be done in spite of a decision to increase enrollment substantially to 2,000, including many more graduate students. To aid in faculty recruitment, the rank of associate professor was added. Previously, assistant professors were promoted directly from assistant to full professorships. The revised system provided immediate and ongoing new strength both in recruiting, and in retaining, highly qualified faculty.

The trustees had agreed upon a new category of trustee emeritus, leaving room for a new generation of community leaders to be named to the governing board. William A. Kirkland, Gus Sessions Wortham, Dr. Frederick Rice Lummis, Harry Carothers Wiess, and Lamar Fleming, Jr., were soon elected, along with two other men who were to become active in the changes under way at the Institute: Harry C. Hanszen and George R. Brown. Hanszen had replaced the deceased Captain James A Baker in May 1942; George Brown was named to the trusteeship of Robert Lee Blaffer after the death of Blaffer, a founder of the Humble Oil & Refining Company in October 1942.

There had been no new construction at Rice during World War II. The last of the U.S. Navy V-12 students had left in July 1946, as the four-month, year-round terms came to an end. It was already apparent, however, that the physical plant would have to be expanded as soon as possible to accommodate the many former students returning after absences dating back to 1940, the new enrollees, and the postwar expansion of the student body.

The greatest need was for a library. Alice Dean, mathematics instructor from the Class of 1916, had been acting librarian for a third of a century and had been promoted to librarian in 1946, one year before her retirement. Beginning with an annual budget of $10,000, she and her assistant, Sarah Lane, had built the collections to more than 150,000 books. But the books were in almost a dozen campus locations, including having spilled over from the original location on the second floor of the Administration Building to the first floor and basement of that structure.

The obvious priority was the construction of a new central library. Rice had joined a new postwar consortium on the planning and construction of libraries at colleges and universities. There was general agreement that a classroom building, as well as an additional engineering laboratory, also ranked high on a list of needs. However, the significance of a library building soon took preference. Claude W. Heaps, senior professor in the Physics Department, had been named chairman of the faculty Library Committee. President Lovett decided to send Dr. Heaps and William Ward Watkin on a nationwide tour of institutions that were planning or already had new libraries.

Fortunately, the financial picture at the Rice Institute had improved most dramatically during World War II. This had come about largely through the efforts of Roy M. Hofheinz of the Class of 1932. The so-called "boy wonder" of area politics was serving as judge of Harris County when the estate of W.R. Davis, a veteran oil wildcatter, was filed in his court for probate. Davis had hit a potentially big strike in Starr County, near the Mexican border in the upper Rio Grande Valley. This was named the Rincon Field. Davis had borrowed about $5 million to bring these wells into production and provide a pipeline to the remote location, as well as for building a shipping terminal at the Port of Brownsville. He owned a 50% working interest in Rincon and nearby leases. Dan Moran's Continental Oil Company held the rest.

Davis' heirs and Judge Hofheinz had found it difficult to settle the estate, primarily because a high tax rate then in effect would apply to any corporate purchase of the property. The $5-million debt (at a time when a million dollars had a great deal more impact than today) was also a considerable deterrent to a proper and satisfactory sale agreement.

Judge Hofheinz decided that the solution might well be to sell Davis' holdings in the Rincon Field to a tax-exempt entity, specifically to the Rice Institute. He brought the matter to the attention of George Brown of Brown & Root, and to Harry Wiess, a founder of the Humble Oil & Refining Company who would become a Rice trustee two years later, after the death of William Marsh Rice II.

Brown and Wiess were invited to discuss the possible purchase of the oil field before a meeting of the governing board of the Institute. The detailed analysis that followed indicated that W.R. Davis' share of production from Rincon would justify a substantial cash offer to the heirs plus assumption of the $5-million debt. It was decided to offer $1 million in cash, if this could be raised quickly, in addition to the debt assumption.

A group of prominent Houstonians including George Brown and his brother Herman, Harry Wiess and Harry Hanszen, the Farish brothers (Stephen Power and William Stamps), and H.R. Cullen gave a total of $200,000. Colonel W.B. Bates and the other trustees of the Monroe D. Anderson Foundation agreed to provide another $300,000. It was agreed that this sum would apply to a campus building that would be a memorial to M.D. Anderson if the $300,000 could be recovered from operating the Rincon Field. The Rice Institute trustees then provided another $500,000 from endowment funds, to make up the total of $1 million in cash offered the Davis heirs.

The heirs accepted the offer just a week before Christmas Day 1942, and signed over almost one-half of the working interest in Rincon to the Rice Institute. This turned out to be an extremely profitable investment. The entire loan against Rincon was paid off within five years, in addition to the $1 million in cash for W.R. Davis' heirs. Net returns since, almost 50 years after the acquisition on December 18, 1942, have been a major factor in the improvement of cash flow and net asset totals at Rice. And, because of this fortunate development, coupled with some sizable gifts, the postwar program of building much needed new facilities for the Rice Institute made remarkable progress between 1946 and 1950.

Happily, the new surge of planning and construction on the campus included important new architectural consultantships for William Ward Watkin. These commissions involved Anderson Hall (1947), the Abercrombie Engineering Laboratory (1948), and the Fondren Library (1947–1950).

On all three projects, Watkin worked with the architects John Delabarre Staub and John T. Rather, Jr., partners in Staub & Rather. Staub had been the architect for many fine homes in Houston. Rather, a graduate of the Class of 1919 at Rice, had been one of Professor Watkin's most talented and active students, as well as a leader in the Architectural Society and its many undertakings on campus.

Anderson Hall, on the north side of the Academic Quadrangle, was ready for occupancy in August 1947. Its classrooms and faculty offices would include the new location of the Department of Architecture and were invaluable in relieving the overcrowding on campus. Ground was broken late in 1947 for the Fondren Library, financed in part by a $1-million gift from Mrs. Walter William (Ella) Fondren. It was to be for a memorial for her deceased husband, another of the founders of the Humble Oil & Refining Company. The estimated cost of the long-needed facility was $1.8 million. In addition to almost $100,000 from an Alumni Association Fund, a substantial part of the deficit of $800,000 was soon covered from an unrestricted bequest dating back more than a decade. E.L. Bender, a prosperous lumberman better known as the owner-operator of the downtown Hotel Bender (famous for its Sunday dinners), had left $200,000 to the Institute when he died in 1934.

Watkin, with Staub and Rather, had hoped to place the Fondren Library in the location envisioned in Cram's original master plan of the campus. This would have been west of the site on which it was actually built. The extremely long vista created back in 1910 by Cram & Goodhue was based on a central axis running from the main entrance through the sally port and the statue of the founder on west, almost to the eastern edge of today's Rice Stadium parking lots.

Faculty members, and a majority of the Library Committee, pointed out that it would be a long hike indeed from classrooms and offices to a library so located, especially in Houston's heat, humidity, thunderstorms, and wet northers. Their view prevailed, magnificent though a longer vista would have been. The Fondren Library was placed at the end of a shortened Academic Quadrangle, north and slightly west of the original Commons. Ralph Adams Cram and Bertram Grosvenor Goodhue's central axis, on which William Ward Watkin had worked as a draftsman beginning his architectural career in Boston as early as 1909, had been considerably shortened.

Mr. and Mrs. James S. Abercrombie and their daughter Josephine (of the Class of 1946 at Rice) provided $500,000 for the Abercrombie Engineering Laboratory. Completed late in 1948, this facility was badly needed as postwar enrollments in science and engineering continued to expand. It included, as an ornamental feature, a sculpture by William M. McVey of the Class of 1927, the first alumni sculpture on the campus. The work depicted the various ways in which the engineer changes, delivers, and stores the natural energy of the sun in the differing forms required by our heavily industrialized civilization. McVey would later receive recognition nationally for another important commission, a statue of Sir Winston Churchill for the British Embassy in Washington, D.C.

During these first postwar years, Watkin was busy adding to faculty of the Department of Architecture for the anticipated jump in enrollment. James Morehead and James K. Dunaway had both returned to Rice from active duty in the fall of 1946, at the same time that Thomas FitzPatrick left for Iowa State. The resumption of the traditional academic schedule for 1946–1947 helped restore more normal operations, but the return of veterans from pre-war classes was a new and major matter. Students returned who had left the Department of Architecture over various periods from their freshman year to the final months of the fifth-year master degree program.

The Rice Institute felt an obligation to help those now returning from the war to complete their degrees as soon as possible, and get on with their lives. However, when these veterans from a wide range of classes were added to those who had remained in course and to the usual list of new applicants, Watkin and his postwar faculty faced formidable problems of scheduling, manpower, and facilities.

A.A. Leifeste, Jr., who had gone into service with the U.S. Navy after completing his master's degree in architecture at Rice in 1936, was the next postwar addition to the faculty. He replaced Claude Hooton, who remained in New Orleans instead of returning to Rice.

James Morehead took over Stayton Nunn's key area of structures. Nunn, the most considerate of colleagues, continued to teach a class from time to time, but was very much involved in his private practice, especially as consulting architect to the Houston Independent School District, which had a major postwar expansion under way. James Karl Dunaway was assigned city planning, which Milton McGinty had taught during his welcome pro tempore assistance during the war. Dunaway spent more time, however, in sophomore and junior design as the full impact of Tom FitzPatrick's departure was felt.

The two final additions to the architectural faculty during this postwar era were Anderson Todd and Robert Folsom Lent, in the fall of 1949. Todd, an architectural graduate of Princeton in 1943, had completed the master's degree there in 1949, after military service. Lent, also a veteran, earned four degrees in architecture and fine arts. He graduated from Cornell and the Massachusetts Institute of Technology before postwar studies abroad, the latter at the Ecole Americaine des Beaux-Arts in Fontainebleau and at the American Academy in Rome.

After World War II, the Archi-Arts balls resumed. The Traveling Scholarship was now funded by patron gifts and private donations from the very active Rice Architectural Alumni Society, as the alumni began to prosper in their new and growing firms [13]. After the war, the architectural graduates of the 1930s had returned home to start their own practices in Houston, just as the postwar building boom was beginning in the 1950s (which extended into the next two decades). As a group, these Rice architects enjoyed much success and have left their mark on the architecture of Houston.

Meanwhile, William Ward Watkin had been invited to join a long-range advisory committee in Houston charged with planning the location of hospitals and support facilities in the mushrooming Texas Medical Center. Rapid and continuing growth of the new center directly south of the Rice Institute campus would make it, in time, one of the largest concentrations of medical facilities in the world. Until the late 1940s, for decades the only establishment there was the original Hermann Hospital.

Also while in the midst of consulting on the three Staub & Rather buildings at Rice, Watkin received a new church commission located near one of his first major buildings, the Museum of Fine Arts. This was the Central Church of Christ, a functional and beautiful place of worship covering much of the 4100 block on the west side of Montrose Boulevard. Here again, he had the opportunity to put into practice many of his recommendations in his 1936 book, *The Church of Tomorrow.*

In 1949, the American Institute of Architects held its annual meeting for the first time in Houston. It had been almost 40 years since Watkin, finding that the Houston Chapter of the AIA had become inactive in 1913, worked with Birdsall Briscoe and Olle Lorehn to restore it to active status. The new AIA charter had been granted to Houston in 1924. The silver anniversary of the Houston affiliate was celebrated in Houston with the well-attended national convention. At this 1949 meeting, Watkin was named a fellow of the AIA.

The certificate granting this honor recalled Watkin's many accomplishments as an architect, educator, and author. Graduates of the Rice Institute Department of Architecture, who were now leading architects themselves, watched from the audience as the certificate was presented to their mentor. Frank Lloyd Wright, architect of international distinction and an acquaintance of Watkin's for many years, was awarded the preeminent Gold Medal of the AIA at the meeting. Known for his acerbic wit, he was asked what he thought of the then-new Shamrock Hotel, site of the AIA convention. "It is the first time," he replied, "that I have been inside a jukebox."

In the same year, Watkin received an honor from his beloved alma mater. President Harold Stassen of the University of Pennsylvania appointed him to be a member of the Special Advisory Committee to the School of Fine Arts (which included the Department of Architecture). He looked forward to attending meetings of this group in Philadelphia.

After the Central Church of Christ was completed, Watkin entered into a new partnership with two of his former students, Milton McGinty and Stayton Nunn. In 1947, he helped secure for the firm one of the partnership's principal commissions: the new Methodist Hospital in the Texas Medical Center. The hospital would also incorporate a lovely chapel, the Wiess Chapel.

Watkin was particularly interested in designing the chapel. It was built as a memorial to Harry Carothers Wiess, an active member of the Rice governing board during the crucial postwar era at the Institute from 1944 until his death August 6, 1948.

Milton McGinty, the first Rice Institute Traveling Scholarship winner, had just completed a project of great consequence to his alma mater and to the city of Houston. This was the new 70,000-seat Rice Stadium at the extreme western boundary of the campus. It was a strikingly handsome and thoroughly functional structure of brick and soaring concrete, built at a cost of $3.3 million by Brown & Root, the world renowned engineering firm headed by Trustee George R. Brown and his brother Herman.

This stadium had been built in record time. The elapsed time from ground breaking until the first game in the new facility, the 1950 home season opener against Santa Clara, was an amazingly short eight months. The Institute had progressed from the old dirt practice field on which Philip Arbuckle's teams played before a few hundred spectators, to one of the finest football stadiums anywhere. In time, it would be the site of historic speeches by U.S. presidents Dwight D. Eisenhower and John F. Kennedy, as well as a speech by General Douglas MacArthur and a crusade by Billy Graham. It would also be the site of a future Super Bowl.

X.

As has been noted, William Ward Watkin had rejoiced over the safe return of his son from years of war in the South Pacific. Now Bill was thoroughly enjoying the new phase of his career as a faculty member at the U.S. Military Academy. On weekends, he and a colleague at West Point often went into New York City for a break from teaching. On one of these brief visits he met the roommate of his friend's fiancée. She was Carol Snyder, a young designer from Burlington, Iowa, and an art graduate of the University of Iowa, who had come to Manhattan to make her own career.

Lieutenant Colonel Watkin and Carol were immediately attracted to one another. They were married in Burlington in February 1949. In February 1950, she presented him with their first son, William

Ward Watkin III, born at West Point. The baby's grandfather was understandably delighted, and Bill and Carol soon brought William Ward III for a visit to Houston.

After World War II, Watkin had begun working on a new book on modern church architecture. The F.W. Dodge Corporation of New York City, well known as publishers for the profession, had produced a series of illustrated books, the popular "Building Types Studies in Architectural Record." In the fall of 1951, F.W. Dodge published Watkin's *Planning and Building the Modern Church*. In the well-illustrated volume, Watkin first examined the "evolution of modern church planning from 1900 to 1950." He then proceeded through the practical steps, from the organization and functions of a church building committee through the many stages resulting in a new church. These included selection of an appropriate site, preliminary studies, materials, the chancel ("heart of the church"), actual construction, and such detailed matters as walls and towers, lighting, heating and air conditioning, and furnishings. The book concluded, ". . . let us hope that . . . there shall be seen by all men a symbol above all and visible to all . . . . In the simple geometry of the cross it shall represent, not boundaries of creed, but universal understanding and justice."

The book illustrated the work of such internationally known architects such as Ralph Adams Cram, Bertram Grosvenor Goodhue, Eero Saarinen, Charles D. Maginnis, and Alden B. Dow. Among the illustrations were the Cadet Chapel at West Point (photographed by William Watkin, Jr.), the Princeton University Chapel, Our Lady Queen of Martyrs at Forest Hills, and the East Liberty and West Liberty Presbyterian Churches in Pittsburgh, designed by Cram.

Also represented were designs by a number of rising young architects who had studied under him. Among these were Talbott Wilson, S.I. Morris, Harold Calhoun, Harvin C. Moore, Hermon Lloyd, and Mace Tungate. Professor Watkin included illustrations of his own designs: St. Mark's Episcopal Church at Beaumont, the Golding Chapel, and the Wiess Chapel.

Watkin's basic philosophy was that great architecture is an architecture "of all the ages." This was made clear again in *Planning and*

Building the Modern Church, as it had been in Watkin's teaching, practice, and writing.

In the 1960s, Ray Watkin Hoagland, recalling her father's career of a half-century, noted that during perhaps the most transitional period in American architecture, he had succeeded in spanning a time of remarkable change "with flexibility."

Here was a man trained at the University of Pennsylvania under Paul Cret, from Lyon's historic Ecole des Beaux-Arts; and by Ralph Adams Cram, the apostle of Gothic tradition; and by Bertram Grosvenor Goodhue, Cram's partner and gifted designer. Yet as the decades moved on, her father "followed with interest the new movements in architecture of Le Corbusier and Frank Lloyd Wright."

Further, William Ward Watkin ". . . encouraged the new approach to design in his teaching and writing," while at the same time professing his basic philosophy: the belief that great architecture remains an architecture of all the ages. Watkin's daughter found this philosophy of her father best expressed in his poem at the beginning of Chapter IV of his book, *The Church of Tomorrow*:

> "To ages past we raise
> Our toast . . .
> And to our age the hope;
> Creative mind with reverent warmth
> Will find its course
> True, clear and new in manner
> As in the spirit fresh,
> One with the old as yet the old
> Is one with all the ages."

XI.

On January 21, 1952, William Ward Watkin celebrated his sixty-sixth birthday and the beginning of a new year that marked four decades as the organizer and chairman of the Department of Architecture at the Rice Institute. He was still carrying his full teaching and administrative responsibilities, and looked forward to a continuing practice with his new firm, which had just completed the new building of the Methodist Hospital. He and Josephine lived content-edly at 5009 Caroline, and looked forward to letters and occasional visits from the children, their spouses, and the grandchildren.

There was a new Watkin at Fort Belvoir, Virginia, where Bill and Carol were now stationed with the Corps of Engineers inside Washington, D.C. A second son, Thomas Snyder Watkin, had arrived in July 1951. Bill Watkin, promoted to full colonel, was serving as deputy commander of the Officer Candidate School for the Corps of Engineers at Fort Belvoir.

Ray and Carl Biehl were still in New Orleans, but Rosemary and Nolan Barrick had moved from Iowa State to the University of Texas, where he was a professor of architecture. They had adopted a son, Bruce Watkin Barrick, and were in the process of adopting another child, a girl to be named Anne Hester Barrick.

Then, as the academic year neared its end. Watkin suffered a painful but seemingly minor injury. On March 31, 1952, he fell in a revolving door at the Shamrock Hotel and broke his kneecap. Taken to his new Methodist Hospital, he was given emergency treatment. It was decided that surgery was necessary. Tragically, he developed a virulent staphy-lococcus infection in his knee from the operation. This led to blood poisoning (septicemia), which grew progressively worse and did not respond to antibiotics. Watkin died on June 24, 1952, in the Methodist Hospital, with his three children and Josephine at his bedside.

Forty-two eventful years had passed since William Ward Watkin had first arrived in Houston, fully expecting to return to Boston and the prestigious firm of Cram, Goodhue & Ferguson after the shortest time necessary to build a new institute along flood-prone Harris Gully in a fledgling Texas city. It seemed, to his family, that he should have had many more fruitful years of life. But today they are confident that his lasting contributions to his university, his two generations of students, his adopted city, and his profession will live on as a permanent legacy to the future.

Notes:

1. President Lovett read an excerpt from a postcard sent to him by the first graduate of Rice Institute to "reach the Western Front." On furlough, the

young soldier had written, ''. . . Old buildings fine, but Paris has changed. The Louvre is closed!'' ''Hear his complaint,'' Lovett told his audience. After attending Art League exhibitions since his days in a Houston grammar school, the soldier reported that the change he most noted and regretted in Paris was the closing of the city's great art museum during the war. The very first project of what was originally the Houston Public School Art League had been to place good reproductions of the great masterpieces of painting in classrooms. The project had a lasting impact.

As Houston moves on into the 1990s, national critics point out that the city has joined New York, Chicago, Los Angeles, and other major cities in having a thoroughly professional and well-established symphony, opera, ballet, resident theater, and museum organizations.

The Museum of Fine Arts predates all of the four other groups except for the Houston Symphony Society, founded in 1913. It has obviously had a major effect in bringing the city widespread recognition as an expanding nucleus of cultural accomplishment. Meanwhile, the Houston Symphony Society is acclaimed for concerts held as far away as Hong Kong. Offerings by the city's opera, ballet, and resident theater are seen in our nation's largest cities, as well as increasingly abroad.

2. The National Youth Administration program was administered in the Lone Star State by a lanky, energetic, and ambitious young man from the Hill Country named Lyndon Baines Johnson. LBJ, of course, moved on from secretary to Congressman Richard Kleberg, to the U.S. House of Representatives and the Senate, to the vice presidency, and six years as the thirty-sixth president of the United States.

3. Gaylord Johnson was well liked and respected by John T. McCants, the new chairman of the renamed Faculty Athletics Council, by Watkin, who continued to serve for a time as a member, and by the administration. He had known many of the faculty as an honor student at Rice and had been one of the few doctoral candidates in the first decade of the Institute. Johnson believed that intercollegiate athletics should play an important role at the Rice Institute. Further, he was convinced that such a program would find substantial support, not only on campus, but in the community as a whole.

4. The championship was won under Jimmy Kitts, a highly successful coach in charge of both football and basketball at Rice. The Owls had opened the 1934 season far from home against Purdue, favored to repeat as Big Ten champions. The Boilermakers lost in a major upset, 13–0. They were never able to stop John McCauley or Bill Wallace,who were to win All-American honors for Rice. On November 24, 1934, the Owls were still undefeated in SWC play. A victory over TCU would assure them the title.

Rice lost the game 2–7, and the opportunity to hear a victory speech by Edgar Odell Lovett. A faithful fan, always in his midfield box with his family (the Watkins were in an adjoining box), Dr. Lovett had been asked to speak to the team after the expected win over the mediocre TCU Frogs. In spite of his innate modesty, he agreed. There would be, however, a second chance for the Owls. The championship was still theirs if they could win over the Baylor Bears at Waco on December 1.

President Lovett spoke to Jimmy Kitts' footballers before the Baylor game. He knew that the coach's real name was Jason, and as a scholar of Greek mythology took as his theme the ancient story of the hero Jason, his ship, the *Argo*, and crew of 11 Argonauts. The *Argo* was built under the supervision of the goddess Athene, whose three owls dominate the shield of the Rice Institute. The crew included sons of the greatest gods and heroes of antiquity: Zeus, Poseidon, and Hermes.

It was a brief yet fascinating comparison between 'Jason' Kitts' Owls and mythology. One of their most important victories had been over the Texas Longhorns. The Argonauts had also "subdued beasts with horns." There had been a thunderstorm during the win over Purdue, and a norther threatened outside for the Baylor game. The *Argo* faced many foreboding and "auspicious signs of thunder and lightning" in pursuit of the "Golden Fleece" (conference championship).

Happily, the Baylor Bears were soundly defeated, 32–0. Rice had won its first SWC football crown, four years into what was to be a decade of glory for intercollegiate athletics at the Institute. Stars of the very first Owl teams, including Ervin (Tiny) Kalb, Isham (Ike) Wilford, Marion Lee (Preacher) Lindsey, and A. M. (Tommy) Tomfohrde would watch with pride as Rice's success continued, not only in football, but in basketball, baseball, track and field, tennis, and golf.

Harry Fouke is one of the few remaining members of the 1934 gridiron champions. He remembers the historic victory over Baylor at Waco, but even more the presence of the dignified and scholarly, yet thoroughly human President Lovett, who compared his Owls to another Jason's Argonauts of legendary fame.

5. William M. McVey's statue of Jim Bowie is a continuing attraction in Texarkana, where it was installed in 1936. Texarkana, a thriving city of almost 100,000, partly in Texas and partly in Arkansas, was selected because it is the center of population, agribusiness, and industry of Bowie County.

The Texas Legislature established Bowie County in 1841, in the pre-statehood days of the Republic, to honor the hero of the Alamo. The county seat at Boston is now a hamlet of 200, almost 20 miles northwest of Texarkana. Although small in population, it adjoins the Red River Arsenal and is a pleasant community in the center of the county. Arkansas inhabitants point out that Colonel Bowie, a native of Georgia, was in their state in 1819, even before it became a territory. And the famed Bowie knife, in use throughout the frontier after Jim Bowie invented the long, deadly weapon, is still called the "Arkansas toothpick."

6. The young, handsome, and mustached Dick Dowling owned the "Bank of Bacchus," which he opened on the corner of Main and Congress, in the heart of downtown Houston early in 1860. This popular "bank" actually dealt in ". . . the exchange of liquors for gold, silver, and [trustworthy] banknotes." When the War Between the States broke out, Houston's sizable Irish population organized quickly to provide enthusiastic support for the Confederate cause. Lieutenant Dowling, a native of County Galway, commanded an all-Irish outfit: Company "F" of the Texas Heavy Artillery. It was part of the Davis Guards, a volunteer battalion known as the "Fighting Irishmen."

   Union forces had captured Galveston late in 1862, and blockaded the vital port, only to have it retaken by the Confederate General John Magruder on New Year's Day 1863. General Magruder knew that the Yankees would be back, and they were, in tremendous force. The first day of September 1863, spies confirmed that 20 ships carrying an estimated 4,000 men were en route from New Orleans to Galveston, and due at Sabine Pass in less than a week. The Pass, guarded by Fort Sabine, was the key to entering the Gulf of Mexico in force, and recapturing Galveston.

   General Magruder ordered Lieutenant Dowling to march immediately to Fort Sabine and destroy the installation, with its six long-range cannon, to prevent them falling into the hands of the invading enemy. Instead, the Fighting Irishmen strengthened the fort as best they could, cleaned and oiled the cannon, stacked the ammunition ready for firing, and otherwise prepared for unwelcome visitors. They then took pains to make Fort Sabine look as if it had been deserted for some time.

   When the *Sachem,* first of the Union gunboats, moved into range to destroy any shore batteries and clear the way for landing troops from following transport ships, the seemingly deserted cannon atop Sabine Pass opened fire. For almost an hour, Dick Dowling's artillerymen sent a ruinous hail of some 150 rounds into the enemy gunboats. The *Sachem* was soon dead in the water, and surrendered along with the *Clifton.* A third gunboat, the *Arizona,* turned tail and led the transports back to New Orleans. It was a glorious victory for Dowling and Company "F." Union casualties included more than 60 dead, wounded, and missing, with two gunboats and some 300 prisoners taken. Galveston and its port remained in Confederate hands, as it would for the remainder of the war. The Battle of Sabine Pass, on September 8, 1863, was part of Texas history.

7. The long conflict, including several truces and the resumption of hostilities, continued well over a century, until 1453. It was clear that by its very length and ongoing destruction, the war tended to sap the resources and accomplishments of both nations. Henry V of England seemed to have finally conquered the French in 1419, when his invading forces took possession of both

Normandy and portions of Aquitaine. Then came Joan of Arc's epic victory at Orleans a decade later, and driving the English and their Burgundian allies out of everything except the port of Calais, to thwart the triumph they had seemed to have in their grasp.

8. The founders of the Cistercian order were former Benedictine monks who returned to the ascetic life and manual labor required by the original Rule of St. Benedict. Many abbots, however, were appointed by the reigning monarch, and exempted from the solitary and self-denying existence of the other monks. This was particularly true of those presiding over the first churches in a capital city such as Paris.

9. Howard Hughes, Jr., had already produced such memorable motion pictures as *Scarface* and *Hell's Angels* in Hollywood, while still in his twenties. Other successes would follow for him. As early as 1935, his inventive mind allowed him to design the plane he piloted to a world record of 352 miles per hour. Three years later, he flew a new Lockheed 14 around the world in little more than 90 hours. And in the late 1930s, he had already started acquiring what finally amounted to a half-billion-dollar stake in Trans-World Airlines.

10. "O.D." Wyatt had been one of the popular men on campus, well known for his participation in an experiment before a capacity audience in William Ward Watkin's Chemistry Lecture Hall. Professor Frank A. Pattie, a renowned psychologist and authority on hypnosis, put Wyatt into a hypnotic state during a featured lecture and demonstration. He then took a half-dollar from his pocket, handing it to a nearby student to prove that it was at room temperature. Pattie advised O.D. that the coin would be too hot to pick up. The coin was then spun down a long table. When Professor Pattie did this, he ordered O.D. to pick it up. The hypnotized subject did so, only to cry out in pain and drop the half-dollar. On examination, there were fresh blisters on his index finger and thumb.

    Fort Worth, his hometown, honored Lieutenant Wyatt by naming a postwar high school for him, located near the new Kimbell Art Museum.

11. Charlie Lykes grew up at 12 Remington Lane in Shadyside. He and Bill had known one another at Kinkaid School. They met again at Camp Pickett, Virginia, where the 31st Division was undergoing final training before being shipped out to the South Pacific. On one of their last evenings at Camp Pickett, they "double dated." Charlie Lykes' date was Mason Mallory, whom he later married after he returned from overseas. They made their home in Tampa, Florida.

    John Harris Meyers' wife, Alice Baker, and Ray and Rosemary Watkin, had been childhood friends, first at Kinkaid School. They were also together as campers one summer at Camp Quinbeck in Vermont. And during World War II, the three of them were living in Houston, as temporary "war widows.'' These were the years of sharing letters from Bill, John, and Charlie (through his mother, Mrs. J.M. Lykes), the three Texas friends who found themselves fighting together in the Dixie Division, halfway around the world from Houston. The news in their letters, which were few and far between as the campaigns in the South Pacific intensified, was eagerly exchanged between the Watkin, Meyers, and Lykes families.

12. Aitape was the key to Hollandia, where the enemy had a major base and hundreds of planes. When the U.S. invasion of Aitape succeeded, more than 200,000 Japanese troops were sent in waves from Wewak, about 100 miles to the east, in a series of counterattacks. The counterattacks failed, and were discontinued in August 1944. This left Hollandia to be overrun and captured by Douglas MacArthur, who had been promoted to the highest rank of general of the army. His forces made simultaneous landings just above and below Hollandia after the destruction of almost 400 enemy planes at the huge base. The failure of Japanese counterattacks on Aitape from Wewak had made this victory possible.

13. In the mid-1960s and the beginning of the Vietnam War, interest in the Archi-Arts Ball began to languish again due to the seriousness of the war. It was at this time—realizing that the Traveling Scholarship might become a war casualty—that Professor Watkin's daughter, Ray, made the decision to permanently endow the Watkin Traveling Scholarship. It continues to be awarded annually to the winner of a design competition among the fourth-year students by the School of Architecture.

E P I L O G U E

July 9, 1990

I.

There it stood, in ongoing splendor: Lovett Hall, the Administration Building of the Rice Institute. Sir Julian Huxley had described it during the dedicatory ceremonies of October 10–12, 1912, as ". . . brilliant, astounding, enduring—rising out of the brown prairie."

During more than three quarters of a century, this magnificent architectural concept of Ralph Adams Cram and his partner Bertram Grosvenor Goodhue, brought to reality by Cram's personal representative William Ward Watkin, had come to represent academic excellence at Rice Institute, now the internationally renowned Rice University. George Will, the Pulitzer Prize-winning author, columnist, and television commentator, summed it all up in his syndicated column in 1988: "Those who say Rice is Houston's Harvard should be told that Harvard is the Rice of the Northeast."

Edgar Odell Lovett and his successors in the presidency [1] at Rice University (the change from the original appellation of Rice Institute became effective on July 1, 1960), in concert with Captain James A. Baker and those who followed on the governing board, had led faculty, staff, and student body to high levels of achievement.

Now, on a blistering hot day in midsummer 1990, Rice University and its first building received attention from around the world. The seven chief executives of the Western world [2] were officially opening the Economic Summit of Industrialized Nations at a plenary session in the Founder's Room of Lovett Hall. U.S. President George Bush, once an adjunct professor in Rice's Jesse H. Jones School of Administration, led the procession of his peers across a red carpet and through the sally port.

Hundreds of journalists provided worldwide television, radio, and print coverage during the three days of the Summit. Some of the television coverage included breathtaking views of the exterior of Lovett Hall, lit during the evenings by floodlights. The lights brought into sharp focus the remarkable details of this stunning masterpiece of roseate-pink brick, pale gray granite, richly toned marbles, and colorful tiles.

Among the building's details, which William Ward Watkin had shown to his students many times during outdoor tours of the architecture of the campus, was the sculpture work of Oswald Lassig. The Austrian sculptor had carved the images of the leaders of academic disciplines in the capitals of the Lovett Hall cloisters [3].

Lovett Hall, indeed the entire campus, had never looked more attractive than it did as the Economic Summit opened. Watkin would have especially appreciated the careful attention given the grounds that he had supervised for so many years as chairman of the Committee on Buildings and Grounds. There was no evidence of the "brown prairie" that Sir Julian Huxley had found surrounding the first buildings at the dedicatory ceremonies seventy-eight years earlier.

Even the imposing Italian cypress trees that formed the long vista of the academic quadrangle west to the statue of William Marsh Rice had been replaced, so that they were now where they had originally stood. A devastating freeze in December 1989 had caused major damage that made this replanting necessary. More than an acre of new grass was also planted on the campus, along with thousands of blue periwinkles and contrasting deep red begonias.

At the Summit's closing ceremonies on July 11, 1990, President George Rupp could look back on what he described as ". . . a double opportunity: . . . a chance to participate in an historic event, and an occasion for Rice to be in the international spotlight." Much of Dr. Rupp's 1990 President's Report is devoted, appropriately, to the Economic Summit, and the sentences concluding a special section on the Summit epitomize how well the opportunity that this unique event presented was realized:

"We are a model," President Rupp told a representative of United Press International, "for what higher education at its best can be. What distinguishes Rice from virtually all of the 3,000 other colleges and universities in the country is that we are committed to embodying both kinds of institutions—the liberal arts college and the major research university. Our aim is not a compromise between the two. Instead, we intend to be both kinds of institutions in full strength."

The President's Report concludes: "It is a message that was sent around the world, even as, for three days in July, the world came to Rice."

Edgar Odell Lovett, the traveler who had journeyed so far in 1908 and 1909 to bring the Rice Institute to the attention of leaders of higher education and government from Ireland to Japan, would surely have been pleased that the Economic Summit had come to Rice.

II.

There had understandably been many changes within the Watkin family in the 38 years since William Ward Watkin's death in 1952. Ray, the firstborn, was divorced from her first husband in 1955. In 1961, she married Henry ("Harry") W. Hoagland, a native of Colorado raised in California, and a graduate of Stanford University, the Stanford Law School, and the Harvard Business School. They first lived on Beacon Street in Boston, very near the office of Cram & Goodhue where William Ward Watkin had begun his architectural career in 1908.

Henry Hoagland was a venture capitalist, first with American Research & Development Co., and then with Fidelity Venture Associates, both in Boston. Since his retirement in 1978, the Hoaglands live in Houston and Kennebunkport, Maine, while spending part of the winter in Tucson, Arizona. They travel widely and have many interests including family, friends, genealogy, the Republican Party, and their respective alma maters. Henry is an overseer of the Hoover Institution on War, Revolution & Peace, an internationally recognized organization funding research scholars and a fine collection of archives in its own library building at Stanford University. He has also served on the board of visitors of the Stanford Law School.

Ray Watkin Hoagland has always maintained her keen interest in Rice University, her alma mater and the locus of so much of her father's career. While on the campus attending the 1961 inauguration of President Kenneth S. Pitzer, she resolved to proceed with a project long under consideration. Her objective was to augment the limited records on hand of William Ward Watkin's life and his works in the field of architecture, both at the Rice Institute and in the city of Houston, and to store them in the Fondren Library archives at Rice.

Ray started in 1962 at the Institute itself by locating scattered campus files, portions of her father's considerable correspondence, other papers, publications, work orders, original drawings, and photographs, dating back to 1908, that related to his role in the planning and building of the new university. She also assembled papers relating the history of the Department of Architecture, founded in 1912 by Watkin, and papers concerning his varied private practice as well.

An invaluable ally to Ray in the Rice Library in the 1960s was Pender Turnbull, Class of 1919, long in charge of the archives dealing with the Institute's history, which included the "Lovett Papers," faculty records, and other materials then located in the basement of the Fondren Library.

Meanwhile, Ray also turned to other sources: John T. McCants, bursar emeritus and first historian of the Rice Institute; architectural faculty members and graduates; fellow architects who had known her father; records of private commissions; files of the Houston Chapter of the American Institute of Architects; clients; old newspaper and magazine clippings and articles; and so forth. She herself recorded interviews with architectural alumni, who were especially helpful.

After Ray's effort had resulted in the establishment of the collection of Watkin Papers of the Fondren Library (which were later the principal basis for this book) with the excellent help of Nancy Boothe, director of the Woodson Research Center, there was another development: Stephen Fox, an architectural historian of marked ability and an architectural graduate of the Class of 1973 at Rice, wrote *Monograph 29* in the series "Architecture at Rice," using the Watkin collection for a great part of his research. The formal title of this work is *The General Plan of the William Marsh Rice Institute and Its Architectural Development.* A superbly researched, written, and illustrated publication that was published in 1981, it made clear William Ward Watkin's crucial role in the planning and construction of the Institute's remarkable original buildings.

Another area of Ray's successful efforts in discovering and preserving the history of Rice has been her activity in collecting and safeguarding items of and for Rice alumni archives for the pleasure of future generations. She began this work in 1975 with the encouragement of H. Malcolm Lovett and the help of Carolyn Hooton Wallace, Class of 1953 and alumni director at that time, and many other interested alumni. Lovett, son of Edgar Odell Lovett and graduate of the Class of 1921, served many years as chairman of the Board of Trustees of Rice, and in many other key positions for his alma mater, and remained especially active in alumni activities.

In 1975, Ray formed the Alumni History Committee—now called the Alumni Archives Committee—which has been successful in carrying out many projects relating to collecting Rice's history and traditions. Of particular interest are the significant number of alumni "treasures," such as scrapbooks and photographs, which are on permanent display in the Alumni Association office and used for special Homecoming presentations each year.

Ray hopes that this valuable alumni collection will be kept together, protected, and enlarged by donations—memories of older alumni and faculty can be taped and added. Most importantly, it is hoped that a permanent, appropriate, and spacious home for the collection can be found on the campus so that the collection will be easily available to interested campus visitors. Ray has donated cabinets and bookcases to accommodate the papers, and a large table and chairs to accommodate the users.

The collection, with its interesting old photos, could serve as excellent source material for a possible future book on the history of Rice's changing campus life. It will be of particular interest as Rice's centennial year approaches.

Ray would also like to see the formation someday of a Rice Historical Society, with programs presented on Rice's history, which would be of interest to all.

William Ward Watkin, Jr., completed more than three decades of distinguished active duty with the U.S. Army, which had begun as a "plebe" at West Point in 1938. He retired as a brigadier general in the Corps of Engineers in 1971. General Watkin had an illustrious career in World War II and Vietnam and in the years following. Upon retirement, he became director of the Delaware River Port Authority in Philadelphia. He was back in the gracious and historic city where his father had studied at the University of Pennsylvania. After heading shipping, rail, and toll bridge operations in Philadelphia for the DRPA for a decade, General Watkin retired in 1982 and was appointed by President Reagan as a director of the Panama Canal Commission. This Commission, established by the U.S. Congress, operates and maintains the Panama Canal. Attesting to his experience as an engineer and port director, William Ward Watkin, Jr., continues to serve on the executive committee of the Commission under President Bush's administration.

General Watkin and his wife, the former Carol Snyder, later had two other sons who joined William Ward III and Thomas. They are Andrew Townsend (remembering his maternal grandfather), born in 1952, and John Kock, born in 1958. William Ward III, 41 years old as this book goes to press and a graduate of West Point, is now a major in the U.S. Army Engineers. He and his wife, the former Corinne Lapeyre Barry of New Orleans, have five children, including William Ward IV. Major Watkin and his family are stationed in Heidelberg, Germany as this is written [4].

Another William Ward Watkin great-grandson has been born to John Watkin and his wife, the former Barbara Nieukirk. He is John K. Watkin, Jr., a family name still known in Northampton, England. John K., Jr., was born in Durham, North Carolina, May 9, 1990.

Rosemary Watkin, the wife of Professor Nolan E. Barrick, dean of the Department of Architecture at Texas Technological University, died in 1984 at Lubbock, Texas, where she and Professor Barrick had made their home for many years. In 1925 her father had designed the general plan for Texas Tech University. She left her husband and two children, Bruce and Anne (Mrs. Charles A. Smith).

William Ward Watkin's second wife and widow, Josephine, continued to live in Houston, where she died in 1987 at the age of 95 after a full and active life. She had continued to follow with interest the accomplishments of the School of Architecture at Rice.

The School of Architecture has prospered and grown in the almost forty years since William Ward Watkin's death in 1952. It has been headed successively by James Morehead, Donald Barthelme, William Caudill, Anderson Todd, David Crane, O. Jack Mitchell, Paul Kennon (who died shortly after taking over), and by his successor and the present dean, Alan Balfour. Under each of these men, the School has grown in size and reached new heights of achievement. A new building for the School of Architecture was built in 1981 as an adjunct to Anderson Hall, and designed by the well-known British architect, James Sterling. The School of Architecture today enjoys a prominent national standing and it looks forward to continuing to build upon its excellent foundation.

Notes

1. Dr. Lovett resigned the presidency he had held since 1908 upon reaching his seventieth birthday on April 14, 1941. However, he agreed to remain in office until a successor was chosen. This was not done until 1946, when William Vermillion Houston, a distinguished physicist at the California Institute of Technology, became the second president of Rice. Edgar Odell Lovett died on August 13, 1957, after a brief illness. He was 86. He had maintained an office on campus almost until his death, and had continued to enjoy visits from members of the faculty and administration.

   Dr. Houston (his name, ironically, was pronounced "How-stun") resigned the presidency in September 1960 after suffering a heart attack. He was succeeded in June 1961 by Kenneth S. Pitzer, an eminent research chemist from the University of California-Berkeley. President Pitzer resigned in 1969 to become the chief executive at Stanford University.

   The fourth president was Norman Hackerman, another distinguished chemist, who left the presidency of the University of Texas to come to Rice in 1970. Dr. Hackerman retired in 1985 after fifteen years marked by exceptional progress in both achievement and recognition for Rice University.

   President Hackerman was succeeded in 1985 by George Erik Rupp, at the time of his appointment dean of the School of Divinity at Harvard University. Dr. Rupp is now in the sixth year of an administration that has already brought noticeable new accomplishments to the university.

2. President Bush's guests at the 1990 Economic Summit were Brian Mulroney of Canada, François Mitterand of France, Margaret Thatcher of Great Britain, Giulio Andreotti of Italy, Toshiki Kaifu of Japan, and Helmut Kohl of West Germany. Also in attendance was Jacques Delors of the European Economic Community.

3. Lassig's carvings on the Lovett Hall capitals depict, among others, Sir Francis Galton, anthropology; Louis Pasteur, chemistry; Sir William Kelvin, physics; Charles Darwin, biology; Thucydides, history; Michelangelo, art; St. Paul, theology; and Edgar Odell Lovett's mentor at the University of Leipzig, Sophus Lie, mathematics and astronomy.

4. The children of Major and Mrs. William Ward Watkin III are Corinne Snyder, born March 1, 1978, Katherine Lapeyre, born June 13, 1980, William Ward IV, born December 16, 1983, Bryan Barry, born April 19, 1987, and Thomas

Cunningham, born April 27, 1988. Rosemary Watkin Barrick's daughter, Mrs. Charles A. Smith (Anne), has one son, Austin William Smith, born April 25, 1984.

The Projects of William Ward Watkin

Architectural projects by Cram, Goodhue & Ferguson and Cram & Ferguson on which William Ward Watkin was involved as Ralph Adams Cram's representative

1909   General plan of the William M. Rice Institute
            Houston

            Administration Building
            William M. Rice Institute, Houston

            Mechanical Laboratory and Power House
            William M. Rice Institute, Houston

1911   Residential Group for Men (South Hall and Commons)
            William M. Rice Institute, Houston

            Entrance gates and fence for entrances 1, 2, and 3
            William M. Rice Institute, Houston

1912   Physics Building
            William M. Rice Institute, Houston

1913   East Hall, Residential Group for Men
            William M. Rice Institute, Houston

            Project: President's House
            William M. Rice Institute, Houston

1914   Parish group master plan and Parish House, St. Mark's
               Church
            670 Calder Avenue, Beaumont, Texas

1915   West Hall, Residential Group for Men
            William M. Rice Institute, Houston

            Project: President's House
            William M. Rice Institute, Houston

1916   *Project:* President's House
            William M. Rice Institute, Houston

Mendelsohn Apartments (for the Scanlan Family)
1317-1321 Crawford Street, Houston

1919   Trinity Episcopal Church
3419 Main, Houston

1920   Field House (William Ward Watkin, architect; Ralph
        Adams Cram, consulting architect)
William M. Rice Institute, Houston

1922-23 Chemistry Building
William M. Rice Institute, Houston

1923   *Project:* President's House
William M. Rice Institute, Houston

1926   Founder's Memorial
William M. Rice Institute, Houston

1927   *Project:* Library Building
William M. Rice Institute, Houston

        Project: Classroom Building
William M. Rice Institute, Houston

Architectural Projects by William Ward Watkin

1912   *Project:* Landscape plan for Allie (Kinsloe) and James L.
        Autry
Houston

        Landscape plan, walls, and gates for Courtlandt
        Improvement Co.
Courtlandt Place, Houston

1913   2-story business and apartment building for Fred M.
        Lege, Jr.
Galveston, Texas

1914   Alterations and additions to house for John M. Bennett, Jr.
409 West Dewey Place, San Antonio, Texas

House for Annie Ray (Townsend) and William Ward Watkin
5009 Caroline Street, Houston

1915   Repairs to house of Cora and Walter J. Crawford, damaged in the 1915 hurricane
1494 Broadway, Beaumont, Texas

Building at West Texas State Teachers College
Canyon, Texas

Science Building, Sam Houston Normal Institute
Huntsville, Texas

ca. 1915 House for Sadie and Perry M. Wiess
1872 Calder Avenue, Beaumont, Texas

1916   Southern Drug Company Building
1511-1517 Preston Avenue, Houston

Alterations and additions to house of William L. Priddie
892 Liberty Avenue, Beaumont, Texas

House for Mr. and Mrs. Robert Nicholson
4800 Drexel Drive, Highland Park, Texas

1917   House for Allene (Gano) and Howard R. Hughes, Sr.
3921 Yoakum Boulevard, Houston

YWCA Building
660 Calder Avenue, Beaumont, Texas

Sul Ross State Teachers College
Alpine, Texas

ca. 1917 Guion Hall, Texas A & M College
College Station, Texas

1918   Parish House, St. Peter's Church
Brenham, Texas

1919   Edson & Feray Co. Motorcar Showroom
2300 Main Street, Houston

Alterations to house of William W. Munzesheimer
602 Sul Ross Avenue, Houston

Miller Bros. Building
1615-1619 Preston Avenue, Houston

House for Nena (Wiess) and William A. Priddle
675 Fifth Street, Beaumont, Texas

ca. 1919 House for Edith R. and Robert G. Caldwell
5218 Bayard Lane

1920   Field House (Cram & Ferguson, consulting architects)
William M. Rice Institute, Houston

Thirty houses for Humble Oil & Refining Co.
Baytown, Texas

The Museum of Fine Arts, Houston, plans begun (Ralph Adams Cram, consulting architect)
Main Boulevard and Montrose Boulevard, Houston

Ye Old College Inn
6545 Main Boulevard, Houston

Project: Houston Public Library Building
Houston

1921   Autry House (in association with Cram & Ferguson)
6265 Main Boulevard, Houston

YWCA Activities Building (with Maurice J. Sullivan and Birdsall P. Briscoe, architects; Wm. F. Thompson, associated architect)
1320 Rusk Avenue, Houston

Additions to the South Texas Commercial National Bank Building
213 Main Street, Houston

Miller Memorial Outdoor Theater, Hermann Park
Houston

ca. 1921 House for Carrie Lou and Clayton B. Deming
1106 Palm Avenue, Houston

1922   House for Hazel and Harry B. Weiser
        5202 Bayard Lane, Houston

        House for Libbie (Johnston) and Neill T. Masterson
        5120 Montrose Boulevard, Houston

        House for Beulah and Max L. Hurvitz
        4203 Montrose Boulevard, Houston

        Windward Court Apartments
        901 Rosalie, Houston

        House for Augusta L. and Ernest William Greundler
        4218 Yoakum Boulevard, Houston

        Subdivision plan and landscape plan for Southampton
            Place
        Houston

        Houston Public Library (in association with Louis A.
            Glover and Cram & Ferguson)
        500 McKinney, Houston

1923   House for Kate (Holloway) and John G. Logue
        1101 Milford Street, Houston

        YWCA Building (F.B. & A. Ware, consulting architects)
        21st Street and Church Street, Galveston, Texas

        House for Blanche (Wood) and Frederick A. Heitmann
        1 Longfellow Lane, Houston

        House for Ethel (Campbell) and Edward M. Armstrong
        1128 Bissonnet Avenue, Houston

        House for Louise (Thomson) and J. Virgil Scott
        1122 Bissonnet Avenue, Houston

        Texas Technological College master plan (in association
            with Sanguinet, Staats & Hedrick)
        Lubbock, Texas

1924   The Museum of Fine Arts, Houston, opening
            (The wing completed 1926)
        Houston, Texas

        Kinkaid School Lower School Building
        1317 Richmond Avenue, Houston

Texas Technological College (original buildings in
   association with Sanguinet, Staats & Hedrick)
   Administration Building
   Agronomy Building
   Home Economics Building
   Judging Building
   President's House
   Textile Engineering Building
   Project: Dining Hall
   Project: Girls Dormitory
Lubbock, Texas

Consulting Architect for Houston Public Schools
   John H. Reagan Senior High School (John F. Staub
      and Louis A. Glover, architects)
   Jefferson Davis Senior High School (Briscoe &
      Dixon and Maurice J. Sullivan, architects)
   Jack Yates Colored High School (Henry F. Jonas &
      Tabor, architects)
   James S. Hogg Junior High School (Briscoe &
      Dixon and Maurice J. Sullivan, architects)
   Albert Sidney Johnson Junior High School
      (Sanguinet, Staats, Hedrick & Gottlieb, architects)
   George Washington Junior High School (Endress &
      Cato and Joseph Finger, architects)
   Sidney Lanier Junior High School (R.D. Steele and
      Henry F. Jonas & Tabor, architects)
   Stonewall Jackson Junior High School
Various locations, Houston

Southampton "Electrical Home"
1931 Sunset Boulevard, Houston

1925   House for Elizabeth (Darden) and Egbert O. Hail
1 West Eleventh Place, Houston

Ritz Theater
911 Preston Avenue, Houston

House for Laura (Ghent) and Marvin L. Graves
11 Shadowlawn Circle, Houston

House for Edna (Daffan) and Brian Brewster Gilmer
1318 North Boulevard, Houston

First Methodist Episcopal Church, South (in association with Sanguinet, Staats & Hedrick and Charles J. Pate)
909 Tenth Street, Wichita Falls, Texas

1926 House for Norrie (Webb) and Perryman S. Moore
1615 North Boulevard, Houston

Victoria Junior College Building
2200 East Red River, Victoria, Texas

Project: Park View Apartments (associate for Sibley & Featherstone, architects)
Houston

Project: 7-story office building for Scanlan Estate
400 block of Main Street, Houston

"Casa de Mañana" for Mr. and Mrs. W.T. Eldridge
806 Lakeview Drive, Sugar Land, Texas

1927 Princess Louise Hotel
1001 North Water Street, Corpus Christi

Warehouse for Scanlan Estate
1902 Congress Avenue, Houston

House for Annie Vieve (Carter) and E.L. Crain
2605 North Calumet Drive, Houston

Project: Public Library Building
Corpus Christi, Texas

Cohen House (Ralph Adams Cram, consulting architect)
William M. Rice Institute, Houston

Edward Albert Palmer Memorial Chapel
6221 Main Street, Houston

ABC Stores #5
2112-2120 Main Street, Houston

Texas Technological College (in association with Wyatt
C. Hedrick)
Agricultural Building
Chemistry Building
Greenhouse
Practice House
West Engineering Building
Lubbock, Texas

Project: Houston Cotton Exchange Building
Houston

1928   Girls Dormitory (in association with Shirley Simons)
College of Industrial Arts, Denton, Texas

Watkin Building
4001-4007 Main Street, Houston

ca. 1928   Roos-Carter-Crain-Bryan Monument, Glenwood
Cemetery
Houston

1930   Alterations to South Hall for P.E. students' study hall
William M. Rice Institute, Houston

1931   1-story commercial building for Palmer Hutcheson
3715 Harrisburg Boulevard, Houston

William C. Hogg Memorial Tablet
The Museum of Fine Arts, Houston

Wilson's Stationery & Printing Co. Building
1018-1020 Prairie Avenue, Houston

1932   *Project:* 5-story office building for Scanlan Estate
Houston

1932-33   F.W. Heitmann office building
412 North Main, Houston

1933   MacGregor Park cenotaph and entrance markers
MacGregor Park, Houston

1935   *Project:* 3-story building for Scanlan Estate
Houston

Agnes Lord and Robert I. Cohen Memorial, Hebrew
  Cemetery
Galveston, Texas

1936   Base of Lt. Richard Dowling Monument (Herring Coe,
          sculptor)
        Sabine Pass, Texas

        Base of James Bowie Monument (William McVey,
          sculptor)
        Texarkana, Texas

        Balustrade and bench for Garden Club of Houston
          (William McVey, sculptor)
        The Museum of Fine Arts, Houston

1937   Cook Paint & Varnish Co. Building for Frederick A.
          Heitmann
        1816 Main Street, Houston

        Recreation Building
        Root Square Park, Houston

        Recreation Building
        Proctor Square, Houston

        Project: Addition to Cohen House
        William M. Rice Institute, Houston

1938   Rice Stadium
        William M. Rice Institute, Houston

        Recreation Building, Bath House, and Swimming Pool
        Emancipation Park, Houston

        Houston Garden Center Building
        Hermann Park, Houston

        Chancel recontruction and Golding Memorial Chapel
        Christ Church, Houston

1939   Additions to Institute Commons
        William M. Rice Institute, Houston

        House for Fanetta (Wortham) and James A. Hill
        1515 South Post Oak Lane, Houston

St. Mark's Church (Stone & Pitts, associate architects)
670 Calder Avenue, Beaumont, Texas

Central Church of Christ
4100 Montrose Boulevard, Houston

ca. 1940 Hughes Monument, Glenwood Cemetery
Houston

Alterations and additions to house of Esther (Meyer) and
George S. Cohen
607 Kipling Street, Houston

1941 *Project:* Library and Bender Hall
William M. Rice Institute, Houston

Naval Reserve Officers Training Corps Building
William M. Rice Institute, Houston

1945 Fondren Library and M.D. Anderson Hall (consulting
architect to Staub & Rather, architects)
William M. Rice Institute, Houston

Methodist Hospital (in association with Stayton Nunn,
Milton McGinty, and Vance D. Phenix, architects,
completed 1951)
6516 Bertner Avenue, Houston

Kinkaid High School Building
1317 Richmond, Houston

1947 Abercrombie Engineering Laboratory (consulting
architect to Staub & Rather, architects)
William M. Rice Institute, Houston

Alterations to First Church of Christ, Scientist
1710 Main Street

ca. 1947 Nena E. Stanaker Branch Library (in association with
Louis A. Glover)
611 North 69th Street, Houston

1948 World War II Memorial
Christ Church, Houston

Select Bibliography

Barnes, Marguerite Johnston. *A Happy Worldly Abode.* Houston: Gulf Publishing Company, 1965.

Book of the Opening, Volumes I, II, and III (a Rice Institute publication). New York: De Vinne Press, 1914.

Brown, Chester A. *My Best Years in Architecture.* Boston: Published privately, 1971.

Brown, Rev. Dr. Lawrence L. *The Episcopal Church in Texas, Volume 2.* Austin, TX: Eakins Press, 1985.

Campanile, Volumes I-XXXVII (a Rice Institute publication). Houston: Gulf Publishing Company, 1916–1952.

Clark, James A. *A Biography of Robert Alanzo Welch.* Houston: Clark Book Company, 1963.

Cram, Ralph Adams. *Excalibur: A Medieval Drama.* Boston: Published privately, 1921.

____. *Heart of Europe.* New York: Charles Scribner's Sons, 1915.

____. *The Substance of Gothic.* Boston: Marshall Jones Company, 1925.

Fehrenbach, T. R. *Lone Star: A History of Texas and Texans.* New York: Macmillan Publishing Company, 1980.

Fox, Stephen J. *Monograph 29: Architecture at Rice (The General Plan of the William Marsh Rice Institute and Its Architectural Development).* Houston: Wetmore & Company, 1981.

Garwood, Ellen Clayton. *Will Clayton: A Short Biography.* Austin, TX: University of Texas Press, 1958.

Guerard, Albert. *L'Avenir de Paris.* Paris: Published privately, 1928.

Hoagland, Ray Watkin. "William Ward Watkin." *Rice University Review*, Spring 1969.

McAshan, Marie Phelps. *A Houston Legacy.* Houston: Hutchins House, 1985. (Distributed by Gulf Publishing Company.)

McCants, John Thomas. *Some Information Concerning The Rice Institute.* Houston: Published privately, 1955.

Meiners, Fredericka. *A History of Rice University.* Houston: Rice University Studies, 1982.

Meyer, Leopold L. *The Days of My Life*. Houston: Universal Printers, 1975.

Muir, Andrew Forest. *William Marsh Rice and His Institute*. Houston: Rice University, 1971.

Nicholson, Patrick J. *In Time: An Anecdotal History of the University of Houston*. Houston: Gulf Publishing Company, 1977.

____. *Mr. Jim: The Biography of James Smither Abercrombie*. Houston: Gulf Publishing Company, 1983.

Santangelo, Susan Hillebrandt. *Kinkaid and Houston's 75 Years*. Houston: Gulf Publishing Company, 1981.

Thresher, Volumes I-XXXVII (a Rice Institute publication). Houston: John L. Scardino & Sons and various other printers, 1916–1952.

Tucci, Douglass Shand. *Ralph Adams Cram, American Medievalist*. Boston: Boston Public Library (Stinehour Press), 1975.

Watkin, William Ward. "Architectural Tradition in The Rice Institute." *Slide Rule*, Volume 13, Number 7 (July 1943), et sequens.

____. *The Church of Tomorrow*. New York and London: Harper Brothers, 1936.

____. *Planning and Building the Modern Church*. New York: F.W. Dodge, 1951.

____. *Architectural Development of the William Marsh Rice Institute*, Houston, Texas; Southern Architectural Review; November, 1910.

____. *Architecture in Texas*, London *Times*; February 9, 1925.

____. *The Work of William Ward Watkin, Architect* (Photographic brochure with foreword); Privately published; Houston; 1926.

____. *Impressions of Modern Architecture* (a series of three lectures): *The Search for a Direct Manner of Expression in Design; The New Manner in France and Northern Europe; The Advent of the New Manner in America*): Rice Pamphlet; volume XVIII, number 4.

____. *Impressions of Modern Architecture* (reprints): Pencil Points; May, June and July, 1931.

____. *Are We Making Progress in our Church Architecture?* Pencil Points; March, 1931.

____. *The Early History of the Rice Institute*. Privately published; Houston; 1937.

____. *The Middle Ages: The Approach to the Truce of God:* Rice Pamphlet; volume XXIX, number 4.

____. *The College Buildings:* Rice Owl; December, 1944.

____. *Architectural Traditions Appearing in the Earlier Buildings of the Rice Institute:* Slide Rule; July, 1953.

Writer's Project of the Federal Works Agency and Works Project Administration (under sponsorship of the Harris County Historical Society). *Houston: American Cities Series.* Houston: Anson Jones Press, 1942.

I N D E X

Abbey of St. Denis, 269, 270
Abbot Suger (of St. Denis), 269, 270
Abercrombie Engineering Laboratories, 310
Abercrombie, James S., 16
Abercrombie, Leland Anderson, 25n
Academic Quadrangle, 159
Administration Building (Lovett Hall), 1, 3, 52, 84, 85, 89, 90, 91, 92, 94, 95, 96, 99, 104, 159, 184, 202–207, 219, 236, 306, 307, 322, 323
Airmail chess game, 302, 304
Aitape, 304, 321n
Aked, Reverend Charles Frederick, 53
Alamo Heights (San Antonio), 137
Allen, Augustus C., 8, 196
Allen, Charlotte Baldwin, 196
Allen, John K., 8, 196
Allred, Governor James V., 266
Altamira y Crevea, 2
Altenburg, Edgar, 237
Alumni Archives Committee, 326
Alumni Association Fund, 309
American Academy (of Rome), 150, 171, 256, 311
American Hospital (Neuilly-sur-Seine, France), 171, 221, 223, 226, 227
American Institute of Architects, 111, 264, 312
American Institute of Architects, Houston Chapter, 166n, 252, 312, 325
American Red Cross, 151, 305
Ames, J. S., 44

Ander, Katherine, 190
Anderson Hall, 309
Anderson, Monroe D. Foundation, 308
Andreotti, Giulio, 328n
Angel, John (sculptor), 233–236
Anson (Jones County), Texas, 17
Appropriations Committee, 296
Arbuckle, Philip H., 106, 110, 146, 161, 162, 170n
Archangel Gabriel, 295, 296
Archi-Arts Ball, 131, 155, 258, 259, 311
Architectural Society (of the Rice Institute), 143, 146, 153, 154
Argo and the Argonauts, 318n
Armstrong, Dr. E. M., 180
Arnold, Dr. E. B., 142
Arrants, Edward, 187
Artillery Ball (Galveston), 134
Art League (of Houston), 135, 188–190, 256, 257, 285, 317n
Asbury, Bishop Francis, 26n
Associate professor (rank of) established, 306
Athene (goddess of the three Owls), 318n
Atkinson, Mrs. A. H., 42
Audubon, John J., 9
Autry, Miss Allie May, 186
Autry House, 156, 185
Autry, James L., Jr., 185
Autry, Mrs. James L., Sr., 185
Avignon, 219
Avignon, School of, 247n
Ayars, Miss Louise (Mrs. Louis A. Stevenson, 99, 134
Axson, Stockton, 151, 189

Baile Español, 155, 258
Baker, Alice Graham, 138
Baker, Graham, 25
Baker, James A., Sr. (father of
    Captain James A. Baker,
    Jr.), 25n
Baker, Captain James A., Jr.
  birth and early life, 16
  charter trustee, 15
  death, 299
  elected chairman, Board of
    Trustees, 18
  and Elizabeth Baldwin Rice
    will, 18, 19
  helps hospitalized Guerard
    family, 249n
  and his successors, 321
  and Kinkaid School, 138
  laying of cornerstone of
    Administration Building,
    206
  and murder of William Marsh
    Rice, 23, 24
  pictured with other trustees, 200
  a principal figure, 4
  settles crucial lawsuit, 24, 25
  and Tony Martino, 157, 159,
    167n
  urges Edgar Odell Lovett to
    accept presidency, 36
Baker, Secretary of State James
    A., 180
Baldwin, Charlotte (Mrs. F. A.
    Rice), 10, 16
Balfour, Alan, 327
Barrick, Anne Hester (Mrs.
    Charles A. Smith), 316,
    327, 329n
Barrick, Bruce Watkin, 316, 327
Barrick, Nolan, 70, 132, 240,
    278, 281, 302, 303, 305,
    316, 327

Barry, Corrine Lapayre (Mrs.
    William Ward Watkin, III),
    327
Barthelme, Donald, 327
Bartino, John, 13
Bates, Colonel W. B., 308
Battle of the Flowers (San Antonio
    celebration and debutante
    ball), 103
Bauhaus movement, 245
Beacon Hill, bellringers of, 113n
Beacon Hill Street, 113n, 324
Beauregard Parish timberlands,
    14, 50n
Beehan, Captain Kermit, 304
Bellaire (City of), Texas, 34
Bellmont, L. T., 161
Belo, A. H., 50n
Bender E. L. bequest, 309
Bender Hotel, 87, 114n, 309
Berengaria, SS, 215
Berenson, Bernard, 46
Bernhardt, Sarah, 88
Bethany College, 31, 49n
Bieber, Alvin C., 151
Biehl, Colonel Carl, Jr., 302, 303,
    305
Biehl, Carl, Sr. 305
Bissonnet Street (formerly West
    11th Place), 180, 181
Blaffer, Robert Lee, 138, 171,
    193n, 306
Blaffer, Jane, John and Cecil
    Amelia (Titi), 171
Blaffer, Sarah Campbell (Mrs.
    Robert Lee), 193n
Blayney, Thomas L., 153, 238
Blois (France), 219, 247
Bodleian Library (Oxford
    University), 217
Bois de Boulogne, 224

Bonner, Miss Garland (Mrs. George Howard), 132, 171
Book of the Opening, I, II and III, 3, 51, 248n
Booth, Edwin, 88
Borden County, Texas, 115n
Borden, Gail, 102, 115n
Borden, Inc., 102
Borden, Texas, 102, 115n
Borel, Emil, 2
Boston (England), 55
Boston *Transcript,* 45
Botts, W. B., 26n
Bouju, Monsieur (Prefect of Paris) and Mlle, 222, 223
Bowie County, Texas, 318n, 319n
Bowie, Jim, 266, 318n, 319n
Boxley, Gertrude (Mrs. Hubert Evelyn Bray), 159, 160
Brady, Chaille Jones (Mrs. Benjamin Botts Rice), 193
Brady, Colonel J. T., 173
Brady, Lucy (Mrs. W. Sperry Hunt), 174
Brady, Sherman, 91, 173, 174, 194n
Brain Trust, The, 147, 154, 155
Bray, Hubert Evelyn, 159, 160
Brazos Hotel, 166n
Bremond, Paul H., 10
Brick, "Brady pink," 95, 173, 174, 193n
Bright, Dennis, 58, 61, 63, 67, 73n, 119
Bright, Lucy Reay (Mrs. Dennis), 58, 61, 63, 119
Briscoe, Colonel Andrew H., 87
Briscoe, Birdsall, 87, 111, 194n, 312
Broadacres, 180, 181
Brown, Chester A., 75–77

Brown, George Rufus, 306, 308, 313
Brown, Herman, 308, 313
Brown, John H., 12
Brown and Root, 313
Browne, Charles L., 151, 231, 232, 241, 244
Browne, Frederic, 244
Brugler, J. H., 64, 253
Bryan, Mrs. Jack, 87, 194n
Bryn Mawr College, 246
Buildings and Grounds, Committee on, 100, 156, 157, 165, 215, 230, 232
Bureau of University Travel, 303
Bush, President George W. H. (adjunct professor, Rice University), 322
Bute, James and Company, 113n
Byzantine Renaissance, 114n

Caldwell, Edith (Mrs. Robert G.), 136
Caldwell, Robert G., 117, 180, 254
Calhoun, Harold, 314
California Institute of Technology, 305, 306, 328n
Cambridge, MA, 55
Cambridge University, 39, 151
Camp Logan, 184
Camp Quinibeck, 140
Campbell, Alexander, 32
Campbell, Thomas, 32
Capitol Hotel, 12, 17
Carnegie, Andrew, 70
Carnegie Institute of Technology, 143, 298
Carpenter, John, 197
Carroll, Robroy, 240, 243, 244
Carter, Miss Annie Vieve, 98, 139
Carter, E. Finley, 194n
Carter, Mrs. Samuel Fain, 139

Carter, W. T., 42
Caruso, Enrico, 88
Caudill, William, 327
Central Church of Christ, 294, 312
Chambord (France), 219, 247
Chandler, Asa, 237, 238
"Chateaux country," 219
Chatham Hall, 235, 240
Chemistry Building, 172, 173,
    174, 175, 193n, 212, 213,
    230, 243
Chemistry Department, 230
Chickering (concert grand piano),
    57, 72n
Children of Rice faculty members,
    127
Chillman, James Henry, Jr., 144,
    150, 171, 190, 191, 215,
    229, 244, 256, 257, 286,
    298, 303
Chopin, Frederic, 166
Christ Church (Cathedral), 28n,
    87, 112, 174
Christmas party (at Cram,
    Goodhue & Ferguson), 77,
    124
Church of the Holy Sepulchre, 54
Church of the Holy Spirit, 249n
Church of St. John the Divine
    (New York City), 77, 233,
    269
Church of Santa Maria dei
    Miracoli (Venice), 186
Church of St. Trophime, 258
Church of Tomorrow, The, 197,
    217, 245, 268, 269–273,
    312, 315
Churchill, Ernest Charles, 55,
    59–61
Churchill, Sir Winston, 69, 310
Clark, James A., 113n
Clark, James B. (Champ), 31

Clayton, Julia, 117
Clayton, Susan Vaughan (Mrs. W.
    L.), 117
Clayton, William Lockhart, 117,
    138, 139
Clemson College, 231, 232, 298
Cleveland, Frank, 78
Cleveland W. D. and Company, 14
Clyce, W. P., 153
Coahuila y Tejas, 101, 102
Cochran, Annie (Mrs. W. S.), 140
Cochran, Billy, 140
Coe, Herring (sculptor), 267
Cohen, Agnes Lord (Mrs. Robert
    I.), 186, 213
Cohen, George S., 186, 194n,
    195n, 213, 278
Cohen House, 186, 187, 213,
    214, 219, 278
Cohen, Robert I., 186, 213
Cohn, Arthur B., 19, 21, 43, 244,
    254–256
Colby's Restaurant, 87, 114n
College of Industrial Arts
    (Denton, Texas), 183
College of William and Mary,
    249n
Colonial architecture, 78, 79
Columbia University, 305
Columbus, Texas, 102, 141, 142
Command and General Staff
    College (USA), 305
Commencement (First, June 12,
    1916), 146
Commons, 92
Compiegne, Forest of, 216, 220,
    228, 229
Conklin, Edwin G., 44
Constantine the Great, 270
Constantinople's Hagia Sophia,
    272
Cooper Union, 13

Copley Square (Boston), 45, 78
Cornell, Ezra, 70
Cornell University, 31, 37, 311
Courtlandt Place, 93, 177
Craig, Reverend Robert E. L., 174, 175
Crain, E. L., Sr., 139, 181
Cram and Ferguson (C&F), 100, 155, 172, 175, 176, 182, 184, 191, 235, 268
Cram and Goodhue (C&G), 302, 309, 324
Cram, Goodhue and Ferguson (CG&F), 4, 39, 43, 44, 47, 48, 52, 75–86, 97, 100, 104, 113n, 124, 155, 158, 172, 173, 217, 316
Cram and Wentworth, 47
Cram, Wentworth and Goodhue, 47
Cram, Ralph Adams, 4, 39, 43–49, 52, 66, 68, 75–85, 95–97, 100, 113n, 114n, 124, 154, 155, 175, 183, 186, 191, 194n, 200, 214, 217, 233–236, 310, 314, 322
Crane, David, 327
Cret, Paul Philippe, 64–68, 73n, 96, 97, 143, 144, 188, 268
Crillon Hotel (Paris), 215
Cripple Creek, SS, 214, 247n
Crooker, John H., Sr., 180
Cullen, Hugh Roy, 308
Cullinan, Joseph H., 178, 179, 181, 185, 188
Culver Military Academy, 277
Cypress trees (Italian), 323

Dallas News, 50n
"Dance of the Nymphs," 190
Daniell, Percy John, 106, 110, 111, 254

Danville, PA, 56, 63, 64, 66, 119, 121
Darwin, Charles, 3, 328n
DAR, 252
Davis, Jefferson, 12
Davis, W. R. (Rincon Field), 307–309
Dean, Alice, 307
Dedication ceremonies (October 10–12, 1912), 1–4, 51–53, 208, 209, 322
Delors, Jacques, 328n
de Martel, Dr. Charles, 225, 227
Democratic National Convention, 196, 197
Department of Architecture (School of Architecture as of September 19, 1965), 52, 99, 105, 106, 111, 112, 142–144, 153–155, 192–193, 229–230, 232, 240–241, 257, 258, 266, 298, 299, 309–311, 315, 324, 327
Department of Physical Education, 261
Depression, The Great and its effects, 244, 245, 253–256
de Vries, Hugo, 2
de Soulis, Simon (Earl of Northampton), 54
Dickensheets, Lavone (Mrs. Mark Edwin Andrews), 240
Dill, Frank, 240
Disciples of Christ (Christian Church), 31
Dodge, F. W., 314
Doge's Palace (Venice), 171, 172
Douty, T. B., 240
Dow, Alden B., 314
Dowling, Lt. Richard H. (Dick), 267, 268, 319n
Drexel Institute, 30

Dudley, Miss Marjorie, 132
Dunaway, James K., 298, 310
Dunn, Mr. & Mrs. DeWitt, 215
Dunn, Miss Bessie, 215
Dunn, Miss Dorothy, 215

East Hall (James A. Baker
    College), 100, 104
Ecole Americaine des Beaux-Arts,
    311
Ecole des Beaux-Arts (de Paris),
    151, 231
Economic Summit of
    Industrialized Nations, 322,
    323
Edward I, King of England, 54,
    55, 74n
Edwards, William Franklin, 106,
    111
Eighth Naval District, 296
Eisenhower, President Dwight D.,
    313
Eldridge, W. T., Jr., 181
Eleanor Crosses, 55–56, 74n
Eleanor of Castile, 54–55, 74n
Elkins, Judge J. A., 16
Elliott, C. G., Jr., 240
Elliott, Mary Alice Loan Fund,
    278
Ellis, Hudson, 238
Endress & Watkin, 174, 182, 192
Engineering Laboratories, 296
Enola Gay, 304
Episcopalian (High Anglican), 46
Episcopalian Diocese of Texas,
    184, 185
Eusebius, Bishop of Caesarea,
    114n
Evans, Griffith Conrad, 106,
    115n, 152, 236, 254
Evans, Isabelle (Mrs. G. C.
    Evans), 136
Excalibur, 113n

Faculty Curriculum Committee,
    248n
Faculty Library Committee, 307
Faculty salaries, 10% reduction in
    and effects, 253–256
Faculty Women's Club, 135
Farish, Stephen Power, 308
Farish, William Stamps, 87, 138,
    308
Farrington, William, 243, 244
Federal Triangle (Buildings), 264
Federation of Garden Clubs, 276
Fendley, Francis T., 153
Ferguson, Frank W., 48, 91
Fidelity Venture Associates, 324
Field House, 155, 156, 176
Finger, Joseph, 243
Finn, A. C., 266
First Methodist Church (of
    Wichita Falls), 191
FitzPatrick, Thomas K., 298, 299,
    310
Fleming, C. C. (Pat), 194n
Fleming, Lamar, Jr., 306
Fleming, Sir Alexander, 67
Florida Chapel, 102
Foard, Major Robert, 103
Foley Brothers, 186, 278
Foley, John, 56, 57
Fondren Library, 14, 36, 115n,
    309, 310, 324, 325
Football stadium (of 1938), 263
Fort Sabine, 319n
Fort Sam Houston, 302
Foster, Marcellus E. (Mefo), 88,
    89
Fouke, Harry, 318n
Founder's Room, 322
Fox, Stephen, 79, 114n, 181, 183,
    186, 187, 189, 218, 325
Frazier, Major Joseph, USA
    (Ret), 148

Freiherren Cram (German home of), 45
French Gothic, 175, 268–270
French Romanesque, 175, 220, 258
Fuller, Reverend Andrew, 72n

Gabert, Leonard, 153
Gables, The, 87, 201, 241, 260
Gail (Borden County), Texas, 115n
Galton, Sir Francis, 328n
Galveston, 3, 8, 21, 22, 53, 100, 115n, 186, 195n
Galveston hurricane, 92
Galveston *News,* 50n, 102
Gano, Allene (Mrs. Howard R. Hughes, Sr.), 193n
Garden Club of Houston, 246, 252
General Court (of Massachusetts), 6
Gerard, James W., 23
Gilman, Daniel C., 37
Gilmer, B. B., 180, 181, 291
Girard College, 13, 30
Girard, Stephen, 13
Glendower Iron Works, 57, 71n
Glover, Louis, 182, 191
Godwin, Edward W., 55
Golden Fleece (Southwest Conference football championship), 318n
Golding Memorial Chapel, 294
Goodhue, Bertram Grosvenor, 47–48, 53, 78, 80, 100, 113n, 183, 217, 310, 314, 315, 322
Gothic style, 45, 47, 48, 65, 77–79, 175, 197, 219, 245, 247n, 249n, 268–272, 315
Graham, Reverend Billy, 313
Graustein, W. C., 237
Graves, Dr. M. L., 180
Gray, Peter, 26n

Gray, William Fairfax, 26n, 273
Greenwood, Dr. James, Jr., 168n
Greenwood, Joe, 168n
Greenwood, Mary Owen (Mrs. Ben M. Anderson), 132, 168n
Grove Park Inn, 112, 139, 170
Guerard, Albert Joseph, 135, 165n, 166n, 223, 224, 227
Guerard, Albert Leon, 111, 117, 135, 136, 152, 154, 222, 238, 249n
Guerard, Mrs. Albert Leon, 221–223, 227, 249n
Guerard, Miss Therina, 222
Guildhall (of Northampton, England), 54, 65, 70
Gulf Building, 197

Haakon VII, King of Norway, 40
Hackerman, President Norman, 328n
Hale, Major Henry M., 32, 143
Hale, Mary Ellen (Mrs. Edgar Odell Lovett), 32, 143
Hall, Josiah (maternal grandfather of William Marsh Rice), 7
Hamilton, Sr. William Rowan, 39, 50n
Hancock, Mary Matilda (Mrs. Frederick W. Watkin), 58–62, 229
Hancock, William (William Ward Watkin's maternal grandfather), 55–60
Hannah, David, Sr., 42
Hanszen, Harry, 308
Harper's Weekly, 45
Harper, William Rainey, 37
Harris Bayou, 93
Harris Gully, 52, 90, 93, 94, 159, 176, 316
Hartford Insurance Company, 194n

Harvard Business School, 305, 324
Harvard College, 2
Harvard University, 44, 159
Havens Creek, 102
Heaps, Claude W., 135, 307
Heaps, Belle (Mrs. Claude W.),
 135, 136
Hedrick, Wyatt C., 182, 191
Heisman, John W., 162–165,
 168n, 169n, 172, 260–262
Heisman Trophy, 164
Heitmann, Frederick A., 177,
 178, 243, 290
Hermann, George, 35, 38, 41,
 188, 189
Hermann Hospital, 184, 312
Hermann Park, 38, 182, 189,
 195n
Herrick, Ambassador Myron T.,
 225, 227
Hill, Albert R., 31
Hirsch, General Maurice, 88
Hirsch, Miss Rosetta, 88
Hoagland, H. W. (Harry), 324
Hobby, Governor and Mrs.
 William Pettus, 179
Hodges, L. A., 153
Hofheinz, Judge Roy M.,
 307—308
Hogg, Miss Ima, 88, 135, 142
Hogg, Governor James Stephen,
 88, 181
Hogg, Mike, 181
Hogg, Will C., 181, 190
Holcombe, Mayor Oscar F., 182
Hollandia, 321n
Holt, Orren T., 13, 18, 19, 21, 24
Hooton, Claude, 130, 215, 224,
 227, 228, 244, 256–258,
 298, 311
Hoover Institution on War,
 Revolution and Peace, 324

Hopkins, Johns, 70, 225
Hotel Argencon (Paris), 130, 227
Hotel-de-Ville (City Hall of
 Paris), 222
Hotel Savoy (London), 39
Houlgate (France), 72
House, Edward M., 27n
House, T. W., 27n
Houston and Central Texas
 Railroad, 12
Houston Chamber of Commerce,
 34, 53, 86, 197
Houston *Chronicle,* 88, 89, 114n
Houston, City of, 5–9, 53, 85–88,
 97, 98, 184, 188, 196, 197
Houston Cotton Exchange, 189,
 191
Houston *Gargoyle,* 141
Houston Independent School
 District (HISD), 192, 195n,
 257
Houston Municipal Band, 2
Houston *Post,* 88, 89, 108, 114n
Houston *Post-Dispatch,* 43
Houston Public Library, 182,
 191–192, 283, 284
Houston School Board, 14
Houston Symphony Orchestra, 88
Houston Symphony Society, 136,
 317n
Houston, President William
 Vermillion, 306, 328n
Houstoun, J. Patrick, 193n, 194n
Howard, Mr. and Mrs. George,
 171
Hoyle, Alexander, 76
Hudspeth, Chalmers, M., 115n
Hudspeth, Demaris DeLange
 (Mrs. C. M.), 115n
Hughes, Arthur, 115n, 152
Hughes, Howard R., Sr., 176,
 177, 193n, 194n, 288, 295

Hughes, Mrs. Howard R., Sr. (Allene Gano), 176, 177, 193n, 194n, 288, 295
Hughes, Howard R., Jr., 194n, 278, 288, 289, 295, 320n
Hughes Tool Company, 176, 177, 277
Humble Oil and Refining Company, 87, 191, 306, 308
Hundred Years War, 269, 319n
Huntsville, Texas, 16, 25n
Hutcheson, Palmer, Sr., 240
Huxley, Sir Julian, 3, 106, 109, 115n, 151, 172, 322, 323
Huxley, Thomas Henry, 109

Ideson, Julia Building (Houston Public Library), 192
Imperial Academy (of Japan), 40
Intercollegiate athletics, 146, 156, 160–165, 317n, 318n
Iowa State, 298, 305, 310
Italian Romanesque architecture, 79, 177

Jackson, Graham, 240
Jamieson, James R., 179
Japan, mass bombing of, 304
Jason (Kitts) and the Argonauts, 318n
Jefferson Davis Hospital, 34
Jett, Joe, 249n, 250n
Johns Hopkins University, 44
Johnson, C. A., 232, 242, 243
Johnson, Francis Ellis, 107
Johnson, Dr. Gaylord, 241, 260, 262, 263, 317n
Johnson, President Lyndon Baines, 317n
Jones, Alice Baker (Mrs. J. H. Meyers), 303
Jones, Charles F. (Charlie), 20–24
Jones, Sir Harry, 3

Jones, Inigo, 101
Jones, Jesse Holman, 86, 113, 196, 239
Jordan, David Starr, 37, 145, 146

Kaifu, Toshiki, 328n
Kalb, Ervin (Tiny), 318n
Keally, Francis X., 143, 144
Kelvin, Sir William, 328n
Kennedy, President John F., 313
Kennebunkport, ME, 324
Kennon, Paul, 327
Kessler, George E., 179
Kidder's *Manual of Construction,* 154
Kikuchi, Baron Dairoku, 40
King Louis VI of France, 269
Kinkaid, Margaret (Mrs. William J.), 138, 240
Kinkaid School, 138, 140, 171, 182, 224, 229, 240, 287
Kinsolving, Bishop George H., 175, 274
Kirkland, William A., 306
Kitts, Jimmy, 318n
Kleberg, Congressman Richard, 317n
Kuldell, General Rudolph, 277

LaFarge, Christopher, 269
Lane, Sarah, 307
Laplace, La Pierre Simon, 39
Lassig, Oswald J. (sculptor), 96, 187, 322, 328n
Le Avenir de Paris, 265
Le Corbusier, 315
Ledbetter, Mrs. Hazel, 142
Lee, Dr. Umphrey, 247
Lefevre, Arthur, 31
Leifeste, A. A., 310, 311
Leighton Buzzard (England), 69
Lent, Robert F., 311
Leon Springs, Texas, 147, 148

Library Board (of the City of Houston), 191

Lie, Marius Sophus, 32, 33, 40, 328n

Lind, Jenny, 70

Lindeberg, Harrie T., 194n

Lindsey, Marion Lee (Preacher), 318n

Link, John Wiley, 177

Lloyd, Hermon, 314

Lombardi, Cesar, 14

Lorehn, Olle, 111, 112, 252, 312

Louisberg Square, 113n

Louisiana Street property (of William Marsh Rice), 34

Lovett, Adelaide, 37, 42

Lovett, Edgar Odell
  accepts presidency of the Rice Institute, 36–37 (photograph, 200)
  a "journey around much of the world," 38–41
  another trip to Europe, 97
  applies for unit of ROTC, 147
  approves Department of Architecture, 99
  and Art League of Houston, 256, 257
  as King Nottoc XIII, 98
  at University of Virginia, 32, 33
  awarded Ph.D at University of Leipzig, 32
  birth and early life, 31, 32
  choosing an architect, 38, 39
  and dedication ceremonies of October 10–12, 1912, 2
  "difference of opinion," with Cram, Goodhue & Ferguson, 80–83
  death of, 328n

  exchange of letters with William Ward Watkin, 299–301
  marries Mary Ellen Hale, 32
  meteoric rise at Princeton, 31–34
  on the job in Houston, 37
  and Phi Beta Kappa Chapter at Rice Institute, 220, 247n, 248n
  reads first Rice Institute paper in Dublin, 39
  reclaims Harold A. Wilson from Glasgow, 237
  residence in Plaza Hotel, 243
  retires on seventieth birthday, 299
  and "rigorous academic standards," 112
  speaks of the "first Rice graduate to reach the Western Front," 316n, 317n
  and succeeding presidents, 328n
  tells the football Owls of Jason and the Argonauts, 318n
  the "Lovett Papers," 325
  through western Europe to Moscow, 40
  to Japan via the Trans-Siberian Express, 40–41
  "university, or technical institute?," 37, 38, 49n
  visits Houston for first time (April, 1907), 34
  will be succeeded by William V. Houston, 306

Lovett, Mary Ellen (Mrs. Edgar Odell Lovett), 37, 136, 143

Lovett Hall, 2

Lovett, Henry Malcolm, 37, 42, 325, 326

Lovett, Laurence Alexander, 37

Lovett, Robert S., 16
Lummis, Frederick Rice, M.D., 193n, 194n
Lykes, Charles, 303, 320n
Lykes, Mr. and Mrs. James McKay, 303, 321n
Lyons (France), 65, 74n, 268

McAshan, Harris, 27n
McAshan, James E., 18, 27n
McAshan, Samuel Maurice, II, 27n
McCants, John Thomas, 110, 117, 215, 230, 260, 261, 317n, 325
McCants, Julia (Mrs. J. T.), 135
McCauley, John, 318n
McCormick, Catherine (William Ward Watkin's paternal grandmother), 55
McFaddin, Caldwell, 275
McGill University, 107, 136
McGinty, Milton, Sr., 214, 230, 241, 242, 247n, 249n, 258, 299, 312, 313
McVey, William M. (Bill), 132, 215, 266, 267, 310, 318n

MacArthur, General Douglas, 304, 305, 313
Maginnis, Charles D., 314
Maidwell (Northamptonshire, England), 53
Majestic Theater, 166
Mitterand, Francois, 328n
Mallet-Stevens, Robert, 265
Marian, General Francis (the "Swamp Fox"), 101
Marsh, Reverend William, 6
Marshall, General George Catlett, 301
Martino, Salvatore (Tony), 157–160, 167n–169n, 210, 230, 236

Martyrs Memorial of Oxford (England), 54
Massachusetts Institute of Technology (MIT), 78, 89, 96, 194n, 236, 305, 311
Masterson, Reverend Harris, Jr., 184, 185, 191
Masterson, Neill T., 290
Matamoros (Mexico), 11
Mather, President W. T. (University of Texas), 169n
Mayfield, KY, 32, 42
Meachum, Miss Lucile, 132, 140
Meachum, Mrs. McDonald (Lucile), 87, 140
Meachum, Senator McDonald, 87
Meagher, Jack, 262, 263
Mechanical Engineering Building, 99, 194n, 203
Medieval art and architecture, 79, 217, 218
Meiji, Emperor of Japan (Mutsuhito), 41
Memorial Park, 184
Merchants and Planters Company, 22
Methodist Church, 6
Methodist Hospital, 139, 287, 312, 316
Methodist Society, 6
Meyers, John Harris, 303, 320n
Michelangelo, 75, 188, 328n
Military Affairs Committee, 296
Miller, Jesse Wright, 189, 195n
Miller Memorial Theater, 182, 276, 280
Miller, William and Sons, 90–92, 94
Missouri State University, 31
Mindanao, 304
Mitchell, O. Jack, 326
Moluccas (Halmaheras), 304

Monterrey, Mexico, 11
Montour Iron Works, 56
Montrose Place, 177
Moore, Harvin C., 314
Moran, Dan, 307
Morehead, James, 298, 310, 311, 327
Morotai, 304
Morris, Seth I., 240, 314
Muchakonoga Peak, 115n
Muir, Andrew Forest, 21
Mulroney, Brian, 328n
Mulvey, Carl, 274
Murrow, Edward R., 303
Museum of Fine Arts, Houston (MFA), 182, 188–191, 252, 286, 298, 303, 317n

Napoleon, 74n
National Architectural Advisory Board (NAAB), 263–265, 302
National Bureau of Standards, 44
National Collegiate Athletic Association (NCAA), 262
National Youth Administration, 259, 260, 317n
Naval Reserve Officers Training Corps (NROTC), 287, 296, 297
Neuhaus, Hugo V., Sr., 194n
Neville, Mrs. Daphne Palmer, 185, 186
New Harmony, IN, 49n
New York *Times*, 24
Nichols, Ebenezer, 27n
Nobel, Albert, 70
Nobel Prize, 3, 40
Northrup, Joseph W., Jr., 89, 95, 96, 115n, 180
Northampton, England, 53, 120, 327
Northamptonshire, England, 53

Norman Gothic architecture, 175
Notre Dame des Doms, 247n
No-Tsu-Oh (Carnival), 98, 99, 168n
Nunn, A. Stayton, 192, 215, 232, 244, 256–258, 298, 311, 312

Oelker, Mlle Marie (Tante Marie), 216, 219–222, 227, 228, 249n
O. Henry (Sidney Porter), 114n
Old England Store, 223
Old South Church (Boston), 78
106th Engineer Battalion, 304
Opera Comique, 223
Order of the Alamo, 99, 103
Outdoor Sports, Committee on, 100, 156, 160, 165, 215, 260, 261
Owen, Robert, 49n
Oxford, England, 172, 214
Oxford University, 39, 217

Paderewski, Ignace Jan, 88
Palace of the Popes, 219, 247n
Palmer, Edwin Albert, 185
Palmer Memorial Chapel (Church), 183, 185, 186, 276, 292, 293
Panama Canal Commission, 327
Pan American Round Table, 136
Pan American Union, 96
Panic of 1837, 7
Paris, France, 171, 215, 216, 221–227
Pasteur, Louis, 328n
Parker, Edwin B., 181
Patrick, Albert T., 20–24, 65
Pavlov, Ivan Petrovich, 40
Pearl Harbor, 296, 301
Peden, E. A., 114n
Peden Iron & Steel, 114n
Pencil Point Magazine, 245, 258

Pennsylvania Academy of Fine Arts, 143
Pennsylvania *Enquirer,* 64
Perry, Albert C., 89, 95, 96, 180
Pershing, General John J., 169n
Philadelphia, 246
Philosophical Society of Texas, 9
Physics Amphitheater, 148
Physics Building, 96, 104, 111, 136, 211, 218
Physics Department, 307
Pillot Opera House, 88
Pitsford, Northamptonshire, England, 55
Pitzer, President Kenneth S., 324, 328n
Planning and Building the Modern Church, 314, 315
Plans A, B, C, 79–82
Plaza Hotel, 243
Plotinus, 54
Poincaire, Henri, 115n
Port of Houston, 86
Power, Reverend James T., 87
Power Plant, 203
President's Home, 42, 92
Princeton, 13, 33, 34, 39, 42, 48, 65, 93, 249n, 311
Pulitzer Prize, 322
Purcell, Bishop John, 49n
Pyle, Ernie, 303

Quin, Reverend (later Bishop) Clinton Simon, 175, 184, 186, 274

Ramsay, Sir William, 3
Raphael, Emanuel, 15, 27n, 30
Raphael, Rabbi Samuel, 27n
Rather, J. T., 153, 309
Raynham Hall (Norfolk, England), 101
Reagan, President Ronald, 327

Renaissance architecture, 65
Renwick, James, 47
Rice Alumni Association, 326
Rice Architectural Alumni Society, 311
Rice *Campanile* (yearbook), 259
Rice & Nichols, 26n
Rice, Benjamin Botts, 234, 235
Rice, Mr. and Mrs. Benjamin Botts, (Chaille Jones Brady), 193n
Rice, David (father of William Marsh Rice), 6, 7, 26n
Rice, David, Jr., 10, 26n
Rice, Elizabeth Baldwin Brown (Mrs. William Marsh), 11, 13, 24, 29
Rice, Frederick Allyn, 10, 15, 23, 26n
Rice Historical Society, 326
Rice Hotel, 37, 92
Rice, Margaret Bremond (Mrs. William Marsh Rice), 10, 11
"Rice of the Northeast," (Harvard), 322
Rice, Patty Hall (mother of William Marsh Rice), 6
Rice Stadium, 313
Rice *Thresher,* 145–147, 164, 297
Rice University, 322
Rice, William Marsh
  Buffalo Bayou, Brazos & Colorado Railroad, 9
  comes to Houston in 1838, 8
  early life in Springfield, MA, 7, 8
  expands into many fields, 9, 11
  first marriage, 10
  headright grant in Harrisburg, 9
  in Havana, 11
  in New York City, 12, 13
Rice, William Marsh (continued)

listed in New York *Social Register,* 12
a magnificent legacy, 4
moves to New York City, 12, 13
murdered, 22, 23
Orphans Institute, 14
second marriage, 11
statue by John Angel, 233–237
trustees receive estate of
  $4,621,439.00, 29
William Marsh Rice Company
  sold at auction, 11
Rice, William Marsh, II (nephew
  of William Marsh Rice), 13,
  30, 34, 35, 37, 49n, 234, 235
Richardson, Alfred S., 16
Richardson, C. J., 45
Richardson, O. W., 107
Rincon Field, 307, 308
Roberts, L. W. (Chip), 246, 264
Roberts, John A., 95
Robinson Springs, MS, 61, 62
Rockefeller, John J., 70
Rockne, Knute, 162, 262
Rockwell Endowment, 195n
Rockwell, Henry, 195n
Rockwell, James, 195n
Rocky Creek, 103
Romanesque style of architecture,
  269, 270
Roosevelt, President Franklin
  Delano, 264
Roosevelt, President Theodore,
  30, 31
Rossetti, Dante Gabriel, 45
Round Top (Townsend), Texas,
  102, 142
Royal Society of London, 3
Rupp, President George Erik,
  323, 328n
Ruskin, John, 45, 46

Saarinen, Eero, 258, 314

Sabine Pass, Battle of, 267, 319n
St. Jean de Luz, 129, 219–221
St. Luke's Monastery (Stiris,
  Greece), 104, 114n, 187,
  217–219
St. Mark's Church (Venice), 104
St. Mark's Episcopal Church
  (Beaumont, Texas), 293
St. Patrick's Cathedral (New York
  City), 47
St. Paul the Apostle, 328n
St. Thomas Episcopal Church,
  New York City, 269
sally port (Sallyport), 1, 52, 322
San Antonio, 103, 112, 134, 137
San Antonio *Express,* 134
San Antonio & Aransas Pass
  (SAAP) Railroad, 94
Sanford, Clarence M., 153, 192,
  215, 232
Sanford, S. M., 153
Sanguinet, Staats and Hedrick, 281
San Jacinto, Battle of, 102, 141,
  174
San Jacinto Inn, 141
San Jacinto Monument, 266
Scanlan Building, 43, 87, 155,
  174, 188, 192, 210, 215,
  232, 238, 275, 279
Scott, Sir George Gilbert, 71n
Scott, Sir Giles Gilbert, 71n
Scott, John Virgil, 180
Sears, Reverend Peter Gray, 185
Second (2nd) Infantry Division,
  301
Seiyojin (men of the western seas),
  41
Seville, 171, 181
Sgraffito technique, 178
Shadowlawn Circle, 180
Shadyside, 35, 177, 179, 180,
  188, 194n

Shamrock Hotel, 312, 316
Sherman, General Sidney, 173, 174
Sherman, Lucy, 174
Shawnee Indians, 73n
Shult, Ernest, 178, 184, 243
Sidis, William J., 115n, 117
Simons, T. Shirley, 153, 183
Slaughter, J. W., 135, 194n, 195n, 246
Slaughter, Margaret (Mrs. J. W.), 135, 246, 252
Slime Parade, 169n
Smith, Governor Alfred E., 196–197
Smith, Secretary of State (Texas) George W., 299
Smyth, Marjorie Peterson (Mrs. Harold A. Wilson), 108
Snyder, Carol (Mrs. William Ward Watkin, Jr.), 313, 314, 327
Southampton (subdivision), 179
South End, 181, 189
Southern Methodist University (SMU), 245, 246
Southern Pacific Railroad, 93, 112, 141, 215
Southern *Review,* 135
South Hall, 92, 104, 144
Southmore (subdivision), 177
Southwest Conference (SWC), 156, 161, 168n, 169n, 260
Southwest Conference football championships, 263
Spain, 171, 180, 181, 191
Spanish Renaissance architecture, 79, 191
Spindletop, 177
Springfield (MA), 6
Springfield (MA), Armory, 6, 7
Springfield (MA), *Republican,* 7
SS *Paris,* 228

Stagg, Alonzo, 162, 163
Stanford Law School, 324
Stanford University, 31, 146, 222, 238, 324, 328n
Stassen, Harold, 312
Staub, John Fanz, 194n, 309
Staub and Rather, 309
"Stepping stone strategy" in South Pacific, 302, 304
Sterling, James, 328
Stevenson, L. A., 194n
Stewart, James and Company, 94, 95, 104
Stewart, James Christian, 114n, 115n
Stratton, Samuel H., 44
Streetcars (Eagle Avenue), 184
Student Army Training Corps (SATC), 150
Student Association, 149
Student Honor Council, 263
Sul Ross Normal, 174, 182, 280
Sunderland (England), 56
Super Bowl, 313
Susquehanna Indians, 63, 73n
Swenson, S. M. and Sons, 23
Swenson, Eric, 23

Teas, Edward, 167n
Teas Nursery, 167n
Technology Chambers (Boston), 78
Telegraph and Texas Register, 102
Terry, Colonel Benjamin Franklin, 50n
Texas Intercollegiate Athletic Association (TIAA), 168n
Texas Military Institute, 25n
Texas Secretary of State, 15
Texas Society of Architects (TSA), 252, 265
Texas Tech (Texas Technological University), 70, 182, 183, 264, 281, 282, 327

T-shaped rail, 56
Thalian Club, 114n
The Knight Errant, 113n
Thirty-First (Dixie) Infantry
    Division, 302–305
Thomas, Congressman Albert,
    277, 296
Thompson, Cathryn (Mrs. Ernest
    Shult), 243
Thomson, Captain Thaddeus,
    USN, 296
Three Hundred and Eleventh
    (311th) Engineer Battalion of
    the 86th Infantry Division,
    305
Tidden, John Clark (Jack), 143,
    144, 149, 150, 154, 155
Todd, Anderson, 311, 327
Tombs, The (New York City
    prison), 23
Tomfohrde, A. M., Sr. (Tommy),
    318n
"Toonerville Trolley" (from Eagle
    Avenue to Rice campus),
    115n
Townsend, Asa, 102
Townsend, Benedictus, 101
Townsend brothers of Long
    Island, NY and Lynn, MA
    (Henry, John, Thomas and
    Richard), 115n
Townsend, Annie Ray (Mrs.
    William Ward Watkin), 98,
    99, 101, 112
Townsend, Elizabeth Stapleton,
    101
Townsend, Floribel, 113, 140
Townsend, Mrs. Foard, 99
Townsend, John 101
Townsend, Light, 101
Townsend, Moses Solon, 102, 103
Townsend, Rebecca, 102

Townsend, Robert Foard, 103,
    140, 141
Townsend, Senator Marcus
    Harvey, 103, 112, 138
Townsend (Round Top), Texas,
    102, 142
Trans-Siberian Railroad, 40
Traveling Scholarship in
    Architecture, 258, 311
Travis, Colonel William Barrett,
    266
Trianon Palace Hotel (Paris), 223
Trinity Church (Boston), 45
Trinity Church (Houston), 112,
    174, 175, 176, 292
Trinity Church (New York City),
    47
Trinity College (Dublin), 40
Trustees emeriti named, 306
Tsanoff, Corinne (Mrs. R. A.
    Tsanoff), 136, 137
Tsanoff, Katherine, 136
Tsanoff, Nevenna, 136
Tsanoff, Radislov Andrea, 118,
    136, 137
Tucci, Douglass Shand, 113n
Tucson, AZ, 324
Tufts University, 159
Tungate, Mace, 314
Turnbull, Pender, 325
Turner, N. P., 180
Twining, Mr. and Mrs. Harvey,
    227
Two Hundred and Thirty-Ninth
    Engineer Construction
    Battalion, 304

United States Military Academy
    (USMA), 39, 48, 277, 313
University of Amsterdam, 2
    California, 254
    Chicago, 160
    Christinia, 3

Glasgow, 3
Houston, 34, 244
Illinois, 97
Iowa, 313
Leipzig, 3, 31
Liverpool, 111
London, 3, 115n, 151
Minnesota, 144
Oviedo, 2
Paris, 2
Pennsylvania, 64, 67, 96, 111, 122, 123, 142, 144, 154, 246, 256, 312
St. Thomas, 177
Southern California, 192
Tokyo (Imperial), 3
Uppsala (Sweden), 40
Virginia, 31, 32, 78, 298
Washington, 111
UNESCO, 115n
University Extension Lecture Series (Sunday afternoon lectures at Rice), 248n, 252
United Press International (UPI), 323
Upjohn, Richard, 47

Vesey, Francis, 131, 215, 242, 243
Vieux Moulin (France), 216, 219, 249n
"Villa Lalo," 129, 130, 219–221
Viollet-Le-Duc, Eugene, 46
V-J Day, 304
Volterra, Vito, 115
von Johnson, Kurt, 296

Waggaman, Adele, 139, 140
Wagner, Richard, 45
Waldo, Wilmer, 93, 94, 179
Wallace, Carolyn Hooton, 326
Warnecke, August, 42
Watkin, Albert, 55

Watkin, Annie Ray (Hoagland), 112, 116, 124, 125, 131, 136–138, 165, 216, 224, 240, 245, 259, 277, 301–303, 305, 315, 316, 321n, 324–326
Watkin, Annie Ray (Townsend), 118, 126, 135, 136, 140, 141, 220–228
Watkin, Charles Francis, 55
Watkin, Frederick William (William Ward Watkin's father), 55, 59–62, 116, 118, 253, 301
Watkin, Mrs. Frederick William (Mary Matilda Hancock, mother of William Ward Watkin), 58–62, 118, 201, 202, 229, 239, 252, 253
Watkin, Henry, 55
Watkin, Hepsibah (Mrs. Ernest C. Churchill), 55, 59–62, 64, 69, 252, 253
Watkin, John (the builder), 54, 71
Watkin, Reverend George (vicar of the Church of the Holy Sepulchre, Northampton, England), 71
Watkin, Reverend John (also vicar of the Church of the Holy Sepulchre), 71
Watkin, Rosemary, 117, 125, 132, 133, 139, 141, 165, 259, 277, 278, 305, 316, 327
Watkin, William (Ward) (grandfather of William Ward Watkin who came from Northampton to New York City in the early 1840s), 54
Watkin, William Ward arrival in Houston, 5, 51

Watkin, William Ward
(continued)
as invaluable link between
Baker, Lovett and Cram, 4
as subdivision planner, 179–182
as supervising architect, HISD,
192, 195n
at age 22, 123
at age 66, full teaching and
administrative duties, 316
attacks of scarlet fever, 67, 84
a vision of Houston, 181
birth (in Cambridge, MA), 55
birth of daughter Ray, 112
birth of daughter Rosemary, 116
birth of son William Ward, Jr.,
116
"Brady pink" bricks, 173, 174,
193n
civic activities and
commissions, 181–183
Cohen House, 186, 187
and Committee on Outdoor
Sports, 100, 156, 160, 165,
215, 260, 261
campus plan for permanent
maintenance and
depreciation, 232
a dangerous bout with
pneumonia, and
convalescence, 228, 229
death of, 316
dedication ceremonies of
October 10–12, 1912, 4, 322
dedication of book to daughter
Ray, 273
design of Abercrombie
Engineering Laboratory,
Anderson Hall and Fondren
Library, 309
designs base for Dick Dowling
statue, 267

designs 1938 football stadium,
263
a devout Episcopalian, 98
dramatic improvement in
financial picture at Rice
Institute, 307
a dreadful trip across the icy
Atlantic, 228
emphasis on education for
Watkin children, 239, 240
enters University of
Pennsylvania in fall of 1903,
65
establishment of Rice (later
Watkin) Traveling
Scholarship in Architecture,
192, 193, 214
European trip with family in
1925, 126, 171, 172
an example of neoclassicism,
189
exchange of letters with
President Lovett, 299–301
Golding Memorial Chapel,
275, 294
Great Depression, 238–239
growing up in Danville, PA,
63, 64, 119
and John W. Heisman, 163–165
and HISD (Houston
Independent School District),
192, 195n, 257
and his maternal ancestors in
Staffordshire, England and
Danville, PA, 55–57
and his need for closeness
within the family, 277
and his paternal ancestors in
Northamptonshire, England,
53–56
and his wife's worsening
illness, 220–227

and Houston Garden Center, 276
and important new
consultantships, 309
in France and Italy, 220–221
interviewed by Ralph Adams
Cram in Boston (1908), 68
Julia Ideson Building (of the
Houston Public Library), 192
". . . a larger portion of my
time to devote to my
children," 238
". . . a limited but selective
practice, emphasizing
creative opportunity," 273
as a link between Rice Institute
and the Museum of Fine
Arts, 188–191
marries Annie Ray Townsend,
112
and the Model T Ford, 138,
139
and Mayor R. H. Fonville, 192
a meaningful letter, 64
moving into the family home at
5009 Caroline, 128
named chairman of two key
campus committees, 100
named FAIA (fellow of the
American Institute of
Architects), 312
named to National Architectural
Advisory Board (NAAB),
263–265
named to Special Advisory
Committee, University of
Pennsylvania, 312
named to Texas Centennial
Advisory Commission, 266
and nationwide tour of
libraries, 307
and new campus assignments in
national emergency, 298

and new Methodist Hospital,
312, 313
and NROTC Building at Rice,
296, 297
offered position at Cram,
Goodhue & Ferguson, 69
and organization of Rice
Faculty Club, 187
Palmer Memorial Chapel
(Church), 185, 186
partnership with Milton
McGinty and Stayton Nunn,
312
personal assistance for his
students, 241–244
*Planning and Building the
Modern Church,* 314
policies regarding
intercollegiate athletics,
260–262
promoted to assistant professor,
143
and Quin, Reverend (later
Bishop) Clinton Simon,
175–176
records of his life and his
works, 323
and residential commissions,
177–182
restoration of Christ Church
Cathedral, 273–275
St. Mark's Episcopal Church
(Beaumont, Texas), 275–276
sharing plans and ideas with
President Lovett, 217, 218
and the Southwest Conference
(SWC), 156, 161, 168n,
169n, 260
and Spain (Granada with
George Howard family),
127

Watkin, William Ward (continued)
  statue of William Marsh Rice
    and relationship with John
    Angel (sculptor), 233–237
  and Sunday Lecture Series at
    Rice, 188
  Tony Martino, 157–160,
    168n–170n, 210, 230, 236
  Traveling Scholarship in
    Architecture named for
    Professor Watkin, 259, 321
  Trinity Episcopal Church,
    175–177
  at USMA (United States
    Military Academy)
    graduation of his son, 133,
    301
  vacations in Vermont, 141
  visits relatives in England
    (1908), 69, 70
  Watkin children in 1920, 125
  Watkin Papers (in Fondren
    Library), 133, 324
  Wiess Chapel, 313
  Wright, Frank Lloyd, 131, 312
Watkin, Brigadier-General
    William Ward, Jr., 73n,
    116, 125, 126, 130, 133,
    134, 138, 140, 165, 277,
    278, 301, 302–305, 313,
    314, 316, 321n, 326, 327
Watkin, Major William Ward, III,
    125, 134, 314, 327
Watkin, Mrs. William Ward
    (Josephine Cockrell), 246,
    252, 327
Watkin, William Ward, IV, 326
Weber, Charles, 25n
Weems, Captain Benjamin
    Francis, 50n
Weems, Fontaine Carrington, 39,
    50n, 110

Weiser, Dorothy, 136
Weiser, Harry Boyer, 118, 136,
    152, 172, 173, 181, 230,
    246, 254
Weiser, Hazel (Mrs. Harry B.),
    136
Weiser, Marjorie, 136
Welch, Robert Alonzo, 113n, 114n
Welch, Robert A. Foundation,
    114n
Wentworth, Charles Francis, 47
Western Kentucky College, 32
West Hall, 155
Westmoreland Place, 177
Westminister Abbey, 55
West Point (USMA), 39, 48, 49,
    83, 277, 278, 302, 305, 313
West Texas State College, 174
White, Lloyd Y., 154
Wiess, Harry Carothers, 177,
    289, 306, 308
Wilford, Isham (Ike), 318n
Will, George, 322
Williams College, 111
Williams, John D., 194n
Wilson, Harold Albert, 107, 108,
    115n, 118, 152, 237
Wilson, Marjorie (Mrs. Harold
    A.), 108, 137
Wilson, Jack, Joan, Kathleen and
    Stephen, 137
Wilson, Talbott, 240, 314
Wilson, President Thomas
    Woodrow, 31, 34, 35–37,
    42, 49n, 248n
Winedale Inn, 142
Winedale Museum, 142
Wolverhampton, England, 69
Womack, Kenneth, 138, 194n
Woodruff, L. J., 154

World, western, chief executives of (at Economic Summit), 322

World War I, 145–154

World War II, 296–305

Wormser family, 227

Wortham, Gus Sessions, 306

Wren, Sir Christopher, 214

Wright, Frank Lloyd, 131, 265, 312

Wyatt, Lieutenant Oscar Dean, 296, 320n

Ye Olde College Inn, 243

YMCA Center (Galveston), 191